CERTIFICATE

ECONOMICS

First edition 1991
Third edition September 1993

ISBN 0 7517 4002 0 (previous edition 0 86277 472 1)

British Library Cataloguing-in-Publication Data

A catalogue record for this book is
available from the British Library

Published by

BPP Publishing Limited
Aldine House, Aldine Place
London W12 8AW

We would like to thank Angela Hatton for her contribution to the preparation of the first edition of this book.

We are grateful to the Chartered Institute of Marketing, the Chartered Association of Certified Accountants, the Chartered Institute of Management Accountants and the Institute of Chartered Secretaries and Administrators for permission to reproduce past examination papers. The suggested solutions have been prepared by BPP Publishing Limited.

CONTENTS

PREFACE

The examinations of the Chartered Institute of Marketing are a demanding test of students' ability to master the wide range of knowledge and skills required of the modern professional marketer. The Institute's rapid response to the pace of change is shown both in the content of the syllabuses and in the style of examination questions set.

BPP's experience in producing study material for professional examinations is unparalleled. Over the years, BPP's Study Texts & Practice and Revision Kits, now supplemented by the Password series of multiple choice (objective test) question books, have helped students to attain the examination success that is a prerequisite of career development.

This Study Text is designed to prepare students for the Certificate in Marketing examination in Economics. It provides comprehensive and targeted coverage of the syllabus (reproduced on pages (vii) to (ix)) in the light of recent developments and examination questions (analysed on pages (ix) to (xi)).

BPP's Study Texts are noted for their clarity of explanation. They are reviewed and updated each year. BPP's study material, at once comprehensive and up to date, is thus the ideal investment that students of the Certificate in Marketing can make for examination success.

The September 1993 edition of this Study Text

Changes made in this edition include the following.

(a) There is added coverage of recent economic developments.
(b) The index has been extended to cover more topics and terms.
(c) The bank of illustrative questions and suggested solutions has been revised.

BPP Publishing
September 1993

For details of the BPP Password title relevant to your studies for this examination, please turn to page 377. If you wish to send in your comments on this Study Text, please turn to page 378.

INTRODUCTION

SYLLABUS

Economics

This syllabus has been designed to provide students with an introduction to the basic principles of economics and to demonstrate their relevance to the marketing manager.

The syllabus covers basic concepts and theories from both micro and macro economics. (Micro refers to a study of individual decision makers and households, whereas macro looks at the economic decisions and influences at a national level.)

Both aspects are important to the marketer.

(a) Micro concepts provide a useful insight into consumer behaviour and the operation of business units.

(b) The macro level aspects provide an essential understanding of the economy, how it operates and affects business decisions.

Aims and objectives

(a) To provide students with an understanding of the economic concepts, theories and policies which are of particular relevance to them as practising managers and as managers in the international business community.

(b) To encourage students to examine economic principles in a business context and as a fundamental theoretical framework for the development of many marketing skills and techniques.

(c) To provide students with an understanding of the economic environment and its impact on business organisations and their markets.

By the end of their study students will be able to:

(a) understand the basic economic concepts and be able to apply them in different economic situations;

(b) demonstrate a working knowledge of the economic theories and concept which are of direct relevance and value to the marketing practitioner;

(c) illustrate economic theories and concepts with relevant commercial examples;

(d) be able to use the basic terminology and tools of the economist with confidence;

(e) understand, explain and illustrate the economic aspects of a variety of marketing tools and strategies;

(f) show a sufficient understanding of how the economy operates and the main 'causes and effects' so that they can demonstrate an understanding of economic problems and policies and their likely impact on the business unit; and

(g) understand the economic issues involved with international trade and the effect of trade policies on export industries and the development of international and multi-national companies.

INTRODUCTION

INTRODUCTION

THE FORMAT OF THE EXAMINATION PAPER

The CIM Certificate Economics paper consists of ten questions, of which any five must be answered. All questions carry equal marks, and three hours are allowed.

ANALYSIS OF PAST PAPERS

The topics examined in the eight most recent examination papers set up to June 1993 are summarised below. Note that the syllabus was revised with effect from the June 1991 sitting; the revisions to the syllabus emphasised a practical and marketing-oriented approach to the subject. However, the move towards this kind of approach had been evident in earlier papers as well.

INTRODUCTION

June 1993

1 Economics and marketing; practical benefit of economics to marketers
2 Demand and supply analysis
3 Explanation, using diagrams, of effects of successful marketing; marketing mix
4 Oligopoly in the retail food sector and the effect on marketing mix
5 The contribution of economics to the pricing process
6 Balance of trade over the last 10 years (in a country of your choice); policies to improve the balance of trade
7 The problems of inflation and anti-inflation policies
8 Environmental policies (on recycling and packaging)
9 Factors determining national income; international comparisons of national income

December 1992

1 Analysis of the consumer's economic problem; its relevance to the marketer
2 Explanations of any two of: kinked demand curve; backward-sloping demand curve; price elasticity of demand of -2.5
3 Explanations on the trade cycle
4 Income elasticity of demand
5 Marketing and economic implications of advertising
6 Benefits of international trade and policies to stimulate export activity
7 Benefits of promotional activities to a monopoly firm
8 Causes and effects of unemployment; policies on unemployment
9 Marketing strategy and the product life cycle
10 Advantages and disadvantages of fixed and flexible exchange rates

June 1992

This paper is given in full at page 300. Only a brief outline of topics is set out below.

1 Price elasticity of demand
2 The economic problem
3 A firm's long run costs
4 Market demand
5 Cartel; oligopoly
6 Shift from direct to indirect taxation
7 European Exchange Rate Mechanism
8 Economic growth
9 Reducing the size of the public sector
10 Inflation

December 1991

1 Evolution of the marketing concept using demand and supply analysis
2 Long run average costs of firms
3 Economic explanation of individual purchase decisions
4 Correcting a balance of payments imbalance
5 Effect of exchange rates on profit and pricing strategy of exporters
6 The business cycle
7 Distinction between micro and macro economics and how they help the marketer
8 Price elasticity of demand and pricing strategies of an oligopolist and a price discriminating monopolist
9 Product differentiation
10 Describe the state of your country's economy and the prospects of firms in it

INTRODUCTION

June 1991

1   Relevance of economics to a marketer
2   Apply demand and supply analysis to the product life cycle
3   Oligopolistic markets
4   Factors determining price an export customer must pay
5   Influence of marketing on the demand curve for a product
6   Economic significance of branding
7   Policy choice between inflation and unemployment
8   Factors influencing a firm's level of investment
9   Application of economic theory to pricing strategy and tactics
10 Protectionist trade policies

December 1990

1   Allocation of resources in a mixed economy
2   Inferior goods; sustaining demand for them by marketing
3   The concept of opportunity cost and its application in marketing
4   Advantages and disadvantages of direct taxation compared with indirect taxation
5   Determinants of demand for a product; the marketer's influence on demand
6   Methods and reasons for controlling the money supply
7   Relevance of elasticity to the international marketer
8   Sources of finance available to private sector firms
9   High unemployment as the cost of controlling inflation
10 Price discrimination

June 1990

1   Problems in forecasting demand for a product
2   Relationship of price of a product to quantity demanded
3   Why a firm must cover total costs in the long term, variable costs in the short term
4   Consumer sovereignty and its relevance to the marketer
5   Advantages of product branding
6   Macroeconomic equilibrium: savings = investment
7   Price discrimination
8   Means of correcting a balance of payments deficit
9   Comparative advantage and its relevance to foreign trade
10 Implications of increasing concentration in retailing

December 1989

1   Value added (GDP); its equality with sum of factor incomes and total final expenditure
2   Price elasticity and income elasticity; their importance in marketing
3   Speed of response of prices in oligopolistic markets
4   Reasons for continued existence of small firms
5   Accelerator theory: investment as a function of changes in income
6   Advertising as a waste of resources
7   Barriers to entry of new firms in established markets
8   The reasons why firms introduce new products
9   Reasons for correcting an imbalance in a nation's balance of payments
10 Methods of finance for private sector firms

INTRODUCTION

STUDY NOTES

Guidance from the Senior Examiner

The following comments from the Senior Examiner were made in *Marketing Success* (September 1990) and are reproduced here with minor amendments.

'There has been a significant revision of the economics syllabus, which will become effective from the June 1991 examination. The intention is to encourage you to look at the economic concepts and content which is most directly relevant to you as a marketer and business person. The syllabus has lost much of its detailed theoretical content. For example you will no longer be required to answer a whole question on accelerator theory. You will, however, still be expected to know all about the trade cycle, the accelerator principle within it and the implications of trade cycle theory for business.

'This apparent reduction of the syllabus is intended to ensure that it is more directly relevant to marketing managers - not to make the paper easier!

'If you fail to answer questions in economic context you are unlikely to be successful. "Is advertising a waste of resources?" is not an opportunity for you to submit a stock marketing answer. You will be expected to develop your argument from an economist's view of resources and the economic role of advertising.'

Coverage of topic areas

Typically, you can expect a fairly even split of questions between micro- and macro-economics. Increasingly there has been a tendency to have two parts to each question, the first requiring an understanding of the economics, the second its business application and relevance. Questions on the macroeconomic section are likely to be set mainly from the perspective of the firm.

Diagrams

You will notice as you read through this study text, particularly in the chapters on microeconomics, that there are a large number of diagrams or graphs. This might make you wonder how many graphs you will be expected to learn and reproduce in your examination.

The major purpose of diagrams in economics is to explain or clarify a point which would perhaps be too complex in narrative alone. In other words, diagrams are intended to be a help not a hindrance. Credit will be given in the examination for diagrams which are used relevantly and which help communicate your answers with more clarity.

Keeping up-to-date

It is important for you to be able to relate your economics studies to current issues in economics and current affairs. Questions in the examination may ask specifically about current events. Even when they do not, practical examples drawn from your knowledge of recent events can be used to illustrate many theoretical points in economics. It is therefore important that you keep up-to-date: this can be done by reading the financial press or a quality newspaper.

INTRODUCTION

Using this Study Text

This Study Text is structured in a logical order to help you to work through the syllabus in progressive stages.

Each part of the Text is divided into chapters which deal with the individual subjects in the syllabus. At the beginning of each chapter is a list of the sections in the chapter. At the end of each chapter you will find a number of short questions which test your knowledge of the material which you have just read.

If you can provide complete answers to each of these short questions then you should try the relevant illustrative question(s) for the chapter. The relevant question number(s) is indicated at the end of each chapter.

Once you have worked through our solution and have checked and understood any differences when compared with your own solution then you are ready to proceed to the next chapter or part of the Text.

This systematic approach will ensure that you have a thorough understanding of each area of the syllabus before you move on to a fresh one.

In addition to the illustrative questions referred to at the end of each chapter, the June 1992 examination paper is set out in full at page 300 with full suggested solutions starting on page 302. We recommend that you attempt this paper under simulated examination conditions as part of your final preparation for the examination.

INTRODUCTION

STUDY CHECKLIST

This checklist is designed to help you chart your progress through this Study Text and thus through the Institute's syllabus. You can record the dates on which you complete your study of each chapter, and attempt the corresponding illustrative questions. You will thus ensure that you are on track to complete your study in good time to allow for revision before the exam.

	Text chapters Ch Nos/Date Comp	Illustrative questions Ques Nos/Date Comp
The nature and scope of economics		
Economics and marketing	1	1-2
Solving the economic problem	2	3-4
Microeconomics		
Demand, supply and the market mechanism	3	5-6
Further aspects of demand and supply	4	7-8
Costs, revenue and profits	5	9-10
Market structures	6	11-12
Business organisation and business finance	7	13
Macroeconomics		
Determining national income	8	14-15
Techniques for controlling the economy	9	16-18
Employment, inflation and growth	10	19-20
The international dimension		
International trade	11	21
The balance of payments	12	22
Exchange rates	13	23-24

PART A
THE NATURE AND SCOPE
OF ECONOMICS

Chapter 1

ECONOMICS AND MARKETING

> **This chapter covers the following topics.**
>
> 1. The relevance of economics
> 2. The framework of economic theory
> 3. Resources, scarcity and choice

1. THE RELEVANCE OF ECONOMICS

Why economics?

1.1 Business people, including marketing managers, have to make decisions within the context of a rapidly changing economic environment. The rate of interest, the level of employment and government policy on taxation are just a few of the variables which might affect the financial health and fortunes of an organisation. It is therefore important that all managers appreciate the dynamics of economics. For students of marketing, the need for a thorough understanding is particularly important as marketers are frequently required to forecast future demand in the marketplace.

1.2 But economics has an even greater contribution to make. Like marketing, economics is built upon an understanding of consumer behaviour and on a study of the exchange process. Economic theory is the root of much marketing and it provides a valuable framework on which marketers can develop a model of consumer behaviour. Although easily criticised for its 'assumptions' and a lack of grounding in the 'real world', the predictions of economic theory do tend to hold true in general terms. The contribution economics makes to marketing cannot be ignored and should not be under estimated.

Economics and marketing

1.3 Economics is a social science concerned with finding solutions for 'the economic problem'. This problem exists because the needs and wants of individuals and societies are not limited while the resources available to them are limited. Economics is concerned with how resources can be allocated so that people get the most benefit from them.

1.4 Marketing is also about allocating resources. For the organisation to get the maximum benefit from its limited resources, it needs to ensure that the goods and services it produces are not wasted. The role of marketing is to identify and anticipate customer needs and wants so that the operation can use its skills and other resources to satisfy them. In doing this both the firm and the individual will benefit from 'mutually profitable exchange'. The customer's need or want is satisfied and the organisation achieves its objective, be that to sell more, earn more profit, increase revenue, or for example to increase the number of travellers using a public transport facility.

1.5 It can be seen then that marketing represents a system or approach which may help to solve the economic problem, by ensuring resources are allocated to provide goods and services which meet the identified needs and wants of customers. As you work through this study text, your attention will be drawn to aspects of economic theory which are directly relevant and contribute to marketing.

Exercise

Explain why marketing professionals might benefit from studying economics.

Outline solution

Economics and marketing both involve a study of the market place.

Both are concerned about ensuring that resources are allocated in such a way that the maximum benefits are derived from their use.

(a) Economists express this as the optimum allocation of resources.
(b) Marketers express this as maximising consumer satisfaction.

Economics helps us to identify and understand what happens to demand when conditions in the marketplace change.

Marketing people use that knowledge to help them influence demand and forecast what is likely to happen to their business in the future.

Customers and businesses exist in a wider environment and their behaviour is significantly affected by changes in the economy, altering their purchasing power, cost structures and so on. All business students need an understanding of how that economy works and of government's role in it.

---

2. THE FRAMEWORK OF ECONOMIC THEORY

2.1 Economic theory provides a framework of analysis for interpreting facts about the real world, but as with other social sciences, there are certain problems with the application of the science.

2.2 Since 'laboratory' testing is not possible for most aspects of economics, observation of and data collected in the real world must often be relied upon. In the real world it is often impossible to isolate the specific factors that we are interested in. Other factors will influence the situation and the outcomes, and so the results are unlikely to be conclusive.

2.3 A social science deals with very different phenomena from a natural science like physics or chemistry. It is often extremely difficult to formulate theories and predictions about what people will do, and therefore forecasts and predictions will often be based on certain assumptions. Often economists need to express some proposition subject to the proviso 'ceteris paribus' which means 'other things being equal', so that a situation can be considered in which only one variable changes at a time.

2.4 An economic model tries to capture the key elements of a real world situation by focusing on the most important elements or variables. Although such a model will not describe the real world situation completely, it is often a very useful explanatory tool in economics.

Rationality

2.5 One of the important assumptions in economics, on which much economic theory is based, is the rationality of human behaviour. In order to make predictions about their economic behaviour, economists assume that human behaviour is 'rational' and that consumers and producers act rationally, for example in deciding what to buy or produce at any given price so as to maximise their satisfaction (consumers) or their profit (producers).

2.6 The assumptions of rationality can be challenged in many particular instances. Although the cynical may claim that marketing actually attempts to encourage consumers to act irrationally, the rationality assumption contains a basic truth, that people try to act rationally in accordance with an objective or goal. Assuming that people act rationally does make theorising in economics a lot easier.

2.7 The assumption of the rationality of human behaviour, and that people will take decisions and actions which are directed towards a rational objective, leads us to the concept in economics of the _optimum._ The optimum means the best possible, and the following are underlying assumptions in much economic analysis.

(a) Producers will seek to maximise their profits and returns.

(b) Consumers will seek to maximise the benefit (or 'utility') they obtain from using the income at their disposal.

(c) Governments will seek to maximise the well-being of their population, eg maximise the national income per head of the population.

2.8 The world is dynamic and the optimum is always changing. For example, the maximum utility for a consumer, ie the maximum 'enjoyment' a consumer can obtain by buying a mixture of goods and services with his income, is unlikely to be the same at one point in time as at a later time. The consumer's tastes and preferences will change, and new products will come on to the market and be available. The consumer will now want to buy a different mix of products and services that will maximise his utility. The dynamic nature of the economic environment makes it difficult in practice to identify the optimum at any point in time. It also demonstrates the difficulties of the marketing manager trying to satisfy those changing tastes and preferences with his or her portfolio of products.

Positive and normative economics

2.9 You might already have strong personal views about what sort of economic society we should have, for example whether a free market 'capitalist' economy is desirable or whether a centralised 'command' economy is preferable. In the study of economics, it is easy for us to be influenced in our views by our ideas of 'what ought to be'.

(a) *Normative economics* is concerned with the expression of value judgements by economists, of what they would like to happen, eg what sort of economic society they would like to see in operation.

(b) *Positive economics* is concerned with objective statements about what does happen or what will happen. A positive approach is more objective, and it is the approach we shall try to take in our study of economics here. We shall try to keep our value judgements, whatever they might be, to one side.

Microeconomics and macroeconomics

2.10 The study of economics is divided into two parts, *microeconomics* and *macroeconomics*.

(a) 'Micro' comes from the Greek word meaning small, and microeconomics is the study of individual economic units or particular parts of the economy. For example how does an individual household decide to spend its income? How does an individual firm decide what volume of output to produce or what products to make? How is the price of an individual product determined? How are wage levels determined in a particular industry?

It is this part of economic theory which provides the marketer with an insight into consumer behaviour. Micro-level economics and marketing are both very interested in demand, what determines it and what factors influence it.

(b) 'Macro' comes from the Greek word meaning large, and macroeconomics is the study of 'global' or collective decisions by individual households or producers. It looks at a national or international economy as a whole, eg total output, income and expenditure, unemployment, inflation, interest rates and the balance of international trade, and at what economic policies a government can pursue to influence the condition of the national economy.

Macro-economics

This part of economic theory provides all business people with an understanding of the economy, providing them the information they need to forecast the impact of future economic developments on their operations. For example what if the rate of interest changes. How will it effect consumer spending, and investment levels of industry?

3. RESOURCES, SCARCITY AND CHOICE

Scarcity

3.1 A fundamental concept in economics is the *scarcity of resources*. There are not enough resources to meet all the needs of consumers, producers and communities.

3.2 Some resources are not scarce. You would not expect fresh air to be scarce, for example, unless you were trapped underground or under water. Ice is not scarce in the Arctic, and sand is more than plentiful in the Sahara Desert.

3.3 Most resources, though, are scarce, and there are not enough resources to meet all the needs of consumers and communities.

(a) In the case of consumers, the scarcity of goods and services might seem obvious enough. Everyone would like to have more, another car, a bigger home, more domestic goods, better food and drink and so on. There simply is not enough to go round to satisfy the potential demand.

(b) In the case of producers, there are four scarce resources:

(i) natural resources, referred to collectively as 'land' by the economist;
(ii) labour;
(iii) capital, eg equipment and tools;
(iv) enterprise or entrepreneurship.

Scarce resources mean that producers cannot make unlimited quantities of goods and services.

(c) The community also wants more: more schools, better hospitals, roads and improved provisions for the elderly. The resources available to the public sector are also limited so some of these wants have to remain unsatisfied.

3.4 Since resources for production are scarce and there are not enough goods and services to satisfy the total potential demand from either consumers (private sector) or the community (public sector), choices have to be made.

Choice is only necessary because resources are scarce, ie because of the economic problem of unlimited needs and wants but limited resources.

(a) Consumers and communities must choose what goods and services they will have.
(b) Producers must choose what to produce with the limited resources available to them.

Opportunity cost and utility

3.5 Choice involves sacrifice. If there is a choice between having more schools or improved hospitals and a country chooses hospitals, it will be giving up the opportunity of improved schooling for better healthcare. The cost of one option can be seen in terms of the alternative options now available.

3.6 The cost of an item measured in terms of the alternative foregone is called its *opportunity cost*.

3.7 Opportunity cost does not just compare the financial cost of different options, but looks more broadly at the relative benefits which different options offer. The rational consumer, producer or government will choose the alternative which provides the most 'benefit'. If I have the choice of spending £8 on an evening out at the cinema or of spending the same money on an evening at a restaurant, I can see the opportunity cost of the cinema trip as being the restaurant meal foregone. I'll choose the option which benefits me most - ie the option which I *prefer*.

3.8 As consumers, we often make choices based on the relationship between utility and opportunity cost. We might for example choose to make a journey by rail instead of by car if it works out cheaper, taking account petrol costs and additional 'wear and tear' on the car. Or we might buy a ready prepared meal at greater cost than buying the separate ingredients to prepare ourselves because we value the additional convenience and time saved more than the value of the difference in price.

3.9 Economists use a concept known as *utility* to provide a measurement of benefit or satisfaction. Utility is an abstract concept. Precise measurement of 'utility' is difficult, but we can compare the utilities gained from different choices. We do this as consumers when we make decisions on what to spend or consume. It is more difficult to make 'interpersonal' comparisons of utility. For example, how can we establish whether I will derive more utility from eating a bar of chocolate than you will?

3.10 'I prefer this brand to that', 'I prefer dark chocolate to milk chocolate', and 'I do not like fish' are all statements which imply that the individual has ranked products in some way. These are statements which we make or think about as consumers and they express our perception of the utility we will derive from different choices.

3.11 When individuals talk about something being 'good value for money', they have added another dimension to their assessment of benefit, price or exchange value. If you imagine you can measure how many units of satisfaction - perhaps 'utils' - a cup of coffee would give you, then you can consider that in relation to its price and calculate value for money.

$$\text{Value for money} = \frac{\text{utility}}{\text{price}}$$

3.12 Value implies utility or benefit. Do not assume that resources with low or no price (free goods like air and seawater) have no value. Air is essential to life and so provides important benefits. It is free because it is not scarce - there is an unlimited supply of it. Price is determined by both how badly people want something (demand), and how much of it is available (supply). We will be looking at the mechanism of demand and supply in Chapter 3.

4. CONCLUSION

4.1 Economics is a social science concerned with how resources are allocated and how choices are made about resources. Economic decisions are about what gets produced, what gets consumed and who gets what.

4.2 The need to make economic decisions (about what to produce or what to buy) arises because economic resources are scarce. Making decisions involves the sacrifice of benefits that could have been obtained from using resources in an alternative way: the benefits foregone are called opportunity costs. (In economics, 'costs' of production are measured as opportunity costs, which is a different concept from the concept of cost used by the accountant in recording the profit of a firm.)

4.3 The concept of utility is the foundation of economists' models of consumer behaviour. Utility is an abstract measure of the want-satisfying power of any particular good or service.

4.4 In the next chapter we will take a more detailed look at how individuals, firms and communities go about solving the economic problem by making choices and deciding on their priorities.

TEST YOUR KNOWLEDGE
The numbers in brackets refer to paragraphs of this chapter

1 What is the economic problem? (1.3)

2 What is the distinction between micro and macro economics. (2.10)

3 Why is microeconomics valuable to the marketer? (1.2)

4 What does *ceteris paribus* mean? (2.3)

5 What is the difference between positive and normative economics? (2.9)

6 What are the four scarce resources available to producers? (3.3)

7 Why is economic choice necessary? (3.4)

8 What is the meaning of 'opportunity cost'? (3.6)

9 What do economists call the benefit or satisfaction derived from using up a product? (3.9)

10 How would you calculate value for money in terms of utility? (3.11)

Now try illustrative questions 1 and 2 at the end of the text

Chapter 2

SOLVING THE ECONOMIC PROBLEM

The chapter covers the following topics.

1. The community's choice
2. The firm's choice
3. The individual's choice

---

1. THE COMMUNITY'S CHOICE

Alternative economic systems

1.1 Scarcity of resources within the community as a whole (ie limited amounts of land, labour, capital and enterprise) means that decisions have to be made about how those limited resources should be allocated. This comes down to three basic <u>resource allocation decisions</u> for a country.

    (a) *What goods and services should be produced?* This will depend on what consumers want to buy, and what they will pay for each product or service. The decisions about what will be produced relate to demand and supply.

        (i) demand means the demand from customers or consumers, and satisfied demand is *consumption*;

        (ii) supply of goods and services is referred to as *production*.

    (b) *How will these goods and services be produced?* The producers or suppliers of goods and services might be small or large companies, 'multinationals' with production facilities in more than one country, state-owned enterprises or the government itself.

        The choice about who will produce the goods and services, and what mix of resources the producers will use, will depend on the costs of resources and the efficiencies of resource utilisation.

    (c) *To whom will the goods and services be distributed?* Some goods and services are provided free by the state (eg in the UK, some health care and education) but others have to be paid for. The distribution of goods and services will therefore depend on the *distribution* of income and wealth in society. This in turn will depend on what individuals and organisations earn, and economics is concerned with what rewards are earned by the owners of scarce economic resources: land, labour, capital and entrepreneurship.

1.2 Providing what people want or need most means identifying goods which offer utility and producing them in the most efficient way, ie with the least cost combination of resources. How resources should be produced and allocated is ultimately a political issue although economists may be able to explain why some methods could work better than others.

1.3 Political approaches to the resource allocation problem are broadly polarised, with the extremes being represented by the command economy or centrally planned economy and by the free market economy.

Centrally planned economy	*Free market economy*
● Resources controlled centrally	● Resources controlled by individual consumers and producers
● Decisions on allocation made in accordance with priorities determined collectively as best for the community	● Decisions on allocation made by the 'invisible hand' of price which signals changing demand to producers
● Driving force is often maximisation of social welfare	● Driving force is profit maximisation

Middle ground is held by economic systems which have tried to combine aspects of both these extremes. The result is the mixed economy, which is the most commonly found economic system in practice.

In a mixed economy there is a public sector and a private sector. Resources in the public sector are broadly allocated as they are in the centrally planned economy and in the private sector by the free market mechanism. As already indicated, the mix of private and public economic activity in an economy is essentially a political decision, but it has significant economic implications.

Command economies

1.4 In a centrally planned or command economy, all or most decisions about resource allocation are made by a central planning authority. The government fixes the quantity of each good to be produced and decides how, and at what price (if applicable) it is to be distributed. It sets quotas for each individual production unit. It decides how many resources should be employed in producing the goods. The State even decides how each worker is to specialise. Such a government believes that it knows best how to organise, distribute and co-ordinate a country's resources.

1.5 There is no private profit, because all resources are publicly owned.

The individual consumer, although being able to express a desire for certain types of goods, is unable to influence the production system.

Many of the economies in communist countries have operated as command economies. However, recent developments in the Eastern European bloc of countries have seen the beginning of a dramatic and difficult shift of these systems towards a mixed economic approach.

1.6   In a planned economy, economic efficiency depends in large part on the accuracy of the government's plan in forecasting society's wants and allocating resources to meet them. In such an economy, people may have only limited freedom, if any, in their economic decisions, but in return they have greater security and greater social equality. Basic necessities are intended to be made available to everyone at prices fixed by the government that all can all afford. In practice, shortages of goods may limit their availability to everyone.

1.7   The disadvantages of a planned command economy include the following.

(a) Having a state-controlled system of allocation, it becomes impossible to judge the wants of households and so what gets produced might not be what households want. As a result, shortages and surpluses of consumer goods frequently arise. (It is interesting to note that even in the comparatively restricted planning of the European Community (EC), price fixing by the central governing body has created wasteful overproduction in agriculture, because the price fixed for producers is above the free market price).

(b) Extensive central planning usually involves large bureaucracies which are costly and wasteful of labour resources.

(c) The co-ordination and management of large scale economic plans are difficult in practice because of the enormous scale of the undertaking.

(d) It is arguable that government ownership and the lack of the 'profit motive' which is characteristic of capitalist economies lessens the incentive of individuals and reduces initiative, effort and productivity.

1.8   The role of marketing in a command economy may appear to be limited, but it should be remembered that marketing can be used to help achieve any agreed objectives, whether or not these are inspired by profit. Marketing may be seen as having the role of matching demand and supply. The potential value of the marketing approach in non-profit maximising operations can be seen by considering its increasing use in the public sectors of mixed economies.

Free market economies

1.9   A 'pure' capitalist free market economy is a complete contrast to a centrally planned economy because economic decisions are left largely to individuals. The allocation of resources is the result of countless decisions by producers and consumers in the market-place. The State does not have a role in directing the allocation of resources.

1.10   In a capitalist economy, price acts as a 'signal' to both producers and consumers. It indicates what and how much firms should produce to maximise their profits, and how much consumers should buy to satisfy their wants. If the price is too low, consumers will demand more than is produced so the price will rise, and vice versa. The price mechanism should thus ensure efficiency in the allocation and use of resources.

In a market economy, quantities produced, prices and resource allocation are all 'market-determined'.

1.11 There are disadvantages to a free market capitalist system.

(a) The free market society might result in a socially unacceptable distribution of income. Since all goods are only available at their prevailing market prices, some members of the community might be badly deprived, unable to afford even the basic necessities of life.

(b) Some desirable products may not be produced for lack of profitability (eg motor cars with extensive safety devices).

(c) Some undesirable products may be produced - eg dangerous addictive drugs - free from government controls and restrictions.

(d) Competition may be eliminated by monopolies, oligopolies (firms with a large but not dominant share of their market) and by restrictive practices, reflecting the disproportionate economic power of certain firms and groups in society.

(e) Competition may lead to a waste of resources, through duplication of effort, for example. (Some argue that marketing activities like advertising are examples of that waste).

(f) Private wealth for some may be high at the expense of others. Where such inequalities of wealth exist, resources may be allocated to producing luxury goods to the exclusion of necessities for the poor.

(g) Some vital services (eg police, courts of law and armed forces) cannot or should not be provided by private enterprise, and need to be provided by the government. These goods, whose benefits must be shared by society as a whole, are called *public goods*.

(h) Some other key goods, such as health and education, might be provided in inadequate quantities in a free market society, and provision of these goods by the state will be necessary to create them in adequate quantities.

(i) Some prices of key goods (eg agricultural goods, commodities) might be volatile, subject to big rises and falls, unless measures for price stabilisation are taken by the government.

1.12 In summary, a wholly free market economy might create unsatisfactory outcomes for how wealth is distributed, *what* goods are produced and *how* they are produced.

Consumer sovereignty and the free market

1.13 Consumer sovereignty refers to the freedom of individuals (strictly, the freedom of households) in the free market to decide for themselves what they want to buy. The customer is king, and rules the market. However, when we say 'the customer is king' we do not mean that consumers can order firms (suppliers) what to do. What we *do* means is that in a free market economy or a mixed economy, the freedom of consumers to decide what to buy influences output decisions by suppliers through the price mechanism - ie the interaction of demand and supply.

1.14 The idea of consumer sovereignty is central to the marketing concept. In essence it implies that goods and services will be provided that meet consumer needs, thus achieving 'market orientation'. In practice, where transition to a market orientation has not yet occurred, firms may decide what to produce and then use the techniques of advertising and selling to increase demand so as to sell what is produced. Many companies' monopoly power (when production is concentrated in the hands of one or a few producers) also casts doubt on the supremacy of the consumer: such companies may restrict supply in order to take advantage of their position.

1.15 The role of marketing is obvious in a free market economy, but it should not be equated with just helping the market process to operate through advertising or selling. Marketing has a role to play in helping to influence demand so that the available supply is matched by demand. But it also has a role to play in identifying needs through marketing research, a role which helps to ensure that resources are allocated to activities which will yield the greatest benefits (to both producers and consumer).

Mixed economies

1.16 There are reasons why the government may choose to intervene in a free economy, for example:

(a) to restrain the unfair use of economic power by monopolies or other bodies which might be able to impose their will on the rest of society;

(b) to correct inequalities of the free market system, redistributing wealth between individuals and between regions;

(c) to provide goods and services that private enterprise would be reluctant or unable to provide in sufficient quantities and at an acceptable price - eg:

(i) goods that are socially desirable but unprofitable for private producers - eg special equipment for handicapped people, motorways;

(ii) services that are unsuitable for private enterprise because such ownership would be against the public interest - such as the armed forces or the legal system;

(iii) services that are 'natural' monopolies, being very large and complex - eg the provision of public utilities or the railway system;

(d) to remove socially undesirable consequences of private production - eg pollution control, regional imbalances in employment;

(e) to direct change in the structure of the nation's industries, by retraining programmes, aid to new industries, or investment in research and development, and so on;

(f) to manage inflation rates, employment levels, the balance of payments and the economic growth rate in accordance with social and political objectives;

(g) as we shall see later, to moderate the ups and downs in the trade cycle, by trying to stimulate economic activity during a recession, and to dampen demand when it is so high that steep price inflation occurs.

1.17 Some government intervention is desirable in order to make sure that sufficient economic resources are channelled into industries which provide socially desirable goods or services – such as education and health care. If these industries were left to free market forces, the quantity of education and health care provided, and the price of these services, would be left to the interaction of supply and demand. Some members of the population might then be unable or unwilling to pay for education or health care for themselves or their families.

1.18 Even when essential services have been 'privatised' in the UK concern for the possible consequences of the monopoly power in such industries on the public interest has meant that the activities of many of these companies continue to be subject to government restrictions and monitoring by a public body (for example, in the case of British Telecom and British Gas, consumers' interests are protected by Oftel and Ofgas respectively).

1.19 There are no purely free market economies or purely command economies and most economies are somewhere in the middle. Most western economies are 'mixed' economies, with a large private sector, but a substantial government or public controlled sector as well.

2.   THE FIRM'S CHOICE

Production possibility curves

2.1 A firm faces the problem of how to use its resources most effectively. If we assume that the firm has the choice of producing two products, tables and chairs, but has limited fixed resources, then the production possibilities available can be shown in two dimensions graphically (Figure 1).

Figure 1
Production possibility curve

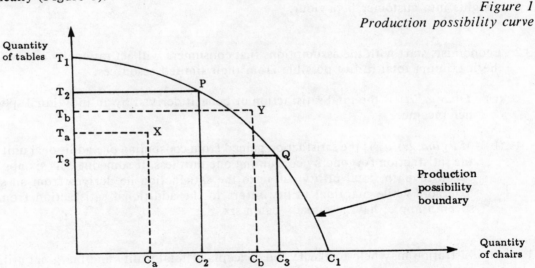

2.2 The curve from T_1 round to C_1 shows the various combinations of tables and chairs the firm can make, if it uses its limited resources efficiently.

(a)   The firm could choose to make:

(i) T_1 units of tables and no chairs;
(ii) C_1 units of chairs and no tables;
(iii) T_2 units of tables and C_2 of chairs (point P on the curve);
(iv) T_3 units of tables and C_3 of chairs (point Q on the curve).

(b) The combination of T_a units of tables and C_a units of chairs plotted at point X is within the production possibility curve. But more than these quantities of either or both tables and chairs can be made.

(c) The combination at Y of T_b tables and C_b chairs is outside the production possibility curve and there are not enough resources in the firm to produce this combination. Point Y is therefore unattainable given the current resources and technology.

2.3 The production possibility curve illustrates the choices to be made about what to produce when there is a scarcity of resources.

2.4 The decision about what combination of chairs and tables will be produced will depend on the benefits which the alternatives are perceived to offer the firm.

Tables may fetch a higher price and cost less to make, or chairs may be demanded by a regular customer. The firm will choose to produce the combination which contributes most to achieving its objectives.

3. THE INDIVIDUAL'S CHOICE

Utility theory

3.1 Each of us as consumers is faced weekly with literally hundreds of choices as we make a wide range of purchase decisions. The marketer is particularly interested in understanding how the consumer chooses goods. Economists' theory of utility provides some valuable and important insights into customer behaviour.

3.2 Economists start with the assumptions that consumers will act rationally and will seek to get the maximum total utility possible from their limited resources.

(a) *Total utility* is the total satisfaction or benefit derived by an individual spending his or her income.

(b) *Marginal utility* is the satisfaction gained from consuming one additional unit of a good or the satisfaction forgone by consuming one unit less. If someone eats six apples and then eats a seventh, total utility refers to the satisfaction he derives from all seven apples together, while marginal utility refers to the additional satisfaction from eating the seventh apple, having already eaten six.

3.3 An illustration may help to clarify the concepts of total utility and marginal utility. Suppose that we are trying to establish the satisfaction that a person gets from a long holiday. An individual is asked to give a total points score out of 100 to show how well her holiday to date matches up to her concept of the ideal holiday. She is asked to give a total score to date after every day of her holiday. She provides the following schedule for her holiday.

Day	*Extra points awarded for the* *Total satisfaction score* *(= total utility)*	*extra day* *(= marginal utility)*
1	19	19
2	33	14 (33–19)
3	45	12 (45–33)
4	55	10 (55–45)
5	64	9 etc
6	72	8
7	78	6
8	81	3
9	82	1

3.4 Total utility would be the total satisfaction she obtains from her holiday and marginal utility would be the extra satisfaction she gets from each additional day on holiday. (In this example you can see that marginal utility gradually falls, and by the end of day 9 she is just about ready to go home and get back to work.)

Utility theory and rationality

3.5 In utility theory, the following assumptions are made about the rationality of consumers:

(a) the consumer prefers more goods to less;

(b) the consumer is willing to substitute one good for another provided its price is right;

(c) choices are transitive. This means that if at a given time a commodity bundle A is preferred to bundle B and bundle B is preferred to bundle C then we can conclude that commodity bundle A is preferred to commodity bundle C.

If we did not make the transitivity assumption, we would have to compare every commodity bundle with every other to derive an order of preference.

Diminishing marginal utility

3.6 As a person consumes more of a commodity, the total satisfaction gained will continue to increase, but the marginal utility derived from increasing consumption will probably fall with each additional unit consumed. The earlier example of someone's holiday provides an illustration of this. The total satisfaction the person gains will increase as her holiday gets longer. She is unlikely, however, to enjoy the second day as much as the first, or the third as much as the second, and so on.

3.7 The 'law' of diminishing marginal utility states that, all other things being equal, the additional satisfaction derived from consuming additional units of a commodity will diminish with each successive unit consumed. Total utility will continue to rise as each successive unit is consumed, but at a decreasing pace.

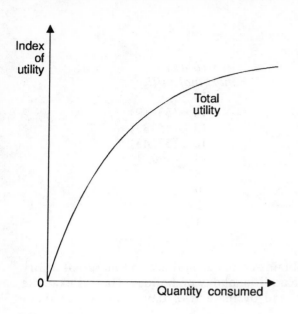

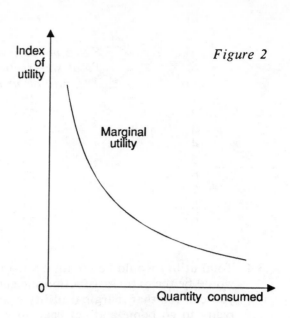

Figure 2

3.8 The law of diminishing marginal utility is very important. It expresses why your first cup of coffee in the morning gives you greater satisfaction than the second or third. It also clarifies the nature of purchase decisions people are really faced with. If you buy a cup of coffee on the way to work and it costs 80p, the first cup may be good value for money. Your second cup still costs 80p but gives less satisfaction: not such a good buy.

It also helps to explain why visitors to your home drink more coffee than they would if they were paying for it. You maximise your total utility by consuming free goods until their marginal utility equals zero.

3.9 The 'law' applies only while the assumptions of fixed household income and fixed tastes of fashion remain valid. If either changes, the 'law' will be temporarily inapplicable until a stable situation is re-established. If income changes, the utility which a consumer obtains from a commodity may be affected by the changing consumption of other commodities and accompanying changes in tastes. A change in tastes, fashion or attitudes may occur as more of a commodity is consumed and marginal utility may increase where such a change is taking place. For example, a person may start acquiring an addiction to a drug, or a person may progress from an occasional buyer of pictures into an obsessive art collector.

3.10 Acting rationally means that the consumer attempts to maximise the total utility attainable with a limited income. To illustrate this point simply, suppose that a man buys two ties for £8 each. If he is maximising the total utility of his spending, we can say that he has chosen to spend £8 on a second tie because he cannot find a more satisfying way of spending £8. If the marginal utility of the second tie were less, he would only buy one tie and spend £8 on other commodities which give greater marginal satisfaction.

In other words, when the consumer considers whether any unit of a good is worth buying he is deciding whether the marginal utility of buying another unit of the good exceeds the marginal utility that would be yielded by any alternative use of the same resources (eg money).

3.11 If a person has maximised his total utility, it follows that he has allocated his expenditure in such a way that the utility gained from spending the last penny on each of the commodities he buys will be equal, ie the consumer will spend his income in such a way that he gets the same marginal utility from the last penny spent on each commodity.

3.12 This proposition can be developed into an algebraic formula using a very simple example. Suppose that a household buys two commodities, X and Y.

Let the marginal utility of a unit of X be Mx
and the marginal utility of a unit of Y be My.

Let the price per unit of X (in pence) be Px
and the price per unit of Y be Py.

The household will attain an utility-maximising equilibrium where the marginal utility from the last penny spent is the same for X and Y, ie where

$$\frac{Mx}{Px} = \frac{My}{Py} \quad \text{............ (1)}$$

Cross multiplying gives

$$\frac{Mx}{My} = \frac{Px}{Py} \quad \text{............ (2)}$$

This is true for any pair of commodities bought by the household. When it holds true for all the goods in the consumer's shopping basket, the consumer has maximised his total utility.

Utility theory and the marketer

3.13 This formula suggests a series of mental calculations which each of us undertakes, comparing value for money in a large number of purchase and consumption decisions. You might have caught yourself trying to decide between two brands of soap powder. But much of the time we may undertake these comparisons almost subconsciously.

3.14 Marketers talk about selling benefits or added value, to improve customer satisfaction. Finding out which benefits will provide the greatest utility will help firms to gain the greatest competitive advantage.

3.15 Utility theory has one very important message for marketing. Decisions are *not* made on price alone, but on $\frac{\text{marginal utility}}{\text{price}}$

Lowering price may improve the ratio, but it is not the only strategy open to the marketer. There are also ways in which consumers' perception of the utility of a good may be increased. Not all of these ways involve changing attitudes to products. For example, if a product is made more convenient to buy, a consumer will derive more net utility from consuming it.

4. CONCLUSION

4.1 Individuals, firms and communities are all faced with decisions caused by the economic problem of how to allocate their limited resources to get the most benefit from them.

4.2 Different countries have different economic systems to provide answers to the problems of what to produce, how best to produce it and who gets to consume it. Most economies in the world are 'mixed' economics which display some of the characteristics of the free market and command systems.

4.3 Firms faced with limited production possibilities will choose a combination of outputs which helps them to achieve the organisation's objectives. The demand for a firm's product depends on the consumer's purchasing decisions. At the basis of these decisions is the notion of utility.

4.4 Rational decision-makers are assumed to maximise utility, subject to constraints which are imposed by their limited income and market prices.

4.5 Marginal utility declines as consumers obtain more and more of a product. A consumer's utility-maximising set of purchases from his or her available income is made where quantities of each product or service bought are such that the relative marginal utility from the last unit of each is the same as their relative prices.

TEST YOUR KNOWLEDGE

The numbers in brackets refer to paragraphs of this chapter

1 What are the three basic problems or questions a community has to solve in order to allocate its resources? (1.1)

2 What are the two parts which combine to form a mixed economy? (1.3)

3 Who owns resources in a planned economy? (1.5)

4 What is meant by 'consumer sovereignty'? (1.13)

5 What does a production possibility curve illustrate? (2.3)

6 What is marginal utility? (3.2)

7 What does the law of diminishing marginal utility say? (3.9)

8 Why do guests drink more coffee than they would if they were buying it themselves? (3.8)

Now try illustrative questions 3 and 4 at the end of the text

PART B
MICROECONOMICS

Chapter 3

DEMAND, SUPPLY AND THE MARKET MECHANISM

This chapter covers the following topics.

1. The concept of demand
2. Marketing and demand
3. Supply
4. The price mechanism
5. Using demand and supply analysis

---

1. THE CONCEPT OF DEMAND

Price theory

1.1 Price theory (or demand theory as it is sometimes referred to) is concerned with how market prices for goods are arrived at through the interaction of demand and supply.

1.2 Goods and services have a *price* because they are *useful* and because they are *scarce*. Their usefulness is shown by the fact that consumers demand them. In a country populated entirely by vegetarians, meat would never command any price, no matter how few cows or sheep there were. Scarcity is revealed by the unwillingness of firms to provide unlimited amounts of a good.

Usefulness and scarcity are the underlying forces which cause prices to exist. The price of a good is determined in the *market* for that good. The usefulness of a good is made apparent through consumers' demand for it and the scarcity of the good is made apparent by the limited volume of supply from firms. Price is determined by the interaction of demand and supply in the market.

1.3 In this chapter we will look in detail at demand. It is very important that marketers, whose work is concentrated on influencing demand, have a thorough appreciation of the concept and nature of demand.

What is demand?

1.4 Demand is an assessment or forecast of how much of any commodity would be demanded in a period at a range of prices.

3: DEMAND, SUPPLY AND THE MARKET MECHANISM

The demand curve

1.5 The relationship between demand and price can be shown graphically as a *demand curve*. The demand curve of a single consumer is derived by estimating how much of the good the consumer would demand at various hypothetical market prices. Suppose a consumer has the following demand schedule for potatoes.

Demand schedule

Price per kilogram £	Quantity demanded (kilos)
1	9¾
2	8
3	6¼
4	4½
5	2¾
6	1

This schedule could be referred to as an 'if' schedule. It does not mean that 6¼ kilos are being bought at a price of £3. It simply says that 'if' the price were £3 we would expect 6¼ kilos to be demanded. At this stage we have no idea what the price actually is, so no idea of actual demand.

1.6 This schedule is based on forecasts of effective demand – a desire to buy backed by the purchasing power to do so.

1.7 We can show the above schedule graphically, with:

(a) price on the y axis; and
(b) quantity demanded on the x axis.

Figure 1
Graph of a demand schedule

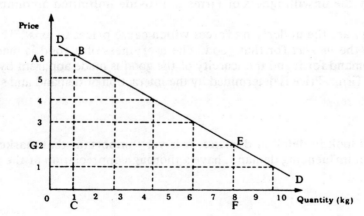

The areas of rectangles in Figure 1 represent consumers' total money outlay at the price in question. For example, at a price of £6, demand would be 1 kilogram and total spending would be £6, represented by rectangle ABCO, where O is the origin of the graph. Similarly, at a price of £2, demand would be 8 kilograms and the total spending of £16 is represented by rectangle GEFO.

24

1.8   If we assume that there is complete divisibility, so that price and quantity can both change in infinitely small steps, we can draw a demand curve by joining the points shown in Figure 1 by the continuous line, DD.

1.9   In Figure 1, the demand curve happens to be a straight line, and straight line demand curves are often used as an illustration in economics because it is convenient to draw them this way. In reality, a demand curve is more likely to be a concave (or 'convex to the origin') curved line. A concave demand curve will mean that there are progressively larger increases in quantity demanded as price falls.

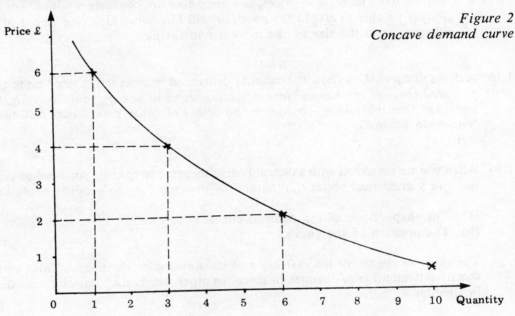

Figure 2
Concave demand curve

1.10   Suppose that the price is £3 per kg. Demand per month would be 6¼ kg.

    (a) If the price were to fall to £2, demand would increase to 8 kg.
    (b) If the price were to rise to £4, demand would decrease to 4½ kg.

1.11   Changes in demand caused by changes in price are represented by movements along the demand curve, from one point to another. The price has changed, and the quantity demanded changes, but the demand curve itself remains the same. Put another way, movements along the demand curve represent extensions or contractions in demand, caused by changes (down or up) in price.

1.12   In this simple example, we are looking at the demand schedule of a single household. A *market demand curve* is a similar curve, drawn from a demand schedule, expressing the expected total quantity of the good that would be demanded by all consumers together, at any given price.

1.13   Market demand refers to the total quantities of a product that *all* households would want to buy at each price level. A market demand schedule and a market demand curve are therefore simply the sum of all the individual demand schedules and demand curves put together. Market demand curves would be similar to those in Figure 2, but with quantities demanded being higher –ie at the level of total market demand.

1.14 The market demand curve generally slopes down from left to right because the lower the price the greater the quantity demanded.

(a) For the individual consumer, a fall in the price of the good makes it relatively cheaper compared to other goods and with his or her limited budget, expenditure will be shifted to the good whose price has fallen. It is the *relative price* of the good that is important. A fall in the relative price of a good results in more being demanded.

(b) A fall in the price of the good means that people with lower incomes will also be able to afford it. The overall size of the market for the good increases. The converse argument applies to an increase in prices; as a price goes up, consumers with lower incomes will no longer be able to afford the good, or will buy something else whose price is relatively cheaper, and the size of the market will shrink.

1.15 A demand curve shows how the quantity demanded will change in response to a change in price *provided that all other conditions affecting demand are unchanged ('ceteris paribus')* - ie provided that there is no change in the prices of other goods, expectations or the size of household incomes.

1.16 When you are presented with a demand curve there are two things you need to look at. These will tell you a great deal about the 'nature' of demand for the product being considered.

(a) The shape/slope of the demand curve.
(b) The position of the curve.

The *shape* of the curve is a reflection of its slope, ie its 'steepness'. This communicates how sensitive demand is to changes in price, in other words its 'elasticity'. We discuss elasticity in Chapter 4.

1.17 The *position* of the curve refers to its position in relation to each axis. We have already seen that changes in price result in movements along the demand curve. If any variable other than price changes, then we need to construct a completely new demand curve. These other variables can be referred to collectively as conditions of demand. When the original demand curve was produced we made the assumption that all these other variables would stay the same - *'ceteris paribus'*.

If one of them changes we have to go back to the marketplace and say, 'Now that your income has gone up, or your tastes have changed, how many would you buy *if* the price was £3.'

1.18 The conditions of demand comprise variables other than price which influence the quantity demanded. They include:

(a) the price of other goods (product and services);
(b) the size of household income;
(c) tastes and fashion;
(d) expectations;
(e) the size of the market (population).

3: DEMAND, SUPPLY AND THE MARKET MECHANISM

Changing conditions of demand

1.19 *The price of other goods - substitutes and complements*

Marketers need to remember that all goods are in competition with each other for the consumer's scarce resource - income. Sometimes goods which may appear unrelated are found to have considerable influence on each others' demand eg demand for summer holidays may be influenced by the price of cars. Many households will be able to afford only one major purchase per year. Changes in price of one consumer durable may affect demand for others.

1.20 However a change in the price of one good will not necessarily change of the demand for another good. For example, we would not expect an increase in the price cocoa to affect the demand for motor cars. But when the market demand is in some way inter-connected, goods are referred to as either *substitutes* or *complements*.

(a) *Substitute goods* are goods that are alternatives to each other, so that an *increase* in the demand for one is likely to cause a *decrease* in the demand for another. Switching demand from one good to another 'rival' good is *substitution*. Examples of substitute goods are:

   (i)   rival brands of the same commodity, eg Coca-Cola and Pepsi-Cola;
   (ii)   tea and coffee;
   (iii) bus rides and car rides;
   (iv)   different forms of entertainment.

(b) *Complements* are goods that tend to be bought and used together, so that an *increase* in the demand for one is likely to cause an *increase* in the demand for the other. Examples of complements are:

   (i)   cups and saucers;
   (ii)   bread and butter;
   (iii) motor cars and car components.

Exercise

Try to work out for yourself a solution to the following problem.

What may be the effect of an increase in the ownership of domestic deep freezers on the price of perishable products?

Outline solution

(a) Domestic deep freezers and perishable products are complements because people buy deep freezers to store perishable products.

(b) Perishable products are supplied in two forms:

   (i)   as fresh produce (fresh meat, fresh vegetables etc.);
   (ii)   as frozen produce, which can be kept for a short time in a refrigerator but for longer in a freezer (eg frozen meat from a supermarket, frozen vegetables, frozen desserts and ice cream).

The prices of both forms of perishable product are likely to be affected by the increased ownership of deep freezers.

(c) Wider ownership of deep freezers is likely to increase bulk buying of perishable products. Suppliers can therefore sell goods in larger packages or bigger units, and offer consumers some price discounts for bulk buying. (The supplier saves some packaging costs.)

The size of household income

1.21 The amount of income that a household earns will affect the demand for a good. More income will give households more to spend, and they will want to buy more goods at existing prices. However, a rise in household income will not increase market demand for all goods and services. The effect of a rise in income on demand for an individual good will depend on the nature of the good.

1.22 Demand and the level of income might be related in one of three ways:

(a) a rise in household income increases demand for a good. This is what we might normally expect to happen, and goods for which demand rises as household income gets bigger are called *normal goods* (Figure 3);

(b) demand increases up to a certain point and then remains unchanged as household income continues to rise (Figure 4). Examples are basic foodstuffs such as salt or bread for which demand can reach a maximum level because there is a limit to what consumers can or want to consume;

(c) demand rises with income up to a certain point but then falls as income rises beyond that point. Goods whose demand eventually falls as income rises are called *inferior goods*, eg tripe and cheap wine (Figure 5). The reason for falling demand is that as incomes rise, demand switches to superior products eg beef instead of tripe, better quality wines instead of cheaper varieties.

1.23 Inferior goods are not necessarily 'shoddy' goods. In themselves they may represent good value for money. But the customer perceives them to be less desirable than a more expensive alternative, for example bus rides as compared with taxi rides.

Figure 3   *Figure 4*

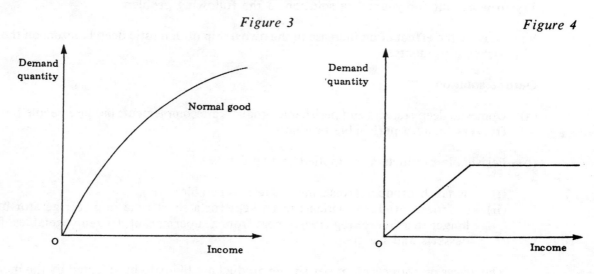

3: DEMAND, SUPPLY AND THE MARKET MECHANISM

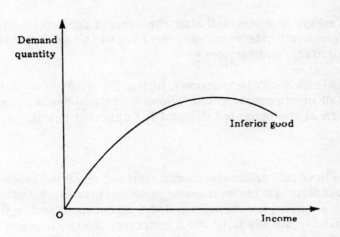

Figure 5

The income effect and the substitution effect

1.24 Two things happen when the price of a good falls. Firstly, the fall in price raises the real income of the consumer, thus increasing the demand for normal goods, but decreasing for inferior goods. This is called the *income effect*. Secondly, now that the good is cheaper, it will tend to be substituted for other goods by the *substitution effect*, leading to a rise in demand for the good. For normal goods, the price fall thus results in greater demand for the good because the two effects work in the same direction.

Other factors

1.25 *The distribution of income*
Market demand for a good can also be influenced by the way in which the national income is shared among households. Consider the patterns of income distribution illustrated in Figure 6. In (a), which has many rich and poor households and few middle income ones we might expect a large demand for Rolls Royce cars and yachts and also for bread and potatoes. In (b), which more closely resembles the actual pattern of income distribution in Britain, we might expect high demand for medium-sized cars and TV sets, and other 'middle income' goods.

Figure 6

(a)　　　　　　　　　　　　　　　　　　(b)

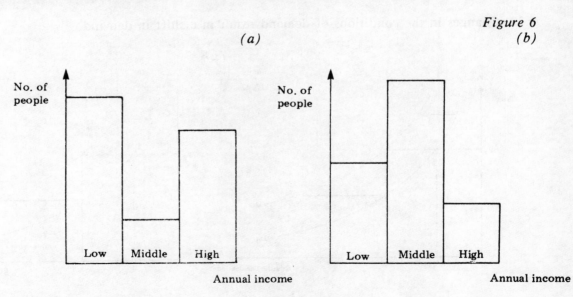

1.26 *Fashion*

A change in fashion or tastes will alter the demand for a product. Major trends towards healthier and 'green' attitudes in recent years have had a significant effect on the demand for a number of products and services.

Some changes in fashion may be temporary, such as the demand for mini skirts or skateboards, or the dramatic fall in egg consumption following the salmonella scare; others could be more permanent, such as the increased demand for unleaded petrol.

1.27 *Expectations*

If consumers believe that prices will change, this can result in short term changes in demand. Prior to a budget there is often an increase in demand for drink and cigarettes if higher taxes are anticipated. Rumour, emergencies and shortages can all lead to these short term demand fluctuations. These frequently bring about temporary changes in price. This phenomena is most easily observed in the stock market, where share prices are frequently influenced by the changing expectations of investors.

1.28 *Changing market size*

If the number of potential customers in a market place changes, this is likely to result in a change in total market demand.

This fact is particularly valuable to the marketer who uses the concept of market segmentation to target his/her key customers. If the size of a segment changes, demand may change and this is a factor which may be outside the marketers control. Any major demographic trends need careful monitoring to see how population movements may influence demand for categories of products. Currently the UK has an ageing population, bringing a higher demand for products for the over 50's, but a drop in the numbers of those aged 16 to 25.

Strategies to open up new markets, for example export markets, can be used to increase demand by increasing the market size.

Shifts of the demand curve

1.29 Changes in the conditions of demand result in a shift in demand.

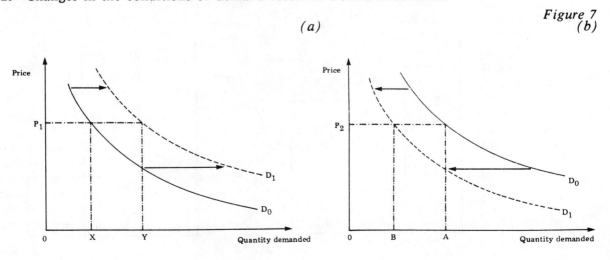

(a)

Figure 7
(b)

Figure 7(a) depicts an increase in demand at each price level, with the demand curve shifting to the right, from D_0 to D_1. For example, at price P_1, demand for the good would increase from X to Y. This shift could be caused by any of the following:

(a) a rise in household income;

(b) a rise in the price of substitutes;

(c) a fall in the price of complements;

(d) a change in tastes towards this product;

(e) an *expected* rise in the price of the product. If the price rise later fails to occur, the shift in demand would be temporary. If the price rise does occur, the demand curve would revert to its previous position, but fewer goods would now be demanded because the price is now higher;

(f) an increase in the size of the market.

1.30 Figure 7(b) depicts a decrease in demand at each price level which is represented by a shifting to the left of the demand curve, from 'old' curve D_0 to 'new' curve D_1. This shift may be caused by the opposite of the changes described in the previous paragraph.

For example, at price P_2 the demand will decrease from A to B.

(a) A shift of the demand curve to the right portrays an increase in the quantity demanded at any given price level.

(b) A shift of the curve to the left portrays a decrease in the quantity demanded at any given price level.

1.31 Note the following.

(a) Movements along a demand curve are caused by a change in price and are referred to as extensions in demand and contractions in demand.

(b) Shifts in the demand curve are caused by changes in the conditions of demand and are referred to as increases and decreases in demand.

2. MARKETING AND DEMAND

2.1 Marketing seeks to control a number of variables which can be used to influence demand. Collectively these are referred to as the marketing mix - the '4 P's' of *product, price, place* and *promotion*. We have seen that the marketer can change the amount demanded by changing the price, one of the four Ps. However, marketers need to remember that the steepness of the demand curve (its price elasticity) will determine how many more or less are bought as price changes. The marketer will prefer a product to be price-insensitive, allowing price to be increased without a significant loss of sales or market share. Consequently one strategy in marketing is to try to influence the shape of the demand curve, making it steeper so that demand will be less sensitive to changes in price.

2.2 Secondly, the marketer is responsible for ensuring there is a match between the demand for a product, and the supply which the organisation is able to make available. Too much demand would simply indicate that a higher price could have been charged for the available output. To do this, the marketer needs to be able to influence the position of the demand curve. This is done by changing the non-price variables. Some of these are outside the control of the marketer, for example income. Others, like taste and fashion, can be influenced by advertising and promotion. The size of the market can be altered by changing the availability of products - the'P of place. Changes in the product itself will change customers' perceptions of the products utility and will also lead to changing demand.

2.3 Normally marketing activity attempts to do two things to the demand curve:

(a) shift it to the right;
(b) change its shape, making it steeper.

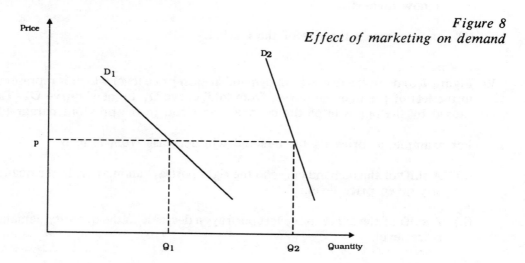

Figure 8
Effect of marketing on demand

2.4 The new curve D_2 is steeper and shows an increase in demand over curve D_1 from Q_1 to Q_2 at price p.

3. SUPPLY

The concept of supply

3.1 Supply refers to the quantity of a good that existing suppliers or would-be suppliers would want to produce for the market at a given price.

The quantity of a good that can be supplied to a market varies up or down, either because:

(a) existing suppliers increase or reduce their output quantities; or

(b) firms stop producing altogether and leave the market or new firms enter the market and begin producing the good.

3.2   If the quantity that firms want to produce at a given price exceeds the quantity that purchasers would demand, there would be an excess of supply, with firms competing to win what sales demand there is. Over-supply and competition would then be expected to result in price-competitiveness and a fall in prices.

3.3   As with demand, supply relates to a period of time - eg an annual rate of supply quantities or a monthly rate.

3.4   As with demand, a distinction should be made between:

(a)   market supply, which is the total quantity of the good that all firms in the market would want to supply at a given price; and

(b)   an individual firm's supply schedule which is the quantity of the good that the individual firm would want to supply to the market at any given price.

Factors which influence the supply quantity

3.5   The quantity supplied of a good depends on:

(a)   the *price* obtainable for the good;

(b)   the *prices of other goods*. An increase in the price of other goods would make the supply of a good whose price does not rise more unattractive to suppliers;

(c)   the *cost of making the good*, which in turn depends on the prices of factors of production - ie wages, interest rates, land rents and profit expectations. A rise in the price of one factor of production (say land), will cause producers to shift away from supplying goods whose costs and profits are closely related to the price of land, towards the supply of goods where the cost of land is less significant;

(d)   *changes in technology*. Technological developments which reduce costs of production (and increase productivity) will increase the quantity of a good supplied;

(e)   *changes in the weather* may affect the availability of supply (eg agricultural goods).

3.6   The factors that affect supply can be summarised briefly as prices and costs, and so profits.

In this chapter, our main interest is in the influence of price on supply and demand. The influence of cost on output decisions by firms, and so on supply to the market, will be discussed more fully in a later chapter.

Supply and the price of a good

3.7   In general, suppliers will want to supply a greater quantity of their output at higher prices.

3.8 For example, if the price of product X is £5 per unit, a supplier might be willing to supply 1,000 units of the product to consumers in the market at that price. If the price of product X now goes up to £10, the supplier will be willing to supply more than 1,000 units of the product. Just how many more than 1,000 they would want to supply would depend on circumstances.

3.9 Why would a supplier be willing to supply more output at a higher price?

It might seem logical to suppose that higher prices should mean higher profits, and so the firm would be attracted by the prospect of bigger profits into supplying more units of output. This is not the full answer, though. We must also ask why, in our example, the supplier was only willing to supply 1,000 units of product X at a price of £5. This means that we have to think about costs as well as prices.

3.10 Why would not the supplier be willing to produce more output for sale at £5? The answer must be that it would not be worthwhile, and that the unit cost of making extra output would exceed the sales price of £5 per unit. At a higher selling price per unit, the output limit where unit costs begin to exceed unit prices will be at a higher level, and so the supplier would now be willing to produce more at the new, higher price.

The supply curve

3.11 A supply schedule and supply curve can be drawn:

(a) for an individual supplier; or

(b) for all firms which produce the good. This total supply curve of all suppliers is the *market* supply curve.

Example

3.12 Suppose that the supply schedule for product Y is as follows.

Price per unit £	Quantity that suppliers would supply at this price units per year
100	10,000
150	20,000
300	30,000
500	40,000

3.13 A supply curve is constructed in a similar manner to a demand curve (from a schedule of supply quantities at different prices) but shows the quantity suppliers are willing to produce at different price levels. It is an upward-sloping curve from left to right, because greater quantities will be produced at higher prices.

3.14 The relationship between output and price, using the data in our example, is shown as a *supply curve* in Figure 9.

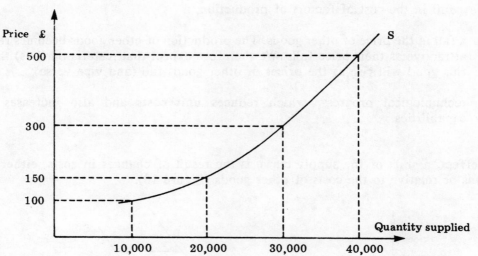

Figure 9

3.15 It is important to note that a supply curve shows how the quantity supplied will change in response to a change in price, provided that all other conditions affecting supply remain unchanged (*ceteris paribus*). If supply conditions (the price of other goods, or costs of factors of production, or changes in technology) alter, a different supply curve must be drawn. In other words, a change in price will cause a change in supply along the supply curve. A change in other supply conditions will cause a shift in the supply curve itself.

The *market* supply curve, remember, is the aggregate of the supply curves of individual firms in the market.

3.16 As with the demand curve, you need to look at two things when faced with a supply curve.

(a) the shape/slope of the curve;
(b) the position of the curve.

3.17 (a) The shape or steepness tells you how much supply will change by as a result of a change in price, ie how price sensitive or price elastic supply is.

(b) The position of the curve tells you whether or not there has been a change in the conditions of supply resulting in a shift in the curve.

Shifts of the market supply curve

3.18 A shift of the market supply curve occurs when supply conditions change. By 'supply conditions' we mean factors influencing supply other than the price of the good itself, eg the price of factors of production, the prices of other goods and technology. Figure 10 shows a shift in the supply curve from S_0 to S_1. A shift to the right of the curve shows an increase of supply and may be caused by:

(a)   a fall in the cost of factors of production;

(b)   a fall in the price of other goods. The production of other goods becomes relatively less attractive as their price falls. We therefore expect that (ceteris paribus) the *supply* of this good will rise as the prices of other goods fall (and vice versa);

(c)   technological progress, which reduces unit costs and also increases production capabilities.

3.19   In effect, a shift of the supply curve is the result of changes in costs, either in absolute terms or relative to the costs of other goods (Figure 10).

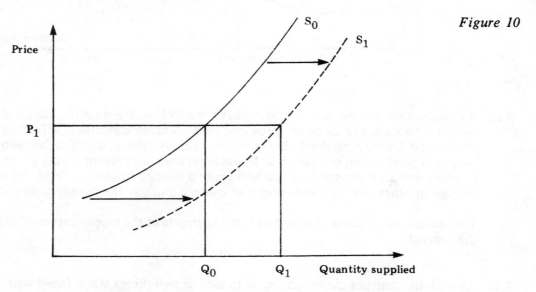

Figure 10

If the price of the good is P_1, suppliers would be willing to increase supply from Q_0 to Q_1 under the new supply conditions.

3.20   Note that we must distinguish between short run and long run responses of both supply and demand. In the short run both supply and demand are relatively unresponsive to changes in price, as compared to the long run.

In the case of supply, changes in the quantity of a good supplied often require the laying off or hiring of new workers, or the installation of new machinery. All of these changes, which will be brought about by management decisions, may take some time to implement.

For example, in the early 1980s there was an excess supply of paper for the UK market and prices fell. Gradually, with short-time working and factory closures, supply decreased so that prices eventually became relatively stable by 1981. Within a few years, however, market conditions changed again, and a shortage of supply of paper in 1984 pushed prices up again.

In the case of demand, it takes time for consumers to adjust their buying patterns, although demand will often respond more rapidly than supply to changes in price or other demand conditions.

3.21 In some markets, responses to changes in price are relatively rapid. In others, response times are much longer. In stock markets for example, supply and demand responds very rapidly to price changes, whereas in the markets for fuel oils or agrichemicals response times are much slower.

3.22 Note that:

(a) movements along a supply curve represent changes in the total quantity of a good that suppliers would want to supply when there is a change in the price of the good;

(b) shifts of the supply curve represent changes in the total quantity of a good that suppliers would want to supply at all prices, because of a change in the cost of supply – eg technological progress, or a change in the price of other goods.

4. THE PRICE MECHANISM

Signals and incentives

4.1 A firm's output decisions will be influenced by both demand and supply considerations.

(a) Market demand conditions influence the price that a firm will get for its output. Prices act as *signals* to producers, and changes in prices should stimulate a response from a firm, to change its production quantities.

(b) Supply is influenced by production costs and profits. The objective of optimising profits provides the *incentive* for firms to respond to changes in price or cost by changing their production quantities.

4.2 People who want goods only have a limited income and they must decide what to buy with the money they have. The prices of the goods they want will affect their buying decisions.

4.3 Firms only have a limited amount of resources with which to produce goods. The supply decisions of firms - ie what goods to supply and in what quantities - will be determined by the profits they can make and these in turn depend not only on the cost of production but also on the prices at which the goods can be sold.

4.4 Decisions by firms about what industry to operate in and what markets to produce goods for, will be influenced by prices obtainable. Although some firms have been established in one industry for many years, others are continually opening up, closing down or switching to new industries and new markets. Over time, firms in an industry might also increase or reduce the volume of goods they sell. Changes in supply are influenced by changes in cost or in price.

4.5 If demand for a good exceeds supply, consumers must either stop demanding what they cannot have, or they must be prepared to pay more for the good. At a higher price, firms will be prepared to supply more of the good. On the other hand, if the price of a good is such that firms want to supply more than consumers are willing to buy, production must be cut back in volume or the price must be reduced so as to stimulate demand.

3: DEMAND, SUPPLY AND THE MARKET MECHANISM

The equilibrium price

4.6 The price mechanism brings demand and supply into equilibrium and the *equilibrium price* for a good is the price at which the volume demanded by consumers and the volume that firms would be willing to supply are the same.

Figure 11

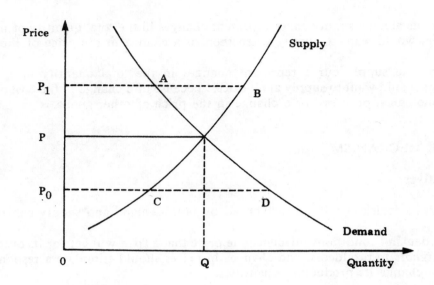

4.7 At price P_1 there is an excess of the quantity that suppliers want to produce over the quantity demanded at that price, equal to the distance AB. The reaction of suppliers as unsold stocks accumulate would be to:

   (a) cut down the current level of production in order to disaccumulate unwanted stocks (ie de-stock); and/or

   (b) reduce prices in order to encourage sales.

4.8 The opposite will happen at price P_0 where there is an excess of demand over supply shown by the distance CD. Output and price would increase.

4.9 At price P the amount that sellers are willing to supply is equal to the amount that customers are willing to buy. There will be no unusual variation in stocks and, unless something else changes, there will be no change in price. P is the *equilibrium price*.

4.10 At the equilibrium price P, consumers will be willing to spend a total of $P \times Q$ - ie PQ - on buying Q units of the product, and suppliers will be willing to supply Q units to earn revenue of $P \times Q$.

4.11 The forces of supply and demand push a market to its equilibrium price and quantity.

   (a) If there is no change in conditions of supply or demand, the equilibrium price will **rule** the market and will remain stable.

(b) If the equilibrium price does not rule, the market is in disequilibrium, but supply and demand will push prices towards the equilibrium price.

(c) Shifts in the supply curve or demand curve will change the equilibrium price and quantity.

4.12 The 'law' of supply and demand is that in a free market, the equilibrium price and output level of a good is the price and output level at which the market demand curve and the market supply curve intersect.

5. USING DEMAND AND SUPPLY ANALYSIS

Illustrating the development of the marketing concept

5.1 In the economics examination you are unlikely to be asked simply descriptive questions about demand or supply. You will need to demonstrate your knowledge of the material in this chapter by applying it in illustrating or forecasting behaviour in a marketplace.

5.2 For example, demand and supply analysis can be used to illustrate economist's view of the development of the marketing concept, tracking the transition of a market from the stage of product orientation through sales orientation to the stage of customer orientation.

Stage 1: Product orientation

5.3 A product-oriented market is characterised by management's emphasis on production and operational issues. The customer is not really considered. This is possible because conditions in the market mean that there has been an increase in demand, without a matching increase in supply.

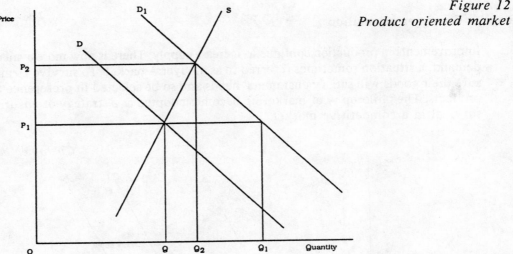

Figure 12
Product oriented market

Supply has not increased to match the new demand illustrated by D_1. At price P_1, Q_1 customers want to buy the product - an excess of demand over supply.

There is no shortage of customers, so firms do not need to worry about them. Prices can be raised to P_2 and they can sell all the product they are able to make - a sellers' market.

A firm in this market which wants to increase profit simply needs to increase output. Collectively the desire to sell more will lead to an increase in market supply.

Stage 2: Sales orientation

5.4   As output increases, so the market nears equilibrium with price falling back again to P_1. There is a closer match between what is demanded and the available output. To be successful a firm needs to be certain customers know about the availability of the firm's product, and so advertising and selling are key elements in the business strategy.

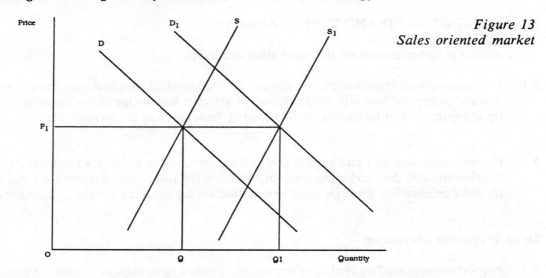

Figure 13
Sales oriented market

As the market for the product matures, so new technologies and new competitors will continue to increase the available supply, moving the market into stage 3.

Stage 3: Customer orientation

5.5   Improvements in production continue to increase supply. There is now more available supply than demand, a situation sometimes referred to as a buyers' market. To survive firms need to make sure their goods will satisfy customers' needs and so be selected in preference to competitors' products. The philosophy of marketing becomes adopted as a strategy of ensuring success and survival in a competitive market.

Figure 14
Customer oriented market

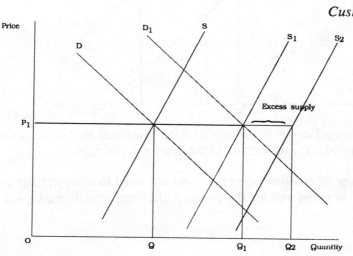

The excess supply over demand at price P_1 is the difference between Q_1 and Q_2. If firms do not reduce their prices, some suppliers will be forced to leave the market. At lower prices some firms will be unprofitable. The only way to survive is to identify customer needs before committing resources to production.

5.6 Demand and supply analysis can also be used to explain and predict changes within particular markets, for example the effect of higher production costs on the market for cars.

6. CONCLUSION

6.1 In a free market, price acts as a mechanism which signals demand and supply conditions to producers and consumers. It therefore determines the activities of both producers and consumers, influencing the levels of demand for and the supply of goods.

> 'The price system was not consciously created. It does not require that anyone consciously oversees and co-ordinates the necessary changes; adjustments occur automatically as a result of the separate decisions taken by a large number of individuals, all seeking their own best interest.' *(R G Lipsey)*

6.2 The *demand curve* is an indication of what consumers are willing to pay - their responsiveness to price. The *supply curve* is an indication of what producers are willing to supply - their responsiveness to price.

6.3 Both the demand curve and the supply curve relate to business:

> *Demand* relates to *revenue*
> *Supply* relates to *cost*

Prices act as *signals* to businesses to guide the decisions on what to produce and how to produce.

6.4 The competitive market process can be summarised succinctly with demand and supply curves. This competitive market process results in an equilibrium price, which is the price at which market supply and market demand quantities are in balance. In any market, the equilibrium price will change if market demand or supply conditions change.

6.5 Appreciating these concepts and this mechanism is vitally important to marketers. Demand theory provides a framework for marketers' understanding of consumer behaviour.

TEXT YOUR KNOWLEDGE
The numbers in brackets refer to paragraphs of this chapter

1   What is the meaning of 'effective demand'? (1.6)

2   What is the market demand? (1.12)

3   Why does a demand curve normally slope down from left to right? (1.14)

4   What is meant by the conditions of demand? (1.17, 1.18)

5   What is the distinction between substitute goods and complements? (1.20)

6   What is an inferior good? (1.22)

7   What does a marketer try to do to the demand for a product? (2.4)

8   What will happen to supply if prices are raised. (3.7)

9   What can change the equilibrium in a market? (4.11)

10 What demand and supply conditions in a market lead to the marketing concept being adopted? (5.5)

Now try illustrative questions 5 and 6 at the end of the text

Chapter 4

FURTHER ASPECTS OF
DEMAND AND SUPPLY

This chapter covers the following topics.

1. Price elasticity
2. Other elasticity measures
3. Elasticities illustrated: agriculture

---

1. PRICE ELASTICITY

The concept of elasticity

1.1 We have already come across the concept of elasticity briefly in Chapter 3. Put simply, elasticity is a way of measuring the degree of responsiveness of either demand or supply to a change in one of the variables influencing demand or supply.

1.2 Without precise measurement of elasticities, we would know that if price is raised sales will fall, but would not know by how much for a particular level of price increase. If people's income goes up, sales will normally increase, but we would not know by how much.

1.3 We have seen that there are a number of variables which can influence demand or supply, and accordingly there are a number of different types of elasticity. All are based on the same standard formula.

1.4 Elasticity is a measure of the responsiveness of demand or supply to a change in one of the variables influencing demand or supply.

Elasticity formula:
$$\frac{\text{change in quantity demanded or supplied as a \% of demand or supply}}{\text{change in the variable as a \% of the variable}}$$

1.5 Economists often find it helpful to use a shorthand to simplify the communication of such formulas as the one above. You need to get used to this type of shorthand, which is used below.

$$\text{elasticity} = \frac{\% \ \Delta \text{ in Q}_{d/s}}{\% \ \Delta \text{ in variable}}$$

Δ = change
Q = quantity
d/s = demand or supply

Examples of elasticity of demand

1.6   The concept of elasticity, applied to demand, is one of the most useful economic concepts to the marketer.

As the marketer uses the elements of the marketing mix, particularly price, to influence demand, it is important to be able to assess how much change is necessary to bring about the required change in demand. Elasticity provides a measure for this assessment.

The price elasticity of demand

1.7   Price elasticity of demand is a measure of the extent of change in market demand Q_d for a good in response to a change in its price. It is measured as:

$$\frac{\text{change in quantity demand, as a \% of demand}}{\text{change in price, as a \% of the price}} \quad \text{or} \quad \frac{\% \ \Delta \text{ in Q}_d}{\% \ \Delta \text{ in P}} = \frac{\Delta \text{ in Q}_d}{\Delta \text{ in P}} \times \frac{P}{Q_d}$$

(Δ = change)

Since normally the quantity demanded goes up when the price falls, and goes down when the price rises, elasticity has a negative value, but it is usual to ignore the minus sign when considering the price elasticity of demand.

1.8   When the formula for measuring elasticity is applied, the value of elasticity may work out to a figure of either above or below 1.

This is important. A value of below 1 denotes *insensitivity* to the variable, and is classified as *inelastic*. A value of above 1 denotes *sensitivity* and is classified as *elastic*.

1.9   The scale of elasticity is depicted in Figure 1 below.

Figure 1

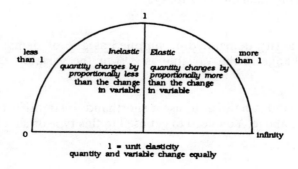

44

1.10 This scale of elasticity is applicable whichever variable is changing and being assessed. Here we will use it to consider the effect on demand of a change in price.

   (a)   For product A over a particular price range,

   Price elasticity of demand $= \dfrac{\% \Delta \text{ in } Q_d}{\% \Delta \text{ in } P} = -\dfrac{1\%}{10\%} = -\dfrac{1}{10} = -0.1$

   Here a 10% change in price brings about a very small change in quantity demanded of just 1%. The demand for this product is very insensitive to price changes - it is price inelastic. The measure of elasticity is just 1/10 or 0.1, and is less than 1.

   (b)   For product B over a particular price range,

   Price elasticity of demand $= \dfrac{\% \Delta \text{ in } Q_d}{\% \Delta \text{ in } P} = -\dfrac{5\%}{10\%} = -\dfrac{1}{2} = -0.5$

   In this example the same price reduction of 10%, brings about a greater change in quantity than in example (a); but it is still fairly small at only 5% more demanded. Ignoring the minus sign, the measure of elasticity is still less than 1, at ½ or 0.5. Therefore the product is still price inelastic.

1.11 On a straight line demand curve, elasticity is different at different points of the curve. But in general, the steeper the curve, the lower the elasticity.

Figure 2

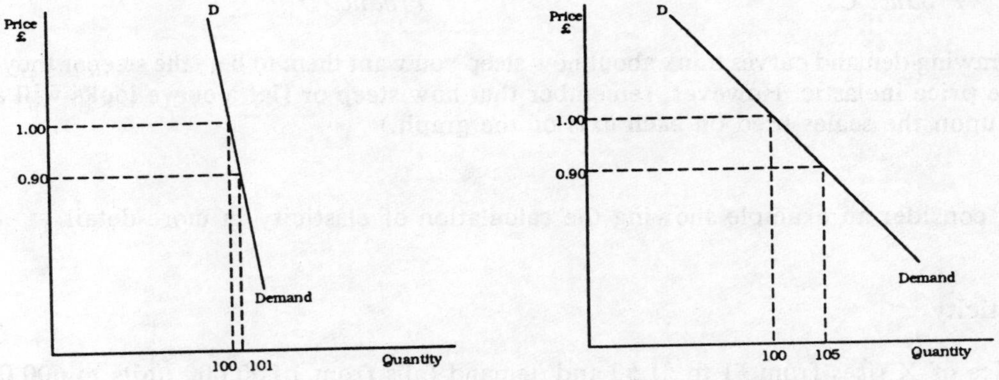

Product A   *Product B*

(η - pronounced 'eeta' - is a symbol used for elasticity of demand.)

1.12 If we now take an example of a product C where the quantity demanded changes more significantly over a particular price range.

   (a) $\dfrac{\% \Delta \text{ in } Q_d}{\% \Delta \text{ in } P} = -\dfrac{11\%}{10\%} = -1.1$

   Here the % change in quantity is greater than the change in price giving an absolute value of elasticity greater than 1. The demand is therefore described as price elastic.

(b)   The bigger the value of elasticity, the greater the sensitivity to price. For product D over a particular price range:

$$\frac{\% \, \Delta \text{ in Qd}}{\% \, \Delta \text{ in P}} = -\frac{20\%}{10\%} = -2.0$$

A value of elasticity of 2 shows that demand changes by twice as much as the change in variable. Both products are price sensitive, ie price elastic, D more so than C.

1.13   These examples C and D would be illustrated by relatively flat demand curves. Both goods are price elastic.

Figure 3

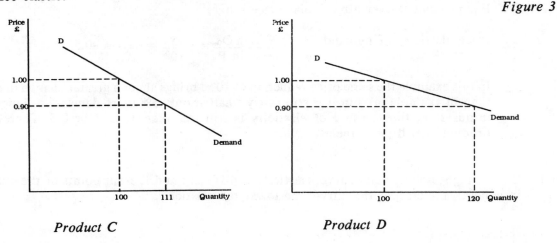

Product C   *Product D*

(When drawing demand curves think about how steep you want them to be – the steeper they are the more price inelastic. However, remember that how steep or flat a curve looks will also depend upon the scales used on each axis of the graph.)

1.14   We now consider an example showing the calculation of elasticity in more detail.

Example: elasticity

1.15   If the price of X rises from £1 to £1.50 and demand falls from 1,000,000 units to 600,000, calculate the price elasticity of demand between these two points on the demand curve.

Solution

1.16   Old demand   1,000,000 units
       New demand   600,000 units
       % change in demand $\dfrac{400,000}{1,000,000} \times 100\%$ =   40%

       Old price   £1.00
       New price   £1.50
       % change in price $\dfrac{50p}{£1.00} \times 100\%$ =   50%

       Price elasticity of demand   = $-\dfrac{40\%}{50\%}$ =   −0.8

Ignoring the minus sign, the price elasticity is 0.8.

The price elasticity of demand over this price range would be said to be *inelastic* because its value is less than 1.

Now try the following example yourself.

Exercise 1

If the price of X rises from £1.40 to £1.80 and the demand falls from 220,000 units to 180,000 units, what would be the price elasticity of demand?

Solution

	Old	New	% change
Quantity demanded	220,000	180,000	$\dfrac{40,000}{220,000} \times 100\% = 18.2\%$
Price	£1.40	£1.80	$\dfrac{40}{140} \times 100\% = 28.6\%$
Price elasticity of demand $=$			$-\dfrac{18.2\%}{28.6\%} = -0.64$

The minus sign is again ignored, and the price elasticity of demand is 0.64.

The price elasticity of demand over this price range is again inelastic, because its value is less than 1.

Elastic and inelastic demand

1.17 As mentioned already, the elasticity of demand will generally have a negative value since normal demand curves are downward sloping. However, the minus sign is often ignored so that elasticity of −1 is usually referred to as an elasticity of 1, or unity. The value of demand elasticity may be anything from zero to infinity.

1.18 Remember that demand is:

(a) *inelastic* if the absolute value is less than 1; and
(b) *elastic* if the absolute value is greater than 1.

1.19 Where demand is price inelastic, the quantity demanded falls by a smaller percentage than price, and where demand is price elastic, demand falls by a larger percentage than the percentage rise in price.

1.20 Generally, demand curves slope downwards. Consumers are willing to buy more at lower prices than at higher prices. Except in certain cases (which are referred to later), elasticity will vary in value along the length of a demand curve.

1.21 At high prices (the top of the demand curve), small percentage price reductions can bring large percentage increases in quantity demanded. This means that demand is relatively *elastic* over these ranges, and price reductions bring increases in total expenditure by consumers on the commodity in question.

1.22 At lower prices (the bottom of the demand curve), large percentage price reductions can bring small percentage increases in quantity. This means that demand is *inelastic* over these price ranges, and price increases result in increases in total expenditure.

Special values of price elasticity

1.23 There are three special values of price elasticity of demand: 0, 1 and infinity.

1.24 $\eta = 0$. *Demand is perfectly inelastic*. The demand curve is a vertical straight line and there is no change in quantity demanded, regardless of the change in price. A near example to this in real life might be the demand for table salt which will be little affected by price changes; we would not expect people to demand significantly more table salt if the price halved nor less salt if the price doubled. This is because salt is not a high priced commodity, and people can afford as much salt as they want.

Figure 4
Perfectly inelastic demand

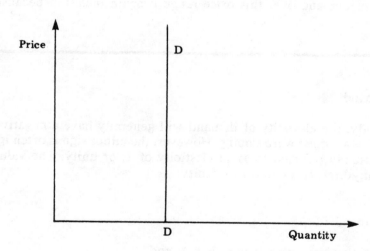

1.25 *Unit elasticity of demand:* $\eta = 1$. The demand curve of a good whose elasticity is 1 over its entire range is a *rectangular hyperbola*. The meaning of this is explained below.

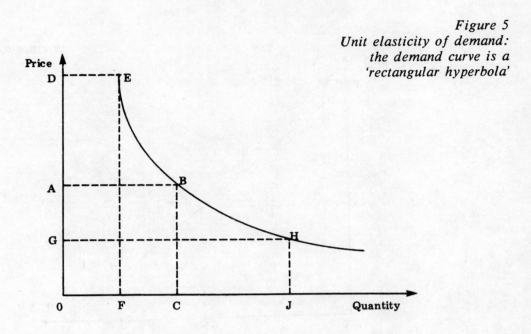

Figure 5
Unit elasticity of demand:
the demand curve is a
'rectangular hyperbola'

Rectangles OABC, ODEF and OGHJ all have the same area.

1.26 *Perfectly elastic demand:* $\eta = \infty$ (infinitely elastic). The demand curve is a horizontal straight line. Consumers will want to buy an infinite amount, but only up to price level P_0. Any price increase above this level will reduce demand to zero. The application of this type of demand curve will be seen in the chapter on perfect competition.

Figure 6
Perfectly elastic demand

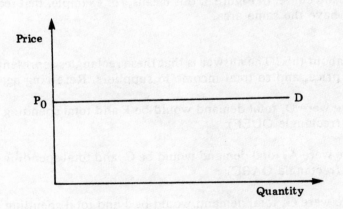

1.27 The different ranges of price elasticity at different places on a straight line demand curve are illustrated in Figure 7.

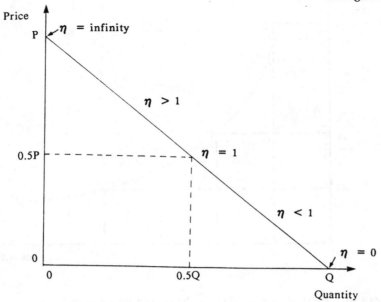

Figure 7
Ranges of price elasticity

The significance of price elasticity

1.28 Price elasticity of demand has a very important practical significance.

As illustrated in Figure 5, when elasticity of demand along an arc of the demand curve is exactly 1, the shape of the demand curve would be a rectangular hyperbola, which means that the size of any rectangle drawn between a point on the curve and the price and quantity axes of the graph would have exactly the same area as any other rectangle drawn in the same way from any other point on the demand curve. In Figure 5, this means, for example, that rectangles OABC, ODEF and OGHJ all have the same area.

1.29 What is so significant about this? The answer is that these rectangles represent total spending by customers at each price, and so total income to suppliers. Referring again to Figure 5:

(a) if the selling price were D, total demand would be F and total spending on the product would be D × F (rectangle ODEF);

(b) if the selling price were A, total demand would be C, and total spending on the product would be A × C (rectangle OABC);

(c) if the selling price were G, total demand would be J and total spending on the product would be G × J (rectangle OGHJ).

1.30 The implications of price elasticity of demand with regard to total revenue is not only important for goods with an elasticity of demand equal to 1.

1.31 When demand is *inelastic,* an *increase in price* would cause a fall in quantity demanded, but *total* revenue obtainable would go up.

In other words, if:

(a) P_0 is the old price;
(b) Q_0 is the old quantity;
(c) P_1 is the new price; and
(d) Q_1 is the new quantity;

then, in Figure 8, $P_1 Q_1$ would be higher in value than $P_0 Q_0$.

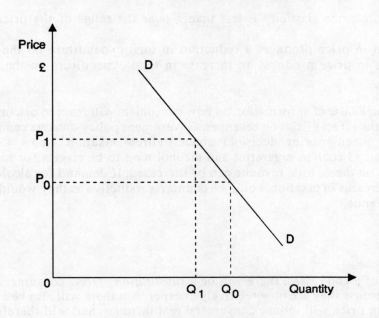

Figure 8
Inelastic demand

1.32 When demand is *inelastic* a *fall in price* would cause an increase in the quantity demanded, but *total revenue would fall*.

1.33 When demand is *elastic*, the opposite is true. An *increase in price* would cause such a large drop in quantity demanded that *total revenue would fall*.

In other words, in Figure 9, $P_1 Q_1$ would be less in value than $P_0 Q_0$.

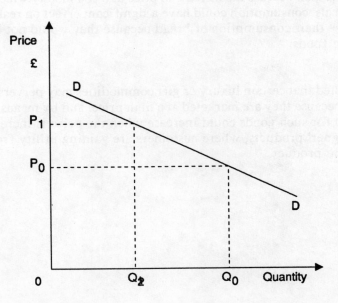

Figure 9
Elastic demand

1.34 When demand is *elastic*, a *fall in price* would cause such a large increase in quantity demanded that *total revenue would increase*.

1.35 For a commodity whose price elasticity is greater than 1 over the range of the price change:

(a) a reduction in price produces an increase in total expenditure on the commodity;
(b) a rise in price produces a reduction in total expenditure on the commodity.

For a good whose price elasticity is less than 1 over the range of the price change:

(a) a reduction in price produces a reduction in total expenditure on the commodity;
(b) an increase in price produces an increase in total expenditure on the commodity.

1.36 Marketers can make use of information on how consumers will react to pricing decisions, not least because of the effect of this on revenues. Government policy-makers can use information about elasticity when making decisions about indirect taxation. Items with a low price elasticity of demand such as cigarettes and alcohol tend to be targets for high taxation: by increasing taxes on these, total revenue can be increased. If demand for alcoholic drinks was price elastic, increases in taxation would be counter-productive as they would result in lower government revenue.

Giffen goods

1.37 When the price of a good rises, there will be a *substitution effect:* consumers will buy other goods instead because they are now relatively cheaper. But there will also be an *income effect* in that the rise in price will reduce consumers' real incomes, and will therefore affect their ability to buy goods and services.

1.38 The 19th century economist Sir Robert Giffen observed that this income effect could be so great for certain goods that the demand curve would be upward sloping. Such goods are called Giffen goods. The price elasticity of demand in such a case would be positive.

1.39 Giffen observed that among the labouring classes of his day, consumption of bread rose when its price rose. This could happen because the increase in price of a commodity which made up a high proportion of individuals' consumption could have a significant effect on real incomes. People would have to increase their consumption of bread because they would not be able to afford other more expensive foods.

1.40 It has also been suggested that certain luxury or gift commodities may perversely be perceived to have value simply because they are marketed at a high price, and by means of this so-called 'snob effect', demand for such goods could increase when the price is increased. This could apply to certain 'designer' products, where customers are gaining utility from the symbolic benefits of buying the product.

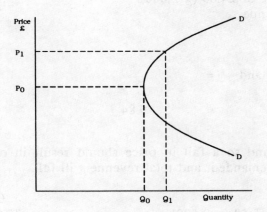

Figure 10
A backward sloping demand curve

1.41 A demand curve might behave normally throughout part of its length but reaches a point P_0, where an increase in price to P_1 actually increases the quantity demanded to Q_1.

Exercise 2

Suppose that there are two products, A and B.

(a) Product A currently sells for £5, and demand at this price is 1,700 units. If the price fell to £4.60, demand would increase to 2,000 units.

(b) Product B currently sells for £8 and demand at this price is 9,500 units. If the price fell to £7.50, demand would increase to 10,000 units.

In each of the two cases, calculate:

(i)   the price elasticity of demand; and

(ii) the effect on total revenue of the change in price if demand is met in full at both the old and the new prices.

Solution

(a) *Product A:*

Price elasticity of demand   =

$$\frac{-300}{0.4} \times \frac{5}{1,700} \qquad = \qquad -2.2$$

Demand is *elastic* and so a fall in price should result in such a large increase in quantity demanded that total revenue will rise.

	£
Revenue at old price of £5 (× 1,700)	8,500
Revenue at new price of £4.60 (× 2,000)	9,200
Increase in total revenue	700

(b) *Product B:*

Price elasticity of demand   =

$$\frac{-500}{0.5} \times \frac{8}{9,500} \quad = \quad -0.84$$

Demand is *inelastic* and so a fall in price should result in only a relatively small increase in quantity demanded, and total revenue will fall.

	£
Revenue at old price of £8 (× 9,500)	76,000
Revenue at new price of £7.50 (× 10,000)	75,000
Fall in total revenue	1,000

Factors influencing the price elasticity of demand

1.42 It is useful for marketers to be familiar with the characteristics which are likely to make demand for a product more or less price sensitive. Some characteristics are set out below. Think of a couple of products and see if you can assess whether demand is likely to be elastic or inelastic, according to these characteristics.

Elastic	*Inelastic*
Luxury	Necessity
Available substitutes	No substitutes
Non-addictive	Addictive
Spending represents a large % of income	Spending represents a small % of income

1.43 Bearing in mind that we are dealing with degrees of price sensitivity and not absolute prices, we can begin to get a feel for the response of individual products. There are no easy substitutes for petrol in the short term, and so demand for petrol will tend to be price inelastic. Cigarettes, alcohol, drugs and gambling all tend to be addictive in nature and likewise have price-inelastic demand. The government is able to take advantage of these characteristics to raise taxation on these goods, without risking significant reductions in their levels of demand.

1.44 Marketers try to build up brand loyalty to encourage 'addiction' to a particular brand, thus making demand for the product less price-sensitive.

Goods which are luxury items can be 'managed without' if their prices rise. Accordingly, business uses promotional strategies to try to convert wants to needs.

1.45 Marketers' ability to make products less price sensitive affects the demand curve, as illustrated in Figure 11.

Figure 11
Reducing price sensitivity

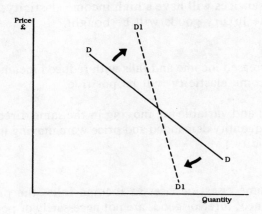

2. OTHER ELASTICITY MEASURES

Income elasticity of demand

2.1 The *income elasticity of demand* for a good indicates the responsiveness of demand to changes in household incomes. It is measured as:

Income elasticity of demand = $\dfrac{\text{\% change in quantity demanded}}{\text{\% change in household income}}$

or $\dfrac{\% \ \Delta \text{ in } Q_d}{\% \ \Delta \text{ in } Y}$

(Y = income)

2.2 (a) A good is *income elastic* if income elasticity is greater than 1 so that quantity demanded rises by a larger percentage than the rise in income. For example, if the demand for compact discs will rise by 10% if household income rises by 7%, we would say that compact discs are income elastic.

(b) A good is *income inelastic* if income elasticity is between 0 and 1 and the quantity demanded rises less than the proportionate increase in income. For example, if the demand for books will rise by 6% if household income rises by 10%, we would say that books are income inelastic.

2.3 For most commodities an increase in income will increase demand. The exact effect on demand will depend on the type of product. For example the demand for some products like bread will not increase much as income rises. Therefore, bread has a low income elasticity of demand. In contrast, the demand for luxuries increases rapidly as income rises and luxury goods therefore have a high income elasticity of demand.

2.4 In general:

(a) necessities of life have a low income elasticity, so that even if household income falls sharply, households will still want to buy the products;

(b) luxury goods and services will have a high income elasticity, so that if household income is low, none of the luxury goods will be bought.

2.5 If demand rises with increased income and falls with reduced income, the good is called a *normal good*. The value of income elasticity will be positive.

The quantity demanded and variable are moving in the same direction giving a positive value (unlike price, where the quantity demanded and price were moving in opposite directions giving a negative value of elasticity.)

2.6 If demand falls as income rises, or rises as income falls, the product is called an *inferior good*. As already mentioned, inferior goods are not necessarily of poor quality, but the consumer perceives that there is a better alternative which is preferred if income increases. For example the public transport system may be well run and comfortable, but as their income rises people may stop using the bus and use their own cars or a taxi instead.

Exercise 3

There are two products, with the same degree of income elasticity of demand. However, Product A has an income elasticity of -1.5 and Product B an income elasticity of +1.5.

Income levels are forecast to rise by 20% over the next five years. How does this information influence the plans for Product A and B over this time?

Solution

Product A is an inferior good whose demand will fall significantly with income.

$$\frac{\% \ \Delta \ in \ Q_D}{\% \ \Delta \ in \ Y} = \frac{-30\%}{+20\%} = 1.5$$

We know that income is expected to increase (+) by 20% and the value of income elasticity for A is -1.5. Therefore that quantity demanded will fall by $1\frac{1}{2}$ times the change in income over the same period, ie by 30%.

Marketing plans may include repositioning the product to help to lose its inferior product image, or there could be plans to diversify into new product areas. Certainly, as things stand, planned reductions in operational levels are essential.

Product B is equally sensitive to income changes. This time the product is a normal good, and so as income rises so does demand. Every 1% increase in income will result in a $1\frac{1}{2}$% increase in demand, a total increase of 30% over five years. Planned expansion of production to meet that demand is strongly advisable.

2.7 *Remember*. A negative value of income elasticity indicates an inferior good. A positive value indicates a normal good.

2.8 The ability to forecast the scale and direction of demand changes is of great value in the planning processes of a business. Information is available about anticipated future income of a country and this can be used by the business planners. However care needs to be taken to ensure national figures are not being applied to regional or demographic market segments, where there may be significant variations from the national average.

2.9 Faced with an inferior good, marketers can adopt strategies to help sustain demand in conditions of rising incomes, eg:

   (a) reposition the product in the market, eg margarine as a healthier product rather than inferior to butter;

   (b) look for new markets with lower current income levels.

Cross elasticity of demand

2.10 *Cross elasticity of demand* refers to the responsiveness of demand for one good to changes in the price of another good. The formula is:

$$\text{Cross elasticity of demand} = \frac{\%\text{ change in quantity of good A demanded*}}{\%\text{ change in the price of good B}}$$

*Given no change in the price of A

   (a) *If the two goods are substitutes, the value of cross elasticity will be positive.* A fall in the price of one will reduce the amount demanded of the other (the quantity and variable moving in the same direction).

   (b) *If the goods are complements, cross elasticity will be negative* and a fall in the price of one will raise demand for the other.

2.11 Cross elasticity involves a comparison between two products. Cross elasticity is significant where the two goods are close substitutes for each other, so that a rise in the price of B, say, is likely to result in an increase in the demand for A.

   Cross elasticity of demand between two complementary products can also be significant because a rise in the price of B would result in some fall in demand for A because of the fall in demand for B.

2.12 Cross elasticity helps the business person to identify the impact of other producers' decisions on the business. It provides an indication of when specific response to competitors' strategies is called for and when there may be opportunities for co-operation and collaboration.

4: FURTHER ASPECTS OF DEMAND AND SUPPLY

Demand elasticity and time

2.13 Elasticity of demand for any good - price elasticity, income elasticity and cross elasticity - can and does change over time. Generally, there are some substitutes for all goods.

Interest rate elasticity of demand

2.14 Another measure of elasticity, which is of some relevance to recent economic conditions in the UK, is *interest rate elasticity of demand*.

$$\text{Interest rate elasticity of demand} = \frac{\text{\% change in demand for a product}}{\text{\% change in interest rate levels}}$$

2.15 Interest rate elasticity should be particularly significant in the case of goods which consumers pay for by obtaining a loan or credit. Higher interest rates might deter consumers from buying such products, and so the demand curve will shift significantly to the left.

2.16 The most notable example of such a product is houses, which are usually bought with mortgage loans.

In the period 1988 to 1990, the UK government's main monetary policy measure for reducing the strength of the 'consumer boom' and inflation was to raise interest rates, in the expectation that higher interest rates would, in time, lead to a fall in consumer demand for goods. The same policy led to a slump in the housing market in 1989 to 1992, with house prices falling in many parts of the country.

Promotional elasticity of demand

2.17 Although not a precise measurement, calculating the amount by which demand changes as a result of a change in promotional spending (the *promotional elasticity of demand*) can help a marketer to measure the effectiveness of a campaign.

$$\text{Promotional elasticity of demand} = \frac{\text{\% change in demand for a product}}{\text{\% change in promotional expenditure}}$$

2.18 A demand-inelastic product indicating little demand change as a result of a campaign could reflect more on the quality of the campaign than on the nature of the demand for the product.

Elasticity of supply

2.19 The *elasticity of supply* indicates the responsiveness of supply to a change in price:

$$\text{Elasticity of supply} = \frac{\text{\% change in quantity supplied}}{\text{\% change in price}}$$

The elasticity of supply will vary between the three illustrated situations below.

2.20 Where the supply of goods is fixed whatever price is offered, eg in the case of antiques, vintage wines and land, supply is *perfectly inelastic*, and the elasticity of supply is 0.

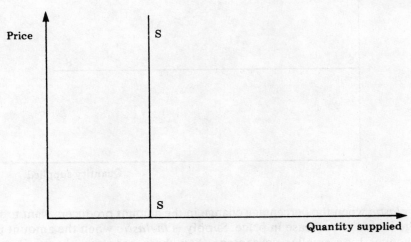

Figure 12
Perfectly inelastic supply

2.21 Where the supply of goods varies proportionately with the price, elasticity of supply equals one. Both supply curves in the following diagram have *unit elasticity* because they are straight line curves passing through the origin.

(Note that a demand curve with unit elasticity along all of its length is not a straight line, but a supply curve with unit elasticity *is* a straight line.)

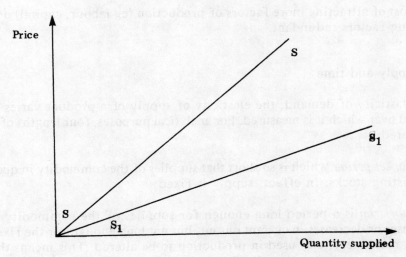

Figure 13
Unit elastic supply

2.22 Where the producers will supply any amount at a given price but none at all at a slightly lower price, elasticity of supply is infinite, or *perfectly elastic*.

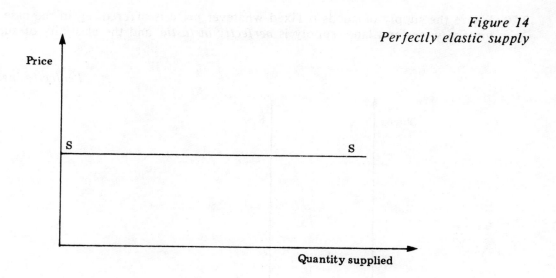

Figure 14
Perfectly elastic supply

2.23 Supply is *elastic* when the percentage change in the amount producers want to supply exceeds the percentage increase/decrease in price. Supply is *inelastic* when the amount producers want to supply changes by a smaller percentage than the percentage change in price.

Factors determining the elasticity of supply

2.24 The factors determining the elasticity of supply include:

(a) the time period;

(b) the range of alternatives open to the producer;

(c) the cost of attracting more factors of production (eg labour, capital) or the saving from making factors redundant.

Elasticity of supply and time

2.25 As with elasticity of demand, the elasticity of supply of a product varies according to the time period over which it is measured. For analytical purposes, four lengths of time period may be considered:

(a) *the market period* which is so short that supplies of the commodity in question are limited to existing stocks. In effect, supply is fixed;

(b) *the short run* is a period long enough for supplies of the commodity to be altered by increases or decreases in current output, but not long enough for the fixed equipment (ie plant, machinery, etc) used in production to be altered. This means that suppliers can produce larger quantities only if they are not already operating at full capacity; they can reduce output fairly quickly by means of lay-offs and redundancies;

(c) *the long run* is a period sufficiently long to allow firms' fixed equipment to be altered. There is time to build new factories and machines, and time for old ones to be closed down. New firms can enter the industry in the long run;

(d) *the secular period* is so long that underlying economic factors such as population growth, supplies of raw materials (such as oil) and the general conditions of capital supply may alter. ('Secular' is derived from the Latin word 'saecula' meaning 'centuries'.) The secular period is ignored by economists except in the theory of economic growth.

These types of time period were postulated by Alfred Marshall in his *Principles of Economics* (1920).

Elasticity of supply and the cost of factors of production

2.26 The cost of factors of production will affect the elasticity of supply. If demand increases, the supplier might attract more factors of production. If the cost of attracting new amounts of the factor is high, the supply curve will be more inelastic than if this cost is low, because suppliers will need a higher price rise to cover these costs, in order to justify an increase in supply. The payment necessary to keep the factor in its current use is termed its *'transfer earnings'*. Any payment in excess of this is called *economic rent*. The higher the elasticity of supply, the less economic rent is paid; where supply is perfectly elastic, all income is transfer earnings.

3. ELASTICITIES ILLUSTRATED: AGRICULTURE

Agricultural markets

3.1 Text books and examination questions on economics often use the example of agricultural produce as an illustration of demand and supply.

3.2 Unless a government intervenes in the market to stabilise prices or agricultural produce, it is likely that the prices of agricultural produce will fluctuate sharply. Why should this be so?

3.3 The reasons are that:

(a) many items of agricultural produce have *inelastic demand*. They are 'necessities of life' and consumers buy them in fairly stable quantities, regardless of price;

(b) agricultural produce has a *perfectly inelastic supply in the very short term, market period*, and at the same time, this total supply is very difficult, or impossible to determine and control, due to uncertainties about the weather or plant diseases that can create anything from a bumper harvest and large, fixed supplies, to a disastrous harvest and very small fixed supplies.

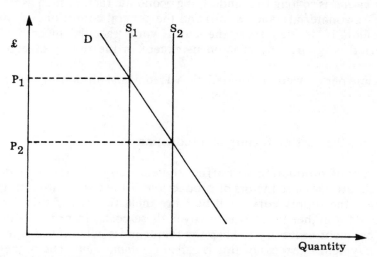

Figure 15

Suppose that the demand and supply for wheat is shown by Figure 15.

(a) Demand is inelastic, as suggested by the steep slope of the demand curve.

(b) Let's suppose that S_1 represents the (fixed) supply of spring wheat in a particular year. Due to a poor harvest, the supply is small and price will be P_1.

(c) Let's suppose that S_2 represents the (fixed) supply of winter wheat in the same year. The harvest is better, and since supply is greater, the price falls to P_2.

Suppliers (farmers) cannot control the very short term supply, and since demand is inelastic, fluctuations in supply can lead to sharp fluctuations in price.

3.4 Another model of how agricultural markets function is illustrated by the *'cobweb cycle'*, which is illustrated in Figure 16.

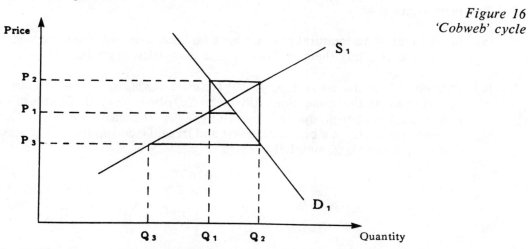

Figure 16
'Cobweb' cycle

It may be that farmers plant crops using as information the prevailing price at the time of sowing (P_1 in Figure 16). But if supply and demand are not in equilibrium and thus demand turns out to be higher after the harvest than it was previously, supply will be insufficient to meet demand at the old price, and prices will rise to P_2. In the second time period, farmers will plant more crops than previously (Q₂) because the price is now higher. Because of this additional supply, price will now fall to P₃ and less will then be sown in the third time period.

In this model, supply is a function of price in the previous time period, while demand is a function of price in the current time period. If the price changes become smaller each time, the market will converge to equilibrium, but if they become bigger each time, prices will fluctuate and the model will be unstable.

Price stabilisation methods

3.5 How can farmers be encouraged to devote enough land to an item of produce, so that supply will never be inadequate for consumers' needs in life? One solution is to try to protect farmers from the uncertainties of price fluctuations by 'guaranteeing' them a price for their produce.

In other words, the government might intervene in the market - ie stop a free market from operating - in order to stabilise prices to farmers.

3.6 There are various methods which are used to provide support for the farming sector; two are described here.

The first is that adopted by the European Community for various farm products. Under this scheme, a 'guaranteed price' is set which consumers in the market *must* pay. In order to maintain that price, the authorities have to be ready to purchase surplus quantities of the commodity, should there by any, to keep the price at its guaranteed level. Figure 17 illustrates such a policy.

Figure 17

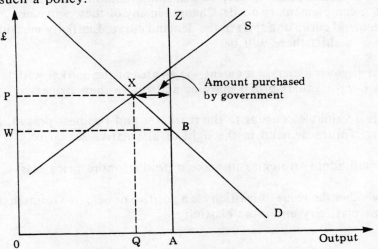

D is the demand curve for a farm product. S is the planned supply curve, showing the amounts which farmers would plan to supply at each price. If there were no government intervention, and no unplanned fluctuations in output, the average price over time would be P and average output would be Q. If the government feels that P is a 'fair' price for farmers it can seek to ensure that the price P will be earned, even if output fluctuates. In that case, government declares P to be the 'guaranteed price'.

3.7 If there is an unexpectedly large harvest, shown by the vertical line Z, then in the absence of intervention price would fall to W. However, since the government has guaranteed the price P it will buy up just enough output to reduce supply to Q and maintain the market price at P. (The amount bought by the government is indicated on Figure 17 as A-Q.) If the government also wishes to use the policy in the other direction, to keep prices down in times of poor harvests, it will have to keep stocks of the commodity in question, so that it can sell from stock in order to keep the price down.

3.8 An alternative approach to price stabilisation is that used in Britain before it joined the EC. Under this policy, known as a 'deficiency payments' scheme, consumers are not forced to pay an artificially high price for the food they consume. Farmers, on the other hand, are given a 'guaranteed price'.

3.9 Assume that government guarantees farmers that they will receive price P, and there is an unexpectedly large harvest shown by the vertical line Z. Under the deficiency payments scheme the price paid by consumers is allowed to fall to W, which 'clears the market' so that there are no surpluses to buy up, and consumers benefit from reduced prices. However, farmers do not suffer, as for each unit of output sold they are paid the difference between the market price and the guaranteed price P.

4. CONCLUSION

4.1 The key points in this chapter are as follows.

(a) Demand for a good depends largely on price, household income and the relative price of substitutes or complementary goods. Changes in any of these will cause either a movement along the demand curve or a shift in the demand curve. Elasticity measures *how much* of a movement or a shift there will be.

(b) If firms can discover a market segment - ie an area of the market with low price elasticity - they can improve their profit margins and revise their prices.

(c) Elasticity is a valuable concept to the marketer and business person. It can be used to help forecast future demand in the light of alternative scenarios.

(d) Marketers will adopt strategies to make a product more price elastic.

(e) Knowing whether the value of elasticity is a positive or negative is important when working with income elasticity and cross elasticity.

TEST YOUR KNOWLEDGE
The numbers in brackets refer to paragraphs of this chapter

1   Why is the concept of elasticity important to the marketer? (1.6)

2   Illustrate what happens to the value of price elasticity along the length of a straight line demand curve. (1.27)

3   What is a Giffen good? (1.38)

4   What characteristics would tend to make a product price elastic? (1.42)

5   What is an inferior good? (2.6)

See the comments on the next page for questions 6 - 9

6   What is meant by the price elasticity of demand for a commodity? What is the significance of this concept to:

(a) the Chancellor of the Exchequer; and
(b) a manufacturer?

7   Why do the prices of agricultural products fluctuate more than the prices of manufactured goods?

8   From the following demand schedule, calculate the price elasticity of demand when

(a) the price falls from £10 to £9
(b) the price rises from £7 to £8

Price per unit £	Demand (units per month)
10	600
9	700
8	800
7	900

9   What will be the effect on price and quantity demanded and supplied of sailing boats, given a significant reduction in income tax?

Test Your Knowledge: comments on questions 6-9

6   The first part of the question can be answered directly from the text of this chapter. A government is interested in elasticity because it should want to know the effects of (an indirect) tax on commodities. For example, do taxes leave prices unchanged or do they cause prices to rise and does the producer or the consumer pay the tax? And so how much tax revenue would be earned? Similarly, if a tax such as VAT is increased from 15%, say, to 20%, will total tax revenue increase or fall? Firms will also be concerned as to the effect on consumer demand, and so on revenue and profits, of a change in the price they charge for their product.

7   This question calls for the application of theory to a specific example.

'*Demand* for agricultural and manufactured goods is likely to be fairly stable, although demand for both may be influenced slightly by seasonal factors. Demand for agricultural produce tends to be more elastic than demand for many manufactured items. On the other hand, *supply* of agricultural goods is likely to be far less stable than manufactured goods. Fluctuations in supply of agricultural goods arise from seasonal factors as well as weather conditions and disease. These seasonal factors can cause major shifts in the supply curves of agricultural goods.' Some reference could be made to price support programmes to stabilise agricultural goods' prices.

8   Price elasticity of demand $= \dfrac{\text{\% change in quantity demanded}}{\text{\% change in price}}$

(a) *£10 to £9:* $- \dfrac{100}{1} \times \dfrac{10}{600} = -1.67$

(b) *£7 to £8:* $- \dfrac{100}{1} \times \dfrac{7}{900} = -0.77$

In this example, demand is inelastic at the lower price level but elastic at the higher price level.

9   The demand curve for sailing boats will shift to the right. Both price and quantity demanded/supplied will go up. The effect of a cut in income tax is to leave households with more to spend. Sailing boats are a luxury good, and the income elasticity of demand is likely to be quite high. The percentage increase in demand for boats is therefore likely to be greater than the percentage increase in after-tax household income.

Now try illustrative questions 7 and 8 at the end of the text

Chapter 5

COSTS, REVENUE AND PROFITS

> **This chapter covers the following topics.**
>
> 1. Costs of production and the firm
> 2. Short run costs
> 3. Long run costs
> 4. Expansion of firms
> 5. Decisions on location
> 6. Adding revenue curves

1. COSTS OF PRODUCTION AND THE FIRM

Introduction

1.1 In this chapter we shall look at the costs and output decisions of an *individual* firm. In other words, we shall look at what the costs of production are for a single firm, and how these are affected by both short-run and long-run factors.

We shall then go on to consider profit and how much output a firm will produce at a given market price. The aggregate amount of goods supplied by every individual firm adds up to the market supply; by studying an individual firm we are looking at the 'building blocks' of market supply.

1.2 The firm is a wide term for any organisation which carries on business. In spite of their structural differences, firms will be treated as single, consistent decision-taking units, and we shall ignore any differences in decision-making procedures and economic structures between them.

1.3 Production is carried out using the factors of production which must be paid or rewarded for their use. The cost of production is the cost of the factors that are used.

Factor of production	*Its cost/reward*
land	rent
labour	wages
capital	interest
entrepreneurship	normal or 'pure' profit

1.4   It is important to note that normal profit is a cost. An accountant, who thinks of profit as the *difference* between revenue and cost might think this odd. But normal profit represents the opportunity cost of enterprise and is a necessary cost without which production will not occur.

Fixed and variable inputs and costs

1.5   Firms combine various input resources to produce a given level of output. By varying the amounts of inputs used, the level of output can be altered. However, not all inputs are equally flexible. Energy, raw materials, the number of labour hours and so on can be combined with each other with a great deal of flexibility, but the size of the factory or number of machines cannot be varied so quickly. For example, output can be increased in the short term by buying extra materials, hiring new labour or working overtime, but the extra work will still be done on the same machines and in the same factory.

1.6   Economists take the view that *in the short run* some factors of production (or 'production inputs') are variable in supply and so have variable costs. Typically, labour is regarded as a variable cost item. On the other hand, some factors of production are fixed in supply and so have fixed costs. Typically, capital is regarded as a fixed cost item.

More precisely, fixed costs are those costs which do not vary directly with output, but which remain constant whether anything is produced or not. Fixed costs do determine the current capacity of an operation - ie the most output which could be produced in a period.

Figure 1

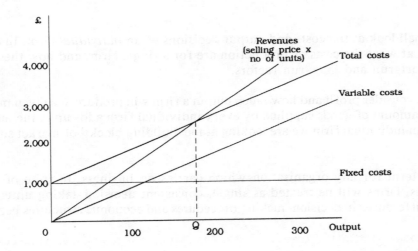

1.7   Figure 1 illustrates the costs faced by a firm in the short run. Some of its inputs are fixed. These have to be paid for (£1,000) whether output is zero or 300 units. Other costs are variable and so change with the volume of output. They are zero at zero output and in this example increase up proportionally with production.

1.8   The firm will want to cover all of its costs, whether fixed or variable. Total costs are the sum of the fixed and variable costs (see Figure 1).

Total costs = fixed costs + variable costs (TC = FC + VC)

5: COSTS, REVENUE AND PROFITS

Break-even analysis

1.9 If a firm just covers all of its total costs, it will 'break even' from the cost accountant's point of view. The volume of sales necessary to achieve this at a price of £15 is shown in Figure 1 as Q. From an economic point of view, a firm will not produce if the price is below average variable cost, ie if revenue is below variable costs.

2. SHORT RUN COSTS

Behaviour of a firm in the short run

2.1 Decisions in business have to be made in the context of the current short run constraints. Today capacity is fixed and it will take time to change it - to buy a new machine, build a new factory and so on. The time period during which we cannot change that capacity is called 'the short run' by economists.

2.2 In business it is normal to want to quantify terms like the short run into a number of years. In plans it is essential that you specify time frames over which objectives are to be achieved. Unfortunately economists cannot be so specific. The actual time involved will vary according to the nature of the business you are in. Building a new nuclear fuel plant would take much longer than expanding a fleet of lorries or the size of a hotel. The economic analysis provides a framework which can be used to understand the mechanisms of decision making in any firm, including investment decisions.

Short-run costs: total costs, average costs and marginal costs

2.3 We now turn our attention to short-run costs - ie costs of output during this time period in which only some resources of production are variable and some resources of production are fixed.

2.4 There are three aspects of cost which must be considered.

(a) *Total cost* (TC).

(b) *Average cost* (AC). Average cost is simply the total cost divided by the total quantity produced (N).

Average cost is made up of an average fixed cost per unit plus an average variable cost per unit.

$$AC = \frac{TC}{N} = \frac{TFC}{N} + \frac{TVC}{N}$$

$$AC = AFC + AVC$$

Average fixed cost per unit (AFC) will get smaller as more units are produced. This is because TFC is the same amount regardless of the volume of output, so as N gets bigger, AFC must get smaller.

If fixed costs are £1,000 and we produce 1 unit:

$$AFC = \frac{£1,000}{1} = £1,000$$

If we produce 10 units:

$$AFC = \frac{£1,000}{10} = £100$$

If we produce 1,000 units:

$$AFC = \frac{£1,000}{1,000} = £1$$

Average variable costs per unit (AVC) will change as output volume increases.

(c) *Marginal cost* (MC). This is the extra cost of producing one more unit of output. For example, the marginal cost for a firm of producing the 50th unit of output is the extra cost of making the 50th unit, having already made the previous 49 units. In other words the MC of the 50th unit is the total cost of making the first 50 units minus the total cost of making the first 49 units.

Numerical illustration of TC, AC and MC

2.5 Let us suppose that a firm employs a given amount of capital which is a fixed (invariable) input in the short run: in other words, it is not possible to obtain extra amounts of capital quickly. The firm may combine with this capital different amounts of labour, which we assume to be an input which is variable in the short term. Thus fixed capital and variable labour can be combined to produce different levels of output.

2.6 Here is an illustration of the relationship between the different definitions of the firm's costs (the figures used are hypothetical).

Units of output n	Total cost TC £	Average cost AC £	Marginal cost MC £	
1	1.10	1.10	1.10	
2	1.60	0.80	0.50	(1.60 – 1.10)
3	1.75	0.58	0.15	(1.75 – 1.60)
4	2.00	0.50	0.25	(2.00 – 1.75)
5	2.50	0.50	0.50	(2.50 – 2.00)
6	3.12	0.52	0.62	(3.12 – 2.50)
7	3.99	0.57	0.87	(3.99 – 3.12)
8	5.12	0.64	1.13	(5.12 – 3.99)
9	6.30	0.70	1.18	(6.30 – 5.12)
10	8.00	0.80	1.70	(8.00 – 6.30)

(a) *Total cost* (TC) is the sum of labour costs plus capital costs, since these are by assumption the only two inputs.

(b) *Average cost* (AC) is the cost per unit of output, ie $AC = \dfrac{TC}{output} = \dfrac{TC}{n}$.

(c) *Marginal cost* (MC) is the total cost of producing n units minus the total cost of producing one less unit, ie (n-1) units.

2.7 There are some important points to notice in this set of figures.

(a) *Total cost*. Total costs of production carry on rising as more and more units are produced.

(b) *Average cost*. AC changes as output increases. It starts by falling, reaches a lowest level, and then starts rising again.

(c) *Marginal cost*. The MC of each extra unit of output also changes with each unit produced. It too starts by falling, fairly quickly reaches a lowest level, and then starts rising.

(d) *AC and MC compared*. At lowest levels of output, MC is less than AC. At highest levels of output, though, MC is higher than AC. There is a 'cross-over' point, where MC is exactly equal to AC. In this small example, it is at 5 units of output.

The relationship between AC and MC

2.8 There are some other relationships between average and marginal costs.

(a) When the average cost schedule is rising, the marginal cost will always be higher than the average cost.

This makes sense. If the marginal cost of making one extra unit of output exceeds the average cost of making all the previous units, then making the extra unit will clearly cause an increase in the average unit cost.

In our example the average cost schedule rises from six units of output onwards and MC is bigger than AC at all these levels of output (6 - 10 units).

(b) When the average cost curve is falling, the marginal cost lies below it.

This follows similar logic. If the marginal cost of making an extra unit is less than the average cost of making all the previous units, the effect of making the extra unit must be a reduction in average unit cost. This happens between production of one and four units.

(c) When the average cost curve is horizontal, marginal cost is equal to it.

When there are five units of output, the average cost stays at £0.50 and the marginal cost of the fifth unit is also £0.50.

The marginal cost curve always cuts through the average cost curve at the lowest point of the average cost curve.

The shape of short-run cost curves

2.9   We can draw a graph of AC and MC, with the x axis representing output quantity and the y axis representing costs.

Figure 2

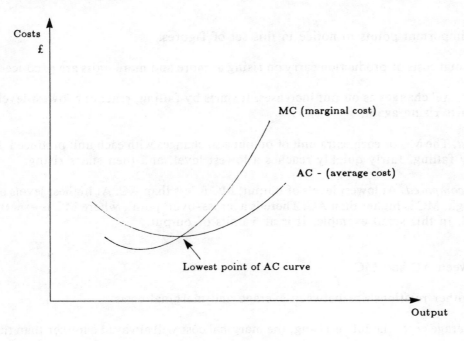

2.10   The short-run average cost (SRAC) curve is always likely to be U-shaped. We now consider why.

2.11   To explain why short run average costs produce this 'U' shaped curve you need to look at what happens to the constituent parts of average costs as you increase output. We have already seen that

$$AC = AFC + AVC$$

2.12   As we have seen, average fixed costs fall as output increases, the same cost being divided by more and more units. However, the fall in AFC at first is more significant, while at higher and higher levels of output, the drop becomes less significant. You can see this from a simple table.

Fixed costs	*Output*	*Average fixed costs*
100	1	100
100	2	50
100	3	33.3
100	4	25
100	5	20

2.13 Average variable costs rise as output rises. However, they are not likely to rise directly proportionally to output, as we assumed in Figure 1. Adding more of a variable factor to fixed factors is subject to an economic law - the law of diminishing returns.

The law of diminishing returns

2.14 Diminishing returns explain why a short run average cost curve begins to rise at a certain level, and the average cost per unit of production gets higher as more output is produced.

2.15 The law of diminishing returns states that, given the present state of technology, as more units of a variable input factor are added to input factors that are fixed in supply in the short run, the resulting increments to total production will eventually and progressively decline.

In other words, as more units of a variable factor are added to a quantity of a fixed factors, there may be some *increasing returns* or *constant returns* as more units of the variable factor are added, but eventually *diminishing returns* will set in.

2.16 The law of diminishing returns can also be expressed as the law of variable proportions, which states that as the proportions of a variable input factor to a fixed input factor are altered, and more of the variable factor is added to the fixed factor, the marginal product attributable to each extra unit of the variable factor will increase at first, but will later diminish and may eventually become negative.

2.17 Two important points to note about the law of diminishing returns are that:

(a) it relates to the short run situation, when some inputs are in fixed supply. It does not relate to the long run;

(b) it is not a law that can be 'proved', but it has been found to apply frequently in practice.

2.18 The law of diminishing returns is expressed in production quantities, but it obviously has direct implications for short run average and marginal *costs*. Resources cost money, and the average and marginal costs of output will depend on the quantities of resources needed to produce the given output.

2.19 Increasing and diminishing returns to a variable factor may provide the reasons why the short run average cost curve is U-shaped.

2.20 If the firm wishes to supply more than Z units to the market place, it can only do so in the short run by accepting higher average costs. This may be acceptable if there was a sudden increase in demand, causing price to rise, but if that increase in demand was likely to be sustained, the firm would want to find a way of reducing average costs in the long term so that they were near the optimum lowest cost level.

Figure 3
U-shaped short run cost
curve and diminishing returns

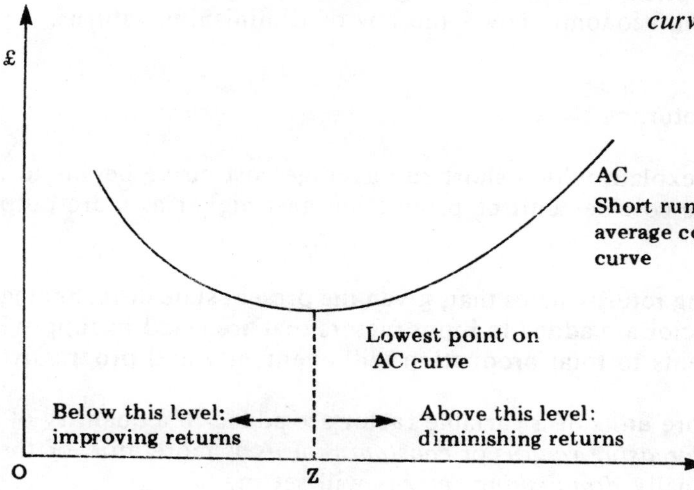

2.21 Average costs start to rise because of the constraints on capacity. To increase output without raising average costs the firm needs to invest in increased capacity, more machines, space, management expertise and so on.

2.22 As soon as this can occur you move to the economist's view of the long run - a time period when fixed costs can vary.

3. LONG RUN COSTS

The long run

3.1 When a firm expands its capacity, its 'fixed' costs are increased. The firm is now faced with a new and short run average cost curve, based on its new cost schedules. Decisions now have to be made in the context of its new expanded operational constraints.

Figure 4
Short run average
costs for a firm

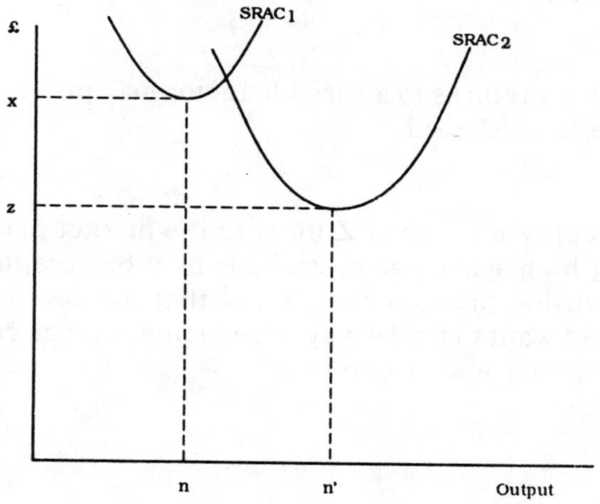

This new curve SRAC₂ (Figure 4) may well indicate lower average costs at increased levels of output £z at output n'. Further increases in capacity will result in still more SRAC curves.

3.2   In effect the long run is made up by a whole series of short run positions and the long run average cost (LRAC) curve can be shown by drawing a line which touches all of the short run curves.

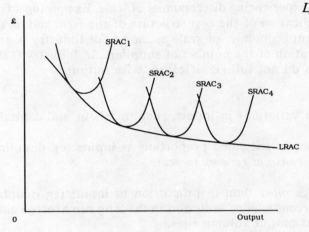

Figure 5
Long run average cost curve

3.3   The long run average cost curve is sometimes referred to as an 'envelope curve'. It 'envelopes' all the short run positions facing the firm at a range of outputs. The LRAC indicates the lowest cost possible for any given output, given the current state of technology.

Why might average costs fall in the long run?

3.4   Unlike the slope of the SRAC curve, which is always 'U' shaped, the LRAC is not always the same shape. Different firms and industries are faced with different shapes of LRAC, with average costs falling more significantly in some cases.

Figure 6

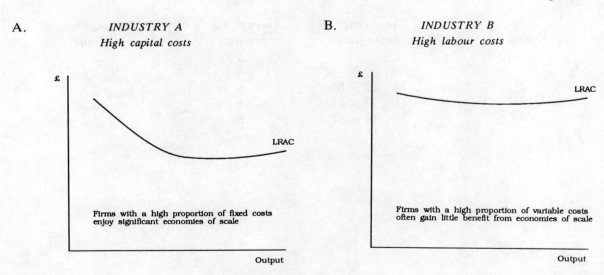

A.   **INDUSTRY A**
                High capital costs

B.   **INDUSTRY B**
                High labour costs

Firms with a high proportion of fixed costs enjoy significant economies of scale

Firms with a high proportion of variable costs often gain little benefit from economies of scale

75

Economies and diseconomies of scale

3.5 For most industries, there will be some reduction of average costs as capacity is increased. The reason for this is in essence very simple - to double output, you do not necessarily double all the fixed costs.

3.6 If costs fall in the long run the firm is enjoying the economies of scale; if costs do not fall or increase, the firm is experiencing diseconomies of scale. Examining a firm's projected LRAC curve gives you an indication of the cost structure of the firm and of the likely structure of the industry. Significant economies of scale as shown for Industry A are likely to encourage mergers, and concentration of the number of suppliers. In Industry B there is less reason for firms to grow as costs do not fall significantly with output.

3.7 Output will vary with variations in inputs, such as labour and capital.

(a) If output increases in the same proportion as inputs (eg doubling all inputs doubles output) there are *constant returns to scale*.

(b) If output increases *more* than in proportion to inputs (eg doubling all inputs trebles output) there are *economies of scale* and in the long run average costs of production will continue to fall as output volume rises.

(c) If output increases *less* than in proportion to inputs (eg trebling all inputs only doubles output) there are *diseconomies of scale* and in the long run average costs of production will rise as output volume rises.

3.8 Returns to scale are, in effect, concerned with improvements or declines in productivity *by increasing the scale of production* - eg by mass-producing instead of producing in small batch quantities.

3.9 A feature of constant returns to scale is that *long run* average costs and marginal costs per unit remain constant. The following figures illustrate this.

Output	Total cost (with constant returns)	Average cost per unit	Marginal cost per unit
	£	£	£
1	6	6	6
2	12 (2 × 6)	6	6
3	18 (3 × 6)	6	6
4	24 (4 × 6)	6	6

Figure 7

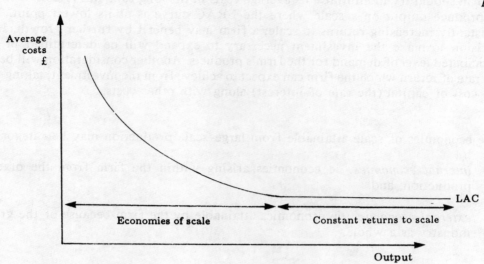

3.10 In the real world, the duplication of all inputs might be impossible if one counts qualitative as well as quantitative characteristics in inputs. One such input is entrepreneurship. Doubling the size of the firm does not necessarily double the inputs of organisational and managerial skills, even if the firm does hire extra managers and directors. The input of entrepreneurship might be intangible and indivisible.

3.11 Figure 7 shows the shape of the long-run average cost curve (LRAC) if there are economies of scale up to a certain output volume and then constant returns to scale thereafter. It may be that the flat part of the LRAC curve is never reached, or it may be that *diseconomies of scale* are encountered.

3.12 Diseconomies of scale might set in when a firm gets so large that it cannot operate efficiently or it is too large to manage efficiently, so that average costs begin to rise.

Figure 8
Long-run average costs; eventual
diseconomies of scale

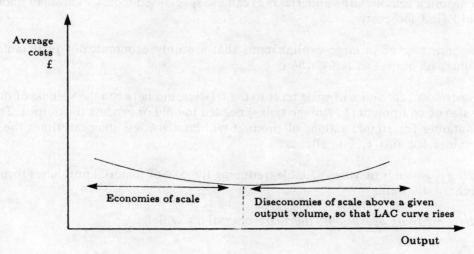

3.13 A firm should try to minimise its average costs in the long run, and to do this it ought to try to produce output on a scale where the LRAC curve is at its lowest point. If there are constantly increasing returns to scale, a firm may benefit by further growth. However the decision to make the investment necessary to expand will be determined in part by the anticipated level of demand for the firm's products. Another consideration will be the level of the rate of return which the firm can expect to achieve from the investment, taking into account the cost of capital (the rate of interest) along with other costs.

3.14 The economies of scale attainable from large-scale production may be categorised as:

(a) *internal economies:* ie economies arising within the firm from the organisation of production; and

(b) *external economies:* ie economies attainable by the firm because of the growth of the industry as a whole.

3.15 *Internal economies of scale* arise from the more effective use of available resources, and from increased specialisation, when production capacity is enlarged.

(a) *Specialisation of labour*: in a large undertaking, a highly skilled worker can be employed in a job which makes full use of his or her skills. In a smaller undertaking, individuals must do a variety of tasks, none of which they may do very well ('Jack-of-all-trades - master of none').

(b) *Division of labour*: because there is specialisation of labour there is also division of labour, ie work is divided between several specialists, each of whom contributes his or her share to the final product. A building will be constructed, for example, by labourers, bricklayers, plumbers, electricians, plasterers, etc. Switching between tasks wastes time, and division of labour avoids this waste.

(c) Large undertakings can make use of *larger and more specialised machinery*. If smaller undertakings tried to use similar machinery, the costs would be excessive because the machines would become obsolete before their physical life ends (ie their economic life would be shorter than their physical life). Obsolescence is caused by falling demand for the product made on the machine, or by the development of newer and better machines.

(d) For a similar reason, large undertakings can use specialised tools which small undertakings would find too costly.

Economists refer to large capital items that are only economically justifiable at high volumes of output as *indivisibles*.

(e) *Dimensional* economies of scale refer to the relationship between the volume of output and the size of equipment (eg storage tanks) needed to hold or process the output. The cost of a container for 10,000 gallons of product will be *much* less than ten times the cost of a container for just 1,000 gallons.

(f) *Buying economies* may be available, reducing the cost of material purchases through bulk purchase discounts.

(g) *Indivisibility of operations*: there are operations which:

(i) must be carried out at the same cost, regardless of whether the business is small or large; these are fixed costs and *average* fixed costs always decline as production increases;

(ii) vary a little, but not proportionately, with size (ie having 'semi-fixed' costs);

(iii) are not worth considering below a certain level of output (eg advertising campaigns, marketing structures).

Set-up costs for batch production are an example of 'fixed cost' items for which average unit costs become lower as the size of the production run gets bigger.

(h) Specialisation of labour and machines result in simplification and standardisation of operations (ie *variety reduction*) which themselves result in lower costs.

(i) *Stock holding* becomes more efficient. The most economic quantities of inventory to hold increase with the scale of operations, but at a lower proportionate rate of increase.

(j) Large firms attract better quality employees if the employees see better career prospects than in a small firm.

(k) Specialisation of labour applies to management, and there are thus managerial economies; the cost per unit of management will fall as output rises.

(l) Marketing economies are available, because a firm can make more effective use of advertising, specialist salesmen, and specialised channels of distribution.

(m) Large companies are able to devote more resources to research and development. In an industry where research and development is essential for survival, large companies are more likely to prosper.

(n) Large companies find it easier to raise finance and can often do so more cheaply. Quoted public limited companies have access to The Stock Exchange for new share issues. They are also able to borrow money more readily.

(o) A large firm can undertake more investments (in fixed assets and new operations) than a small firm; this allows the large firm to spread risks.

3.16 *External economies of scale* occur as an *industry* grows in size. For example:

(a) a large skilled labour force is created and educational services can be geared towards training new entrants;

(b) specialised ancillary industries will develop to provide components, transport finished goods, trade in by-products, provide special services etc. For instance, law firms may be set up to specialise in the affairs of the industry.

The extent to which both internal and external economies of scale can be achieved will vary from industry to industry, depending on the conditions with respect to that industry. In other words, large firms are better suited to some industries than others.

3.17 Internal economies of scale are potentially more significant than external economies to a supplier of a product or service for which there is a large consumer market. It may be necessary for a firm in such an industry to grow to a certain size in order to benefit fully from potential economies of scale, and thereby be cost-competitive and capable of making profits and surviving.

External economies of scale are potentially significant to smaller firms who specialise in the ancillary services to a larger industry. For example, the development of a large world-wide industry in drilling for oil and natural gas off-shore has led to the creation of many new specialist supplier firms, making drilling rigs, and various types of equipment.

A specialist firm may benefit more from the market demand created by a large customer industry than from its own internal economies of scale.

3.18 It is generally accepted that in any industry, there is a minimum scale of production which is necessary for a firm to achieve the full potential economies of scale. Just what this *minimum efficient scale* (MES) is will vary from industry to industry. In the paint manufacturing industry, for example, it might be necessary to have a 15% share of the market in order to achieve maximum scale economies, whereas in frozen food production, a 25% share of the market might be necessary, and so on. If a firm has a production capacity below the minimum economic scale, its unit costs of production will be higher than the unit costs of its bigger competitors, and so it will not compete successfully and it will make lower profits, or even losses. A profit-maximising firm should be attempting to minimise its unit costs, and this means striving to achieve maximum scale economies, which in turn may mean having to grow bigger. The only alternative is to develop a niche in the market providing added benefits at premium prices.

Technological progress and shifts in the long-run cost curve

3.19 The U-shaped LRAC curve predicted by the economic theory of eventual diminishing returns to scale may not exist in fact because of technological progress. Technical progress would shift the LRAC curves over time, as shown in Figure 9, so the LRAC curve observed from empirical data over time would be the L-shaped curve shown by the dashed line.

Figure 9
The LRAC curve shifts over time from
$LRAC_1$ to $LRAC_2$ to $LRAC_3$ as
technological progress is made and so
further economies of scale are created

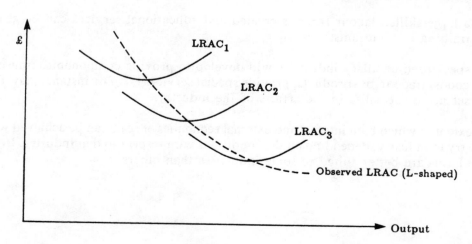

3.20 The reason why technological progress reduces long-run costs is that new technology reduces short-run costs, and since the long-run average cost curve represents a series of short-run cost curves at different output volumes, there will be reductions in the LRAC too.

3.21 Short-run costs will fall because:

(a) the new technology might help in achieving greater economies of scale; it will improve labour productivity too, measured as output per employee over time;

(b) there might be a shift to using cheaper machines from relatively more expensive labour. In other words, new technology can result in lost jobs.

Exercise

Two concepts have now been described about a firm's costs. These are:

(a) diminishing returns to a factor;
(b) economies of scale.

As an exercise, check that you can explain what is the difference between these two concepts.

Solution

Diminishing returns. In the short run, some factors of production are fixed, and some are variable. This means that a firm can increase the volume of its output in the short run, but only within the constraint of having some fixed factors. As a result, the short-run average cost curve is U-shaped, because of increasing and then diminishing marginal returns.

Marginal returns occur within a given production capacity limit. For example, if a company has a given capacity limit of 100,000 units, with fixed costs of £300,000 per period and variable costs of £2 per unit, decreasing average cost per unit, as output is increased eg

Output Units	Fixed costs £	Variable costs £	Total costs £	Average costs £
50,000	300,000	100,000	400,000	8.00
75,000	300,000	150,000	450,000	6.40
100,000	300,000	200,000	500,000	5.00

However, when marginal costs per unit begin to increase above £2 per unit (eg because of overtime premiums on labour costs) there will be diminishing returns to scale.

Economies of scale. In the long run, all factors of production are variable and so a firm can increase the scale of its output in the long run without any constraints of fixed factors. By increasing output capacity in this way, a firm might be able to reduce its unit costs - eg by mass-producing with bigger and more efficient machines or more specialised machines. These cost reductions are economies of scale.

Economies of scale occur when a firm re-organises its production capacity and is able to produce more output. For example, suppose that a firm which has an output capacity of 100,000 units, with fixed costs per unit of £300,000 and unit variable costs of £2, now doubles its output capacity to 200,000 units, when fixed costs are £400,000 and unit variable costs are £1.50. There will be economies of scale, because both average unit costs (above a certain level of output) and marginal costs have fallen.

Output Units	Fixed costs £	Variable costs at capacity £	Total costs at capacity £	Average costs at capacity £
100,000 (old capacity)	300,000	200,000	500,000	5.00
200,000 (new capacity)	400,000	300,000	700,000	3.50

If economies of scale are sufficiently great, average costs and more particularly marginal unit costs will fall to the point where suppliers are able to reduce their selling prices and still maximise profits at the lower selling price. MC has fallen, so MR will fall too, at the profit-maximising output level.

Economies of scale explain the L-shape of a firm's long-run average cost curve.

4. EXPANSION OF FIRMS

Economies of scale and expansion of the firm

4.1 The two broad methods of achieving growth in sales and output volumes and/or growth in profits are:

(a) organic growth - ie growth through a gradual build-up of the firm's own resources, developing new products, acquiring more plant and machinery, hiring extra labour and so on;

(b) growth through mergers and takeovers - ie the combination of two firms into one.

Integration and diversification

4.2 The nature of a merger or takeover can be viewed according to what firms are coming together: are they in exactly the same line of business? Are they in very similar businesses? Are they in related businesses, but operating in different stages of the production and selling process? Are they in unrelated lines of business?

(a) *Horizontal integration.* When two firms in the same business merge, there is horizontal integration. Horizontal integration tends to create monopolies, so that if, for example, All-England Chocolate plc with a 15% share in the UK chocolate market were to merge with British Choc plc which has a 20% share of the UK market, the enlarged company might expect to hold a 35% share of the market.

(b) *Vertical integration.* Two firms operating at different stages in the production and selling process might merge. When they do, vertical integration occurs. For example, the stages in the production of petrol for cars are:

      (i)   Oil extraction;

      (ii)   Shipping (in tanker fleets, or by pipeline);

      (iii) Refining;

      (iv) Distribution (to petrol stations);

      (v)   Retail sales (at petrol stations).

A company which operates exclusively in oil refining might take over an oil shipping company, and perhaps an oil extraction company too. This would be *backward* vertical integration, ie back through stages in production towards the raw material growing/extraction stage.

The same company might take over a company with a distribution fleet of petrol tanker lorries, and perhaps a chain of petrol stations too. This would be *forward* vertical integration, ie forward through stages in production and selling towards the end consumer sales stage.

    (c)   *Conglomerates.* A company might take over or merge with another company in a different business altogether. This form of merger is diversification, and a group of diversified companies is referred to as a conglomerate organisation.

4.3   There is good reason for 'horizontal' mergers when further economies of scale become achievable. Suppose that there are four firms in an industry, each having a 25% share of the total market and each maximising the potential economies of scale. If a new technological process is developed which enables further reductions in unit costs to be achieved but only for firms with output capacity sufficient to satisfy a 50% share of the market demand, it would not make sense for all four firms to double their output capacity. Capacity would then be double the market demand. It would make more sense for the four firms to arrange mergers, to reduce the total number of firms down to two.

Diseconomies of scale

4.4   'Classical' economic theory predicts that there will be diseconomies of scale in the long-run costs of a firm, once the firm gets beyond an ideal size. The reasons for diseconomies of scale are human and behavioural problems of managing a large firm. In a large firm employing many people, with many levels in the hierarchy of management, there are:

    (a)   difficulties with communicating information and instructions;

    (b)   excessively long chains of command;

    (c)   poor morale and motivation amongst staff, which are often much worse than in smaller firms;

    (d)   difficulties for senior management in assimilating all the information he needs in sufficient detail, to make good quality decisions. 'Increases in the scale of the hierarchy result in a reduction of the *quality* of both the information reaching the top co-ordinator and of the instructions passed down by him to lower-level personnel. Moreover, since the capacity of the top administrator for assimilating information and issuing instructions is limited, he can, after a point, only cope with an expansion of the (management) hierarchy by sacrificing some of the detail provided before the expansion' (*Duncan Reekie, Managerial economics*).

ADVANTAGES AND DISADVANTAGES OF DIFFERENT TYPES OF BUSINESS EXPANSION

Advantages

Horizontal expansion or integration

- Economies of scale from larger production qualities, ie. lower costs. Horizontal expansion should enable a firm to achieve:
  - technical economies (use of larger machines or more specialised machines)
  - managerial economies (greater specialisation of middle managers)
  - commercial economies (bulk buying and selling)
  - financial economies (ability to borrow money more cheaply)
  - risk-bearing economies (some greater spread of products made within the same general market should help the firm to spread its risks).

- Possibility of achieving monopoly or oligopoly status, and having greater influence in the market and chance to earn superprofits and raise prices.

Vertical integration

- Gives firm greater control over its sources of supply (backward vertical integration) or over its end markets (forward vertical integration).

- Financial economies of scale and possibly some commercial economies. Otherwise few economies of scale unless production now becomes better co-ordinated through its various stages.

Diversification

- Risks are spread by operating in several industries. If one industry declines, others may thrive.

Disadvantages

- Top management might be unable to handle the running of a large firm efficiently - ie there might be management diseconomies of scale.

- The creation of a monopoly might provoke counter-measures from the government authorities.

- Possible management diseconomies of scale, owing to lack of familiarity with business acquired.

- No economies of scale apart from financial economies.

- Possible management diseconomies of scale, owing to lack of familiarity with business acquired.

4.5 There will not usually be any *technical* factors producing diseconomies of scale. The technology of higher-volume equipment, on the contrary, is more likely to create further economies of scale.

4.6 The implication of diseconomies of scale is that companies should achieve a certain size to benefit fully from scale economies, but should not become too big, when cost controls might slacken and inefficient bureaucratic organisation is likely to develop.

Other problems with large-scale production

4.7 There are some other drawbacks to large-scale production.

(a) In some industries, large-scale production might create a *monopoly*. Although an individual firm might seek a monopoly so as to increase its profits, difficulties may arise from anti-monopoly legislation. In the USA in particular, anti-trust legislation has acted as a barrier to the growth of even larger corporations.

(b) Large-scale production affects the nature and organisation of labour.

   (i) Powerful trade unions can organise the work force and, regardless of how successful they are in improving the real earnings of their members, can disrupt production with strike action or limit efficiency with job demarcation agreements.

   (ii) Many employees become key specialist personnel, and strike action by one small group can disrupt all production. In smaller organisations where specialist skills are less prevalent, individuals cannot act disruptive to such an extent.

(c) Trade unions might resist changes to one part of an organisation's activities by threatening to disrupt the entire organisation. This can prevent management from rationalising large-scale production in order to keep costs down.

(d) A major difficulty with large-scale production is the need to operate at a certain minimum level of capacity to achieve sufficient cost efficiencies. If a large plant works at less than, say 50% capacity, its unit costs of output will be very high.

(e) In an industry where markets tend to be segmented, large-scale organisations making a homogeneous product might have difficulty in competing successfully against smaller firms that specialise in particular segments of the market.

Survival of the small firm

4.8 If there are economies of scale, it is reasonable to ask why small firms continue to exist. In some industries and professions, small firms predominate (eg building and the legal profession) and in some, small and large firms exist.

4.9 Small firms have certain advantages over large firms which may outweigh economies of scale. For example:

(a) Since they are small, they are more likely to operate in competitive markets, in which prices will tend to be lower, and the most efficient firms will survive at the expense of the inefficient.

(b) They are more likely to be risk-takers, investing 'venture capital' in projects which might yield high rewards. Innovation and entrepreneurial activity are important ingredients for economic recovery or growth.

(c) Management-employee relations are more likely to be co-operative, with direct personal contact between managers at the top and all their employees.

(d) Small firms tend to specialise, and so contribute efficiently towards the division of labour in an economy.

(e) The structure of a small firm may allow for greater flexibility (eg an employee or manager can switch from one task to another much more readily).

(f) Small firms often sell to a local market; large firms need wider markets, and incur higher costs of transport.

(g) Managerial economies can be obtained by hiring expert consultants, possibly at a cheaper cost than permanent management specialists.

(h) Some small firms act as suppliers or sub-contractors to larger firms.

(i) Market demand may be insufficient to justify large-scale production.

4.10 There will be some industries to which large-scale organisation will be more suited than small firm competition, notably industries where research and development costs must be high, but it can be argued that government assistance and encouragement for small firms in certain parts of the economy would be a useful policy for economic growth.

5. DECISIONS ON LOCATION

5.1 We now turn to the question of how decisions about the location of a business affect its costs.

5.2 The major factors in a firm's location decision will typically be:

(a) the costs of resources at that location;

(b) the location of customers - ie the nearness of the market to the place of production;

(c) the costs of transportation:

    (i) of raw materials to the place of production;
    (ii) of finished goods from the place of production to the market;

(d) 'agglomeration' economies of scale (bigger industrial units should be able to produce more cheaply);

(e) historical accident;

(f) government regional aid and tax incentives.

5.3 The costs of resources are the costs of land, capital, labour and materials.

(a) The *characteristics* of land only sometimes affect a location decision; however, the cheaper *cost* of land might attract a firm into a particular region.

(b) Capital is a very mobile resource and should not influence the location decision. However, the level of business risk in one region may be very high, so that firms are unwilling to invest capital there.

(c) Labour costs may influence the location decision, provided that sufficient labour skills exist in a number of alternative regions. However, low *wage rates* in one region might be offset by poor *productivity*, so that labour costs can be cheaper in a region of comparatively high wages. (For example, it is cheaper to pay labour £6 per hour for output of 10 units than to pay £5 per hour for output of only 8 units, because unit costs would be cheaper). In an area which has a reputation for militant trade unionism, strikes and absenteeism, the potential costs of disruption to production might deter a firm from setting up its business locally.

5.4 The comparatively low costs of *transporting raw materials* makes the cost of materials in different regions a less important factor in location decisions. By comparison, it is often much more costly to transport *finished goods* from the place of production to the market (because they are more bulky and may require more careful transportation) and the *nearness of markets* will then be more significant than the nearness of raw materials.

5.5 Historical accident explains how some firms have come to be located in a particular place. An example is the decision to site the Morris car production plant at Cowley near Oxford. The location decision was not determined primarily by economic or cost factors, but rather by the location of the home of the firm's owner who started his business in a small workshop in central Oxford.

5.6 There may be economies of scale – economic benefits of large scale operations – which reduce costs when several firms decide to locate their business in the same area. Localisation economies of scale are those which benefit all firms in a particular industry, and may include:

(a) localised specialist component suppliers who produce components for different firms in the same industry;

(b) specialist consultancy firms or legal firms, with expertise in a particular industry, may be created in an area where the industry is centrally located;

(c) local training schemes (eg at technical colleges) might specialise in work associated with the industry, so that skilled labour is available in that particular region.

5.7 These *localisation* or *agglomeration* economies of scale are 'external' economies of scale, as distinct from internal economies. However, you may also come across a distinction between 'localisation' economies (which are benefits of size accruing to all firms in the *same* industry in a particular region) and 'external' economies, which are benefits of size accruing to all firms in any industry in a particular region. Examples of such external economies would be a highly developed infrastructure of fast roads, railways, ports, airline facilities, warehousing facilities, financial services (eg banks, money markets and capital markets) and a pool of skilled general management.

6. ADDING REVENUE CURVES

Costs and revenues

6.1 Marketers are frequently accused of ignoring the cost side of the business equation and concerning themselves mainly with revenue. Given their role in relation to the customers and demand this may be understandable, but it is not justifiable. In your study of economics you will be expected to demonstrate a clear appreciation that profitability is determined by both costs and revenue.

6.2 Having examined a firm's costs, we now turn to an examination of its revenue.

There are three aspects of revenue to consider.

(a) *Total revenue* (TR), which is the total income obtained from selling a given quantity of output. We can think of this as quantity sold multiplied by the price per unit.

(b) *Average revenue* (AR), which we can think of as the *price per unit* sold.

(c) *Marginal revenue* (MR), which is the addition to total revenue earned from the sale of one extra unit of output.

6.3 How much a firm can sell its goods for and how many it can sell are determined by the demand for its output. We need to consider the demand curve facing each firm. The shape of that curve is determined in part by the number and size of the firms which make up the industry.

6.4 An industry made up of a very large number of small firms, none of whom can influence the market with their decisions, is a perfectly competitive market. Here the firm has to accept the market price, but at that price it can choose to sell as many goods as it wants.

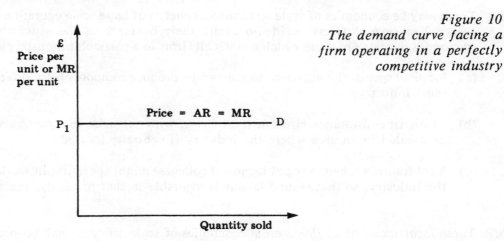

Figure 10
The demand curve facing a firm operating in a perfectly competitive industry

This demand curve, is perfectly elastic. It indicates that the firm can sell as many units as it wants at P_1, but no units at a price above that. This is because the customer has the choice of perfectly acceptable substitutes offered by competitor firms at the lower price of P_1.

(Note that there is no benefit in the firm selling below P_1, because they can sell as much output as they want at the higher price of P_1.)

6.5 In industries where there are fewer firms whose behaviour can influence the market price, firms are faced with a downward sloping demand curve. It is possible for them to sell more, but only by reducing the price (ie the average revenue). Each firm has to make its own decision on price or output.

Firms in these industries can decide either the price or the quantity they will produce, but the market-place, ie the customers, will decide the other. If firms set a high price, customers will decide how many to buy. If they choose to limit output, customers will decide what that output is worth.

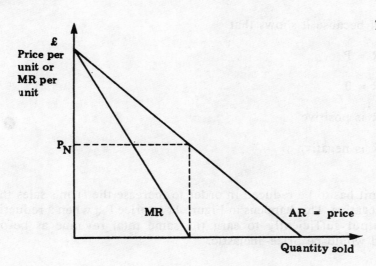

Figure 11
The demand curve facing
a firm operating in an
imperfectly competitive
market

Note that in Figure 11 all units are sold at the same price. The firm has to reduce its price to sell more, but the price must be reduced for *all* units sold, not just for the extra units. This is because we are assuming that all output is produced for a single market, where a single price will prevail.

6.6 The demand curve is downward sloping, indicating that the firm can sell more by lowering its price. The average revenue curve still represents the demand curve, but is no longer the same as the marginal revenue curve, which is to the left of AR and falling more steeply. This can be seen from the figures in the table below.

Price, or Average revenue £	×	Quantity	=	Total revenue £	Marginal revenue £
10.00		10		100.00	–
9.50		11		104.50	4.50
9.00		12		108.00	3.50
8.50		13		110.50	2.50

The steepness of the average revenue curve indicates how price sensitive demand for the firm's product is.

6.7 From the above table you can see that the price and average revenue fall by 50p for each additional unit sold. With each step up in quantity the total revenue increases, but by a smaller and smaller amount. This is indicated by the marginal revenue, which is the increase to total revenue from selling one more unit. Note that the marginal revenue is less than the average revenue, and that it is falling more rapidly.

6.8 Marginal revenue and price elasticity of demand can be related mathematically through the following formula.

$$MR = P \left(1 - \frac{1}{\epsilon} \right)$$

where   MR is marginal revenue
           P is price
           ϵ is the absolute value of price elasticity of demand (ie ignoring the minus sign).

The formula is useful because it shows that

(a)   when $\epsilon = \infty$, MR = P

(b)   when $\epsilon = 1$, MR = 0

(c)   when $\epsilon > 1$, MR is positive

(d)   when $\epsilon < 1$, MR is negative

6.9 When the price per unit has to be reduced in order to increase the firm's sales the marginal revenue can become negative. This happens in Figure 11 at price P_N when a reduction in price does not increase output sufficiently to earn the same total revenue as before. In this situation, the demand would be price-inelastic.

Marginal analysis

6.10 Marginal decision-making is based on the principle of measuring the change in benefits and/or costs that would arise as a consequence of a decision. The change would be worth having if the extra benefits exceeded the extra disadvantages, eg extra money costs or loss of enjoyment.

This is an important aspect of pricing theory which marketers need to understand.

'There is a common element to all decision problems which is expressable in the apparently trivial question, "Is it worthwhile?" A firm considering an improvement in product quality, a consumer considering the purchase of a bottle of win, or a government agency considering the organisation of another research project must all ask the same question - whether the action in question will *add* sufficiently to the benefits enjoyed by the performer to make it worth the cost.'

(Baumol)

6.11 Marginal analysis is based on some fairly simple rules and arithmetical relationships.

Rule 1

When there are no resource limitations, the scale of an activity should be increased if the marginal benefits from the change or increase exceed the marginal costs. Essentially, any activity is worth undertaking if it adds more benefits than it does cost.

In the case of a firm, for example, it would be worth spending extra money on advertising, given no restrictions on the cash available to spend on advertising, provided that the extra profits from the resulting extra sales[*] were higher than the cost of the advertising.
([*] ie extra profits before deducting advertising costs).

6.12 *Rule 2*

Given no resource constraints, it follows that the scale or amount of an activity should be increased if the marginal net yield is positive.

The scale of activity should be extended to the point where the marginal net yield is zero - ie to the point where the extra costs are equal to the amount of the extra benefits.

6.13 *Rule 3*

When there is a shortage of resources, the scale of activity will be restricted to a level where marginal benefits still exceed marginal costs. In this situation, the decision problem will often be to choose between alternative *competing* courses of action - ie between mutually exclusive options.

In the case of a firm with limited resources, should the resources be put into making and selling product A or product B or product C?

To achieve optimisation, each activity should be taken to the level where the marginal (net) yield is *the same for every activity*.

For example, if a firm has £1 to spend, and can spend it on advertising to yield extra profit of £2, or on extra staff to yield extra profit of £1.50, the choice would obviously be to spend the money on advertising.

6.14 A decision in favour of a course of action should be taken if the *incremental revenues* arising from the chosen action exceed the *incremental opportunity costs*. This is an application of marginal analysis.

Profit maximisation: MC = MR

6.15 As a firm produces and sells more units, its total costs will increase and its total revenues will also increase (unless the price elasticity of demand is inelastic and the firm faces a downward sloping AR curve).

(a) Provided that the extra cost of making an extra unit is *less than* the extra revenue obtained from selling it, the firm will increase its profits by making and selling the extra unit.

(b) If the extra cost of making an extra unit of output *exceeds* the extra revenue obtainable from selling it, the firm's profits would be reduced by making and selling the extra unit.

(c) If the extra cost of making an extra unit of output is *exactly equal* to the extra revenue obtainable from selling it, bearing in mind that economic cost includes an amount for normal profit, it will be worth the firm's while to make and sell the extra unit. And since the extra cost of yet another unit would be higher (the law of diminishing returns applies) whereas extra revenue per unit from selling extra units is never higher, the profit-maximising output is reached at this point where MC = MR.

6.16 In other words, given the objective of profit-maximisation:

(a) If MC is less than MR - profits will be increased by making and selling more.

(b) If MC is greater than MR - profits will fall if more units are made and sold, and a profit-maximising firm would not make the extra output.

If MC = MR, the profit-maximising output has been reached, and this is the output quantity that a profit-maximising firm will decide to supply.

6.17 The analysis of a firm's profit-maximising price and output levels by matching MC and MR is a form of *marginal analysis*.

Profit maximisation and the objectives of firms

6.18 The point where MC = MR indicates the output a firm should produce if it wishes to maximise its profits. This point can also be shown by examining the total revenue and cost curves.

We can define profits as *total revenue minus total economic costs* at any level of output. Profits are at a maximum where the (vertical) distance between the total revenue (TR) and total cost (TC) curves in Figure 12 is greatest.

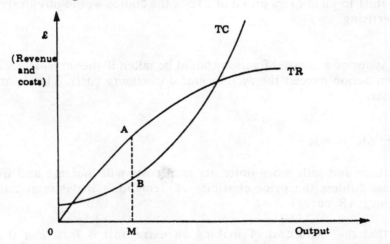

Figure 12

6.19 The common principle applying to competitive firms is the motive of *profit maximisation:* a firm is assumed to produce a volume of output that will enable it to maximise its profits.

6.20 This assumption does not necessarily hold true, but does provide a useful basis for beginning to look at the output decisions of individual firms. In reality firms may set objectives related to long-term survival, expanding market share or security of management jobs, rather than profit maximisation. You should also be aware of the non-profit making objectives of many public sector organisations, to whom marketing is increasingly important.

7. CONCLUSION

7.1 The key points in this chapter are as follows.

(a) A firm's output decision should be seen in both the short term, when some factors of production are fixed, and the long term, when all factors of production can be varied. The effects of investment decisions arise in the longer term.

(b) In the short run, a firm's SRAC curve is U shaped, due to diminishing returns beyond a certain output level. In the short run, a firm will maximise its profits where (short-run) MR = MC.

(c) In the long run, a firm's SRAC curve can be shifted, and a firm's minimum achievable average costs at any level of output can be depicted by a long run average cost curve (LRAC).

(d) The shape of an LRAC depends on whether there are increasing, constant, or decreasing returns to scale. There are some economies of scale, and even if increasing returns to scale are not achievable indefinitely as output rises, up to a certain minimum efficient scale of production (MES) there will be increasing returns to scale. Firms will reduce their average costs by producing on a larger scale up to the MES.

(e) Whether there are constant or decreasing returns to scale beyond the MES will vary between industries and firms. Similarly, whether economies of scale are significant will vary between industries.

(f) Technological progress results in shifts in the LRAC, and since technology changes are continual, a firm's LRAC can probably never be 'stabilised' and unchanging for long.

(g) If economies of scale are significant, there is a strong argument in favour of growth and investment by firms, either through organic growth or through mergers and takeovers.

(h) Firms base their output decisions on their objectives. In economics we normally assume that firms seek to maximise profits, in which case they will increase output until MC = MR.

(i) The demand curve facing an individual firm is determined by the structure of the industry it is part of.

(j) A firm will take account of 'agglomeration' economies of scale in making a location decision. Other factors to be taken into account in the location decision include the costs of transport and the location of customers.

TEST YOUR KNOWLEDGE
The numbers in brackets refer to paragraphs of this chapter

1   What is meant by the short run? (2.2)

2   Why is the SRAC curve for a firm always U-shaped? (2.19)

3   What does a steeply falling LRAC curve tell you about the industry in which the firm is operating? (3.4(a))

4   What are internal economies of scale? (3.15)

5   What happens to the LRAC curve if technical progress occurs in the industry? (3.19)

6   What are the advantages and disadvantages of a firm growing by horizontal rather than vertical integration?

7   If economies of scale occur, why are there so many small firms? (4.9)

8   What will typically be the major factors in a firm's location decision? (5.2)

9   What determines the shape of the demand curve facing a firm? (6.3)

10 What is the shape of the demand curve facing a firm operating in an imperfectly competitive market? (6.5)

11 What is the profit maximising output for any firm? (6.18)

Now try illustrative questions 9 and 10 at the end of the text

Chapter 6

MARKET STRUCTURES

This chapter covers the following topics.

1. The characteristics of markets
2. Perfect competition and monopoly
3. Price discrimination and monopoly
4. Monopolistic competition and non-price competition
5. Oligopoly

---

1. THE CHARACTERISTICS OF MARKETS

1.1 Managers need to make business decisions within the context of the market in which they are operating. Economic theory can provide a useful starting point for examining the structure of industry and identifying the characteristics of firms, competition and marketplace behaviour.

1.2 In this chapter we will examine the different forms of market structure characteristic of both 'perfectly' and 'imperfectly' competitive industries. The distinction between perfect and imperfect competition will be discussed further below.

Figure 1

⟶ Increasingly imperfect markets ⟶

PERFECT COMPETITION	MONOPOLISTIC COMPETITION	OLIGOPOLY MONOPOLY

⟶ Number of firms in the industry decreases ⟶

⟶ Barriers to new firms entering the industry increase ⟶

1.3 The number of firms in an industry in part establishes the characteristics of the market, dictating the firms' ability to influence price and output decisions and how much attention they need to pay to competitors' activities.

1.4 It was explained in the previous chapter that a firm is assumed to want to maximise its profits, and it will do this at the price level and output level where MC = MR.

95

Decisions by a firm about how much to produce are therefore dependent on matters relating to their costs and their revenues.

(a) A firm's *costs* depend on the cost of factors of production, (labour, capital, etc) in both the short run and the long run.

(b) An individual firm's *revenues* depend on:

(i) the *market demand* for its goods; and also
(ii) the *nature of competition* in the market.

1.5 We shall consider the pricing and output decisions by individual firms, and how these are influenced by the competition in the market.

Perfect competition and imperfect competition

1.6 Perfect competition is a theoretical model for predicting behaviour. In its pure form it does not really exist anywhere, although the activities of markets like the stock market probably come fairly close to meeting the characteristics of a perfect market.

CHARACTERISTICS OF PERFECT COMPETITION

- There is a *large number of relatively small sellers (firms) and buyers* in the market. Each firm is producing such small proportion of the total supply of goods to the market that no single firm can make a change in its own output which is sufficiently large to affect the market price of the good that it produces.

- *The product is homogeneous*, which means that all units of a good made by all suppliers are identical to one another and there is no consumer preference for the goods of one supplier over the goods of another supplier. The goods of every supplier are therefore perfect substitutes for each other.

- Both producers and consumers have exactly the *same information* about conditions in the market.

- There is *free entry and exit of firms* into and out of the industry. This means that if a firm wants to start making and selling a particular good, because it sees the chance for higher profits in the market, it can get into the market without hindrance or trouble. And if a firm is making losses, it can get out of the market without hindrance too. *A firm can therefore react quickly to changes in market conditions.*

- There are *no transport costs and no costs of information-gathering*.

- We also assume that *factor markets are perfect*, ie the market for labour, capital and land, and factors of production are homogeneous.

1.7 It is helpful to use perfect competition as a theoretical benchmark against which we can:

(a) judge or predict what firms might do in markets where competition shows some or most of the characteristics of being perfect;

(b) contrast the behaviour of firms in markets that are much more imperfect.

Characteristics of imperfect competition

1.8 In contrast to perfect competition, *imperfect competition* describes a situation in which an individual firm can have a significant influence on the market. Imperfect competition differs from perfect competition in one or more of the following four ways.

(a) There will be one or just a few large firms dominating the market.

(i) A single firm dominating the market is called a monopolist, or monopoly firm.

(ii) When two or several firms jointly dominate the market, there is an *oligopoly* and firms are referred to as oligopolists. (A special case of oligopoly is *duopoly:* this is when precisely two firms dominate the market).

When only one or a few firms dominate the market, most of the market demand will be for their products and the firm has a much bigger say in what the market price should be. The firm can make decisions on price as well as output and the firm is a price maker.

(b) Free entry into the market might be prevented by existing firms in the market. Monopolists and oligopolists can create *barriers to entry*.

(c) In oligopoly markets, oligopolists might act in collusion to keep prices up, and do not necessarily act independently.

(d) In some markets, firms succeed in creating special differences, real or imagined, between their own product and similar products of competitors through *product differentiation*. They seek to create customer demand for their own products in preference to competitors' products by emphasising these differences. Two ways of creating differences are *branding* and *advertising*. There might be small variations in product design. Firms try to create product differences, real or imaginary, because they can then become like monopolists or oligopolists in their own special corner of a large market. This type of competition is therefore referred to as *monopolistic competition* because many firms that ought to be competing with each other are able to act like monopolists.

Perfect and imperfect competition: the key difference

1.9 A key difference between perfect and imperfect competition is that:

(a) in *perfect competition*, no firm dominates the market. There are no consumer preferences for one supplier over another. Consumers will buy at the cheapest price they can, and so a firm must sell at the same price as every other firm; otherwise it won't sell anything at all.

Firms are *price-takers* and must sell all output at the ruling market price. In effect, all firms in the market must raise or lower their prices together;

(b) in all forms of *imperfect competition*, firms have more say. They control all or a large part of the industry's entire output, or they build up strong customer loyalties.

Firms are *price-makers* because they have choice in both what price to charge for their good and how much of it to produce.

1.10 With this key difference between perfect and imperfect competition in mind, we can go on to consider the profit-maximising equilibrium for firms operating under each set of market conditions. We shall begin by looking at firms in perfect competition.

2. PERFECT COMPETITION AND MONOPOLY

2.1 In perfect competition, then, every firm is a price taker. It must accept the ruling market price. Decisions by a firm to increase or lower output will have no effect on demand and supply in the market so no effect on market price. Every extra unit on output will be sold at the same price, which is market price.

2.2 One producer cannot make any difference to the market price of the product. If he sells at a higher price, nobody will buy his goods. If he sells at a lower price he will fail to maximise profits. As we saw in Chapter 4, the demand curve facing an individual producer is therefore perfectly elastic, and he may sell whatever amount he chooses at the given market price P.

2.3 It follows that:

(a) since a firm sells each extra unit of output at the ruling market price, the firm's MR = price, ie MR = AR;

(b) the firm's AR is the same market price at all levels of output, and so its AR = MR curve can be shown on a graph as a line parallel to the x axis.

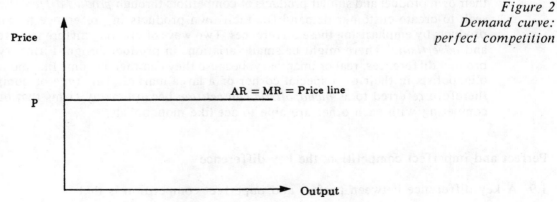

Figure 2
Demand curve:
perfect competition

The MR curve is the same as the demand curve (or AR curve, or price line) because all output can be sold at market price P (Figure 2).

Equilibrium in the short run

2.4 How are price, output and the maximisation of profit determined in the case of the firm operating under conditions of perfect competition in the short run?

2.5 The short run refers to a period in which the number of firms in the market is temporarily fixed. In these circumstances it is possible for firms to make supernormal profits or losses, as the following diagrams show.

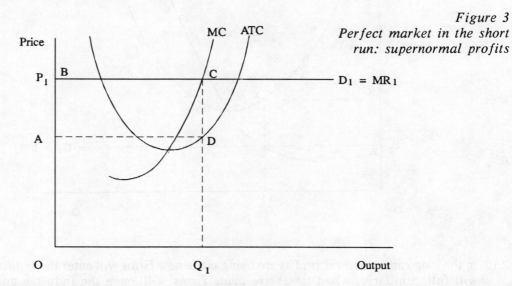

Figure 3
Perfect market in the short
run: supernormal profits

2.6 Figure 3 shows the cost and demand curves of a firm in the short run making supernormal profits. The demand curve is the horizontal line D_1 at price P_1. The curve is a horizontal line indicating that the firm may not influence the price of the goods and has to accept the price that the market as a whole fixes for them. If the firm were to charge a higher price it would lose all its sales and there is no point charging a lower price as it can sell all its output at the given price. The demand curve is thus also the marginal revenue curve; every new unit sold at price P_1 increases total revenue by an amount P_1.

2.7 Figure 3 also shows the average total cost curve (ATC) and the marginal cost curve (MC), with the MC cutting the ATC at the lowest point of the ATC. Given these cost curves and the demand curve D_1, the firm will produce the output Q_1, where the MC curves cuts the MR horizontal curve at the point C. This is the profit maximising point.

2.8 If the firm were to produce fewer units it would be producing at a point where MR was higher than MC and all additional units produced up to the point where MR = MC would similarly have MR greater than MC. The firm should produce these units because so long as MR is greater than MC, each unit shows a profit (additional revenue is greater than additional costs). Similarly it should not expand production past MR = MC because it will be producing where MC is greater than MR, in other words where the additional costs for each unit exceed the additional revenue earned.

2.9 At the output Q_1 (Figure 4) the firm is making supernormal profits indicated by the rectangle ABCD. This will attract new firms into the industry and the price will be bid down, possibly to price P_2 as shown in Figure 4. Here the firm makes a loss shown by the rectangle WXYZ. Once again the firm produces where MC = MR giving an output of Q_2.

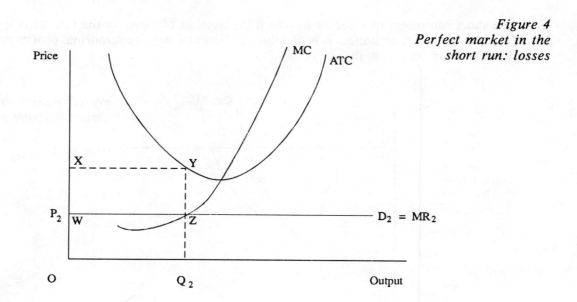

Figure 4
Perfect market in the
short run: losses

2.10 In the long run, whenever profits are being made new firms will enter the industry and the price will fall. Similarly, when losses are made firms will leave the industry and the price will rise.

Equilibrium in the long run

2.11 In a perfectly competitive market in the long run, the firm cannot influence the market price and its average revenue curve is horizontal. The firm's average cost curve is U-shaped. The firm is in equilibrium and earns normal profits only (ie no supernormal profits) when the AC curve is at a tangent to the AR curve as shown in Figure 5(b). In other words, *long-run equilibrium* will exist when supernormal profits and losses are eliminated.

2.12 There is no incentive for firms to enter or leave the industry and the price will remain at P with the firm making normal profits only.

Figure 5

(a) Market as a whole   *(b) Individual firm in a perfectly competitive market*

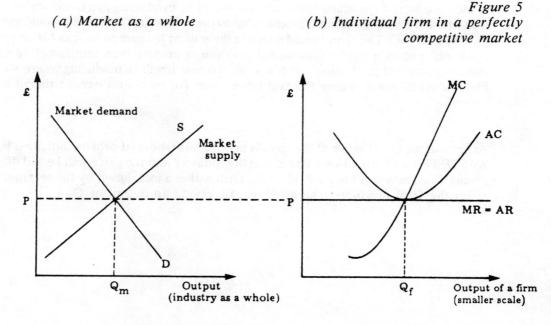

2.13 Note the following points about Figure 5.

    (a)   The market price P is the price which all individual firms in the market must take.

    (b)   If the firm must accept a given MR (as it must in conditions of perfect competition) and it sets MR = MC, then the MC curve is in effect the individual firm's supply curve (Figure 5(b)). The *market supply curve* in Figure 5(a) is derived by aggregating the individual supply curves of every firm in the industry.

2.14 Long-run equilibrium will, then, occur in the industry when there are no more firms entering or leaving the industry because no new firm thinks it could earn higher profits by entering and no existing firm thinks it could do better by leaving. In the *long run*, then, all firms in the industry will have MR = MC = AC = AR = price, as in Figure 5(b).

Assumptions of imperfect competition

2.15 Some of the assumptions of perfect competition were that:

    (a)   there are many independent firms, each so small relative to the market that its decisions cannot affect market price;

    (b)   there is free entry and exit into and out of the market;

    (c)   individual producers and consumers act independently.

With imperfect competition, one or several of these assumptions do not apply. One form of imperfect competition is monopoly

Monopoly

2.16 Monopoly is the complete opposite to perfect competition. In a monopoly, there is only one firm, the sole producer of a good which has no closely competing substitutes, so that the total market supply is identical with the single firm's supply.

2.17 In monopoly the firm faces a downward-sloping average revenue curve because its average revenue curve is the same as the total market demand curve.

2.18 As we saw in the previous chapter, if average revenue is falling, marginal revenue will always be lower than average revenue; if the monopolist increases output by one unit the price per unit received will fall, so the extra revenue generated by the sale of the extra unit of the good is less than the price of that unit. The monopolist therefore faces a downward-sloping AR curve with an MR curve below the AR curve, and falling more steeply than it.

2.19 It is obviously important that you should understand what the MR and AR (demand) curves are showing us. In Figure 6:

    (a)   at output quantity X, the marginal revenue earned from the last unit produced and sold is MR_X, but the price at which all the X units would be sold is P_X. This is found by looking at the price level on the AR curve associated with output X;

(b) similarly, at output quantity Y, the marginal revenue from the last unit produced and sold is MR_Y, but the price at which all Y units would be sold on the market is, from the AR curve for Y output, P_Y.

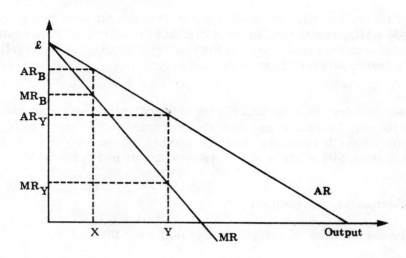

Figure 6
A monopolist's
MR and AR

Profit-maximising equilibrium of a monopoly

2.20 The condition for profit maximisation is, as we have seen, that marginal revenue should equal marginal cost. This is true for any firm. As long as marginal revenue exceeds marginal cost, an increase in output will add more to revenues than to costs, and therefore increase profits. A monopolist might maximise profits:

(a) but make no supernormal profits; or
(b) make supernormal profits.

Situation (a) is rare for a monopolist, but it could happen.

2.21 Figure 7 shows a monopoly equilibrium where the monopolist is earning just *normal profits* and so AC = AR. At this point (Q) the AC curve would have to touch the AR curve at a tangent, at exactly the same output level where MC = MR. Since AC = AR and AC includes normal profits, the monopolist will be earning normal profits but no super-normal profits in this situation.

Figure 7
Equilibrium of a monopoly firm
earning normal profits. (The AR
curve is at a tangent to the AC
curve at exactly the output level
where MC = MR.)

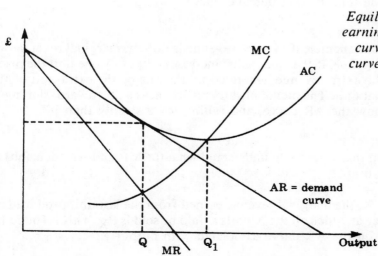

2.22 When this situation occurs, the monopoly will make a loss by producing at output higher than Q, and so, it will be 'forced' to produce at an output level which is below the capacity at which its average costs are minimised (output Q_1).

2.23 Monopolies however, are usually able to earn 'monopoly' or supernormal profits in the long term as well as the short term, and the situation illustrated in Figure 7 will be rare. It *might*, however, represent the long term equilibrium of some monopolies, where barriers to entry into the industry are low, and competition would be attracted into the market if supernormal profits were achievable.

2.24 In perfect competition, a firm should not be able to earn super-normal profits in the long run because they would be 'competed away' by new entrants to the industry. In monopoly, however, the firm can earn super-normal profits *in the long run* as well as in the short run, because there are *barriers to entry* which prevent rivals entering the market. Figure 8 shows a firm earning supernormal profits, equal to the shaded area, which represents $(P - AC) \times Q$ units produced and sold.

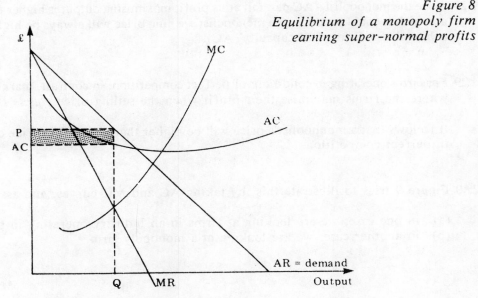

Figure 8
Equilibrium of a monopoly firm
earning super-normal profits

Monopoly and perfect competition: comparison of profit maximising equilibrium

2.25 An important comparison between perfect competition and monopoly is that *if there are no economies of scale for a large-output-volume firm*, then output will be lower, and costs and price higher, under monopoly as compared with perfect competition.

2.26 This is true for a monopoly that is not earning super profits as well as a firm earning super profits. However, the explanation here will concentrate on a monopoly firm where super-normal profits are earned.

2.27 We will compare a monopolist and a perfect competitor of similar size so that their cost curves are the same; and we can compare them on a single graph.

The following points have been made earlier. Check that you understand them.

(a) In conditions of *perfect competition*, a firm will maximise its profits where MR = MC and if there are no short-term supernormal profits, this is also where AR = AC. Since, in perfect competition, an individual firm's AR = MR, then AR = MR = AC = MC.

(b) Since the MC curve always cuts the AC curve at the lowest point on the AC curve, this is at the output level where the firm's short-run AC per unit is at a minimum.

(c) In conditions of *monopoly*, the monopoly firm will also maximise its profits where MR = MC. This will always be at a volume of output which is below the level where the firm's short-run AC per unit would be at a minimum.

(d) The monopolist's selling price at its profit-maximising output level will never be less than the AC per unit. If the monopolist is earning supernormal profits, the price (AR) will exceed the AC.

2.28 Since the monopolist's AC per unit at its profit maximising output is higher than the minimum AC at which it could produce, the monopolist's selling price will always be higher than its minimum achievable AC (or 'full capacity' AC).

2.29 For firms operating in conditions of perfect competition, in contrast, market equilibrium occurs where the firms maximise their profit when the selling price *equals their* AC.

It follows that a monopolist's price will be higher than the selling price of a comparable firm in perfect competition.

2.30 Figure 9 tries to illustrate this, by taking AC and MC curves, and assuming that:

(a) in one case, we are looking at firms in an industry operating in perfect competition;
(b) in another case, we are looking at a monopoly firm.

Figure 9
Monopoly and perfect
competition: output
and price levels compared

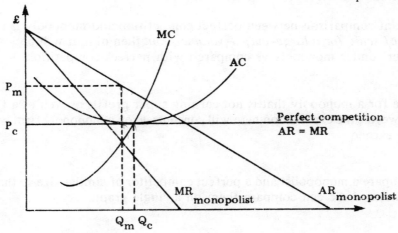

2.31 In Figure 9:

> (a) firms in the industry, if they were operating in perfectly competitive conditions, would maximise profits where AR = MR = MC = AC, and this is:
>
> > (i) at the market price P_c;
> > (ii) at the output volume for the market, Q_c, where AC per unit is minimised;
>
> (b) in contrast, if the industry were controlled by a monopoly firm, the firm would maximise profits where MR = MC, which is:
>
> > (i) at output volume Qm. This is below the output at which the firm could minimise average cost per unit (Q_c);
> >
> > (ii) at price P_m. This is also higher than the cost where AC would be at a minimum - ie it is higher than the perfectly competitive industry's price P_c.

Conclusion: monopoly and perfect competition

2.32 Under conditions of perfect competition;

> (a) price is likely to be lower;
> (b) and output is likely to be higher

than under monopoly conditions.

This is true whether or not the monopolist is able to earn supernormal profits.

2.33 This conclusion is an important argument in support of the view that monopolies are harmful to an economy.

2.34 The conclusion might not be valid, however, if the monopolist is able to take advantage of its monopoly position to achieve economies of scale that perfectly competitive firms could not achieve, due to their relative smallness in terms of the total market output.

This is an important proviso, because it is a theoretical argument *in favour* of monopolies!

It should also be remembered that public sector monopolies will not be operated to maximise profits, but generally to cover costs. They will therefore produce an output at which AC = AR.

3. PRICE DISCRIMINATION AND MONOPOLY

Price discrimination and market segmentation

3.1 Before assessing the positive and negative features of monopolies, we turn our attention to price discrimination and market segmentation.

The term *price discrimination* refers to a situation in which a firm sells the 'same' product at different prices in different markets.

Market segmentation may involve elements of *product differentiation* (eg different brand names) in order to satisfy particular segments of the market. We return to this topic later in this chapter.

3.2 Three basic conditions are necessary for price discrimination to be effective and profitable.

(a) The seller must be able to control the supply of the product. Clearly, this will apply under monopoly conditions. The monopoly seller has control over the quantity of the product offered to a particular buyer.

(b) The seller must be able to prevent the resale of the good by one buyer to another. The markets must, therefore, be clearly separated so that those paying lower prices cannot resell to those paying higher prices. The ability to prevent resale tends to be associated with the character of the product, or the ability to classify buyers into readily identifiable groups. Services are less easily resold than goods while transportation costs, tariff barriers or import quotas may separate classes of buyers geographically and thus make price discrimination possible.

(c) There must be significant differences in the willingness to pay among the different classes of buyers. In effect this means that the elasticity of demand must be different in at least two of the separate markets so that total profits may be increased by charging different prices.

3.3 We can see how the monopolist seller practising price discrimination can maximise revenue using a diagrammatic illustration.

Figure 10

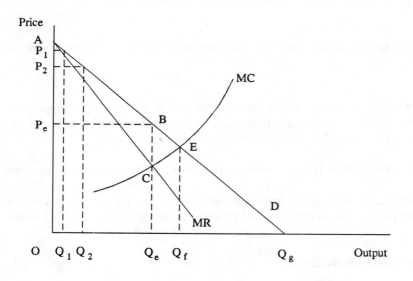

D = Demand curve
MR = Marginal revenue curve without price discrimination
MC = Marginal cost curve

3.4 Figure 10 demonstrates firstly the equilibrium position of a monopolist that does not discriminate. He produces at the point C where marginal cost equals marginal revenue, producing output Q_e and selling at price P_e. His total revenue is given by the rectangle OP_eBQ_e.

Figure 10 also illustrates how the discriminating monopolist can improve on this position, both from the point of increased revenue and increased profits.

3.5 The discriminating monopolist does not charge the same price for all units sold. If we assume that the monopolist can discriminate perfectly, then he can sell each unit for a different price as indicated on the demand curve. Thus he can sell the first unit Q_1 at the price P_1, and the second unit Q_2 at the price P_2. This follows for all units sold so that the demand curve becomes the marginal revenue curve; each extra unit sold is sold for the price indicated on the demand curve, each previous unit being sold for the higher price relevant to that unit.

3.6 The perfectly discriminating monopolist will still maximise profits where MC = MR, but the marginal revenue curve is now the curve D, the demand curve. He thus produces at the point E where marginal cost equals the new marginal revenue, producing Q_f units.

3.7 The additional revenue of the discriminating monopolist is represented by the areas AP_eB plus Q_eBEQ_f. The discriminating monopolist has thus maximised his revenue (consistent of course with maximising his profit). If the monopolist did not wish to maximise profit but wished simply to maximise revenue he would expand production to the point Q_g when his total revenue would be the area OAQ_g.

3.8 Take care not to confuse maximising revenue with maximising profit. Increasing output beyond Q_f in the example will not increase profit as marginal costs exceed marginal revenue for each additional unit sold.

Examples of price discrimination

3.9 Various examples show that these conditions can be met and that it is possible for a monopolist to engage in price discrimination. Markets may be separated by a time barrier, for example British Telecom varies the cost of telephone calls according to the time of day at which they are made. British Rail charges cheaper rates for off peak travel. Holiday companies charge a higher price for a given package holiday at certain times of the year, the price in the summer months being higher than at other times. These are examples of services which cannot be transferred from the cheaper to the dearer market.

3.10 Price discrimination often results where the market is separated by transport costs and tariffs, hence firms may sell their products abroad cheaper than at home. An extreme example of this is known as dumping; this occurs when exports sell in foreign markets at prices below the cost of production. This pricing strategy is designed to drive domestic producers out of the industry so that the foreign producer may achieve monopoly power. The price differential cannot, of course, exceed the cost of transporting the good back to the home market plus any tariff on imports.

3.11 Price discrimination also occurs where it is possible to separate buyers into clearly defined groups. Industrial users of gas and electricity are able to purchase these fuels more cheaply from British Gas and electricity companies than are domestic users. Similarly milk is sold more cheaply to industrial users, for example for making into cheese or ice cream, than to private households.

Exercise

Explain why it is possible for a railway or airline to charge different fares for passengers using the same service.

Outline solution

(a) *Consumers' ignorance:* not all consumers may be aware of the availability of low-rate tickets such as lower prices for booking in advance, special offers and so on. This means that two customers on the same journey and in similar seats might pay different prices because one of the customers is unaware that a cheaper price could have been obtained.

(b) *The nature of the good:*

   (i)   prices can be varied according to the time of day or day of the week. Many customers will be forced to travel at peak times and pay top prices and some will switch to travelling at a cheaper time when the railway or airline has spare capacity to be filled up. Demand for journeys at peak times will be relatively inelastic, since demand will be from commuters who must travel in these periods in order to reach their workplace on time;

   (ii) a cheaper rate might be offered to children. Since a child cannot transfer his ticket to an adult there is no danger that adults can buy cheaper tickets by using children to obtain tickets on their behalf.

(c) *Distance:* a railway can sell cheap travel to customers travelling from say, Manchester to London, but still charge full rates to customers travelling from London to Manchester.

Are monopolies beneficial or harmful?

3.12 We have now seen that:

(a) a monopolist is likely to produce less output but charge a higher price for it than a comparable firm operating in conditions of perfect competition, unless the monopolist can achieve economies of scale that a smaller firm could not;

(b) monopolists can practice price discrimination.

These two points might suggest that monopolies are a bad thing. But there are economic arguments both for and against monopolies.

3.13 The arguments in favour of monopolies are as follows.

(a) A firm might need a monopoly share of the market if it is to achieve maximum economies of scale. Economies of scale mean lower unit costs, and lower marginal costs of production. The consumer is likely to benefit from these cost efficiencies through lower prices from the monopoly supplier.

(b) Economies of scale shift the firm's cost curves to the right, which means that it will maximise profits at a higher output level, and quite possibly at a lower selling price per unit too.

(c) Monopolies can afford to spend more on research and development, and are able to exploit *innovation* and *technical progress* much better than small firms.

(d) Monopolies may find it easier than small firms to raise new capital on the capital markets, and so they can finance new technology and new products. Monopolies will therefore help a country's economy to grow.

(e) There is also an argument that firms which show entrepreneurial flair and innovation deserve rewarding for the risks they have taken and the new products they have made. They should therefore be rewarded by legal protection of the monopoly ie. the award of *patent rights*. Monopolies can spend more on research and development and will therefore tend to be innovative.

3.14 The economic arguments against monopolies are also important.

(a) The profit-maximising output of a monopolist is likely to be at a price and output level which give it large profits or 'superprofits' - ie profits in excess of 'normal' profits. This is a benefit for the monopoly producer at the expense of the consumer.

(b) The profit-maximising output of a monopoly is at a point where:

(i) total market output is lower; and
(ii) prices are higher

than they would be if there were a competitive market instead of a monopoly.

(c) Monopolies do not use resources in the most efficient way possible. Efficient use of resources can be defined as combining factors of production so as to minimise average unit costs. The profit-maximising output of a monopoly is not where AC is minimised (ie at the lowest point of the firm's AC curve), and so monopolies are not efficient producers (see Figure 9).

(d) If there are no economies of scale, a monopoly will produce less and sell at a higher price than the combination of firms in a competitive market would. This might be good for the firms and their owners, but it is not so good for consumers who must pay the higher prices.

(e) Monopolists can carry out restrictive practices, such as price discrimination, to increase their supernormal profits.

(f) The higher prices and super-profits encourage firms in competitive markets to want to become monopolies, and they can do this by trying to create product differentiation - ie differences between their own products and the products of rival competitors. These differences might be real product design or quality differences, or imaginary differences created by a brand name and a brand image. *Product differentiation* allows competing firms to become a sort of monopoly producer, and markets where this occurs are therefore characterised by *monopolistic competition*. This can be beneficial for producers, but at the expense of consumers.

(g) Because they are not threatened by competition and are earning superprofits, monopolies might:

     (i)   become slack about cost control, and inefficient in using resources, so that they fail to achieve the lowest unit costs they ought to be capable of;

     (ii)   adopt a take-it-or-leave-it complacent attitude to innovation, instead of investing in innovation.

(h)   Monopolies might stifle competition, by:

     (i)   taking over smaller competitors who try to enter the market;
     (ii)   exploiting *barriers to entry* against other firms trying to enter the market.

Action by firms to prevent competition is against consumers' interests.

(i)   If a monopoly controls a vital resource, it might make decisions which are damaging to the public interest. This is why governments often choose to put vital industries under state control (eg health care, the fire service, coal mining and the nuclear power industry).

(j)   There might be diseconomies of scale in a monopoly firm.

Barriers to entry

3.15 Monopolists might try to use their size and power or other advantages to prevent competitors from entering the market. Actions that stifle competition are likely to be against the public interest.

Barriers to entry can be classified into several groups.

(a)   *Product differentiation barriers.* An existing monopolist or oligopolist would be able to exploit his position as supplier of an established product that the consumer/customer can be persuaded to believe is better. A new entrant to the market would have to design a 'better' product, or convince customers of the product's qualities, and this might involve spending substantial sums of money on R & D, advertising and sales promotion.

(b)   *Absolute cost barriers.* These exist where an existing monopolist or oligopolist has access to cheaper raw material sources or to know-how that the new entrant would not have. This gives the existing monopolist an advantage because his input costs would be cheaper in absolute terms than those of a new entrant.

(c)   *Economies of scale barriers.* These exist where the long run average cost curve for firms in the market is downward-sloping, and where the minimum level of production needed to achieve the greatest economies of scale is at a high level. New entrants to the market would have to be able to achieve a substantial market share before they could gain full advantage of potential scale economies, and so the existing monopolist/oligopolists would be able to produce their output more cheaply.

The amount of *fixed costs* that a firm would have to sustain, regardless of its market share, could be a significant entry barrier.

(d)   *Legal barriers.* These are barriers where a monopoly is fully or partially protected by law. For example, there are some legal monopolies (nationalised industries perhaps) and a company's products might be protected by patent (eg computer hardware components or software features).

3.16 Examples of barriers to entry are:

(a) patent laws conferring on one firm the sole right to produce a certain commodity;

(b) a government-awarded charter or franchise such as to TV and radio companies. Also nationalised industries are often monopolies;

(c) a 'natural' monopoly may arise because of major economies of scale. An established firm may be able to maintain its monopoly by producing at a cost lower than any cost attainable by a newer and smaller firm. Some natural monopolies are the water supply, gas supply and electricity supply industries;

(d) force - an established monopoly may have the resources to carry out a successful price war against would-be competitors. Putting off would-be competitors by temporarily reducing prices is sometimes called *predatory pricing*. A monopolist might even resort to sabotage and intimidation to prevent competition;

(e) the costs of entry - in a market where there is some product differentiation, there may be high costs of entry for a new competitor wishing to enter the market. For example, initial advertising costs may need to be very high in order to gain 'recognition' from customers;

(f) taking over smaller firms that try to enter the market, just to eliminate the competition.

3.17 With strong entry barriers, existing firms in the market can usually achieve a high market share, and by 'making prices' and keeping output down, they can maximise profits with higher prices than in a perfectly competitive market. Profits would include *supernormal* profits. Barriers to entry can be erected by monopoly firms, oligopoly firms, and, in the short run at least, by firms in markets where there is monopolistic competition.

Inefficiency

3.18 One of the arguments against monopolies is that they are more inefficient than competitive firms, because they never produce at an output level which minimises average costs. This implies that monopolies are inefficient in allocating resources. This inefficiency is called *allocative inefficiency*.

3.19 A second and different criticism of monopolies is that they are wasteful of costs, and spend more than they need to. The lack of competition, perhaps, makes monopolies 'complacent', and resources are not used with maximum efficiency. This 'over-spending' inefficiency is called *X-inefficiency*.

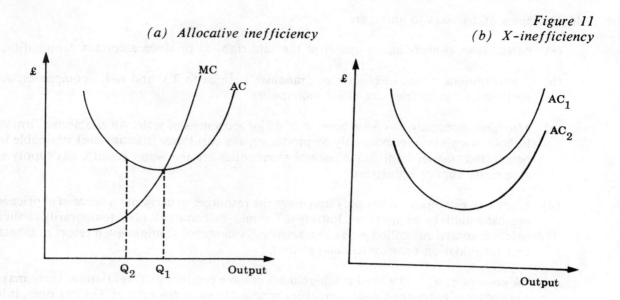

Figure 11

(a) Allocative inefficiency

(b) X-inefficiency

3.20 The difference between allocative inefficiency and X-inefficiency is shown in Figure 11.

(a) *Figure 11(a)*. If a monopolist maximises profit at output level Q_2, there is allocative inefficiency because the firm could minimise its average costs at output Q_1.

(b) *Figure 11(b)*. If a monopolist has an average cost curve AC_1, when it ought to use resources more efficiently and have an average cost curve AC_2, there is X-inefficiency.

3.21 All monopolies might be accused of some X-inefficiency, but there has been a view that *state-owned monopolies* have a tendency to be more X-inefficient than monopolies which are private companies.

Do firms really produce at output levels where MC = MR?

3.22 When a firm is a monopolist in the market, there could be a tendency for·it to develop X-inefficiencies, and also to pursue objectives which are different from profit-maximisation.

3.23 In large companies especially, the management has become divorced from the ownership. Managers are paid to make the decisions about prices and output, but it is the shareholders who expect to benefit from the profits. Managers will not necessarily make pricing decisions that will maximise profits, because:

(a) they have no personal interests at stake in the size of profits earned, except in so far as they are accountable to the shareholders for the profits they make; and

(b) there is no competitive pressure in the market to be efficient, minimise costs and maximise profits.

3.24 Given the divorce of management from ownership, it has been suggested that price and output decisions will be taken by managers with a *managerial aim* rather than the aim of profit maximisation, within the constraint that managers must take some account of shareholders' interests because they are formally responsible for them and so are accountable to shareholders for their decisions.

3.25 One 'managerial model' of pricing and output decisions is *Baumol's sales maximisation model*, which assumes that the firm acts to maximise sales revenue rather than profits (subject to the constraint that the profit level must be satisfactory and so acceptable to shareholders and to provide enough retained profits for future investment in growth). The management of a firm might opt for sales revenue maximisation in order to maintain or increase its market share, ensure survival, and discourage competition. Managers benefit personally because of the prestige of running a large and successful company, and also because salaries and other perks are likely to be higher in bigger companies than in smaller ones. This is described further below.

3.26 Another managerial model is *Oliver Williamson's management discretion model*, which assumes that managers act to further their own interests and so maximise their utility, subject to a minimum profit requirement. Utility may be thought of in terms of prestige, influence and other personal satisfactions. The model states that utility, which a manager aims to maximise, is a function of his own salary and also expenditure on his staff (prestige and influence depend on the numbers and pay levels of subordinate staff), the amount of perquisites (luxurious office, personal secretary, company car, expense account etc) and the authority to make *discretionary investments* (ie new investments other than straightforward replacement decisions). The profit aimed for will not be maximum profit, because of management's wish for expenditure on themselves, their staff and the perquisites of management.

3.27 Cyert and March suggested that a firm is an organisational coalition of shareholders, managers, employees and customers, with each group having different goals, and so there is a need for 'political' compromise in establishing the goals of the firm. Each group must settle for less than it would ideally want to have - shareholders must settle for less than maximum profits, and managers for less than maximum utility, and so on.

Maximisation of sales revenue (Baumol)

3.28 Monopoly firms, or near-monopoly firms, are in a particularly suitable position to pursue alternative objectives. Perhaps the most significant of them is the objective of *sales revenue* maximisation. If a monopolist sets out to maximise sales revenue, it might be furthering its own interests by making it less profitable for other firms to enter the market. Maximising sales revenue is one way of creating a barrier to entry.

3.29 It is not unreasonable to suggest that if a very small number of firms account for a very large share of the market then their main preoccupation may well be to maintain and expand their market share, rather than to maximise their profits. This is not as unrealistic as it may sound at first, because growing market shares, or at least a stable share, ensure both the survival of a firm as a viable unit and also may ensure satisfactory profits. One important reason for that is that economies of scale may in fact require a substantial level of output before costs fall and therefore allow both a competitive price and a satisfactory profit margin.

We shall therefore now briefly consider a model of a firm (an imperfect competitor) which maximises total revenue rather than profits, contrasting it with the profit-maximising model.

3.30 We shall assume that the firm is concerned to maximise total revenue, regardless of profit.

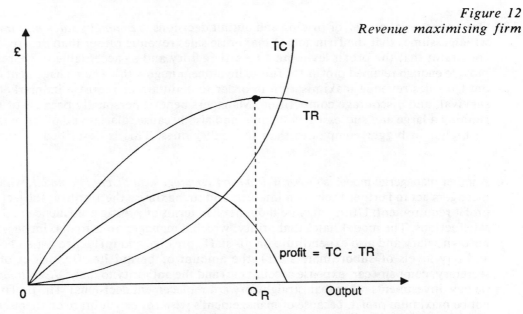

Figure 12
Revenue maximising firm

The firm produces a higher output than a profit-maximising firm. This implies a lower price for its output (and a lower market price if most firms maximise total revenue) than in the case of profit maximisation. The firm will produce Q_R (Figure 12).

3.31 If a revenue-maximising firm is constrained (perhaps by its shareholders) to earn a minimum level of profit, it may have to produce at a level of output below that which maximises total revenue, but its output will still be higher than if it were a profit-maximiser.

Public policy towards private enterprise monopolies

3.32 Since monopolies have both economic disadvantages and economic advantages, there are reasons why a government might wish either to restrict or encourage the development of private enterprise monopolies within its country.

3.33 Monopolies might be harmful or beneficial to the public interest.

(a) A beneficial monopoly is one that succeeds in achieving economies of scale in an industry where the minimum efficiency scale is at a level of production that would mean having to achieve a large share of the total market supply.

(b) A monopoly against the public interest would be one in which cost efficiencies are not achieved, or are negligible. Oliver Williamson suggested that inefficiency in monopolies might occur if 'market power provides the firm with the opportunity to pursue a variety of other-than-profit objectives.'

3.34 There are other reasons for trying to control monopoly growth. A monopoly firm may be a multinational, with its head office in another country. Multinational firms are difficult to control within the context of a government's economic policy requirements and so a government might prefer to see more 'national' firms in a position of some strength in the country's home markets.

3.35 Monopolies might also try to preserve their monopoly position by acting to prevent competition. They might create barriers to entry into the industry against other potential rivals (eg. by taking over small new competitors or purchasing patents to secure a production monopoly). When competition between firms is 'killed off' in this way, the public interest is harmed.

3.36 A monopoly may try to exploit its position by using price discrimination, to charge higher prices for the same good in a different segment of the market. Certain pharmaceuticals manufacturers, for example, have been accused of unfairly charging higher prices in one country than in another. This too can be against the public interest.

Government control over monopolies, mergers and restrictive practices

3.37 There are several different ways in which a government can attempt to control monopolies.

    (a) It can stop them from developing, or it can break them up once they have been created. In the past, there has been a history of 'trust-busting' in the USA. For example, Rockefeller's giant Standard Oil Corporation was broken up by the US government early this century. Preventing monopolies from being created is the reason why a government might have a public policy on mergers.

    (b) It can take them over. Nationalised industries are often government-run monopolies, and central and/or local government also have virtual monopolies in the supply of other services, such as health, the police, education and social services. Government-run monopolies are potentially advantageous because:

        (i) they need not have a profit-maximising objective so that the government can decide whether or not to supply a good or service to a household on grounds other than cost or profit;

        (ii) the government can regulate the quality of the good or service provided more easily than if the industry were operated by private firms;

        (iii) key industries can be protected (eg health, education).

    (c) It can allow monopolies or oligopolies to operate, but try to control their activities in order to protect the consumer. In particular, it can try to prohibit the worst forms of restrictive practice, such as price cartels.

3.38 There are two basic tenets in the thinking behind consumer protection policies.

    (a) Control over markets can arise by firms eliminating the opposition, either by merging with or taking over rivals or stopping other firms from entering the market. The problem here is that when a single firm controls a big enough share of the market it can begin to behave as a monopolist even though its market share is below 100%.

(b) Several firms could behave as monopolists by agreeing with each other not to compete. This could be done in a variety of ways - for example by exchanging information, by setting common prices or by splitting up the market into geographical areas and operating only within allocated boundaries.

3.39 In a perfect monopoly, there is only one firm that is the sole producer of a good that has no closely competing substitutes, so that the firm controls the supply of the good to the market. The definition of a monopoly *in practice* is rather more extensive than this, because governments seeking to control the growth of monopoly firms will probably choose to regard any firm that acquires a certain share of the market as a potential monopolist.

The Monopolies and Mergers Commission in the UK

3.40 In the UK, the Monopolies and Restrictive Practices Act 1948 provided that any firm controlling more than one third of the market for its goods should be investigated as a potential monopoly which was against the public interest. Under the Fair Trading Act 1973, the Director General of Fair Trading is allowed to refer cases to the Monopolies and Mergers Commission (MMC) if any firm controls one quarter of the market, or if any proposed takeover or merger would create a firm that controlled more than one quarter of the market. The Commission will then investigate the proposed merger or takeover and recommend whether or not it should be allowed to proceed.

3.41 Another aspect of the work of the Monopolies and Mergers Commission is to investigate cases where a monopoly is suspected of operating against the public interest and to recommend to the government the steps that should be taken to make the monopoly alter its practices.

3.42 It is significant, however, that a government department, the Office of the Director General of Fair Trading has the power to refer cases to the Commission, which can then prevent a merger or takeover from taking place if it is considered to be against the public interest. The strength of anti-monopoly and anti-takeover activity therefore depends on the attitude of the government of the day, as expressed by the activities of the office of the Director General of Fair Trading.

Breaking up existing monopolies

3.43 You may have noticed that in the UK, public policy has not been aimed at breaking up existing monopolies, although this is an option available to any government. The Conservative government of the 1980s expressed the view that 'de-mergers' - ie the break-up of large firms - might be beneficial and create smaller, more efficient firms - but it has done nothing of substance to encourage de-mergers to happen. The government has also encouraged competition to develop against established monopolies, such as British Telecom, state-owned bus services and the Post Office, but in most cases so far not to the extent that the monopoly firm's position as a monopolist is threatened.

Public policy in favour of monopolies and mergers

3.44 The UK government's policy has mainly been one of trying to control the development of monopolies that are 'against the public interest'. But opinions differ about what monopolies would be good for the country and which ones would be harmful.

3.45 In the modern world of multinational companies, companies need to be big to survive and prosper. Arguably, the UK's industrial strength has declined over the years because the country has failed to nurture enough multinational companies (strengthened by virtual monopolies in their own country) to compete successfully in world markets. Compare Rover cars, as just one example, a very small car manufacturer in world terms, with Fiat of Italy, the largest company in Italy, a big multinational with a virtual monopoly in the Italian car market.

3.46 There have been signs in recent years that the UK government has wanted to encourage the growth of companies in the UK, and many of the proposed 'mega-mergers' - ie mergers between big companies - have not been referred to the Monopolies and Mergers Commission. Government anti-monopoly policy in the UK has accordingly been relatively mild in recent years.

4. MONOPOLISTIC COMPETITION AND NON-PRICE COMPETITION

Monopolistic competition

4.1 Monopolistic competition describes a form of market structure in which:

(a) there are several firms which produce a good that is more or less similar to the goods of other firms, and so there is some competition between the firms;

(b) however, each firm is able to make its good different in some way from those of other firms, at least in the eyes of customers.

    (i) In doing so, each firm is able to achieve a downward-sloping demand curve for its good, and so achieve some of the benefits of being a monopolistic producer, despite the existence of competition.

    (ii) This means that firms do not have to sell their good at a ruling market price, but can exploit product differentiation to decide the price (and output) level of their choice.

Non-price competition

4.2 Firms in monopolistic competition *and* firms in an oligopoly will try to avoid competition on price, in order to preserve their position as a price maker. They will often resort to non-price competition instead. This can take several forms, which include the following.

(a) Product differentiation (eg design differences)
(b) Branding
(c) Advertising and sales promotion
(d) Creating 'add-on' services.

Oligopoly firms might avoid price competition through *collusion* - eg a cartel agreement to restrict output to the market in order to maintain higher prices.

Product differentiation

4.3 Product differentiation describes a situation in which there is a single product being manufactured by several suppliers, and the product of each supplier is basically the same. However, the suppliers try to create differences between their own product and the products of their rivals. These differences might be real (eg small or large design differences) or imaginary, created largely by advertising and brand image.

4.4 Differentiation may take a number of forms, including:

(a) different physical or technical characteristics, satisfying different buyer needs or the same needs in different ways;

(b) different packaging;

(c) different conditions of sale with respect to guarantees, after-sales services, etc;

(d) different geographical location;

(e) different perceptions of the product created through advertising and promotion. This includes *branding* of goods.

4.5 The marketer's role in product differentiation is important and there are many examples. There are several motor car manufacturers who produce a largely similar product which they try to differentiate by a mixture of design differences and advertising. Food manufacturers (eg of baked beans or frozen peas) rely more heavily on brand image and advertising to create product differentiation. Soft drinks can be sold in cartons, bottles and ring-pull cans, and the price differences do not just reflect the cost of each type of packaging.

4.6 But why is product differentiation desirable for producers? The answer is that if all producers made a single homogeneous product, they would operate in a perfectly competitive market. On the other hand, by creating product differentiation they can operate in conditions of monopolistic competition.

Other forms of non-price competition

4.7 There are other ways in which non-price competition can be developed. As the term implies, non-price competition involves competition between firms for customers in the same market, but not on the basis of lowest price (or, at least, not on the basis of low price only). Marketing concentrates on using these non-price variables to influence demand.

(a) *Advertising and sales promotion, or brand imagery.* The aim of advertising, sales promotions or brand image is to increase demand for the good, often at the expense of demand for the goods of other firms in the market.

(b) *Incidental services.* Incidental services are 'extra' services that come as an 'add-on' to the basic good. A firm might make its product more attractive than its rivals' by means of, for example, superior sales services or personal attention. Rival firms can retaliate by offering incidental services too.

(c) *Innovation and technical differences.* A firm may enhance its market share by creating genuine differences through innovation: Brand X is made to have more 'features' than Brand Y, so that customers for Brand Y are encouraged to switch. Here, the opportunity for retaliation by other firms must be limited because innovation is easily the most effective form of non-price competition; however, it is not easily available to firms which produce a basic commodity, such as petrol or farm produce, eg milk or wheat.

Profit-maximising equilibrium of a firm in monopolistic competition

4.8 A firm which operates in conditions of monopolistic competition:

(a) has a downward-sloping demand curve;

(b) unlike a monopoly firm, is often *unable* to create barriers to entry to other firms. (Indeed, the firm already competes with rivals, which can take retaliatory competitive action if the firm makes big profits).

4.9 A firm will therefore have:

(a) a short-run equilibrium, in which it can make supernormal profits; and
(b) a long-run equilibrium.

In the *long run*, the monopolistic competitor cannot earn supernormal profits since there are no entry barriers. Its short-run supernormal profits will be competed away by new entrants. So the firm will eventually be able to achieve normal profits only.

4.10 The short run equilibrium for a firm in monopolistic competition is illustrated in Figure 13. This diagram is identical to a diagram which shows the equilibrium of a monopoly firm earning supernormal profits.

Figure 13
The short run equilibrium of a firm in monopolistic competition. The firm makes supernormal profit of (P - AC) × Q units

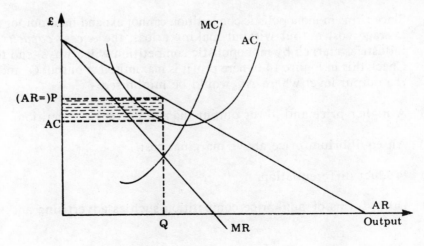

4.11 The long run equilibrium for a firm in monopolistic competition is illustrated in Figure 14. This diagram is identical to a diagram which shows the equilibrium of a monopoly firm which earns no supernormal profits, and so normal profits only.

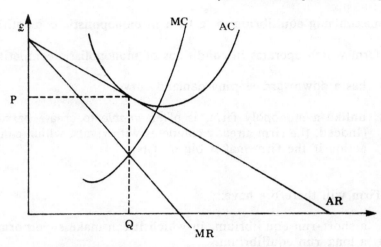

Figure 14
The long run equilibrium of a
firm in monopolistic competition

Price is higher and output lower than in perfect competition for the same reasons described earlier when comparing monopoly with perfect competition.

4.12 Because profit-maximising output is lower in a market with monopolistic competition, and at a point where average costs are not minimised, monopolistic competition, like monopoly, is arguably more wasteful of resources than perfect competition.

Characteristics of monopolistic competition: summary

4.13 Monopolistic competition is characterised by the following.

(a) Equilibrium output below the level at which average costs are a minimum, in the long-run. Monopolistic competitors are said to have *excess* or *unused* capacity.

(b) Since firms in monopolistic competition cannot expand their output to the level of minimum average cost output without making a loss, the *excess capacity theorem* predicts that industries marked by monopolistic competition will always tend to have excess capacity. Check this in Figure 14, where profit is maximised at output Q, and output Q is lower than the output level where AC would be minimised.

(c) A higher price and lower output than in perfect competition.

(d) An equilibrium price above marginal cost.

(e) Product differentiation.

(f) Other forms of non-price competition such as advertising and sales promotion.

4.14 Note that a wide variety of brands of one good is not a guarantee that there is monopolistic competition, for a single firm often produces many brands itself. For example, Proctor and Gamble produces Daz, Tide, Dreft, and many other washing powders. It is fair to describe the market for such soaps and detergents as an oligopolistic one, with Unilever and Proctor and Gamble competing for market leadership.

Is monopolistic competition wasteful of economic resources?

4.15 There are several reasons for suggesting that monopolistic competition is wasteful of economic resources.

(a) It can be argued that it is wasteful to produce a wide variety of differentiated versions of the same product. If a single version of the same product were made, firms might be able to achieve economies of scale with large-volume production (and so shift their cost curves to the right).

(b) Some methods that are used to create product differentiation are a waste of resources. Advertising costs are often cited as an example of this.

(c) Firms in monopolistic competition, like monopolists, produce at an output level below that at which where AC is minimised. (And so there is allocative inefficiency of resources).

4.16 There are other reasons for arguing that monopolistic competition is *not* so wasteful of resources.

(a) Some product differentiation is 'real' - ie there are technical differences between similar goods from rival firms. Buyers/consumers therefore have more to choose from when there is product differentiation. Their requirements are likely to be satisfied better than if there were just a single, basic, low-price good, without any choice.

(b) If product differentiation is entirely imaginary, created by brand image and advertising when the goods of rival firms are exactly the same, rational buyers should opt for the least cost good anyway. Or the imagery could be seen as providing symbolic utility to the consumer, providing him or her with additional benefits, besides functional ones.

5. OLIGOPOLY

The nature of oligopoly

5.1 Oligopoly differs from monopoly in that there is more than one firm in a market, although the number of firms is small. Oligopoly differs from monopolistic competition because the number of rival firms is small.

An oligopoly consisting of only two firms is sometimes referred to as a *duopoly*. Usually industries dominated by up to 10 firms would be classified as oligopolistic.

5.2 Oligopolists may produce a homogeneous product (eg oil) or there may be product differentiation (eg cigarettes, cars).

5.3 The essence of oligopoly is that *firms' production decisions are interdependent*. One firm cannot set price and output without considering how its rivals' response will affect its own profits. There is no simple answer to the question of how an oligopolist will actually set his output and price. The answer depends on what assumption firms make about their competitors' behaviour.

Price cartels by oligopolist producers

5.4 A cartel agreement is an agreement on price and output levels between producers. A price cartel or price ring may be created when a group of oligopoly firms combine to agree on a price at which they will sell their product to the market. The market might be willing to demand more of the product at a lower price, while the cartel agreement attempts to impose a higher price (for higher unit profits) by restricting supply to the market to a level which is consistent with the volume of demand at the price they wish to charge.

5.5 Each oligopoly firm could increase its profits if all the big firms in the market charge the same price as a monopolist would, and split the output between them. This is known as *collusion*, which can be tacit or openly admitted.

5.6 Cartels are difficult to outlaw. There might still be collusive price leadership. This occurs when all firms realise that one of them is initiating a price change that will be of benefit to them all, and so follow the leader and change their own price in the same way.

Cartels: output as well as price collusion

Figure 15
Price cartel
shown by supply curve
S_2 and price P_2

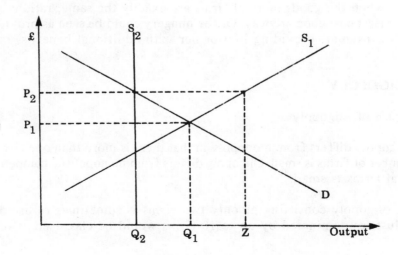

5.7 Figure 15 illustrates how:

(a) in a competitive market, with a market supply curve S_1 and demand curve D, the price would be P_1 and output Q_1;

(b)   a cartel of producers might agree to fix the market price at P_2, higher than P_1. But to do so, the cartel must also agree to cut market supply from Q_1 to Q_2, and so fix the market supply curve at S_2.

5.8   Establishing a cartel depends on:

(a)   the firms in the cartel being able to control supply to the market;

(b)   agreeing on a price (P_2);

(c)   agreeing on how much of the output each firm should produce. In Figure 3, if the market price is fixed at P_2, firms would want to supply output Z in a free market. This cannot be allowed to happen; otherwise market price P_2 could not be sustained.

5.9   The main weakness with cartels is that each firm is still seeking the best results for itself, and so there is an incentive for an individual firm to break the cartel agreement by secretly increasing its output and selling it at the fixed cartel price.

5.10   However, if all firms increased their output in this way, the cartel would collapse because the high price could not be sustained without a restricted output, and excess supply on the market would force down the price.

5.11   This has been the experience in recent years amongst the oil-producing countries of OPEC (the Organisation of Petroleum Exporting Countries). Attempts to agree on a restricted output quota for each country in order to push up oil prices have often broken down because some member countries exceeded their quota, or sold below the cartel's agreed price.

5.12   The success of a price cartel will depend on:

(a)   whether it consists of most or all of the producers of the product;

(b)   whether or not there are close substitutes for the product. For example, a price cartel by taxi drivers might lead to a shift in demand for transport services to buses, cars and trains;

(c)   the ease with which supply can be regulated. (In the case of primary commodities, such as wheat, rice, tea and coffee, total supply is dependent on weather conditions and even political events in the producing country);

(d)   the price elasticity of demand for the product. An attempt to raise prices might result in such a large a fall in demand that the total income of producers also falls if demand is price elastic ie η is greater than 1;

(e)   whether producers can agree on their individual shares of the total restricted supply to the market. This is often the greatest difficulty of all.

The kinked oligopoly demand curve

5.13 Price cartels, whether 'official' or tacit and collusive, do not always exist in an oligopoly market. So how does an oligopoly firm which is competing with a rival oligopoly firm decide on its price and output level?

A feature of oligopoly markets, remember, is that each firm's pricing and output decisions are influenced by what the firm's rivals might do.

When demand conditions are stable, the major problem confronting an oligopolist in fixing his price and output is judging the response of his competitor(s) to the prices he has set. An oligopolist is faced with a downward sloping demand curve, but the nature of the demand curve is dependent on the reactions of his rivals. Any change in price will invite a competitive response. This situation is described by the kinked oligopoly demand curve in the diagram shown here, in which the oligopolist is currently charging price P, for output OQ, which is at the kink on the demand curve DD.

5.14 The kinked demand curve is used to explain how an oligopolist might have to accept price stability in the market.

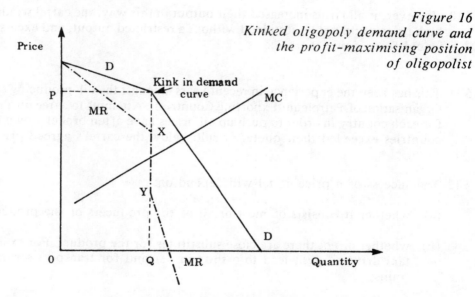

Figure 16
Kinked oligopoly demand curve and
the profit-maximising position
of oligopolist

If he were to raise his prices above P (Figure 16), his competitors would keep their price lower and so many consumers would buy from them instead. An example is the difficulty which individual petrol companies have in raising the price of petrol at garages. If competitors do not raise their prices too, the firm usually soon has to restore its prices to their previous level. The demand curve would therefore be quite elastic at these higher prices.

If, on the other hand, the oligopolist were to reduce his prices below P, competitors would probably do the same. Total market demand might rise, but the increase in demand for the oligopolist's products would probably be quite low, unless the price elasticity of demand in the market as a whole is fairly high. The elasticity of demand at prices below P will be less than the elasticity at prices above P - hence the kink in the demand curve.

5.15 Note that the MR curve is discontinuous at the output level where there is the kink in the demand curve. The kink in the demand curve explains the nature of the marginal revenue curve MR. At price P, output OQ, the MR curve falls vertically because at higher prices the MR curve corresponds to the more elastic demand curve, and at prices below P the MR curve corresponds to the less elastic demand.

5.16 A firm maximises its profit at the point where MR = MC. There is a strong probability that the MC curve will cut the MR curve somewhere between points X and Y (the discontinuous part of the MR curve). The more inelastic the demand curve is below price P, the longer the discontinuous portion (XY) of the MR curve will be.

The oligopolist's cost structure can change, with worsening or improved efficiencies, but as long as the MC curve cuts the MR curve through its vertical portion XY, the oligopolist's price and output decision should not alter. Hence, there will be price and output stability, with cost changes for the oligopoly firm, which change its MC curve, not affecting output and price.

5.17 Only if marginal costs rise far enough for the MC curve to pass through the MR curve above point X in Figure 16 is there a case for raising price, and only if MC falls far enough to pass through the MR curve below point Y is there a case for lowering price.

5.18 In general, oligopoly prices will rise only if all the firms follow the lead of a rival in raising its price, so that the AR curve shifts outwards. The kink rises to the new common price level, which is again stable. The converse holds for price falls, perhaps occurring because of technological advance.

Price leadership and price wars in oligopoly markets

5.19 In oligopoly markets there is a tendency for one firm to set the general industry price, with the other firms following suit. This is called *price leadership*. It is one source of stability in a market where there may be cartels which tend to be undercut, and price wars.

5.20 When demand conditions change, the situation becomes somewhat different and price stability might no longer exist.

(a) If total market demand falls, oligopolists might try to increase their share of the market by cutting prices.

(b) Similarly, if one oligopolist begins to lose his *share* of the market, he might try to restore it by cutting prices. The consequence would be a price war. In the UK in recent years there have been price wars by supermarkets and oil companies, for example. The effect of price wars is usually beneficial to consumers, but they are of limited duration because it is not in the interests of oligopolists to sustain them for long.

5.21 Without the opportunity to compete on price, oligopolistic firms also have to compete through non-price variables.

5.22 However, if firms get out of line with the industry norm for advertising spending or promotional activity, this can also cause adverse competitive responses. Advertising wars can be as damaging to profits as price wars.

6. CONCLUSION

6.1 Perfect competition is an idealised version of competition but it does express many of the realities facing businesses in a 'competitive' environment. The essence of competition is that companies produce a small share of total market output and hence have little influence over price. Competition is generally associated with large numbers of firms.

6.2 The *firm* is in equilibrium under competition when it can do nothing more to increase its profit, ie when MC = MR = Price. The *industry* is in equilibrium when S = D, alternatively when there is no tendency for firms to leave or enter the industry.

6.3 Competitive pressures erode profits. Firms have an incentive to collude and raise prices to the consumer by restricting output. If they can do this their profits will increase.

6.4 In the short term, a *loss-making firm* might stay in the market, hoping that in the longer term, prices will go up or costs will fall. In the short run, the firm will seek to minimise its losses. Provided that AR exceeds AVC (average variable cost), the firm will make some contribution towards covering fixed costs. Contribution will be maximised at the price and output level where MC = MR.

6.5 In the short term, a firm might earn *supernormal profits*, even in a competitive market. In the longer term, it must make decisions about whether to expand capacity to increase total profits and so its cost structure will change. Competition, if it exists, will eventually erode supernormal profits.

6.6 When price competition is restricted, firms usually go in for other forms of competition, for example advertising, product differentiation and market segmentation/price discrimination.

6.7 In some industries, there are many firms, but competition is reduced because each firm seeks to achieve some product differentiation (eg brand image). In doing so:

(a) it is more difficult for new competitor firms to break into the market;

(b) each firm can build up a customer loyalty or market niche, and act in many ways like a monopolist, ie making prices and facing a downward-sloping demand curve.

These market conditions are called monopolistic competition.

6.8 When industries consist of a small number of firms, then one thing that managers will have to consider is the reaction of rivals to their own pricing and output decisions and to the non-price competitive activities which they pursue. This is referred to as *competitor analysis*.

6.9 The kinked oligopoly demand curve may explain why there is price stability (and non-price competition) in many oligopoly markets. Oligopolies might collude and make a formal or informal cartel agreement on the price for the industry and output levels for each firm.

TEST YOUR KNOWLEDGE

The numbers in brackets refer to paragraphs of this chapter

1 What characteristics would you examine to identify how perfect or imperfect the competition was in a given industry? (1.3)

2 What are the conditions necessary for perfect competition to exist? (1.6)

3 Use a diagram to illustrate the long run equilibrium position of a firm operating under conditions of perfect competition. (2.12)

4 What conditions are necessary for price discrimination to be practised? (3.2)

5 What are the arguments in favour of monopolies? (3.13)

6 What is meant by non-price competition? (4.2)

7 How would you explain the shape of the demand curve facing an oligopolistic firm? (5.14)

Now try illustrative questions 11 and 12 at the end of the text

Chapter 7

BUSINESS ORGANISATION AND BUSINESS FINANCE

This chapter covers the following topics.

1. Types of business organisation
2. Sources of business finance

1. TYPES OF BUSINESS ORGANISATION

Types of business and public sector organisation

1.1 Having considered in the previous chapter some theoretical models of markets we can now consider the various types of business and public sector organisations that are found in a mixed economy. There are:

(a) organisations in the private sector, owned by shareholders who may be institutions (such as life insurance companies, unit trusts or pension funds), or private individuals;

(b) organisations in the public sector, owned by the state.

1.2 Private sector organisations include:

(a) commercial 'profit-making' organisations, including:

   (i)   sole trader businesses;
   (ii) partnerships;
   (iii) private limited companies;
   (iv) public limited companies; and
   (v)   co-operatives;

(b) non-commercial organisations with non-profit objectives, such as:

   (i) charities;
   (ii) clubs, societies and associations.

1.3 Public sector organisations comprise:

(a) central or local government owned organisations, such as hospitals, schools, the armed forces, the fire and police services, public libraries, public swimming baths and public museums and art galleries;

(b) state-owned nationalised industries. In the UK, these include British Rail and British Coal. During the 1980's, many previously nationalised industries have been sold into the private sector, or 'privatised' (examples are British Gas, British Telecom, British Airways and the regional water companies).

Sole traders

1.4 A sole trader is a person who enters business on his own account, contributing the capital to start the enterprise, running it with or without employees, and receiving the proceeds or standing the loss of the venture.

His business is a separate entity, but it does not have a legal personality of its own. The sole trader personally is legally responsible for the actions of his business and all its debts.

1.5 Sole traders are to be found mainly in the retail trades (eg corner shops, local news agencies), small-scale service industries (eg garages, plumbers, office cleaning), small manufacturing and craft industries (eg furniture making, bespoke tailoring and pottery).

1.6 The main advantages of sole trading are as follows.

(a) No formal procedures are required to set up in a business (except that for certain classes of business a licence must be obtained, eg retailing wines and spirits, operating a taxi cab and many must or choose to register for VAT).

(b) There is independence and self-accountability with no requirement to reveal the state of the business to anyone (except the Inland Revenue, and Customs & Excise if VAT-registered).

(c) Personal supervision can ensure effective operation.

1.7 Among the disadvantages are the following.

(a) The proprietor has 'unlimited liability', which means that he is personally liable to the full extent of his private assets for the debts of his business.

(b) Expansion capital is usually only provided by ploughing back the profits of the business, although loans may be available from banks or personal contacts.

(c) There is high dependence on the individual which can mean long working hours and difficulties during sickness or holidays.

(d) The death of the proprietor may make it necessary to sell the business in order to pay inheritance tax.

(e) The individual may only have one main skill. A sole trader may be a good technical engineer or craftsman but lack the skills to market his products or maintain accounting records to control his business effectively.

Partnerships

1.8 A partnership is a relationship between two or more persons who decide to carry on business together with a view of profit.

1.9 A partnership is particularly suitable for professional people. Indeed, at the time of writing solicitors, doctors and accountants may only function as sole traders or partnerships. This form of business organisation is also suitable for many other small-scale enterprises such as those operated by sole traders.

1.10 The reasons for taking a partner or partners include the following.

(a) Increased capital is available, permitting more rapid expansion.

(b) Responsibility is spread (both financial and operating).

(c) Wider experience and skill can be contributed to the firm, for instance, a technical person can combine with a marketing person.

(d) The affairs of the business are still private.

1.11 But there are also disadvantages of partnership.

(a) The partners still have unlimited liability for the debts of the business.

(b) The independence of the individual is lost as each partner must consult the others and consider their views every time a decision of any consequence is made.

(c) The death of a partner may cause problems for the partnership if the executors or beneficiaries of the will wish to withdraw the capital from the business.

1.12 The Limited Partnership Act 1907 permits a partnership between active partners and one or more 'sleeping' partners.

The sleeping partner contributes funds to the business and can receive a share of profits, but he does not take any part in the conduct of the business or the management of the firm. In this case, the principle of limited liability applies to the sleeping partner who is liable only to the extent of the capital he has contributed to the business.

Private and public limited companies

1.13 A limited company is an entity separate from its members, this being the essential difference between a limited company and a partnership. Whereas a limited company's members have limited liability for its debts, all partners are fully liable for the partnership's debts. Only the company itself, not its members, is fully liable without limit for its debts. The partner in a firm may have to sacrifice his or her own personal assets, including his or her house, to pay the debts of the partnership. The member of a limited company may lose all of what he or she has paid for the company's shares, but will not lose more than that.

1.14 Public company status offers the advantage that shares in the company may be offered to the general public. A private company is prohibited from doing this. But the price of this advantage is that there are more restrictions placed on public companies by the Companies Act than on private ones.

1.15 A *public limited company* must:

    (a)   have an authorised and allotted capital of at least £50,000;
    (b)   state in its memorandum that it is a public company;
    (c)   obtain a trading certificate before it may commence business; and
    (d)   have at least two directors.

A *private limited company* is any company which is not a public limited company. You can distinguish between them by the fact that the former's name must end with 'ltd' or 'limited' whilst the latter's ends with 'plc' or 'public limited company'.

A mistake which is often made is to confuse public limited companies with *listed* companies. To have shares listed on the Stock Exchange, a company must be a public one (since it is offering its shares to the public), but plc's do not have to be listed, and indeed many are privately owned.

1.16 The reasons for forming a limited company, either private or public, are mainly to obtain sufficient capital (rarely can one person find enough for a large undertaking) and to obtain the benefits of limited liability. The two are inter-related, since if people know their liability is limited to the amount of capital they wish to invest then they are probably prepared to risk that amount in a firm, whereas if they could be called upon to subscribe additional amounts or be responsible for a company's debts they might not invest anything. Hence limited liability companies are a means of bringing capital and enterprise together. It should be borne in mind however that the benefits of limited liability are reduced for many small businesses because their banks often require a charge over director-shareholder's personal assets (eg their house) before lending money to them.

1.17 A company is registered by the Registrar of Companies, who issues a certificate of incorporation.

The certificate of incorporation bestows on the company a separate legal personality. It can then in its own right do things such as own property, employ people, and be involved in legal actions.

1.18 Before a company can begin trading it must secure the capital it requires. In a private company this will largely be contributed by the promoters or founders. For a public company, it can be obtained from the public, either directly, or indirectly through institutional investors such as insurance companies and pension funds. Private companies are not allowed to seek subscription from the public in this way.

1.19 Many companies start in a small way, often as family businesses which operate as a private company, then grow to the point where they become public companies and can invite the public to subscribe for shares. The new capital thus made available enables the firm to expand its activities and achieve the advantages of large-scale production.

1.20 Shares in public companies are freely transferable. However, as noted above, it is by no means compulsory for a plc to trade its shares on a public exchange.

1.21 As a distinct legal person, the company has a separate identity from the shareholders, and it is not managed or run by them. It is controlled by the directors, but the shareholders or members may elect a new board of directors at the annual general meeting if they wish to do so. The shareholders' main functions are the provision of capital and the bearing of the risk that the company will succeed or fail. In return they receive their share of the profits as dividends. If the company fails, they stand to make a loss, but only to the extent of the capital which they have subscribed - their limited liability.

Co-operatives

1.22 A co-operative could be one of two types.

(a) *Consumer co-operative.* This is a group of consumers who organise themselves into a collective group for the purpose of purchasing goods for consumption. A shop or chain of stores might be run as a co-operative whereby goods are purchased collectively in bulk by the co-operative and then re-sold to individual co-operative members. Financial services may also be provided by co-operatives and other forms of mutual organisation. The Co-operative Wholesale Society, with its large retail network, and the UK building societies, which provide loan finance to homebuyers, started in this way.

(b) *Producer co-operative.* This is a group of workers who organise themselves into a collective group in order to produce and sell goods. A well known example in the UK is the Meriden motor cycle factory, which unfortunately went into liquidation in 1983.

1.23 The essential feature of a co-operative is that ownership of the enterprise rests with the people who actually operate it (consumers in a consumer co-operative and workers in a producer co-operative). This feature of ownership is distinct from:

(a) ownership of a private firm, which rests on the amount of capital subscribed by ordinary shareholders, partners or sole trader owners; and

(b) ownership of a public corporation.

1.24 Membership of a co-operative is obtained by subscribing for shares in it. Management of a co-operative is the responsibility of a management committee whose members are appointed from the ranks of the members of the co-operative itself. In some cases, a manager who is an outsider might be appointed.

Clubs, societies and associations

1.25 Clubs, societies and associations provide benefits to their members at a price that enables them to cover their costs. The task of a club or society is to provide benefits to its members which are valued at least as highly as the subscription rates which members are expected to pay for them. To give examples, among the largest in the UK are the Automobile Association and the Royal Automobile Club.

Public sector organisations

1.26 Public sector organisations might be non-profit making, or alternatively might be required to make a profit, or a certain rate of return on assets.

(a) Non-profit making organisations include state schools and the fire services. These must provide a product or service of a certain quality to meet whatever demand there is and, except indirectly through the taxation system, there is no charge for the service to customers. The economic aim of these organisations should be to provide 'value for money'; they should use resources as efficiently as possible so as to provide the quality service at a minimum cost.

(b) Nationalised industries are state-owned, but are expected to make a profit. Some nationalised industries are monopolies (eg the railways) but because they are state-owned the government might restrict their freedom of choice in making pricing decisions, and so a nationalised industry might not be allowed to maximise its profits.

(c) When a nationalised industry is 'privatised' the government might still keep some control over the prices of the industry's products, particularly if the organisation is a monopoly supplier. When British Telecom was privatised in 1984, for example, it was made a condition that any future annual tariff increases by BT should be restricted to 3% below the annual rate of inflation.

Nationalised industries

1.27 Nationalised industries are government-owned businesses which are corporations and get most of their revenue from selling goods or services. A public corporation like British Coal or the electricity supply authorities should not necessarily attempt to maximise profit as if they were in the private sector because it must make allowance for the social implications of its pricing policies. But at the same time, the government may not want the nationalised industries to run at a financial loss, since these losses must be paid for.

1.28 The government pays directly for *social investment* (investment to obtain benefits for society) which is carried out by nationalised industries. For all other investment projects, each industry is told to attain a *required rate of return* on its total investments. In addition, each individual industry is set an *external financing limit* (cash limit) on the amount of money it can borrow to finance investment. A nationalised industry might also be given performance or productivity targets.

There is some indirect pressure to earn reasonable profits in order to finance all the desired investment programmes. Cash limits are in principle set annually, but the government is sometimes forced to increase them during the year.

1.29 There is wide divergence in the performance of nationalised industries. British Gas in the years running up to its privatisation was extremely profitable and was set a *negative* cash limit in some years - it paid money to the government - but British Rail, in contrast, continues to receive large sums of money from the government.

1.30 We can conclude that the nationalised industries have to achieve both:

(a) commercial returns; and
(b) social responsibility.

Since the two objectives are not necessarily compatible, they are approached separately by the industries. In addition, the former objective may be sacrificed for political reasons, or if over-ridden by another of the government's economic aims.

Advantages and disadvantages of state ownership

1.31 The proper mix of public and private ownership or resources in the mixed economy is still a topic debated in Britain today. In broad terms, the Labour Party is in favour of more state control, the Conservatives of less control.

1.32 Possible economic advantages of nationalisation include the following.

(a) Single control over a whole industry enables economies of large-scale production to be achieved.

(b) State ownership may enable an industry to undertake large-scale capital investment which would not be possible if it were privately owned (eg power stations).

(c) Some industries are 'natural' monopolies (eg water, electricity) and state ownership provides a means of controlling these essential services.

(d) Key industries can be protected (eg nuclear power).

(e) Important, though declining, industries can be protected (eg steel).

(f) Employees may prefer to work for a state industry, if they feel that their welfare is better protected.

(g) State ownership can protect the national interest, especially where it would be economically wasteful if the producer were not a monopolist (eg duplication of the railway network would be wasteful).

(h) The government can use the state controlled industries to carry out its economic policies.

(i) The exceptionally high cost of research and development expenditure and of modern highly-sophisticated capital equipment in many sectors of the economy is a barrier to small-scale operations. This is especially true in the aerospace and electronic industries and increasingly it is the case that major developments in these sectors cannot proceed without the financial involvement of the government.

1.33 The economic disadvantages of nationalisation are as follows.

(a) Most nationalised industries suffer from the problems of monopoly:

    (i) there is a loss of consumer sovereignty with the monopolist being in a powerful position as sole or main supplier to the market;

    (ii) costs might not be controlled efficiently;

    (iii) the size of the firm can cause problems of management. It is difficult to control the large undertaking efficiently;

    (iv) strikes can cripple the industry.

(b) Waste may be encouraged since losses are borne by rate-payers or tax-payers.

(c) Politicians and councillors may not be familiar with the operation of the business and political pressures or indecision may influence adversely the decision-making process, both of which can result in inefficiency.

(d) There can be conflict between economy of operation and adequacy of service. The public will demand as perfect a service as possible but may not wish to bear the cost involved.

(e) Because public enterprises are publicly accountable this can lead to excessive caution on the part of managers, which can slow down innovation for fear of being blamed or criticised.

1.34 The economic factors to be considered in deciding whether a nationalised industry should be privatised include the following:

(a) whether the government will be creating a privately-owned monopoly, and if so, whether the monopoly would be economically harmful or beneficial to the community;

(b) how the revenues from the sale of the enterprises would be used by the government to manage the economy, where the private capital subscribe to purchase shares in the privatised enterprises would come from, and who the purchaser would be:

    (i) individuals might use personal savings to buy shares;

    (ii) large firms, including financial institutions, might buy shares instead of subscribing for shares in other companies, or purchasing government securities;

    (iii) overseas investors might decide to subscribe - this may affect the exchange rate for sterling and trade with other countries;

(c) whether the privatisation of government-owned industries would lead to an improvement in the efficiency of factors of production (eg labour) in those industries. The Conservative government in the UK appears to take the view that nationalised industries are inefficient, and therefore that privatisation would improve productivity and cut unit output costs;

(d) whether de-nationalisation would add to unemployment as new profit-conscious managers seek to cut costs by implementing a scheme of rationalisation, involving redundancy and early retirement programmes;

(e)   whether the management of the privatised industries would consider themselves free from any obligation to commit themselves to buying equipment from British suppliers. For example, British Airways might be less inclined to purchase British-made aircraft, and British Telecom less inclined to purchase telephone exchange equipment from a British manufacturer such as GEC;

(f)   whether the government's offer price (selling price) for shares in privatised enterprises would be too low, thereby enabling speculators to make a quick profit at the community's expense.

PRIVATISATION

Arguments for

●   Privatisation can improve efficiency, in one of two ways.

  o   If the effect of privatisation is to increase competition, the effect might be to reduce or eliminate allocative inefficiency.

  o   If nationalised industries are X-inefficient the effect of denationalisation might be to make the industries more cost-conscious, because they will be directly answerable to shareholders, and under scrutiny from Stock Market investors. X-inefficiencies might therefore be reduced or eliminated.

●   Denationalisation provides an immediate source of money for the government.

●   Privatisation reduces bureaucratic and political meddling in the industries concerned.

●   There is a view that wider share ownership should be encouraged. Denationalisation is a method of creating wider share ownership, as the sale of British Telecom, British Gas and various other nationalised industries showed in the UK.

Arguments against

●   The privatisation of natural monopolies such as the water industry and telecommunications enables the privatised companies to charge high prices, thus making supernormal profits at the expense of the consumer.

●   State-owned industries are more likely to respond to the public interest, ahead of the profit motive. For example, state-owned industries are more likely to cross-subsidise unprofitable operations from profitable ones; eg the Post Office will continue to deliver letters to the isles of Scotland even though the service might be unprofitable.

●   Encouraging private competition to state-run industries might be inadvisable where significant economies of scale can be achieved by monopoly operations.

7: BUSINESS ORGANISATION AND BUSINESS FINANCE

Privatisation

1.35 Privatisation takes three broad forms.

(a) The deregulation of industries, to allow private firms to compete against state-owned businesses where they were not allowed to compete before: (eg deregulation of bus and coach services, possible deregulation of postal services).

(b) Contracting out work to private firms, where the work was previously done by government employees - eg refuse collection, hospital laundry work.

(c) Transferring the ownership of assets from the state to private shareholders - eg the denationalisation of British Telecom and British Gas.

1.36 The UK government has carried out a policy of denationalisation in recent years. British Gas, British Telecom and the main Water Authorities have been among the enterprises which have been privatised. In spite of some competition against British Telecom, these organisations are in general 'natural monopolies' and the government has not planned to break their monopoly hold on their markets. Instead, the government has chosen to appoint *consumer watchdog' bodies* - ie organisations set up to protect the consumers' interests, and with some legal powers to control activities of the monopolies which could be against the consumers' interests.

2. SOURCES OF BUSINESS FINANCE

Sources of long-term capital

2.1 When firms wish to invest, they must obtain capital. Long-term investments should be financed by long term funds, and short-term investments (in working capital such as stocks and debtors) should ideally be financed by a mixture of short-term and long term funds.

2.2 The major source of long-term capital funds for UK companies is retained profits.

2.3 When companies need more long-term capital than they can get from retained profits, they must go to the *capital markets* to obtain the extra capital they need.

(a) The 'capital markets' is a term used to describe the institutions which exist to provide long-term and medium-term finance, and the 'financial instruments' - ie the forms that such finance take.

(b) These are distinct from the 'money markets', which are the markets for short-term borrowing.

2.4 Both private firms and the government raise funds in the capital market. To some extent, so too do individuals - in particular, individuals seek finance from building societies and banks in the mortgage market in order to buy houses. We shall concentrate here, however, on capital raised by firms.

2.5 *Firms* obtain long-term or medium-term capital in one of the following ways.

   (a) *Share capital*. Most share capital issued to raise new funds is ordinary share capital, and ordinary shareholders are the owners or 'members' of the company.

   (b) *Loan capital*. Long-term loan capital might be raised in the form of a mortgage or debenture. The lender will usually want some security for the loan, and the mortgage deed or debenture deed will specify the security. Debenture stock, like shares, can be issued on the Stock Market and then bought and sold in 'second hand' trading.

2.6 The *government* borrows from a variety of sources, but two important means of borrowing by central government are:

   (a) issuing gilt-edged securities, or 'gilts'; and
   (b) National Savings.

Capital markets in the UK

2.7 There are several 'market places' for raising capital. In the UK there are the following.

   (a) *The Stock Exchange*. The Stock Exchange provides the main market in which:

      (i) large public limited companies can raise new funds by issuing new shares or loan stock;

      (ii) the government can raise new funds by issuing gilt-edged stock; and

      (iii) investors can buy and sell 'second-hand' stocks and shares. Most dealings on the Stock Exchange are in second-hand securities, rather than in new capital issues, but it is the existence of this ready market for selling shares that makes investors so willing to buy shares in the first place.

   (b) *The Unlisted Securities Market (USM)*. This is a market set up by the Stock Exchange where companies which are not big enough to obtain a full listing on the Stock Exchange can raise new capital by issuing shares. Few companies have been coming to the USM in recent years, and the future of this market is uncertain at the time of writing.

   (c) *Banks*. Banks can be approached directly by firms and individuals for medium term loans. The major clearing banks, many merchant banks and foreign banks operating in the UK are increasingly willing to lend medium term capital, especially to well-established companies.

   (d) *Building societies*. This is a capital market where individuals obtain capital to buy a home with a mortgage.

   (e) *National Savings*. This is a capital market where the government obtains capital by borrowing from private investors.

The Stock Exchange

2.8 The Stock Exchange is an organised capital market which plays an important role in the functioning of the UK economy. It is the main capital market in the UK.

(a) The Stock Exchange makes it easier for large firms and the government to raise long term capital, by providing a 'market place' for borrowers and investors to come together.

(b) The Stock Exchange publicises the prices of quoted (or 'listed') securities. Investors can therefore keep an eye on the value of their stocks and shares, and make buying and selling decisions accordingly.

(c) The Stock Exchange tries to enforce certain rules of conduct for its listed firms and for operators in the market, so that investors have the assurance that companies whose shares are traded on the Exchange and traders who operate there are reputable. Confidence in the Stock Exchange will make investors more willing to put their money into stocks and shares.

(d) The index of share prices on the Stock Exchange acts as an indicator of the market's view of the state of the country's economy.

2.9 The Stock Exchange does little to discourage speculation, which is the buying and selling of stocks and shares in anticipation of short-term price rise or price fall.

The activities of speculators arguably make the stock market more volatile that it would otherwise be, and occasionally put undue pressure on certain shares to rise or fall in price. Nevertheless, speculation is an inevitable feature of any organised market.

Lenders of capital

2.10 The *lenders* of capital include private individuals, who buy stocks and shares on the Stock Exchange, or who invest in National Savings or building societies. However, there are large *institutional investors*. These include:

(a) pension funds;
(b) insurance companies;
(c) investment trust companies;
(d) unit trust companies;
(e) venture capital organisations.

Venture capital organisations specialise in raising funds for new business ventures, such as 'management buy-outs' (ie purchases of firms by their management staff). A venture capital organisation which has operated for many years in the UK is 'Investors in Industry' also known as 'the 3i group'.

Short term borrowing

2.11 Companies might also borrow short term funds. The most common sources of short term funds are:

(a) bank loans and overdrafts;
(b) trade credit - credit from suppliers.

As you know, banks are a major source of short term credit in the UK, and firms and individuals can approach their bank for an overdraft facility or short-term loan.

2.12 The main source of new *lending* to companies, both long and short term, is the banks. New debenture stock is not often issued by companies to raise new funds because this stock must compete with government loan stock (gilts) to attract investors and, because they are more 'high risk', company debentures must generally offer a higher rate of interest than the interest rate on gilts, which has been very high itself in recent years. However, there are signs that firms are becoming more interested in issuing their own debt, especially on eurobond markets.

The money markets

2.13 The 'money markets' in the UK, in which the banks and other financial institutions are active participants, are a source of short-term finance. Although the money markets largely involve borrowing and lending by banks, some large companies, and nationalised industries, as well as the government, are involved in money market operations. The money markets consist of the following.

(a) *The discount market.* This is a market where principally banks buy and sell bills of exchange.

(b) *The interbank market.* This is the 'market' in which banks lend short term funds to one another.

(c) *The eurocurrency market.* This is the market operated by banks for lending and borrowing in foreign currencies on deposit in countries outside their country of origin. Most of the trading is done by banks on behalf of their customers. Firms wishing to borrow in a foreign currency will usually do so from a bank, and will not become directly involved in the eurocurrency markets.

(d) *The Certificate of Deposit market.* This involves banks and their customers in the issuing and purchase of CDs.

(e) *The local authority market.* This is a market in which local authorities borrow short term funds from banks and other investors, by issuing and selling short term 'debt instruments'.

(f) *The finance house market.* This refers to the short term loans raised from the money markets by the finance houses.

(g) *The inter-company market.* This refers to direct short term lending between companies, without any financial intermediary. This market is very small, and restricted to the treasury departments of large companies.

2.14 A distinction is sometimes made between the discount market and all the other money markets, which are referred to collectively as the *parallel markets*.

2.15 In summary, despite the existence of capital markets and money markets, it is not necessarily easy for firms to raise new capital, except by retaining profits. Small firms in particular find it difficult to attract investors. The banks are a major source of funds for companies. The capital markets, however, are also dominated by institutional investors, but these tend to channel their funds into 'safe' investments such as stocks and shares which are traded on the Stock Exchange or USM, and government securities.

3. CONCLUSION

3.1 There are a number of different forms a business organisation can take. Marketing students need to be aware of this.

3.2 Business growth is dependent on access to financial resources. The sources of such funds will vary according to the form the firm has adopted.

TEST YOUR KNOWLEDGE
The numbers in brackets refer to paragraphs of this chapter

1 What are the advantages and disadvantages of operating as a sole trader? (1.6, 1.7)

2 What is the most important difference between a partnership and a limited company? (1.13)

3 What advantages might there be of state ownership of a business? (1.32)

4 List the main capital markets in the UK. (2.7)

5 What are the parallel markets? (2.13)

Now try illustrative question 13 at the end of the text

PART C
MACROECONOMICS

In this part of the Study Text we will be examining the theory and concepts of economics which are classified as macroeconomics. This involves an examination of how the economy as a whole operates. Instead of examining individual or market demand we will be looking at *aggregate* or total demand, expenditure and so on.

A thorough understanding of how the economy as a whole operates is essential. Marketers need to able to forecast future demand and plan business activities. This has to be undertaken in the wider context of the macroeconomic environment. Fluctuations in the rate of inflation, changes in interest rates and changing government policy on economic issues can all have a direct and significant impact on both the costs and revenue of a business.

Studying macroeconomics will provide you with an understanding of the macroeconomic framework to help you to analyse the microeconomic impact of macroeconomic changes and policies.

Chapter 8

DETERMINING NATIONAL INCOME

This chapter covers the following topics.

1. Measuring national income
2. The circular flow of income
3. Fluctuations in the level of economic activity
4. Explaining the trade cycle
5. The trade cycle: implications for economic policy

---

1. MEASURING NATIONAL INCOME

Introduction

1.1 When we measure national income we are attempting to quantify the creation of a nation's wealth.

Serious attempts to measure what was going on in the UK economy began during World War II. Since then three different approaches to its measurement have evolved and are used in the UK.

1.2 These three approaches can be easily understood by considering a very simple economy – the community of 'Smalltown', in which five individuals produce goods which they sell to their neighbours, using the income they earn to buy goods produced by their neighbours. In our model there is no government, no savings and no trade outside the community of five.

Exercise 1

Consider the diagrammatic representation of the 'Smalltown' community below and calculate the following:

(a) the total income earned by the community of five;
(b) the total of all expenditures;
(c) the value of the goods produced by the inhabitants of Smalltown.

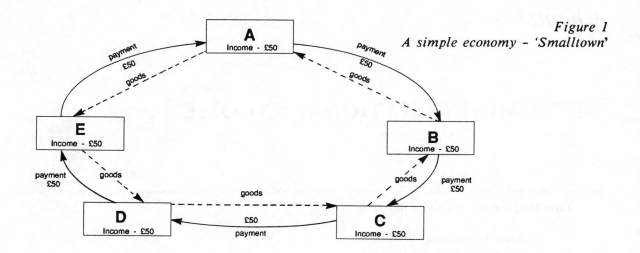

Figure 1
A simple economy – 'Smalltown'

As you can see, in our simple economy A spends his or her income on goods purchased from B, who in turn uses this income to buy goods from C and so on.

Solution

(a) The total of all incomes earned in our economy can be calculated by adding up the individual's incomes, as indicated in Figure 1.

Person	Income
	£
A	50
B	50
C	50
D	50
E	50
	250

The total income of Smalltown is £250.

This is the basis for the first method for calculating national income: simply add up the total of individuals' incomes.

(b) The total expenditure is calculated by adding together the value of all transactions made.

In our model you will find five transactions of £50, giving a total expenditure of £250.

The total income and expenditure will be equal, because one person's expenditure must become another persons income.

    INCOME = EXPENDITURE

(This fundamental principle is basic to macroeconomic theory and policy.)

The expenditure method is the second approach to measuring national income.

(c)   The total value of goods produced may at first not be quite so apparent, but the price paid for a good represents our measure of its value. A paid £50 for goods from B. The value of B's output is therefore £50. You will find that in total 'Smalltown' has a total output of £250 worth of goods. This is the output measure and represents the third approach to quantifying the national income.

All three measures produce the same value of income, because (as you can see in our model):

INCOME = EXPENDITURE = OUTPUT

This single value of income is often referred to as Gross Domestic Product (GDP).

1.3   In practice, the three methods of calculation illustrated in the exercise above do not each produce the same value for GDP/national income in an actual economy. This is because collecting statistics is liable to error. Estimates have to be made when accurate figures are unobtainable, and there are omissions in obtaining some figures: for example, incidence of inaccurate tax returns might be occurring on a large scale. Because of errors, the three approaches will produce slightly different figures, and for practical reasons one of them must be taken as broadly 'correct'. In practice, the expenditure-based figures are considered most reliable, and the income-based and output-based figures are adjusted to the expenditure-based figure by inserting a balancing item known as a residual error.

Difficulties in calculating national income

1.4   The calculation of national income is a complicated statistical process. Difficulties arise because:

(a)   arbitrary definitions must be made, for example:

(i)   production includes goods and services paid for but excludes work done by a person for himself or herself;

(ii)   goods which have a serviceable life of several years are included in national income at their full value in the year they are bought (with the exception of owner-occupied houses, where an annual value is estimated on the basis of the rateable value of the houses);

(iii) government services which are not paid for directly (eg police services and education) are included in national output at cost;

(b)   data from which the national income figure is estimated are full of errors and are incomplete (eg because of false or inaccurate income tax returns). The value of the unmeasured 'black' or 'shadow' economy which is kept hidden from officialdom might be very high;

(c)   there is a danger of double counting. If a firm buys vegetables from a farmer in order to produce soup, the output of the farmer (vegetables) will be included in the output of the firm (soup) although the vegetables, of course, are produced only once. A firm's output needs to be valued after excluding the value of bought-in materials, otherwise double counting results. In practice, errors can easily occur in estimating the 'value added';

(d) transfer payments, that is the transfer of income from one person to another (eg pensions and social security payments), do not affect national income and must not be included;

(e) services provided 'free' to the public by the government, such as policing, health services and much education are valued at cost, whereas output of private firms include profit in their valuation. A country with a strong government services sector might therefore arguably be undervaluing the national income because so much output would be valued at cost;

(f) when a country is suffering from inflation, comparison of figures becomes difficult. In the UK a second set of 'deflated' figures is produced to try and redress the impact of inflation.

1.5 The derivation and treatment of each set of figures are as follows.

(a) *Income*
Income figures are derived from income tax returns, but adjustment must be made to:

(i) deduct transfer payments (income such as gifts, social security payments, unemployment benefits, and pensions, which represent income received without a corresponding contribution towards output of goods or services);

(ii) add profits from publicly-owned enterprises (including local authority activities).

(b) *Expenditure*

(i) The Census of Distribution provides data on the value of shop sales.

(ii) The Census of Production provides data on the values of investment goods produced and additions to stock.

Since the censuses are not taken annually, estimates are made from various other government sources (eg data on retail sales). Since the market price of sales includes indirect taxes (VAT etc) but excludes subsidies, adjustments are made for these items.

(c) *Output*
The value of consumer goods and services plus investment goods produced in the year must be estimated so as to avoid double-counting. For example, if firm A makes a component which it sells to firm B for £100, and firm B uses the component to make an item that it sells for £200, the full value of output is only £200, but there would be a danger of double-counting output as £300.

Who creates economic wealth?

1.6 The methods described above consider how to measure economic wealth, but they also provide clues about what activities lead to the creation of wealth.

(a) People or organisations who spend money on goods and services are involved in the creation of wealth.

In our simple model at Figure 1 this was restricted to the five inhabitants of a community. In the real world economy spending is done not just by consumers (or households), but by companies, the government and by overseas buyers.

(b) Some classes of people *earn* the wealth, ie:

    (i)   labour, who earn wages for the work they do;
    (ii)   providers of capital, who earn interest on the capital they invest;
    (iii) owners of 'land', who earn rent on the land they provide for economic use;
    (iv) entrepreneurs, who earn profits for the business risks that they take.

(c) The creators of wealth can also be identified as the firms (or government departments or public corporations) which *produce* the goods or services in the national economy.

1.7 The government has several functions within the national economy, and so plays several different roles in the circular flow of income.

(a) It acts as the *producer* of certain goods and services instead of privately owned firms, and the 'production' of public administration services, education and health services, the police force, armed forces, fire brigade services, and public transport are all aspects of output. The government in this respects acts, like firms, as a producer, and must also pay wages to its employees.

(b) It acts as the *purchaser* of final goods and services and adds to total 'consumption' expenditure. National and local government obtain funds from the firms or households of the economy (eg in the form of taxation) and then use these funds to buy goods and services from other firms.

(c) It *invests* by purchasing capital goods - eg building roads, schools and hospitals.

(d) It acts as a means of transferring wealth or income from one section of economy to another - eg by taxing workers and paying pensions, unemployment benefits and social security benefits to other members of society.

Items (a), (b) and (c), but not (d), contribute to the creation of economic wealth.

It is also important to note that most government have an objective of growth as a key element in their macroeconomic policy.

Why is national income so important?

1.8 National income is an important measure because it is an aggregate of personal incomes. The bigger the national income in a country, the more income its individual inhabitants will be earning on average. More income means more spending on the output of firms, and more spending (ignoring inflation) means more output - goods and services. The economy as a whole will be more active. The bigger the national income, the bigger the economy.

1.9 National income is calculated for several purposes:

(a) to measure the total wealth (standards of living) of a country. National income is commonly measured in terms of national income per head of population;

(b) to compare the wealth of different countries;

(c) to measure the improvement (deterioration) in national wealth and the standard of living;

(d) to assist central government in its economic planning.

National income, economic wealth and economic welfare

1.10 There is a difference between economic wealth and economic welfare. Economic welfare is a measure of the well-being or quality of life of society's members, and should take account of matters such as the amount of leisure time for individuals, pollution levels and the quality of the environment. Therefore, national income may turn out to be a poor indicator of economic welfare.

(a) National income may be high even when a government spends much of its own income on defence and other items of expenditure, which do not have any immediate relevance to the economic wealth of individuals in the society. In other words, if a government spends, say, two thirds of its income on armed forces, national income might be high but the general standard of living low.

(b) National income is a money measure, and in a country where much trade is done by barter, or leisure activities are pursued, figures for national income would not reflect the contribution of the barter economy nor leisure activities to the standard of living.

(c) A country might have a considerable stock of existing wealth, but a low national income. Wealth earned in the past is not apparent from current figures for national income. Similarly, national income figures do not indicate whether a country has potential wealth-earning resources for the future. For example, a country with large amounts of unexploited natural resources would have a potentially strong economy, but current national income figures may not show this.

Comparisons between different countries

1.11 When evaluating international marketing opportunities, national income figures are very important to the marketer. It is therefore important to appreciate the factors to consider when analysing comparative data.

1.12 The national income figures say nothing about the distribution of income in the country. We have to be careful when comparing countries like the UK with a small Middle Eastern oil producer which may have a very high per capita income. We cannot conclude that on average people in the UK have a lower standard of living. The income in the Middle Eastern state may not filter through to the majority of the population.

1.13 When comparing countries there is the problem of converting national income calculated in one currency to that of another. This is not necessarily as straightforward as it sounds and may make conclusions about such comparisons difficult to reach.

1.14 If Country X has a national income valued at US $200,000 million and Country Y has a national income valued at US $100,000 million, it might seem that Country X is twice as rich as Country Y and so the standard of living in X twice as high as in Y.

However, if the population of X is 40 million people and the population of Y is 8 million, the national income per head of the population would be:

X US $5 per capita
Y US $12.5 per capita.

Income is on average two and half times higher in Y than in X.

1.15 The relative standard of living of different countries is better compared by means of national income per capita than by means of total national income.

(a) Every country will have difficulty in obtaining accurate data about output and income. Thus a country with a strong 'black economy' will be much wealthier than its official income per head of population might suggest. Given differences in the strength of the black economy from country to country, their figures for national income will not be properly comparable.

(b) The needs of people in one country will differ widely from the needs of people in another country. This will be due to differences in social attitudes, customs and habits, religious beliefs, climate, density of population and so on. One country might have thriving industries for tobacco and alcoholic goods, for example, whereas another country might ban these entirely. Inhabitants of a country with a hot climate might spend large sums on air conditioning and similar products, whereas a country with a cool climate will want central heating and insulation products instead. When people in different countries want and need entirely different things, it is not really possible to presume that their comparative standards of living can be measured on a single money scale.

(c) Countries will produce items that are of little direct relevance to their standards of living. Spending on defence equipment and space programmes are examples. These add to income per head of the population without people in the population getting any easily quantifiable benefit out of them. The income per capita of a country with high defence spending and one with little such spending might not be properly comparable.

1.16 These drawbacks to using income per head of population for international comparisons mean that simpler and more direct comparisons may be used instead. One way of doing this is to select a number of products which are universally in demand in every country (or at least most countries). Examples might be television sets and motor cars. Measurements can then be obtained of:

(a) the average number of cars or TV sets per household or per head of the population; and

(b) how long it takes an 'average' worker to earn enough in wages to buy a car or a TV set, for example.

1.17 The overall size and rate of growth of a country's national income depends on several factors, which include:

(a) the natural resources of the country (eg mineral deposits, fertility of the soil);

(b) the nature of the labour force (eg its size in relation to the total population, its energy, skill, ability and mobility);

(c) the amount of capital investment (which may depend on the sophistication of a country's banking system and money/capital markets);

(d) whether the factors of land, labour and capital are combined in an efficient way;

(e) the ability of the country to produce innovative ideas (eg new technologies);

(f) political stability; and

(g) the availability of foreign loans.

These will all affect the *potential* size of national income and are factors marketers need to take into account when forecasting the future market potential of a particular international market segment.

Understanding national income statistics

1.18 There are various ways in which national income statistics can be modified to include or exclude certain items. This results in a variety of measures which are in common use.

If you are fully to appreciate the economic commentary in the media or understand any national accounts you are presented with, you need to appreciate the differences between these various measures.

1.19 The UK national income can be defined as 'the sum of all incomes of residents in the UK which arise *as a result of economic activity*, that is from the production of goods and services. Such incomes, which include rent, employment income and profit, are known as *factor incomes* because they are earned by the so-called factors of production: land, labour and capital.' (CSO)

1.20 National income is also called *net national product*.

(a) The terms 'income' and 'product' are just two different aspects of the same circular flow of income.

(b) The term 'net' means 'after deducting an amount for capital consumption or depreciation of fixed assets'. We shall return to this point later.

Gross domestic product (GDP)

1.21 Most UK national income is derived from economic activity within the UK. Economic activity within the UK is referred to as total *domestic income* or *domestic product*. It is measured 'gross' - ie before deducting an amount for capital consumption or depreciation of fixed assets - and the term *gross domestic product* therefore refers in the UK to the total value of income/production from economic activity within the UK.

Gross national product (GNP)

1.22 'Some national income arises from overseas investments while some of the income generated within the UK is earned by non-residents. The difference between these . . . items is *net property income from abroad*.' (CSO)

Gross national income or gross national product (GNP) is therefore the gross domestic product (GDP) plus the net property income from abroad - or after subtracting the net property income from abroad, if it is a negative value.

The relationship between GDP, GNP and national income

1.23 The relationship between GDP, GNP and national income is thus as follows.

	GDP
plus	Net property income from abroad
equals	GNP
minus	Capital consumption
equals	National income (net)

2. THE CIRCULAR FLOW OF INCOME

A simple model

2.1 The simple model illustrated in Figure 1 demonstrated the basic principle of the circular flow of income. However, we did not build into that model the complexities of a business sector, government or foreign trade. We must now expand that simple model to take these real factors into account, but we will build them in gradually, starting by considering the economic model with just two sectors, households and firms. We will still make some assumptions.

(a) All income is spent.

(b) There are only two sectors in the economy - consumers and producers - which will be referred to using the terms 'households' and 'firms'.

(c) The economy is 'closed': there is no trade with other countries.

2.2 The circular flow of income describes the way in which income flows backwards and forwards between households and firms.

(a) The income of firms is the sales revenue from the sale of goods and services.

(b) The income of households is the income arising from the ownership of the factors of production - wages or salaries as labour, rent as owners of land, interest as owners of capital and profits as owners of businesses.

2.3 Firms must pay households for the factors of production, and households must pay firms for goods. This creates a circular flow of income as follows.

Figure 2
Circular flow of income

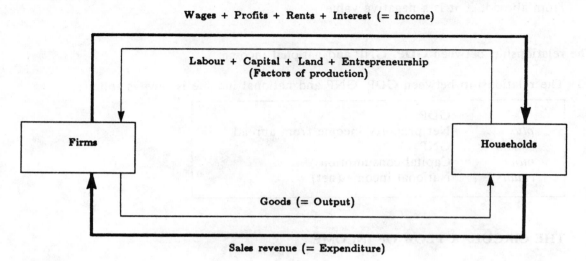

Wages + Profits + Rents + Interest (= Income)

**Labour + Capital + Land + Entrepreneurship
(Factors of production)**

Firms

Households

Goods (= Output)

Sales revenue (= Expenditure)

2.4 The system is 'closed' and all income is spent; if households receive £100m in factor payments they will spend £100m purchasing goods and services. Income is circulating around the system and the flow at the bottom (expenditure) will be equal to the flow at the top (income). When this balance exists in a system we refer to it as *equilibrium*. Equilibrium will exist in this system unless something happens to disturb it.

2.5 Remember the equilibrium condition:

    Total income   =   Total expenditure

2.6 We have said nothing yet about the size of the income flow or expenditure flow. Obviously equilibrium can exist if the flow is £50m, £500m or £5,000m providing the flow at the 'bottom' of the system is equal to the flow at the 'top' of the system. A low level of activity implies underemployment of factors, spare capacity within firms and relatively small flow of goods and services to households. A high level of activity implies full employment of resources, factories and firms working 'flat out' and a large volume of goods and services being produced.

2.7 To measure the level of activity in the circular flow, we can measure:

    (a)   the flow of spending on goods and services; or
    (b)   the value of goods and services produced; or
    (c)   the flow of incomes.

    As we have already seen, these three alternatives are the three methods of calculating the national income – the expenditure method, output method and income method.

A more realistic model

2.8 So far we have a very simple model of the real world created by three assumptions which we can now relax. Let us now allow people to decide whether or not to spend all of their incomes. Some people will spend less than they earn and this amount we will call 'savings'. On the other hand, some may decide to spend more than they earn. Traditionally, spending more than current income was undertaken almost exclusively by firms and so in the circular flow we refer to this activity as investment. If savings occur, money is removed from the flow and disequilibrium is created. However, this can be counter-balanced by additions to the flow which will come from investment.

Figure 3
Circular flow with savings and investment

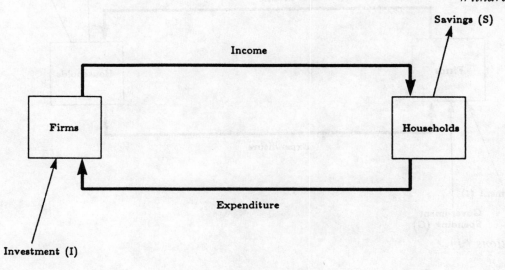

Withdrawals (W)

Injections (J)

2.9 Now, instead of just income and expenditure flows, we have an addition or injection to the flow and a withdrawal from it. It should be clear that as long as the loss through savings is matched by an equal addition through investment, equilibrium will still exist.

2.10 The equilibrium condition is best described as

Savings (S) = Investment (I)
or
J (injections) = W (withdrawals)

2.11 In a modern mixed economy the government plays an important part. The effect of introducing the government into the circular flow is that we have another withdrawal from the system in the form of taxation and another injection in the form of government spending.

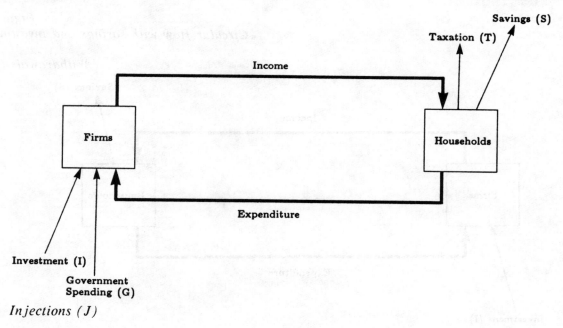

Figure 4
Circular flow with government intervention

2.12 The equilibrium condition has changed with the addition of the government to the circular flow. Now, as long as savings and taxation are equal to investment and government spending, we have a stable situation. As long as:

J (injections)   =   W (withdrawals)

then equilibrium is maintained.

2.13 Our final assumption to be relaxed involves the 'closed economy'. The UK is heavily involved in trade with other countries and this further complicates the model of the circular flow. When we buy goods/services from other countries this represents a withdrawal from our system. When people in other countries buy our goods/services this represents 'new' money coming into our system. We now have an additional withdrawal and an additional injection.

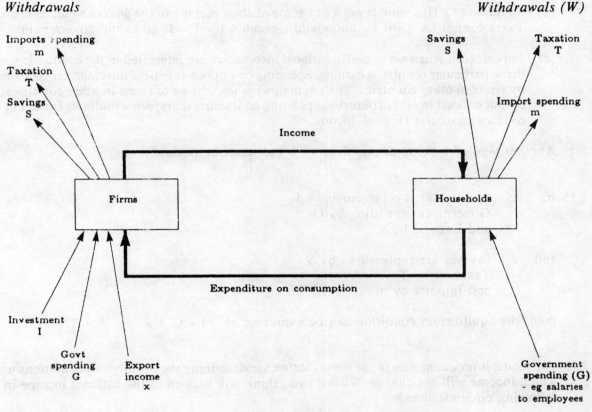

Figure 5
Circular flow of income showing
all withdrawals and injections

2.14 We now have a much more realistic model of the economy. The equilibrium condition can still be represented by

$$J \text{ (injections)} \quad = \quad W \text{ (withdrawals)}$$

except that now there are three injections.

(a) *Investment* (I). Investment in capital goods is a form of spending on output, which is additional to expenditure by households. Just as savings are a withdrawal of funds, investment is an injection of funds into the circular flow of income, adding to the total economic wealth that is being created by the country.

(b) *Government spending* (G). Government spending is also an injection into the circular flow of income. In most mixed economies, total spending by the government on goods and services represents a large proportion of total national expenditure. The funds to spend come from either taxation income or government borrowing.

(c) *Exports* (x). Firms produce goods and services for export. Exports earn income from abroad, and therefore provide an injection into a country's circular flow of income.

And there are three withdrawals.

(a) *Savings* (S). Households do not spend all of their income. They save some, and these savings out of income are withdrawals from the circular flow of income quite simply because savings are not spent.

(b) *Taxation* (T). Households must pay some of their income to the government, as taxation. Taxes cannot be spent by households, because the funds go to the government.

(c) *Imports* (m). When we consider national income, we are interested in the economic wealth that a particular country is earning. Spending on imports is expenditure, but on goods made by firms in other countries. The payments for imports go to firms in other countries, for output created in other countries. Spending on imports therefore withdraws funds out of a country's circular flow of income.

Another way of looking at this is to view the items individually.

2.15 If: Investment is represented by I
              Government spending by G
              and Exports by x

     and: Savings are represented by S
              Taxation by T
              and Imports by m

then, the equilibrium condition can be expressed as: $I + G + x = S + T + m$

2.16 The model is now complete in the sense that we are describing the equilibrium conditions under which income will not change. What do you think will happen to the national income in the following circumstances?

(a) Total injections (J) exceed total withdrawals (W).
(b) Total withdrawals (W) exceed total injections (J).
(c) Total injections (J) = total leakages (W).

2.17 The level of national income is like the water in a sink. Injections represent the water coming from the tap and withdrawals the amount going down the plug hole.

(a) If injections exceed withdrawals the income level will rise.
(b) If withdrawals exceed injections the income level will fall.
(c) When the two are equal the income level remains unchanged.

2.18 We have not shifted from the basic principle of:

     Income (Y) = Expenditure (E).

What we have done by producing a more realistic circular flow model is to recognise that in the real world there are four sectors within the economy who can buy goods and therefore influence total expenditure.

(a) *Consumers/households*, whose spending is referred to as consumption (C).

(b) The *business sector/firms*, whose spending is categorised as investment (I).

(c) The *government sector*, whose spending is abbreviated as (G).

(d) The *balance of foreign trade*, ie the difference between the value of imports and the value of exports. This is shown in short form as (x - m). This can, of course, be a negative value if imports exceed exports or a positive value if exports exceed imports.

This more complete model of income = expenditure can therefore be shown as:

$$Y = C + I + G + (x - m)$$

ie, Income = consumption + investment + government spending + the balance of foreign trade.

Changing the level of income

2.19 In principle, if a government wishes to influence the level of national income they simply have to manage the balance of injections and withdrawals. This simple economic model illustrating the circular flow of income lies at the heart of all government macroeconomic policy.

2.20 The economist who first analysed the workings of the macroeconomy and proposed that government should try to influence income was John Maynard Keynes, who can be considered the founder of macroeconomics. Until his work in the 1920s and 1930s governments adopted a broadly 'hands off' policy to economic management. This is known as a *laissez faire* approach. The belief in the microeconomic market mechanism was such that it was believed that left alone the market would provide the optimum allocation of the nation's resources and would eventually reach an equilibrium.

2.21 Pre-Keynesian economists had tried to explain unemployment as a temporary phenomenon. They believed that if there is a surplus of labour available (ie, unemployment) the forces of demand and supply, through the wages (price) mechanism, would restore equilibrium by bringing down wage levels, thus stimulating demand for labour. Any unemployment would only last for as long as the labour market was adjusting to new equilibrium conditions. The pre-Keynesian theory was discredited during the 1930s. If pre-Keynesian theory was right, wages should have fallen and full employment restored. However, this did not happen, and the Great Depression continued for a long time.

2.22 It was in this economic situation that Keynes put forward his new theory. Its fundamental advance on earlier theory was to explain how *equilibrium* could exist in the macroeconomy, but there could still be persistent (long term) unemployment and slow growth.

2.23 Keynes' *General Theory of Employment, Interest and Money* (1936) revolutionised economic analysis. Keynes put forward his ideas following a period in which there was an economic boom (after the First World War), followed by the Wall Street Crash in 1929, and the Great Depression in the 1930s when unemployment levels soared.

2.24 Keynes also tried to explain the causes of 'trade cycles' which are the continuous cycles of alternating economic boom and slump. Why does an economy not grow at a steady rate, or remain stable, instead of suffering the harmful effects of trade cycles?

3. FLUCTUATIONS IN THE LEVEL OF ECONOMIC ACTIVITY

3.1 The Keynesian analysis of aggregate demand and supply provides the framework for understanding the causes of the cyclical movements in economic activity.

Aggregate demand and aggregate supply

3.2 Keynes argued that the level of overall output and employment depends on the level of *aggregate demand* in the economy. His basic idea was that demand and supply analysis could be applied to macroeconomic activity as well as microeconomic activity.

   (a) *Aggregate demand* means the total demand in the economy for goods and services.
   (b) *Aggregate supply* means the total supply of goods and services in the economy.

3.3 Aggregate supply depends on physical production conditions - the availability and cost of factors of production and technical know-how. Keynes was concerned with short-run measures to affect the economy, and as he also wrote in a period of high unemployment there was effectively little constraint on the availability of factors of production. His analysis therefore concentrated on the *demand side*. (You might hear the phrase 'supply side economics' to describe the views of economists who do not subscribe to the Keynesian approach to dealing with the problem of national income and employment, and prefer instead to concentrate on 'supply side' - ie production factors). We shall discuss the approach of supply side economists again in a later chapter.

3.4 The *aggregate supply curve* will be upward sloping, for the reasons applying to the 'microeconomic' supply curves mentioned in earlier chapters. A higher price means that it is worthwhile for firms to hire more labour and produce more because of the higher revenue-earning capability. So at the macroeconomic level, an increasing price level implies that many firms will be receiving higher prices for their products and will increase their output.

3.5 In the economy as a whole, supply will at some point reach a labour constraint, when the entire labour force is employed. When there is full employment, and firms cannot find extra labour to hire, they cannot produce more even when prices rise, unless there is some technical progress in production methods. The aggregate supply curve will therefore rise vertically when the full employment level of output is reached (AS in Figure 6).

3.6 *Aggregate demand (AD)* is the total desired demand in the economy, for consumer goods and services, and also for capital goods - no matter whether the buyers are households, firms or government. Aggregate demand is a concept of fundamental importance in Keynesian economic analysis. Keynes believed that national economy could be 'managed' by taking measures to influence aggregate demand up or down.

3.7 Aggregate demand is the total desired demand, just as a 'microeconomic' demand curve represents the desired demand for a particular good at any price level. The AD curve will be downward-sloping because at higher prices, total quantities demanded will be less.

3.8 Keynes argued that a national economy will reach equilibrium where the aggregate demand curve and aggregate supply curve intersect.

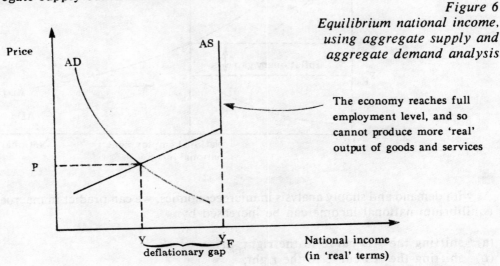

Figure 6
Equilibrium national income,
using aggregate supply and
aggregate demand analysis

The economy reaches full employment level, and so cannot produce more 'real' output of goods and services

3.9 The actual level of national income will be at the intersection of the AD curve and AS curves - ie at Y. The difference between the equilibrium national income Y and the full employment national income Y_F shows how much national income could be increased with the resources at the economy's disposal. This 'gap' between actual equilibrium national income and full employment national income is called a deflationary gap. Price levels will be P. Y therefore represents the level of 'satisfied' demand in the economy.

Note. The aggregate demand function assumes constant prices.

3.10 Two points follow on immediately from this initial analysis.

   (a) Equilibrium national income Y might be at a level of national income below full employment national income. This is the situation in Figure 6.

   (b) On the other hand, equilibrium national income Y might be above full employment national income, in which case, the economy will be fully employed, but price levels will be higher than they need to be (they will be P but could be lower at P_F), and there will be inflationary pressures in the economy, as shown in Figure 7 below, if aggregate demand is AD_1.

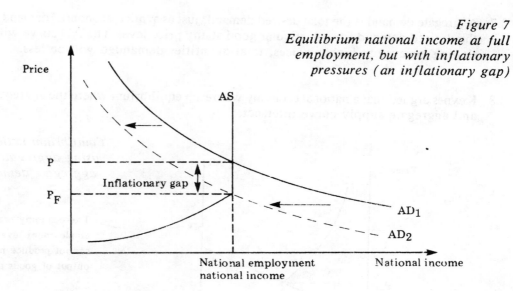

Figure 7
Equilibrium national income at full employment, but with inflationary pressures (an inflationary gap)

3.11 As with demand and supply analysis in microeconomics, we can predict in macroeconomics that equilibrium national income can be increased by:

(a) shifting the AD curve to the right; or
(b) shifting the AS curve to the right;

ie, expanding either AD or AS in the economy. As suggested already, Keynesian economists concentrate on shifts in AD.

You should also note that a shift in the AD curve or the AS curve will not only change the national income, it will also change price levels (P). In Figure 7, an inflationary gap can be removed by shifting the aggregate demand curve to the left, from AD_1 to AD_2.

3.12 If you are not sure about this point, a simple numerical example might help to explain it better. Suppose that in Ruritania there is full employment and all other economic resources are fully employed. The country produces 1,000 units of output with these resources. Total expenditure (ie aggregate demand) in the economy is 100,000 Ruritanian dollars, or 100 dollars per unit. The country doesn't have any external trade, and so it can't obtain extra goods by importing them. Because of pay rises and easier credit terms for consumers, total expenditure now rises to 120,000 Ruritanian dollars. The economy is fully employed, and cannot produce more than 1,000 units. If expenditure rises by 20%, to buy the same number of units, it follows that prices must rise by 20% too. In other words, when an economy is at full employment, any increase in aggregate demand will result in price inflation.

3.13 The Keynesian economic argument is that if a country's economy is going to move from one equilibrium to a different equilibrium, there needs to be a shift in the aggregate demand curve. To achieve equilibrium at the full employment level of national income, it may therefore be necessary to shift the AD curve to the right (upward) or the left (downwards).

Deflationary and inflationary gaps

3.14 In a situation *where there is unemployment of resources* there is said to be a *deflationary gap*. Prices are fairly constant and real output changes as aggregate demand varies.

A deflationary gap can be described as 'the extent to which the aggregate demand function will have to shift upward to produce the full-employment level of national income.'

(Lipsey, *Introduction to positive economics*)

3.15 In a situation where resources are fully employed, there is said to be an *inflationary gap*, if changes in aggregate demand have caused price changes and not variations in real output.

An inflationary gap can be described as 'the extent to which the aggregate demand function would have to shift downward to produce the full employment level of national income without inflation ... .'

(Lipsey)

The 'ideal' equilibrium national income

3.16 If one aim of a country's economic policy is full employment, then the 'ideal' equilibrium level of national income will be where AD and AS are in balance at the full employment level of national income, without any inflationary gap - ie where aggregate demand at current price levels is exactly sufficient to encourage firms to produce at an output capacity where the country's resources are fully employed. This is shown in Figure 8, where equilibrium output will be Y (full employment level) and price levels P.

Figure 8

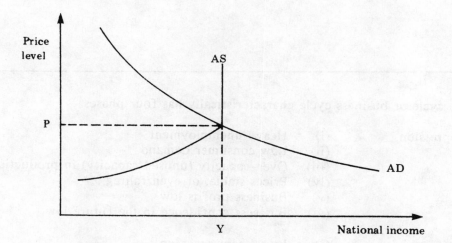

(A country will also seek economic growth, but to achieve a real increase in living standards, both AD and AS curves will now have to shift to the right. Economic growth can be defined as an increase in our capacity to produce goods, in other words we can supply more with the same level of inputs, for example, following technological advances.)

The trade cycle

3.17 What Keynes was trying to establish with his analysis was a clear picture of what was happening to an economy as it moved through the stages of the trade cycle. The fluctuations in economic activity were well recorded and documented and Keynes could clearly see that the economy did not find itself in an equilibrium position and stay there, as microeconomic analysis might indicate.

3.18 Left on its own, economic activity fluctuated in a regular and cyclical pattern known as the trade or business cycle. Some highs or booms were higher than others and some lows, as in the recessions of the 1930s and early 1980s, were more severe than other, but the pattern remained the same.

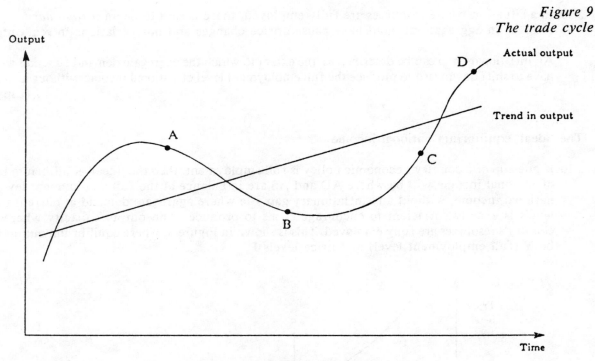

Figure 9
The trade cycle

3.19 A trade cycle or business cycle characteristically has four phases.

(a)	Depression	(i)	Heavy unemployment
		(ii)	Low consumer demand
		(iii)	Over-capacity (unused capacity) in production
		(iv)	Prices stable, or even falling
		(v)	Business profits low
		(vi)	Business confidence in the future low.
(b)	Recovery	(i)	Investment picks up
		(ii)	Employment rises
		(iii)	Consumer spending rises
		(iv)	Profits rise
		(v)	Business confidence grows
		(vi)	Prices stable, or slowly rising
(c)	Boom	(i)	Consumer spending rising fast
		(ii)	Output capacity reached: labour shortages occur
		(iii)	Output can only be increased by new labour-saving investment
		(iv)	Investment spending high
		(v)	Increases in demand now stimulate price rises
		(vi)	Business profits high

(d) Recession	(i)	Consumption falls off
	(ii)	Many investments suddenly become unprofitable and new investment falls
	(iii)	Production falls
	(iv)	Employment falls
	(v)	Profits fall. Some businesses fail
	(vi)	Recession can turn into severe depression.

3.20 The Keynesian analysis in effect takes a snapshot of the economy at different stages in the cycle. During recession and depression the economy is suffering a deflationary gap. Demand is insufficient to general full employment of the factors of production (as illustrated in Figure 6). Deflationary gaps typically bring with them the economic problems of unemployment and no economic growth. (Economic growth results from an increased capacity to produce goods; this in turn requires investment. A firm unable to sell its existing output because of a depression is unlikely to want to invest in machinery which will further increase output.)

3.21 Keynes' analysis was clear and it told government that if they did not want to have the economic problems associated with the downturn then they had to 'manage the level of demand' in the economy. This could be achieved by planning for injections to exceed withdrawals in the circular flow, so boosting income to the desired full employment level. These are known as reflationary policies.

3.22 The booms and periods of recovery are illustrated in Figure 7 as the inflationary gap. Too much demand will cause higher prices and a balance of payments deficit. (This is when imports exceed exports. High prices and unsatisfied demand in the home market tends to discourage exports and attract imports, leading to a balance of payment problem.)

3.23 Again, if government wish to avoid these difficulties it is clear that they need to take action which will reduce the level of demand in the economy - ie deflationary policies. By planning for withdrawals to exceed injections, expenditure and therefore income can be reduced to the level necessary to sustain full employment.

3.24 Keynes' call for government intervention in controlling the level of economic activity through a process of 'demand management' was really only dealing with the symptoms of the trade cycle and did nothing about the underlying causes of it. To understand more fully the nature of cyclical problems and the eventual failure of Keynesian interventionist policies, it is necessary to take a more detailed look at the trade cycle, and its underlying causes.

4. EXPLAINING THE TRADE CYCLE

The dynamics of the trade cycle

4.1 Keynes wanted to suggest why the volume of national income might change, by how much, and what would be the consequences of such a change. When national income grows, we have economic growth. Since economic growth might be an economic objective of government, the reasons for economic growth will obviously be of crucial importance for the government's economic planners.

4.2 The level of national income might increase or decrease for a number of reasons; for example, there might be a pay rise for workers or an increase in the country's exports. Keynes showed that if there is an *initial* change in expenditure, say an initial increase in exports, or government spending or investment or consumer spending, a new equilibrium national income level will be reached.

The eventual total increase in national income will be greater in size than the initial increase in expenditure.

This is an important point. A small initial increase in expenditure will result in a bigger total increase in national income before equilibrium is re-established.

4.3 The principle behind this concept is the *multiplier* and can be seen by returning to our very simple 'Smalltown' model of income flow from Figure 1 in this chapter.

Here we are considering what would happen if there is a change in expenditure which injects say £200 into the economy. If we assume there is still no taxation or foreign trade influencing our model, any extra income has to be either spent or saved.

4.4 The proportion of additional income which a community will tend to spend is known as the marginal propensity to consume (MPC). If we assume in our economy that out of every £1 of additional income there is a tendency to spend 90p, the MPC is 90% or 0.9. The balance of the £1 must be the amount which will be saved ie the marginal propensity to save (MPS).

4.5 As people can only do two things with their income, spend it or save it, so the marginal propensity to consume (MPC) plus the marginal propensity to save (MPS) must equal one.

MPC + MPS = 1

Figure 10
The multiplier in a 'closed'
economy with no taxation

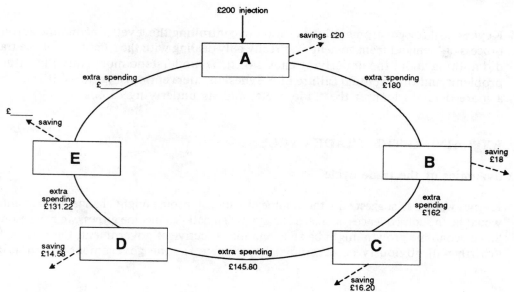

4.6 How much will E save and how much will his spending increase by (Figure 10)? What you can see is that at each round of spending, 10% is leaking out of the circular flow in the form of savings and so the amount of additional income is getting progressively smaller. This process will continue on the second and third circuit of our simple model until the whole of the injection has leaked away, in other words when injections = leakages the national income will stop changing.

4.7 If you were to set out all the stages and follow the process until all the £200 injections had leaked out on savings you would find the following:

			Increase in expenditure £	Increase in savings (withdrawals) £
Stage	1	Income rises	200.00	–
	2	90% is consumed	180.00	20.00
	3	A further 90% is consumed	162.00	18.00
	4	"	145.80	16.20
	5	"	131.22	14.58
	6	"	118.10	13.12
	7	etc	etc	etc
		Total increase in income	2,000.00	200.00

This long hand method of calculating the eventual increase in expenditure as a result of the injection is obviously too cumbersome to be practical in a more complex case. The multiplier provides a formula for its easy calculation.

The multiplier

4.8 The ratio of the total increase in national income to the initial increase in national income is called the *multiplier*.

$$\text{Multiplier} = \frac{\text{Total increase in national income}}{\text{Initial increase in national income}}$$

The multiplier can be defined as a measure of the effect on total national income of a unit change in some component of aggregate demand, in particular, I, G or x - ie investment spending, government spending or exports.

4.9 There are two formulae for calculating the value of the multiplier (k):

$$k = \left(1 - \frac{1}{MPC} \right) \text{ or } \frac{1}{MPS}$$

4.10 In our example the MPC was 0.9 and the MPS was 0.1 so the multiplier can be calculated as either:

$$k = \frac{1}{(1 - 0.9)} \text{ or } \frac{1}{0.1} = \frac{10}{1}$$

The value of the multiplier is the reciprocal of the marginal propensity to save 0.1, ie 10/1.

In an economy with an MPS of 0.1 and therefore a multiplier of 10 will find that national income changes by 10 times the original injection. £200 injection results in an increase in expenditure and therefore income of £2,000.

4.11 The multiplier in a national economy works in the same way. An *initial* increase in expenditure will have a snowball effect, leading to further and further expenditure in the economy. Since total expenditure in the economy is one way of measuring national income, it follows that an initial increase in expenditure will cause an even larger increase in national income. The increase in national income will be a multiplier of the initial increase in spending, with the size of the multiple, ie the size of the multiplier, depending on factors which include the marginal propensity to save.

4.12 If you find this hard to visualise, think of an increase in government spending on the construction of roads. The government would spend money paying firms of road contractors, who in turn will purchase raw materials from suppliers, and sub-contract other work. All of these firms employ workers who will receive wages that they can spend on goods and services of other firms. The new roads in turn might stimulate new economic activity - eg amongst road hauliers, housebuilders, shop builders, estate agents and house buying.

4.13 By considering the impact on national income if there was the same injection of £200, but different marginal propensities to save within the economy you will see why knowing the speed with which an injection will leak out of the circular flow is important.

Exercise 2

Try and calculate for yourself the value of the multiplier if the marginal propensity to save was:

20p	in the £, ie 20%	or 0.2
25p	in the £, ie 25%	or 0.25
33.3p	in the £, ie 33.3%	or 0.33
50p	in the £, ie 50%	or 0.5

Solution

Marginal propensity to save	Multiplier calculation $\dfrac{1}{\text{MPS}}$	Effect of a £200 injection on national income £
0.2	$\dfrac{1}{1/5} = \dfrac{5}{1} = 5$	1,000
0.25	$\dfrac{1}{1/4} = \dfrac{4}{1} = 4$	800
0.33	$\dfrac{1}{1/3} = \dfrac{3}{1} = 3$	600
0.5	$\dfrac{1}{1/2} = \dfrac{2}{1} = 2$	400

Note. As the MPS increases and people save more of their additional income, so the total increase in national income through extra consumption will be less. The richer the economy the higher the MPS.

4.14 Other factors which influence the relative size of MPC and MPS in an economy are the income distribution, the age distribution of the population, expectations for the future and a variety of socio-economic factors. For example, in the UK over the last 20 years or so there has been a shift away from savings towards spending. This has lowered the MPS.

4.15 Depending on the size of the multiplier, an increase in investment would have repercussions throughout the economy, increasing the size of the national income by a multiple of the size of the original increase in investment.

4.16 If, for example, the national income were £10,000 million and the average and the marginal propensity to consume were both 75%, in equilibrium, ignoring G, T, x and m:

Y =	£10,000 million
C =	£7,500 million
I = S =	£2,500 million

Since MPC = 75%, MPS = 25%, and the multiplier is 4.

An increase in investment of £1,000 million would upset the equilibrium, which would not be restored until the multiplier had taken effect, and national income increased by 4 x £1,000 million = £4,000 million, with:

Y =	£14,000 million	
C =	£10,500 million	(75%)
I = S =	£3,500 million	(25%)

4.17 A 'downward multiplier' or 'de-multiplier' effect also exists. A reduction in investment will have repercussions throughout the economy, so that a small disinvestment (reduction in expenditure/output) will result in a multiplied reduction in national income.

The importance of the multiplier

4.18 The importance of the multiplier is that an increase in one of the components of aggregate demand will increase national income by *more* than the initial increase itself. Therefore if the government takes any action to increase expenditure (eg by raising government current expenditure, or lowering interest rates to raise investment) it will set off a general expansionary process, and the eventual rise in national income will exceed the initial increase in aggregate demand.

This can have important implications for a government when it is planning for growth in national income. By an initial increase in expenditure, a government can 'engineer' an even greater increase in national income, (provided that the country's industries can increase their output capacity), depending on the size of the multiplier.

4.19 In the real economy, the size of the multiplier depends on the flow of leakages from the circular flow ie:

(a) the marginal propensity to save (MPS);

(b) the marginal propensity to import – because imports reduce national income, and if households spend much of their extra income on imports, the 'snowball' increase in total national income will be restricted because imports are a 'withdrawal' out of the circular flow of income. One of the reasons for a low multiplier in the UK is the high marginal propensity to import that exists in the UK; and

(c) tax rates – because taxes reduce the ability of people to consume and so are likely to affect the marginal propensity to consume and the marginal propensity to save.

The multiplier in an open economy

4.20 In the UK, where the marginal propensity to consume has been estimated to be 83%, the multiplier is not 5 but nearer 2 or 3. Any increase in income is subject to tax, thereby reducing the amount available for consumption, and a large proportion of extra consumption is on imported goods, which benefits other countries and does not increase national income. The existence of T and M, in addition to S, as withdrawals from the circular flow of income reduce the size of the multiplier.

4.21 Whereas the multiplier in a closed economy is the reciprocal of the marginal propensity to save, the multiplier in an open economy – ie taking into account government spending and taxation, and imports and exports – will be less. This is because government taxation and spending on imports reduces the multiplier effect on a country's economy.

For an open economy

$$\text{multiplier} = \frac{1}{s + m + t}, \text{ where}$$

s   is the marginal propensity to save
m   is the marginal propensity to import
t   is the marginal propensity to tax – ie the amount of any increase in income that will be paid in taxes.

Limitations of the multiplier

4.22 Keynes developed the concept of the multiplier in order to argue that extra government spending on public works, financed by a budget deficit, would have a 'pump-priming' effect on a demand-deficient economy, so that:

(a) demand would be increased and National Income would increase by more than the amount of the initial injection into the economy of the extra government spending; and

(b) because demand would be increased, unemployment would be reduced.

4.23 However, there are several important factors that limit the significance of the multiplier for economic management.

(a) It is of more relevance to a demand-deficient economy with high unemployment of resources, than to an economy where there is full employment. If there is full employment, any increase in demand will be inflationary.

(b) The leakages from the circular flow of income might make the value of the multiplier very low, and so 'pump priming' measures to inject extra spending in the economy would have little effect. This is relevant to the UK, where there is a high marginal propensity to import (m).

(c) There may be a long period of adjustment before the benefits of the multiplier are felt. If a government wants immediate action to improve the economy, relying on demand management and the multiplier could be too slow.

(d) The consumption function in advanced economies is probably more volatile than Keynes believed. If consumption is unpredictable, measures to influence National Income through the multiplier will be impossible to predict too.

The accelerator principle

4.24 The accelerator principle is another principle that deals with changes in national income. It pre-dates Keynes in the economic literature, and is concerned with the size of changes in investment spending.

The accelerator principle states that if there is a small change in the production output of consumer goods, there will be a much greater change in the production output of capital equipment required to make those consumer goods. This change in production of capital equipment - ie investment spending - speeds up the rate of economic growth, or slump.

4.25 A numerical example might help to illustrate this principle. Suppose that a firm makes biscuits and has 100 ovens in operation. If the life of each oven is 5 years, 20 ovens must be replaced each year.

(a) If the demand for the consumer good (biscuits) is constant, 20 items of the capital good (ovens) will be made each year.

(b) If the demand for biscuits now rises by, say 10% the firm will need 110 ovens in operation. During the first year of the increase, the demand for ovens will be 30, ie

(i) replacement of 20 ovens;
(ii) extra requirement of 10 ovens to bring total to 110.

A 10% rise in demand for consumer goods results in a 50% rise in demand for capital goods - in the short-term. The accelerator is at work! The accelerator principle indicates how, when the demand for consumer goods rises, there will be an even greater proportional increase in the demand for capital goods. This speeds up growth in national income.

(c) If demand for biscuits now remains constant at the new level, annual replacement of capital equipment will average 22. There is consequently the danger that there will be over capacity in the oven-making industry because the short-term peak demand of 30 ovens pe. annum is not maintained.

(d)   This means that unless the rate of increase in consumer demand is maintained, over-capacity in capital goods industries is likely to occur.

4.26 The accelerator also works in reverse. A decline in demand for consumer goods will result in a much sharper decline in demand for the capital goods which make them.

4.27 The accelerator implies that national income remains high only as long as investment is high, but investment is high only as long as income and consumption are *rising*. As income approaches the peak level dictated by available capacity, new investment will fall towards zero, reducing aggregate demand and hence national income. (The sharp fall in investment caused by the fall in consumption, due to the accelerator effect, will be compounded by the 'de-multiplier' - so that the accelerator and the de-multiplier will combine to reduce national income more severely than the initial fall in consumption.) The recovery in investment when demand stops falling will stimulate the economy again and cause income and thus demand to rise again.

4.28 Note carefully that the accelerator comes into effect as a consequence of changes in the rate of consumer demand.

4.29 The extent of the change in investment depends on:

(a)   the size of the change in consumer demand;

(b)   the *capital-output ratio*. This is the ratio of capital investment to the volume of output - ie how much capital investment is needed to produce a quantity of output. For example, if the capital output ratio is 1:3, it would need capital investment of £1 to produce an extra £3 of output p.a., and so if demand went up by say, £3 billion, it would need an extra £1 billion of investment to produce the extra output to meet the demand.

The multiplier and the accelerator

4.30 Keynes suggested that a *combination of the multiplier and the accelerator* explained the upswings and downswings of the trade cycle.

Suppose that there is an actual or even an *expected* increase in consumption, so that a small initial increase in national income occurs or is expected to occur. If firms are to be able to meet the extra demand from consumers, they will have to invest in more capital equipment, and therefore there will be an increase in investment, which in turn increases spending and national income. The investment which is thus caused by changes in output is called *induced investment*. *Autonomous investment*, such as government expenditure on infrastructure, on the other hand, is unrelated to changes in income/output and is usually long-term investment.

4.31 The multiplier comes into effect and the small initial increases in consumption and investment result in an even bigger total increase in national income. As national income grows, investment grows faster than the growth in consumption because of the accelerator.

4.32 A numerical example might help to illustrate this. Suppose that the initial increase in consumption raises demand from £10 million in year 1 to £12 million in year 2 and £16 million in year 3, and to produce the output to meet this demand industry must invest £2 per £1 of annual demand. The increase in demand will result in bigger increase in investment (accelerator multiple = 2) as the following table shows.

Year	Demand C £m	Total investment needed C × 2 £m	Change in investment I £m		National income C + I £m
1	10	20	-		10
2	12	24	(24-20)	+ 4	(12+4)	16
3	16	32	(32-24)	+ 8	(16+8)	24
4	16	32	etc	0	etc	16
5	14	28		- 4		10

4.33 In year 4, we will suppose that consumption peaks at £16 million and so no extra investment is needed. The reduction in new investment immediately causes a cut in national income and so consumption demand begins to fall too. This in turn puts the accelerator into reverse, with disinvestment occurring, in this example, at twice the rate of the fall in the demand.

4.34 Since the multiplier effect increases (or decreases) national income as a result of increases (or decreases) in injections to the circular flow, the accelerator effect also comes into operation, and investment demand rises (or falls) as a result of actual and expected changes in consumption.

4.35 The connecting link between the change in consumption, the level of investment and national income is the view that entrepreneurs take about whether the increase in demand will be maintained in the future - and so whether it is worth investing more capital. If an increase in demand is only expected to be temporary, firms might decide not to invest, so that the extra consumption spending will be met by higher imports. (The value of imports per £1 spent, as mentioned earlier, has a bearing on the size of the multiplier.) Although not quantifiable, the level of confidence of business people and their expectations have a considerable impact on the strength and length of any boom or depression.

4.36 Combined together, the multiplier and accelerator build up the momentum of initial small changes in demand - so that the multiplier - accelerator process explains the cumulative tendencies of upswings and downswings in the economy - ie trade cycles.

4.37 The implications of Keynes' analysis, and in particular of multiplier-accelerator theory, are that large increases or decreases in national income occur because of small initial changes in consumption or investment. Even *expected* changes in demand should result in new investment and the multiplier and accelerator would then come into operation.

8: DETERMINING NATIONAL INCOME

Floors and ceilings

4.38 Although business upswings and downswings can be large and rapid, there will eventually be a limit to the upswing or the downswing. A ceiling or a floor in the level of national income will be reached.

4.39 Why should this be so?

(a) *Ceilings*. Ceilings are reached when the full employment level of national income is reached. Unless firms can invest in new labour-saving equipment, or increase labour productivity, the total volume of output will eventually be restricted to the limited availability of labour. If labour is fully employed, it can't produce more unless it becomes more productive, or unless machines can be introduced to do work that labour did before.

(b) *Floors*. A floor will also be reached. At its worst level - and this never occurs in the 'real world' - business confidence will be so low that firms do not invest at all. If investment is nil, savings will fall to zero too, and national income will equal consumption only. There must always be some consumption, and national income could never fall below this minimum fixed consumption level.

4.40 *Turning points* in upturns and downturns can be explained by accelerator theory.

The multiplier-accelerator effect, combined with floors and ceilings, could explain how there might be never-ending business cycles of upturns and downturns in a national economy.

What keeps the business cycle moving?

4.41 Keynes wanted to suggest why a nation's economy might go through cycles of boom and depression instead of achieving a national income equilibrium and staying there. The point was made earlier that he suggested that a reason for trade cycles, and the failure to achieve an equilibrium in national income, is the short-term differences between withdrawals and injections into the circular flow of income.

4.42 It also follows that temporary imbalances *can be made to happen, if required, by the government*. The government can try to reduce the upswing of a trade cycle or limit the downswing by taking action to reduce or increase national income. This can be done by:

(a) encouraging new investment so as to give a boost to I. If private investment cannot be encouraged, the government can invest itself;

(b) increasing government spending, G, and financing the extra spending with borrowing instead of matching the increase in G (an injection) with an increase in tax, T (a withdrawal) to pay for it. *Borrowing* by government to finance extra spending is necessary in order to create the imbalance between injections and withdrawals that is needed to bring the multiplier and accelerator into action;

(c) reducing taxes so as to encourage more consumer spending, but keeping government spending at the same level - and so run a 'budget deficit'. The difference between (b) and (c), which both call for a budget deficit, is whether the extra spending should be done by the government or by consumers.

4.43 In this way Keynes explained how governments could adopt policies which would limit the impact of the trade cycle through a process of demand management.

5. THE TRADE CYCLE: IMPLICATIONS FOR ECONOMIC POLICY

Practical problems of evening out the trade cycle

5.1 Keynesian analysis of the causes of the cyclical fluctuations experienced by the economy was sound. His recommended solutions were theoretically very straightforward:

(a) depression indicates insufficient demand, so government adopts policies which increase injections and reduce withdrawals so that after allowing for the multiplier and accelerator effect, demand is increased sufficiently to generate full employment;

(b) booms are the result of excessive demand and the reverse policies are called for.

5.2 In practice the application of this approach caused a number of difficulties.

(a) Forecasting the precise timing and shape of the trade cycle was impossible. It was not possible to calculate how deep the natural cycle was or how long it would last.

(b) Time lags between adopting policies and their impact on the economy meant that policies to add demand in a depression failed to have an impact until recovery was already under way. The result was that demand was further increased in a very buoyant economy, forcing the eventual boom even higher.

(c) The policy options available were far from accurate. Reducing taxation was known to increase consumption, but by how much and when this should be done was far from certain.

(d) Although there was support for tackling insufficient demand with reflationary policies, there was less enthusiasm for deflationary measures in times of boom. Reducing demand and the likelihood of thereby increasing unemployment was seldom seen as a politically attractive option.

5.3 Keynesian policies adopted throughout the 1960s and 1970s failed as a result to flatten or even limit the impact of the cyclical nature of income fluctuations. The sudden and dramatic shifts in policy reacting to the economic upturns and downturns became known as *stop/go policies* (Figure 11).

5.4 The practical difficulties described above meant that demand management in practice served to actually exaggerate and extend the fluctuations, increasing business uncertainty and reducing their willingness to invest.

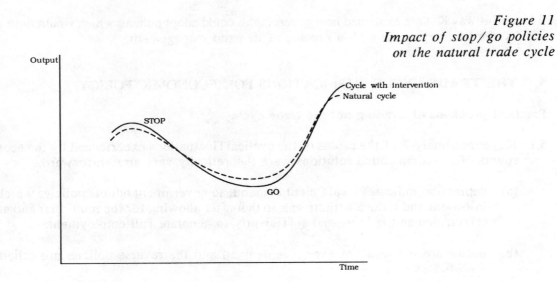

Figure 11
Impact of stop/go policies
on the natural trade cycle

Implications for business

5.5 Both the existence of the trade cycle and an understanding of governments' likely responses to its fluctuations are important to the business and marketing person. Movements in the trade cycle will be reflected in similar demand fluctuations across a wide range of markets, eg the size and speed of the accelerator has significant implications for those in the business of industrial capital goods.

5.6 Marketers need to ensure that they are aware of the way in which the trade cycle impacts on their market demand and then build into future demand forecasts the expected impact of the general economic fluctuations.

5.7 It is important for managers to recognise that the national picture can hide some much more dramatic fluctuations in a region or within a particular market segment. A fall in income of 5% is not likely to be shared out equally across all sectors of the community. Within a depression or recession it is still possible for some groups to do will, whilst in other industries or areas there is high unemployment. Monitoring the fluctuations within a market is therefore still important.

5.8 Marketers also need to recognise how purchasing behaviour for their products changes during the various stages of the trade cycle. An understanding of this allows pro-active marketing strategies to be developed and launched as the cycle unfolds. For example, customers are always likely to be more price and value conscious during a depression. Standard models are likely to sell better than deluxe ones and promotional activities geared to increased quantity or money-off are likely to be well received.

5.9 A surprisingly large number of companies will admit they do not take economic forecasts into account as part of their planning process. Ignoring this critical aspect of the external macroeconomic environment is like trying to plan with your head in the sand. Fluctuations in income and economic activity can be predicted and a good business should be prepared. The strength of fluctuations may on occasions surprise managers as is the case in the recession of 1990 to 1992, but more attention to the forecasters may have helped reduce the number of business casualties.

6. CONCLUSION

6.1 The following are key points.

(a) There is a circular flow of income in an economy which means that expenditure, output and income will all have the same total value.

(b) There are withdrawals from the circular flow of income (savings, taxation, import expenditure) and injections into the circular flow (investment, government spending, export income). In formula terms:

$$W = S + T + m$$
$$J = I + G + x$$

(c) National income can be measured by an expenditure method, income method or output method. Allowing for statistical errors in collecting the data, all three methods should give the same total for GDP, GNP and national income.

(d) A useful formula to learn is the expenditure method: $Y = C + I + G + (x - m)$.

(e) National income figures can be used to measure growth in the economy, although 'real' growth can only be measured by 'taking out inflation' and using figures on a common price basis.

(f) The creation of economic wealth is perhaps best measured by GDP, GNP or national income per head of the population. National income is a measure of *annual* income, not the nation's total stock of wealth.

6.2 For reasons mentioned in this chapter, national income has serious limitations as a measure of economic wealth and welfare. It remains an important indicator nonetheless, and in planning its economic policy, a government will probably seek to improve the standard of living of its population by setting as targets:

(a) growth in national income; and
(b) growth in national income per head of the population.

6.3 We have looked at the Keynesian model, as a way of explaining how national income is determined, and how national income equilibrium is reached.

Note the following points:

(a) To achieve full employment national income, it might be possible for a government to take measures to boost aggregate demand in the economy, although some price inflation will probably result. (Remember, $Y = C + I + G + (x - m)$).

(b) When there is inflation in the economy, measures should be taken to suppress aggregate demand.

(c) Changes in national income begin with a small change in expenditure, leading to an even larger eventual change in national income, due to the multiplier effect.

(d) The value of the multiplier is $\frac{1}{s}$ in a closed economy with no government sector.

6.4 Trade cycles are explained by Keynesian economists as the combined effect of the multiplier and the accelerator.

(a) Upturns and downturns in the economy are caused by short term differences between withdrawals and injections into the circular flow of income – by a balance of trade deficit, by a difference between savings and investment or by a difference between government tax income and government spending.

(b) Keynes argued that government intervention to stimulate investment, if necessary by direct government spending on investment financed by a budget deficit, was a solution to economic depression. He brought fiscal policy to the forefront of government economic policy. Although his ideas have now been questioned, because they have not provided adequate solutions to the world's economic problems of the 1970s and 1980s, they remain very important in economic theory.

6.5 Business people need to take economic forecasts into account when developing business plans.

TEST YOUR KNOWLEDGE

The numbers in brackets refer to paragraphs of this chapter

1   What are the three methods used to calculate the creation of a nation's wealth? (1.3)

2   What are the main difficulties encountered when trying to measure national income? (1.4)

3   In what ways is national income not a good indicator of wealth? (1.10)

4   Why does care need to be taken when making international comparisons of national income and what would make a better basis for comparison? (1.11–1.16)

5   What is the relationship between GDP, GNP and national income? (1.23)

6   What are the three injections and the three leakages from the circular flow of income? (2.14)

7   Illustrate an inflationary and a deflationary gap. (3.9, 3.11)

8   What are the characteristics of the four stages of the trade cycle? (3.19)

9   Explain what is meant by the multiplier. (3.33)

10   How do you explain the floors and ceilings in the trade cycle? (4.39)

11   What factors limited the success of flattening out trade cycle fluctuations? (5.2)

Now try illustrative questions 14 and 15 at the end of the text

Chapter 9

TECHNIQUES FOR CONTROLLING
THE ECONOMY

This chapter covers the following topics.

1. Fiscal policy
2. The incidence of taxation and implications for business
3. Monetary policy
4. Implications of monetary policy for business

---

1. FISCAL POLICY

Introductory note

1.1 We saw in the last chapter how the level of economic activity will fluctuate if market forces are left to their own devices. We also identified the major economic problems associated with the cyclical up and down swings. Since the time of Keynes, governments have accepted the desirability of adopting policies to try and control the economy and so to reduce or eradicate the impact of the associated economic problems.

1.2 The macroeconomic objectives of government are generally concerned with solving the problems of:

(a) unemployment
(b) inflation
(c) lack of growth
(d) imbalance of payments.

In the next chapter we will be looking at each of these in more detail. Here we identify the techniques available to a government wishing to influence the operation of the economy. The first area of policy which we consider is fiscal policy.

Fiscal policy

1.3 *Fiscal policy* relates to anything which affects the income or expenditure of a government. The word 'fisc' means the state treasury or the public purse. The UK government's fiscal policy for the forthcoming year is announced annually by the Chancellor of the Exchequer in the Budget.

1.4   Government spending has to be financed by government revenue and any shortfall made up by borrowing. These three then represent the three elements of public sector finance.

Government expenditure = Revenue + Borrowing

(a)   *Expenditure*

The government, at a national and local level, and through the nationalised industries, spends money.

Expenditure by the government has several purposes, eg

(i)   to provide goods and services, such as a health service, public education, a police force, roads and public buildings, and to pay its administrative work force;

(ii)   to provide payments to certain members of society, such as old age pensioners and the unemployed;

(iii)   on a small scale, perhaps, to provide finance to encourage investment by private industry, eg by means of grants.

(b)   *Income*

Expenditure must be financed, and the government must have income.

(i)   Most government income comes from taxation.

(ii)   Other income comes from profits of the nationalised industries and charges made by the public sector.

(iii)   Revenue from the sale of shares in previously nationalised companies such as British Telecom and British Gas.

(c)   *Borrowing*

To the extent that a government's expenditure exceeds its income, it must borrow to make up the difference. The amount that the government must borrow each year is referred to as the Public Sector Borrowing Requirement or PSBR.

However, a government might choose to raise more income than it needs for its expenditure and the PSBR can be negative. When the government raises more income than it needs for spending, surplus income will be used to repay some of the country's debts (the National Debt). When the UK did this in the late 1980s, the negative PSBR was called a PSDR - ie Public Sector Debt Repayment.

These three elements make up what we might call the fiscal triangle.

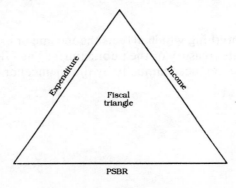

1.5 Fiscal policy is action by the government to spend money, or to collect money in taxes, with the purpose of influencing the condition of the national economy. Remember that government spending is an injection into the economy, adding to aggregate demand = expenditure = national income, whereas taxes are a withdrawal. A government might intervene in the economy by:

(a) spending more money and financing this expenditure by borrowing;

(b) collecting more in taxes without increasing public spending;

(c) collecting more in taxes in order to increase public spending, thus diverting income from one part of the economy to another.

1.6 Demand management, you will remember, is a term used to describe the economic policy of a government when it attempts to influence the economy by changing aggregate demand and was the policy favoured by Keynes and most UK governments before 1979.

1.7 Fiscal policy could be used as an instrument of demand management. Government spending and taxation levels could be used to eliminate an inflationary gap or deflationary gap in the economy. A reduction in taxation would give households a larger income, and so domestic consumption (C) would rise: conversely, an increase in taxation would reduce domestic consumption. Extra government spending (G) should create a multiplier effect on national income, although public sector spending might 'crowd out' private sector investment, because of higher rates of interest in the capital markets.

1.8 In Figure 1, an increase in taxation by £T, without any matching increase in government expenditure, would reduce the aggregate expenditure in the economy from AD_1 to AD_2 and so the money value of national income would fall from Y_1 to Y_2. This would result in either a fall in real output or it would dampen inflationary pressures.

Similarly, a reduction in taxation without any reduction in government spending would increase the money value of national income. This would either cause real output to increase, or it would give a boost to price rises and inflation.

Figure 1
The 45° line on this diagram indicates points at which income and expenditure are equal

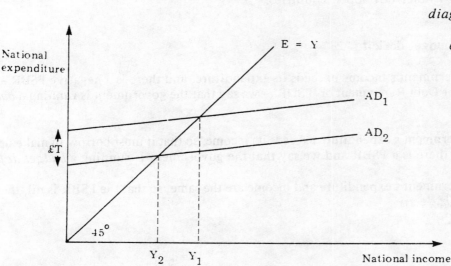

181

Taxation as a deterrent to economic growth

1.9 In most modern societies, some taxation is essential, because governments have to raise money somehow to carry on their own activities – running the country, providing defence forces, a police force, a fire service, a health service, education, roads and so on. Governments can use tax revenues to invest directly in new enterprises, or to fund important research.

1.10 The proportion of income controlled by central and local government in this way indicates the size of the public sector. Much of the thinking behind the 'Thatcherite' years in the UK (1979 to 1990) was based on the belief that many of the UK's problems lay in a public sector which had grown too large and was deterring growth.

Fiscal policy should be formulated within the guidelines that:

(a) taxes should be high enough to allow the government to carry on its functions; but

(b) they should not be set so as to deter private investment and initiative.

Fiscal policy and the Budget

1.11 A government must *plan* what it wants to spend, and so how much it needs to raise in income or by borrowing. It needs to make a plan in order to establish how much taxation there should be, what form the taxes should take and so which sectors of society (firms or households, high income earners or low income earners etc) the money should come from. This formal planning of fiscal policy is usually done once a year. The taxation aspects are set out in the Budget. In between Budgets, a government must resort to other non-fiscal policy instruments to control the economy, such as influencing interest rate levels.

In the UK, decisions on public *expenditure* for the coming financial year have been announced some four months earlier than the Budget in the Autumn Statement. However, in the 1992 Budget, it was announced that taxation and expenditure decisions would be brought together and announced at the same time in a Budget which would take place towards the end of each year. The first such Budget is due to be presented in November 1993. This change brings practice in the UK into line with that of most other developed countries.

Budget surplus and budget deficit

1.12 (a) When a government's income exceeds its expenditure, and there is a negative PSBR – ie a Public Sector Debt Repayment or 'PSDR' – we say that the government is running a *budget surplus*.

(b) When a government's expenditure exceeds its income, so that it must borrow to make up the difference, there is a PSBR and we say that the government is running a *budget deficit*.

(c) When a government's expenditure and income are the same, so that the PSBR is nil, there is a *balanced budget*.

Fiscal policy in the UK

1.13 In the 1950s and 1960s in Britain, fiscal policies were thought to be the *only* real method of controlling the economy. Some economists thought that frequent small changes to the level of government spending and taxation would be sufficient to keep national income at a full employment level. The influence of Keynes was very important in forming this attitude.

The fiscal policy of frequent (perhaps annual) changes in government expenditure and taxation to control national income and employment is known as *fine tuning* the economy - the economy was considered to be in reasonably good shape, but *minor adjustments* made by means of fiscal policy would help the economy to settle at exactly the right level of income.

During this time governments' use of monetary policy (the other main mechanism for influencing the economy) was limited to a mainly supportive role.

1.14 There have been changes in the attitude of government to fiscal policy since then.

(a) By the 1970s it was recognised increasingly that demand management and fine tuning alone were not sufficient to correct the underlying weaknesses in the economy.

(b) The years of Thatcherism represented a dramatic change in economic thinking. Monetarist policies were adopted, where the main emphasis was controlling the money supply, which concentrated on influencing purchasing power rather than expenditure. Fiscal policy was regulated to a supporting role and even its influence in microeconomic issues and problems was limited by a government which advocated non-interference with the market mechanism. During these years the objective was to have a budget surplus or at worst a balanced budget.

(c) After the resignation of Mrs Margaret Thatcher as Prime Minister in 1990, there were indications of change. One of the most significant recent developments in the UK economy was the entry of sterling into the European exchange rate mechanism (the 'ERM'). ERM membership limited the government's freedom to use rates of interest to influence economic activity making fiscal policy more important. Sterling's departure form the ERM in September 1992 changed the situation radically again, making interest rates a more flexible policy option. While allowing interest rates to fall to help the UK out of recession, the government intends to maintain anti-inflationary policies, including a tight control of government spending.

(d) The government has accepted the need for a short term budget deficit to help the economy out of the current recession. However, the medium-term financial strategy is still for a balanced budget.

Taxation policy and its effects

1.15 To the marketer, government changes in taxation may have a direct effect on plans and strategy.

1.16 The functions of taxation include the following:

(a) *to raise revenues for the government*, local authorities and similar bodies (eg the European Community). The revenues are used to provide goods and services that the market economy either does not provide at all (eg defence) or will not provide in sufficient quantities (eg education) and to pay for the upkeep of government administration;

(b) *to discourage certain activities regarded as undesirable.* The imposition of Development Land Tax in the United Kingdom in the mid-70s was partially in response to the well-publicised growth in property speculation;

(c) *to cause certain products to be priced to take into account their social costs.* For example, smoking entails certain social costs, including the cost of hospital care for those suffering from smoking-related diseases, and so the government sees fit to make the price of tobacco reflect these social costs;

(d) *to redistribute wealth.* The higher rates of income tax up to 1979 and Capital Transfer Tax were designed to transfer wealth from the better off to the less well off through higher social security benefits. Some politicians favour a wealth tax;

(e) *to protect industries from foreign competition.* If the government levies a duty on all imported goods much of the duty will be passed on to the consumer in the form of higher prices, making imported goods more expensive. This has the effect of transferring a certain amount of demand from imported goods to domestically produced goods, but it runs the risk of encouraging trade wars and after 1992 will not be possible between European countries.

(f) *to provide a stabilising effect on national income.* Taxation reduces the effect of the multiplier*, and so can be used to dampen upswings in a trade cycle - ie higher taxation when the economy shows signs of a boom will slow down the growth of money GNP, and so take some inflationary pressures out of the economy.

* The size of the multiplier, remember, is $\left(\dfrac{1}{s + m + t}\right)$ where t is the marginal rate of taxation.

(g) taxation can be used to *support particular regions or industries* through rebates, incentives and subsidies and so can help achieve microeconomic objectives of government, such as through small business initiatives.

Qualities of a good tax

1.17 Adam Smith in his *Wealth of Nations* ascribed four features to a good tax system.

(a) Persons should pay according to their ability.

(b) The tax should be 'certain' and easily understood by all concerned.

(c) The payment of tax should ideally be related to how and when people receive and spend their income (eg PAYE is deducted when wages are paid, and VAT is charged when goods are bought).

(d) The cost of collection should be small relative to the yield (by this criterion, the car road tax is an inefficient tax).

Further features of a good tax are that:

(a) it should be adjustable so that rates may be altered up or down;
(b) it should not harm initiative;
(c) evasion should be difficult;
(d) it should be equitable.

1.18 *A regressive tax* takes a higher proportion of a poor person's salary than of a rich person's. Television licences and road tax are examples of a regressive tax since they are the same for people of all wealth classes. A poll tax or community charge is also a regressive tax because it takes a greater proportion of the income of a poor person than a rich person, even though individual charges can vary from one local authority to another, and in spite of some rebates for the least well-off groups.

A proportional tax takes the same proportion of income in tax from all levels of income. Schedule E income tax with a base of tax at 25% is proportional tax, but only within a limited range of income.

A progressive tax takes a higher proportion of income in tax as income rises. Income tax as a whole is progressive, since the rate of tax increases in steps from 20p in £1 to 40p in £1 as taxable income rises above threshold levels. However, income tax in the UK is now less progressive than it has been in the past.

Figure 2 illustrates these distinctions.

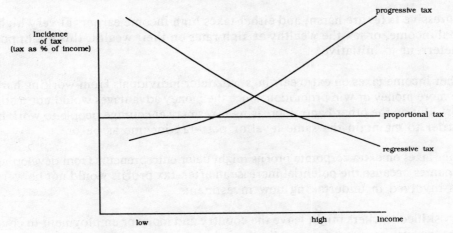

Figure 2

Advantages of progressive taxation

1.19 There are several arguments in favour of progressive taxes.

(a) They are levied according to the ability of individuals to pay. Individuals with a higher income are more able to afford to give up more of their income in tax than low income earners, who need a greater proportion of their earnings for the basic necessities of life. If taxes are to be raised according to the ability of people to pay (which is one of the features of a good tax suggested by Adam Smith) then there must be some progressiveness in them.

(b) Progressive taxes enable a government to redistribute wealth from the rich to the poor in society. It is likely that there will be little redistribution of wealth among the middle-income ranges of society, but there should be some redistribution of wealth from the richest members of society to the poorest. Such a redistribution of wealth might be regarded as a matter of social justice but it will also alter the consumption patterns in society since the poorer members will spend their earnings and social security benefits on different types of goods than if the income had remained in the hands of the richer people.

(c) Taxes on expenditure (such as value added tax) tend to be regressive and progressive taxes are needed to counterbalance regressive taxes in the tax system, and so make the tax system as a whole more fair.

(d) Progression in taxation is a matter of degree. In the UK, income tax is progressive, but currently only mildly so. As long as the progression is not harsh or 'unfair' to the wealthy, society as a whole will accept that there is social justice in a progressive tax system.

The disadvantages of progressive taxation

1.20 There are some arguments against progressive taxes.

(a) Some would argue that in an affluent society, there is less need for progressive taxes than in a poorer society, and there is less need to redistribute wealth from the very wealthy to the fairly well-to-do.

(b) When progressive taxes are harsh, and either taxes high income earners at very high rates on marginal income, or tax the wealthy at high rates on their wealth, this might possibly act as a deterrent to initiative.

   (i) Higher income taxes on extra earnings will deter individuals from working harder to earn more money or win promotion, since the money advantages would not justify the effort. But on the other hand, increasing taxes may encourage people to work harder in order to maintain the same level of post-tax income as before.

   (ii) Higher taxes on extra corporate profits might deter entrepreneurs from developing new companies because the potential increase in after-tax profits would not be worth the risks involved in undertaking new investments.

   (iii) Many skilled workers might leave the country and look for employment in countries where they can earn more money: the 'braindrain' was a significant phenomenon of the 1970s.

(c) It is also sometimes argued that individuals and firms suffering from high taxes might try to:

   (i) find loopholes so as to avoid paying tax - eg non-taxable perks;

   (ii) evade taxes - ie withhold information about their income or wealth from the authorities;

   (iii) transfer their wealth to other countries, or establish companies in tax havens where corporate tax rates are low.

   But of course some people will try to avoid or evade tax whether it is high or not so high.

Advantages and disadvantages of a proportional tax

1.21 The advantage of a tax which is proportional to income is primarily that it can be seen to be fair.

1.22 The disadvantages of a proportional tax are as follows.

(a) A large administrative system is needed to calculate personal tax liabilities on a proportional basis. Income tax, for example, can be a costly tax to collect where individuals (especially self-employed people) require detailed tax assessments.

(b) The tax rules may need to be quite complex in order to be proportional.

(c) Such a tax does not contribute towards a redistribution of wealth among the population.

Advantages and disadvantages of a regressive tax

1.23 The main disadvantage of a regressive tax is that it is not equitable, because a greater tax burden falls on those least able to afford it.

1.24 The main advantage of a regressive tax is that it can be relatively easy to administer and collect. However, a regressive tax could also be expensive to collect. Arguments against the 'poll tax' (community charge) in the UK were that it was both regressive and also expensive to administer.

Direct and indirect taxes

1.25 A *direct tax* is paid direct by a person to the Revenue authority. Examples of direct taxes in the UK are income tax, corporation tax, capital gains tax and inheritance tax. A direct tax can be levied on income and profits, or on wealth. A wealth tax can be levied on newly-acquired wealth (eg capital gains tax, or inheritance tax) or existing wealth (eg some politicians advocate a wealth tax). Direct taxes tend to be progressive or proportional taxes. They are also usually unavoidable, which means that they must be paid by everyone, and everyone knows how much tax they are paying.

1.26 An *indirect tax* is collected by the Revenue authority (eg Customs & Excise) from an intermediary (eg a supplier) who then passes on the tax to consumers in the price of goods they sell. Indirect taxes include VAT, excise duty on spirits and beer, and customs duties on goods imported from countries outside the European Community. *Indirect taxes tend to be regressive* (unless they are charged exclusively on luxury items). They are also usually avoidable, which means that people can choose not to pay the tax, by not buying the goods or services on which the tax is levied. The tax element being charged is not always evident to the consumer.

Comparison of direct and indirect taxation: summary

1.27 A government must decide how it intends to raise tax revenues, from direct or indirect taxes, and in what proportions tax revenues will be raised from each source.

(a) Direct taxes have the quality of being progressive or proportional. Income tax is usually progressive, with high rates of tax charged on higher bands of taxable income. Indirect taxes can be regressive, when the taxes are placed on essential commodities, or commodities consumed by poorer people, in greater quantities.

(b) Direct taxes might act as a disincentive. Corporation tax might discourage firms from seeking higher profits if the rate of tax is too high. Since firms need retained profits in order to invest in new projects, direct taxes on firms might discourage new investments - unless suitable capital allowances are provided to help firms to mitigate or delay the tax burden. It is important to bear in mind that higher taxes on company profits, by reducing the profitability of new investments and also leaving firms with lower profits to reinvest, will probably reduce the volume of new investment in the economy.

(c) Excessive indirect taxes on commodities will reduce the demand for them.

(d) In the UK, the major indirect tax is VAT, and the government is able to reduce its administrative burden of tax collection by having tradespeople and businesspeople act as tax collectors on the government's behalf.

2. THE INCIDENCE OF TAXATION AND IMPLICATIONS FOR BUSINESS

The incidence of taxation

2.1 The *incidence* of a tax is the distribution of the tax burden. A tax's *formal* incidence can be distinguished from its *actual* incidence.

(a) In the case of income tax, formal and actual incidence are the same - unless workers negotiate a higher post-tax wage, in which case employers bear some of the tax burden. Employers might then raise their product price and pass some of the tax burden on to consumers.

(b) Corporation tax falls formally on profits and so on shareholders; but the tax could be passed forward to consumers in the form of a price rise following on a reduction in supply and the actual incidence of the tax would then fall on the consumers.

(c) According to economic theory, producers will not pass the burden of a profit tax on to consumers because they are already producing at a profit-maximising level of output and the marginal condition MR = MC is not affected by a tax. However, it might be more plausible to suppose that producers would regard the tax as an additional cost, in which case it would justify a reduction in output and rise in price. The consumers would in this case bear some of the burden.

(d) A general indirect tax on all goods would be borne by consumers, since they cannot buy alternative goods which are not taxed. VAT is the closest equivalent to a general indirect tax in Britain. Only necessities are exempt from VAT or zero-rated, eg food, fuel and power, transport, health services - and books!

2.2 We shall consider below the incidence of a *selective* indirect tax, ie an indirect tax which is levied on one good but not on others.

Incidence of a selective indirect tax

2.3 If an indirect tax is imposed on one good, the tax will shift the supply curve to the left. This is because the price to consumers includes the tax, but the suppliers still only receive the net-of-tax price.

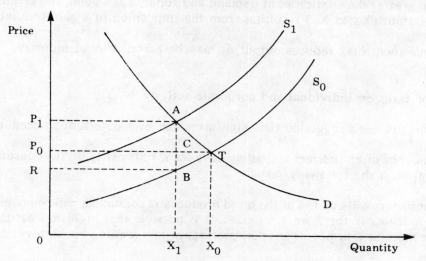

Figure 3
Incidence of selective indirect tax

(a) The vertical distance between the old supply curve S_0 and the new curve S_1 is equal to the rate of tax.

$$\text{Tax} = AB = P_1R$$

(b) Before the tax, output is X_0 and price is P_0. Total expenditure is shown by the rectangle OP_0TX_0.

(c) After the tax has been imposed, output is X_1 and price is P_1. Total expenditure is OP_1AX_1, of which RP_1AB is tax revenue and $ORBX_1$ is producers' total revenue.

(d) At the new equilibrium:

   (i)   price to the customer has risen from P_0 to P_1;

   (ii)   average revenue received by producers has fallen from P_0 to R;

   (iii) the tax burden is therefore shared between the producers and consumers, with CB borne by the supplier and AC borne by consumers.

2.4 Consumers pay P_0P_1AC of total tax revenue and producers pay RP_0CB. It can be shown that:

$$\frac{\text{Consumers' share of tax}}{\text{Producers' share of tax}} = \frac{\text{elasticity of supply}}{\text{elasticity of demand}}$$

(though proof is omitted here).

Thus if a selective indirect tax of 10p is placed on a product where supply elasticity is 1.2 and demand elasticity is 0.8, the price of the good would rise by 6p, ie:

(a) the consumer would pay 6p of the 10p (ratio 1.2:0.8);

(b) the supplier would pay 4p because the price increase of 6p is insufficient to pay the full tax of 10p per unit.

2.5 Further points to note are as follows.

   (a) The greater the elasticities of demand and supply for a good, the greater will be the loss of output (X_0 to X_1) resulting from the imposition of a selective indirect tax.

   (b) Since such a tax reduces output, it may be harmful to an industry.

The effect of taxes on individual and corporate activity

2.6 It has already been suggested that high taxes can be a deterrent to economic activity.

The incidence of an indirect tax, as we have seen, falls partly on the consumer and partly on the firm, with the following result.

   (a) Consumers will buy less of the taxed product and consumers will be unable to afford to buy as much as if there were no taxes. It is possible that high indirect taxes will increase the amount that people save in preference to spending on highly-taxed goods.

   (b) Firms will maximise their profits at a lower volume of output - and lower profits - than if there were no taxes.

Taxation and the redistribution of wealth

2.7 Another aspect of taxation is the extent to which it can be used to redistribute wealth, and the consequences this would have for economic activity. Suppose, for example, that a country has no taxation, and most national income is earned by a very small and wealthy proportion of the population. The expenditure pattern within the country would probably be:

   (a) fairly substantial spending by the wealthy few on luxury goods and specialist services (eg domestic servants etc);

   (b) substantial spending by the poor majority on cheap basic necessities for living, such as simple food and cheap clothing.

2.8 Now suppose that a progressive income tax is imposed, which successfully redistributes wealth among the population, so that general income levels rise. The result should be a general rise in living standards, with:

   (a) greater demand for some items; and

   (b) some switch in demand from inferior goods to more expensive substitutes;

   (c) less demand for luxury goods or a reduction in saving from the affluent classes who will seek to maintain their previous consumption levels. Lower savings can result in more expensive borrowing and therefore may be a disincentive to investment and further economic growth.

Implications for marketing – taxes on specific goods

2.9 A government can make a significant and unexpected impact on a product's marketing plan with a change in fiscal policy. One of the problems facing the marketer is that fiscal policy, announced annually in the Budget, tends to remain a well guarded secret prior to the Budget speech. As a result, marketers can be faced with the equivalent of immediate price rises with little or no warning. Marketing plans need to be flexible enough to respond to such events.

2.10 Companies producing goods which are likely to attract the attention of the Chancellor need to pay particular attention to government opinion. Marketing skills will be used to lobby political opinion in order to influence such decisions.

Traditionally such goods as cigarettes, alcohol and gambling have been those which government has taxed heavily. In the future any company offering products which, though perceived to be luxuries do in fact have relatively price inelastic demand curves, could be subject to the same treatment. Foreign holidays would be an example of such a product.

In the 1991 Budget the Chancellor unexpectedly made mobile telephones a taxable benefit – undoubtedly having an impact on demand for such products.

Implications for marketing – taxes on market segments

2.11 Indirect taxes can be targeted at specific goods and sectors, but direct taxation is likely to have an impact on the purchasing power of broader market segments. A change of government can significantly influence the policy on taxation and shifts from progressive to regressive taxes can have far reaching effects on demand in many markets. Such taxation changes alter individuals' disposable income and so represent a change in the conditions of demand. Forecasting the impact of such a change is dependent on the marketer having an awareness of the income elasticity of demand for their products.

A note on industrial markets

2.12 Government can target fiscal changes to help stimulate growth, investment, and employment in industries and regions. For those marketing business-to-business products changes in business taxation policy could generate as many threats and opportunities as do changes in personal taxation.

2.13 The marketer cannot, then, afford to ignore governments' fiscal policies. Scenario planning to prepare in advance for sudden changes in taxation is well advised. Budget day is important and its wider implications need to be identified quickly and strategies and plans modified where necessary.

3. MONETARY POLICY

3.1 By the mid 1970s, Keynesian demand management strategies which had depended in the main on fiscal policy were coming to be questioned. The economy was suffering from low growth, rising inflation and unemployment and a persistent and serious balance of payments deficit. The increase in the UK's international indebtedness led eventually to intervention from the International Monetary Fund, which helped to force a political change of focus away from an economic priority of maintaining full employment to one of containing and reducing inflation.

3.2   With this change in priority came a change in economic thinking which we now associate strongly with the Thatcher years – a move towards a monetarist approach to the economic management of the economy. Monetary policy had always existed, but previously it had been used to support fiscal policy. Its main purpose had been to keep a stable rate of interest to help stimulate investment.

What is monetary policy?

3.3   Monetary policy is any government action which changes either:

(a)   the rate of interest ie the price of money; or
(b)   the quantity of money ie the available purchasing power in the economy.

Monetary policy is only possible if the government has a 'monopoly' control of the supply of money. If this is the case the government can choose to either control the price or the quantity of money.

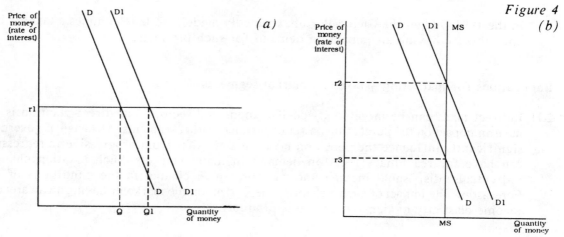

Figure 4

Figure 4(a) shows that the government can fix the rate of interest by expanding the purchasing power in the economy as aggregate demand shifts from D to D_1. This was broadly the approach which Keynes advocated. But increasing the supply of money faster than the economy is growing leads in the long run to inflation.

Figure 4(b) illustrates the monetarist view, which involves controlling the amount of purchasing power in the system and letting the rate of interest move in line with changes in aggregate demand.

Money supply and prices – the link

3.4   Turn back to Chapter 8, Figure 1, which showed our model of 'Smalltown'.

Exercise

Try and answer the following questions.

(a)   What is the supply of money in Smalltown?

(b)   What is the velocity of circulation? (ie the number of times money changes hands in the time period)

(c)   If the average price of products sold was £5, how many transactions were there?

Solutions

(a)   The money supply is £50. This £50 changes hands within the community, but there is just £50 money supply.

(b)   Money changes hands five times in our model A–E and so the velocity of circulation is 5.

(c)   Money supply (M) × velocity of circulation (V) = national income, and

income   =   expenditure,   therefore

MV   =   PT

If average prices are £5 and our economy has an aggregate expenditure of £250,

$$\frac{250}{5} = 50$$

transactions have taken place. Average price (P) × number of transactions (T) = expenditure.

3.5   The 'equation' or identity of the quantity theory of money is MV = PT: this is the fundamental concept of monetarism. As you can see it is in essence only a way of analysing our basic circular flow model of income = expenditure.

What would happen in Smalltown if the money supply suddenly increased to £100. Assume there is no change in the velocity of circulation.

MV   =   PT
100 × 5   =   ? × ?
500   =   500

Income has now increased to £500. Therefore expenditure must also be £500 and either P or T has to change. If T increases to 100 the average price would be unchanged at £5, but this would represent a doubling of the economic activity of Smalltown. It is unlikely that output could go from 50 to 100 units within one time period of say one year, because bottlenecks and timelags will prevent industry from being that responsive. This would after all represent an economic growth of 100%. If T cannot change by that much, some of the change in M will be reflected by a change in P. If T remained completely unchanged average prices would rise to £10, representing inflation of 100%.

Milton Friedman, a leading monetarist economist, argues that in an advanced economy T is likely to be able to change by 3–5% per annum. Then any growth in M above that will be reflected in higher prices.

3.6 Monetarists believe that if the government allows purchasing power (ie the money supply) to grow more quickly than economic output, the result will always be inflation. Equally the government can control the economy, output and inflation by maintaining tight monetary control.

3.7 One way of describing the purpose of monetary policy is as the maintenance of stability of income and prices - in other words, *to keep the rate of inflation under control*. In addition, monetary policy may be applied to help the economy to grow in real terms. Economists do not know fully what makes an economy grow, but it is generally accepted that:

(a) economic depression or recession; and
(b) rapid and variable rates of inflation,

are harmful to the prospects of economic growth. Monetary policy, like any other economic policy tool, might be used to avoid an economic depression, or at least to make it less deep, or to provide a way of reducing the rate of inflation.

The role of monetary policy is perhaps best thought of as a means towards the achievement of an intermediate economic target, which in turn is a means towards the achievement of an ultimate economic objective.

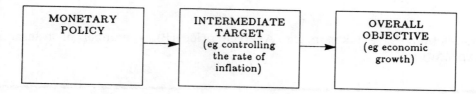

3.8 Monetary policy in the UK has for some years been directed primarily at the intermediate objective of keeping the rate of inflation under control.

The Governor of the Bank of England has said (16 October 1986):

'The role of monetary policy is progressively to squeeze out inflation, ... as an essential precondition for any sustained expansion in (economic) activity and employment.'

3.9 If monetary policy is dependent on the government's ability to control the supply of money it is obviously important to be able to define and measure the money stock.

What is M?

3.10 The money supply is the total amount of money in the economy. It is also referred to as the money stock.

3.11 A *monetary aggregate* is a total of the money stock or money supply. The aggregates currently published for the UK economy are called M0, M2 and M4. Statistics are also now published for 'liquid assets outside M4'.

3.12 The main purpose of measuring a monetary aggregate is to discover by how much (and how rapidly) the money supply is rising in the economy, and to predict from this rise what future changes in economic activity might be. Another purpose may be to discover whether past changes in the money supply help to explain changes in economic activity which have already occurred.

There is also the monetarists' view that controlling M is the key to controlling the economy, making it necessary to know what M actually is.

3.13 You might accept at this stage that it is useful to measure the money supply, defined as a monetary aggregate. However, you might well be wondering why we need different monetary aggregates. Why is one not enough?

3.14 The UK government and the Bank of England have admitted that there is considerable difficulty in defining an acceptable aggregate for the money stock or for the liquid assets held by various sectors of the economy. There are several reasons for this difficulty.

(a) Money is both a means of payment and a store of wealth. To be a means of payment, money must be liquid. However, as a store of wealth, the requirement for liquidity is not so immediate. People are prepared to sacrifice some liquidity to obtain higher interest. A problem in defining a monetary aggregate can be stated as:

'When does a financial asset become so non-liquid that it cannot be classed as money?'

(b) There are so many different financial instruments in the UK that no matter where the line is drawn between money and non-money there will always be borderline cases where the difference between items included and excluded is small.

(c) The government has found from experience that there is no single monetary aggregate which is good enough on its own to show the relationship between changes in the money supply and other economic activity. Instead, it relies on different monetary aggregates and uses each one in appropriate situations.

The different monetary aggregates

3.15 The definitions of UK monetary aggregates are shown on the next page.

3.16 Note the following points about the monetary aggregates in current use.

(a) M0 is the 'narrowest' definition of money, the great majority of which is made up of notes and coin in circulation outside the Bank of England. M0 is now the only monetary aggregate for which a target is set by the government (this is referred to again below).

(b) M2 is effectively a measure of all sterling deposits used for *transaction* purposes (as distinct from 'investment' purposes).

(c) M4 is a 'broad' definition of money, including deposits held for savings as well as spending purposes. M3H is a broadly similar European equivalent to M4. Statistics for various 'liquid assets outside M4' are published for the benefit of those who are interested in a still broader definition of the money stock. The government does not set a target for growth in M4, although it does 'monitor' its growth.

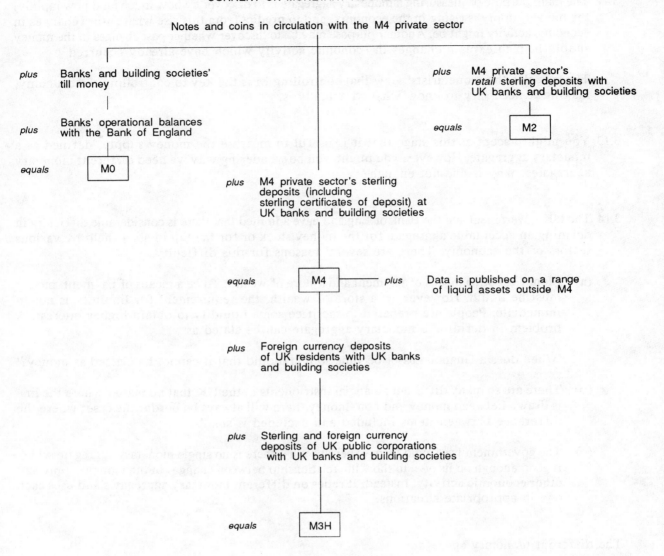

CURRENT UK MONETARY AGGREGATES

Notes and coins in circulation with the M4 private sector

plus Banks' and building societies' till money

plus M4 private sector's *retail* sterling deposits with UK banks and building societies

plus Banks' operational balances with the Bank of England

equals M2

equals M0

plus M4 private sector's sterling deposits (including sterling certificates of deposit) at UK banks and building societies

equals M4 — *plus* Data is published on a range of liquid assets outside M4

plus Foreign currency deposits of UK residents with UK banks and building societies

plus Sterling and foreign currency deposits of UK public corporations with UK banks and building societies

equals M3H

Note: The 'M4 private sector' means the non-bank non-building society private sector, comprising UK domestic residents and UK based businesses.

Targets of monetary policy

3.17 Targets are quantified aims for achievement and targets might be set by a government for:

    (a)   its overall economic objectives, eg:

        (i)   to achieve real growth of 3% per annum;
       (ii)   to reduce unemployment by 100,000 per annum;

(b) its intermediate objectives, eg:

(i) to restrict price inflation to 5% per annum;
(ii) to achieve a surplus each year in the balance of payments current account;

(c) its policies, eg:

(i) if a government decides to try to restrict the growth of the broad money supply as a means of keeping inflation under control, it might set a target growth rate in the money supply of, say, no more than 6% per annum;

(ii) a government might decide to try to maintain the exchange rate for its national currency within a certain target range, as a means of influencing the country's balance of payments and interest rates.

3.18 When a government chooses its monetary policy it will express its policy aims in terms of targets for achievement. These targets of monetary policy must be selected and should relate to something:

(a) over which the government or central bank can exert influence; and

(b) which will contribute to the achievement of the government's overall economic objectives.

3.19 Targets of monetary policy are likely to relate to the volume of national income and expenditure.

The targets of monetary policy which might have some influence on national income (ie 'national income', 'GNP' or 'GDP') are:

(a) growth in the size of the money stock (money supply);
(b) the level of interest rates;
(c) the volume of credit or growth in the volume of credit;
(d) the exchange rate;
(e) the volume of expenditure in the economy (ie national income or GNP itself).

Let's now have a look at some of these possible targets of monetary policy in more detail.

The money stock as a target of monetary policy

3.20 To monetarist economists, the money stock is an obvious intermediate target of economic policy. This is because they claim that an increase in the money supply will raise prices and incomes, and this in turn will raise the demand for money to spend.

It is a crucial aspect of monetarist theory that the link between the money supply and prices, incomes and expenditure is reasonably predictable and stable. In other words, the velocity of circulation must remain fairly stable so that money expenditure and money income are directly influenced by changes in the money supply. If this link is not reliable, government policy to control the growth of the money stock will have unpredictable consequences for both inflation and 'real' expenditure in the economy and so would be a poor weapon of government policy.

3.21 In a government Green Paper *Monetary Control* (1980) the acceptance of such a link was described as follows:

> 'The government considers that a progressive reduction in the rate of growth of the money stock is essential to achieving a permanent reduction in inflation..... The relationship between the growth of prices and incomes is complex. They can diverge in the short run but there are strong grounds for believing that they will not diverge significantly over a period of years.'

3.22 Controlling the growth of the money supply is only a medium-term policy, however, and it cannot work miracle cures for the economy in a short time.

When such a policy is first introduced, the short term effect would be unpredictable because:

(a) the effect on interest rates might be erratic;

(b) there might be a time lag before anything can be done. For example, it takes time to cut government spending, and cuts in the PSBR might be an instrument of monetary policy to control the growth in M0 or M4;

(c) there might be a time lag before control of the money supply alters expectations about inflation and thus wage demands.

3.23 The money stock, if it is a monetary policy target, should therefore be a *medium term* target. When the UK government set targets for the growth of the money supply as a main feature of its economic policy strategy from 1980, it was prepared to wait for some years to see any benefits from its policies and therefore set out its policy targets in a *medium term* financial strategy.

Interest rates as a target for monetary policy

3.24 The authorities may decide that interest rates themselves should be a target of monetary policy. This would be appropriate if it is considered that there is a direct relationship between interest rates and the level of expenditure in the economy.

Although it is generally accepted that there is likely to be a connection between interest rates and investment (by companies) and consumer expenditure, the connection is not a stable and predictable one, and interest rate changes are only likely to affect the level of expenditure after a considerable time lag.

3.25 In the UK, the government's main monetary policy weapon from 1988 to 1991 was the application of high interest rates. High interest rates, it was argued, will help keep down the rate of inflation which is seen to be caused mainly by a boom in consumer spending.

(a) High interest rates will deter consumer borrowing, it is believed. If consumer borrowing can be controlled, consumer spending will be controlled too, at least to the extent that consumer spending is financed by borrowing.

(b) High interest repayments on existing loans will leave borrowers with less money to spend on other things. This effect is particularly important in the UK, where the level of owner-occupation of houses is high and increases in mortgage rates have a large effect on many householders' disposable income.

(c)   High interest rates will tend to keep the value of sterling high. This will tend to keep down the cost of imports, which will include imports of raw materials. It is hoped that this will help to prevent 'import-cost-push' inflation.

3.26 A problem with a policy to control the level of interest rates is that the authorities can only influence *current* rates of interest whereas investment and borrowing are almost certainly influenced by *expectations* of future real *rates of interest*.

Real rates are interest rates after allowing for inflation. Thus, if market rates of interest (eg bank lending rates) are 12% per year and inflation is 8% per year, the real rate of interest is approximately 4% per year.

3.27 It is also important to bear in mind that the government cannot set interest rates at whatever level it wishes. Firstly, it can only set rates at levels which the financial markets will bear: if it sets rates much away from these levels, market forces will exert pressure for a change in rates. For a country in a fixed or semi-fixed exchange rate system, such as the European exchange rate mechanism (ERM), interest rates must be set at levels which keep the currency within its limits in that system. For example, if the value (exchange rate) of the currency falls too low within the system, interest rates may need to be raised to make it more attractive.

3.28 Interest rates can be an effective intermediate target of monetary policy even though the connection between interest rates and economic growth is by no means a clear one. An important reason for pursuing an interest rate policy is that the authorities are able to influence interest rates much more effectively than they can influence other policy targets, such as the money supply or the volume of credit.

The growth in the volume of credit as a target for monetary policy

3.29 The government might decide to restrict credit lending (impose a '*credit squeeze*') and so set targets for limited growth of credit in the economy. An increase in bank lending (ie in the volume of credit) is likely to lead to a rise in the level of expenditure in the economy because people borrow money in order to spend it. Higher bank lending is also likely to result in higher bank deposits and thus an increase in the money stock.

3.30 Control over the total volume of bank credit, and perhaps the total volume of credit of other non-bank financial institutions too, might be:

(a)   a direct way of reducing the level of expenditure in the economy; and

(b)   a way of affecting expenditure in the economy *indirectly* by containing the growth of the money supply.

However, a credit squeeze needs to be efficient and fair. It might be seen as unfair, for example, to restrict banks from giving more credit if similar restrictions are not also placed on non-bank financial institutions that also give credit.

The exchange rate as a target of monetary policy

3.31 A government might have a target for the foreign exchange rate for the domestic currency, as a target of monetary policy.

3.32 If the exchange rate falls, exports become cheaper to overseas buyers and so more competitive in export markets. Imports will become more expensive and so less competitive against goods produced by manufacturers at home.

A fall in the exchange rate might therefore be good for a domestic economy, by giving a stimulus to exports and reducing demand for imports. An increase in the exchange rate will have the opposite effect, with dearer exports and cheaper imports.

3.33 A problem with an exchange rate policy is that the effect of a change in a currency's exchange rate on the value of a country's exports and imports also depends on the price elasticity of demand for both exports in foreign markets and imports in domestic markets. It is conceivable that a fall in the exchange rate could worsen the balance of payments position rather than improve it.

3.34 A further severe problem with exchange rate policy is that:

(a) one country's government, on its own, has a restricted practical capacity to do much to influence its exchange rate, although *concerted intervention in the foreign exchange markets by several countries*, to bring about a currency realignment or to stabilise exchange rates, can be potent, in the short term at least;

(b) but although intervention by governments to influence exchange rates might work in the short term:

(i) it is unlikely to work on its own in the longer term, if target exchange rates differ from the 'economic realities' of the markets and international economies;

(ii) intervention might have to be very large if it is to be effective.

3.35 An important feature of exchange rate policy is that if *all major trading countries of the world* try to stabilise their exchange rates, international trade is likely to benefit and grow more quickly. More international trade is likely to be good for all countries.

Growth in national income itself as a target of monetary policy

3.36 The authorities might set targets for the level of national income in the economy. For example, the policy might be for the growth in the national income (or GNP or GDP) to be X% per annum for Y years. Policy tools for achieving these targets might be control of the money stock, interest rates or credit. However, it takes time to collect information about national income, whereas targets of monetary policy should be items for which statistical data can be collected regularly and easily.

For this reason, although a target growth rate in national income itself might seem to be the most suitable target of monetary policy, it is the least practical because the authorities would always be working with out-of-date information.

The inter-relationship between targets: the money supply and interest rate targets

3.37 If the government does select targets for the money stock, interest rates, credit and the exchange rate, these targets could not be set independently because the growth of the money stock, interest rates, credit and the exchange rate are all interdependent.

3.38 The authorities (the government and the central bank) can set intermediate targets for the growth of the money supply, but to achieve their targets of growth it will be necessary to allow interest rates to adjust to a level at which the demand for money matches the size of the money supply. For example, a policy to cut the growth of the money supply might result in higher real interest rates.

3.39 Alternatively, the authorities might set targets for the level of interest rates. If they do so, they must allow whatever demand for money there is to be met at that rate of interest by allowing the money supply to meet the demand. If they did not, interest rates would then rise above or fall below the target level.

3.40 This means that the authorities can set a target for the money supply or a target for interest rates, but they cannot practicably set independent targets for both at the same time.

The inter-relationship between interest rates and the exchange rate

3.41 As already mentioned the level of interest rates also influences the exchange rate. High interest rates in the UK for example will attract foreign investors into buying sterling denominated securities, and this will bring capital inflows into the UK and so help to strengthen sterling. On the other hand, a policy of low interest rates would encourage investors to pull out of sterling and invest elsewhere, and so weaken sterling.

3.42 Having decided on the intermediate policy targets to pursue, a government must formulate detailed plans for putting the policies into effect. There will be a choice of different policy 'instruments' which might be selected.

Instruments of monetary policy

3.43 A government will set monetary policy targets. But having set a target or targets, how do they set about achieving them? The *techniques* or *instruments* available to the authorities to achieve their targets for monetary policies include:

    (a) changing the level and/or structure of interest rates.
    (b) fiscal policy.
    (c) reserve requirements.
    (d) direct controls, which might be either:

        (i)   quantitative; or
        (ii) qualitative.

    (e) exchange rate controls.

9: TECHNIQUES FOR CONTROLLING THE ECONOMY

Control over the level and structure of interest rates

3.44 When the government uses interest rates as an instrument of policy, it can try to influence either the general level of interest rates or the term structure of interest rates. It could do this by influencing:

(a) *short term interest rates*. In the UK, this is done through the Bank of England's direct participation in the money markets ('open market operations');

(b) *long term interest rates*. This could possibly be done by increasing or reducing the public sector borrowing requirement (PSBR), and so through the government's fiscal policy.

3.45 Influencing interest rates might have one of several policy aims.

(a) High interest rates might be seen as a requirement for controlling consumer spending, so as to keep down the rate of inflation.

(b) Interest rate changes might be used to achieve the government's target levels for the exchange rate. Higher interest rates will attract more investors into buying sterling, and so keep up the exchange rate.

(c) Interest rate 'control' has also been used as a method of trying to control the growth in the money supply, although the effects of controlling short-term interest rates on money supply growth are not easy to identify.

Fiscal policy as an instrument of monetary policy

3.46 Fiscal policy, as we have seen, refers to the government's policy on public expenditure and taxation. Fiscal policy can work in co-operation with monetary policy. For example, a fiscal policy of reducing government expenditure and cutting the PSBR will have the effect of reducing the growth in the broad money aggregate M4.

A major weakness of fiscal policy *as an instrument of monetary policy* is that most aspects of fiscal policy change only once a year, at Budget time, and so for much of the year, the monetary authorities must take fiscal conditions as given.

3.47 The government usually has expenditure in excess of revenues and so in most years, the government borrows.

(a) The additional borrowing each year is the PSBR.
(b) The total cumulative debt of the country is the National Debt.

3.48 The government might wish to reduce the PSBR, as a monetary policy target. A reason for wanting to reduce the PSBR could be because the government wants to cut its spending and reduce the role of government in the economy, leaving the performance of the economy to 'free market forces'.

3.49 The PSBR could be reduced by:

(a) cutting government expenditure; or
(b) raising tax revenues.

Reserve requirements on banks as a means of controlling the money supply

3.50 As another technique for controlling money supply growth, the government might impose reserve requirements on banks. One type of reserve requirement is a compulsory minimum cash reserve ratio (ie ratio of cash to total assets).

3.51 Another form of reserve requirement is that banks should have a minimum ratio of *reserve assets* to total deposits. Reserve assets are types of short term liquid assets, and by insisting that banks hold a certain proportion of these assets in their asset portfolios, the authorities would hope to reduce the volume of bank loans and therefore the volume of bank deposits.

Direct controls as a technique of monetary control

3.52 Yet another way of controlling the growth of the money supply is to impose direct controls on bank lending. Direct controls may be of two kinds:

(a) *Quantitative controls* might be imposed on either bank lending (assets) or bank deposits (liabilities).

For example, the government might put 'lending ceilings' on the clearing banks which restrict the growth of the banks' lending (assets). For example, banks might be forbidden to increase their lending by more than, say, 5% per annum.

(b) *Qualitative controls* might be used to alter the *type* of lending by banks.

For example, the government (via the Bank of England) can ask the banks to limit their lending to the personal sector, and lend more to industry, or to lend less to a particular type of firm (such as, for example, property companies) and more to manufacturing businesses.

Prudential controls

3.53 Prudential control refers to the oversight of banks and other financial institutions by the authorities to ensure that they have an adequate capital structure, liquidity (asset portfolio) and/or foreign exchange exposure.

3.54 The prudential control by the Bank of England as a supervisor of the banking system belongs to a grey area between quantitative and qualitative controls. Prudential controls are not used directly to control the money supply but they might have some indirect influence and so it is useful to mention them here.

Interest rates as the main instrument of monetary policy in the UK

3.55 In a speech, reported in the Bank of England Quarterly Bulletin in August 1986, the Governor of the Bank of England said that there are *practical limits* to the extent to which reliance can be placed on:

(a) government funding and
(b) exchange rate intervention,

as well as limits to their effectiveness. In other words, exchange rate policy and funding policy are not altogether effective instruments of monetary control.

4.   IMPLICATIONS OF MONETARY POLICY FOR BUSINESS

4.1   Unlike the annual fiscal policy announcement, monetary policy is carried out continuously, in part by the Bank of England acting on the Government's behalf. Monetary targets are announced as part of the Chancellor's Budget statement, but the implementation of policy is more flexible than fiscal alternatives.

4.2   The implications for business of the government's monetary policy can be seen only too clearly when looking back over the years from 1988 to 1990.

4.3   The high interest rate policy of the government has had a twofold impact on business:

(a)   it increases costs of borrowing making servicing existing variable-rate debts more expensive for businesses and reducing their ability and propensity to invest;

(b)   it hits customer purchasing power. High mortgage rates left the customers in certain market segments very little disposable income and reduced the attractiveness of shopping with credit. There was the additional indirect effect on some markets, such as consumer durables and household furnishings, that the slump in the housing market resulting from high interest rates reduced demand for items which householders need to buy when they move house.

4.4   As with fiscal policy, marketers need to be alert to government intentions for monetary policy and need to analyse the impact of changes on their target customers.

4.5   Monetary policy decisions also affect the exchange rate and therefore the price of international products. This effect is crucial to many businesses. Raw materials are often priced in the US dollar, a currency which fluctuates in value against European currencies.

5.   CONCLUSION

5.1   The key points in this chapter are as follows.

(a)   Fiscal policy seeks to influence the economy by managing the amounts which the government spends and the amounts it collects through taxation. Fiscal policy can be used as an instrument of demand management.

(b)   Taxation has effects which a government may wish to create in order to promote its policy aims - for example, a redistribution of income or wealth - as well as providing a means of 'fine tuning' the economy.

(c)   A government may use monetary policies to pursue its economic aims. It will do so by setting 'intermediate' targets, for interest rate levels, growth in the money supply, the exchange rate or growth in bank lending and so on.

(d) Tools for implementing monetary policy include influence over interest rates, fiscal policy, exchange rate policy, and the regulation of banks and other financial institutions.

(e) Governments can only influence economic activity through either fiscal or monetary policy. Most governments will therefore use a combination of techniques.

(f) At the microeconomic level, changes in macroeconomic policy can have significant effects on:

    (i)   price of goods
    (ii)   the availability of credit
    (iii)   the disposable incomes of customers
    (iv)   the costs of borrowing.

(g) It follows that marketers need to take government policy into account when developing their own strategies.

TEST YOUR KNOWLEDGE

The numbers in brackets refer to paragraphs of this chapter

1   What are the main macroeconomic objectives which government economic policy is generally concerned with? (1.1)

2   What have been the major changes in the government's attitude to fiscal policy over the last 20 years? (1.14)

3   What are the main advantages and disadvantages of a progressive tax? (1.19, 1.20)

4   How can we calculate how the burden of an indirect tax will be shared between producer and consumer? (2.3, 2.4)

5   What is monetary policy? (3.3)

6   What do monetarists believe causes inflation? (3.6)

7   Why is a number of monetary aggregates necessary? (3.14 - 3.16)

8   What sorts of monetary targets might a government adopt? (3.19)

9   What are the techniques or instruments available to the government to help achieve monetary targets? (3.43)

10   Outline the main implications of monetary policy for business. (4.3 - 4.5)

Now try illustrative questions 16, 17 and 18 at the end of the text

Chapter 10

EMPLOYMENT, INFLATION AND GROWTH

This chapter covers the following topics.

1. Inflation
2. Unemployment
3. Inflation and unemployment: the Phillips curve
4. Economic growth
5. Demand management and supply side economics

---

1. INFLATION

1.1 As we have seen earlier in this part of the text, Keynes identified that left alone, the economy would go through the cyclical swings of the trade cycle, which bring with it the economic problems of unemployment, inflation, lack of growth and an unstable balance of payments.

1.2 Government can adopt policies to tackle these issues but it needs to be remembered that:

(a) policy instruments are imprecise;

(b) there are unpredictable time lags in the system;

(c) policies to improve one problem area can aggravate others (for example, reflationary policies to stimulate employment can lead to higher inflation);

(d) the government needs to be concerned with a balanced economic picture and also has to consider the impact of domestic policy on our international economic position;

(e) although ideally governments would like to solve all economic problems simultaneously, in reality they will prioritise their economic objectives. Before the late 1970s the UK government's priority was to achieve full employment; throughout the 1980s and early 1990s it has been to tackle *inflation*.

Inflation can be defined as a general and persistent rise in money prices (or as a fall in the value of money).

Why is inflation undesirable?

1.3 The disadvantages of inflation can be summarised as follows:

(a) it causes hardship for people with relatively fixed incomes, since the real value of their income falls;

(b) it can disrupt firms' investment plans if they are unable to predict their future cash flows and interest rates;

(c) there are structural and organisational costs associated with frequent price changes, eg re-printing price lists and labels;

(d) inflation can bring benefits to borrowers but disadvantages to lenders since the value of the debt will fall in line with inflation (the financial institutions of the City of London are among the strongest supporters of anti-inflation policy);

(e) if people have different expectations of inflation, distortions may arise in wage bargaining;

(f) if inflation is unpredictable the government may find macro-economic control more difficult. In extreme cases, economic instability can lead to political instability;

(g) higher inflation in one country without a compensating adjustment in foreign exchange rates will make exports more expensive to foreign buyers and thus dampen export trading;

(h) higher inflation in one country will affect the foreign exchange rate for that country's currency and the expectations of further inflation may also have the effect of undermining confidence in the economy and deterring international trade.

Inflation and the functions of money

1.4 Inflation interferes with the functions of money. We can consider the four different functions of money. Money acts as:

(a) a means of exchange;
(b) a unit of account;
(c) a standard of deferred payment; and
(d) a store of value.

1.5 *Money as a means of exchange*
This is the most important function of money in an economy, because without money, the only way of exchanging goods and services would be by means of *barter*, by a *direct exchange* of goods or services. During periods of high inflation, sometimes referred to as hyper-inflation, people can become unwilling to accept money in exchange for goods and so the economy can revert to a commodity money or barter economy. This occurred widely in Germany during the 1930s, when cigarettes became adopted as a medium of exchange.

1.6 *Money as a unit of account*

This function of money is associated with the use of money as a means of exchange. Money should be able to measure exactly what something is worth. It should provide an agreed standard measure by which the *value* of different goods and services can be compared. During periods of inflation the fluctuations in the value of money prevent it from performing this function adequately.

1.7 *Money as a standard of deferred payment*

When a person buys a good or service, he might not want to pay for it straight away, perhaps because he has not yet got the money. Instead, he might ask for credit. Selling goods on credit is not an essential feature of an economy, but it certainly helps to stimulate trade. The function of money in this respect is to establish, by agreement between buyer and seller, how much value will be given in return at some future date for goods provided/received now. Similarly, when a buyer and seller agree now to make a contract for the supply of certain goods in the future, the function of money is to establish the value of the contract, ie how much the buyer will eventually pay the seller for the goods.

1.8 In order to provide an acceptable standard for deferred payments, it is important that money should maintain its value over a period of time. Suppose, for example, that a customer buys goods for an agreed sum of money, but on three months' credit. Now if the value of money falls in the three-month credit period, the sum of money which the seller eventually receives will be worth less than it was at the time of sale. The seller will have lost value by allowing the credit.

1.9 When inflation is high, sellers:

(a) will be reluctant to allow credit to buyers. For example, if a buyer asks for three months credit and inflation is running at 20% inflation, the 'real' value of the debt that the buyer owes will fall by about 5% over the 3 month credit period;

(b) will be reluctant to agree to a fixed price for long term contracts. For example, a house-builder might refuse to quote a price for building a house over a twelve month period, and instead insist on asking a price which is 'index-linked' and rises in step with the general rate of inflation.

(c) may choose to hold on to assets in the hope of making a speculative gain. For example, in a period of high house price inflation, sellers hold on to properties in the hope of selling them at even more inflated prices in the future.

1.10 *Money as a store of value*

Money acts as a store of value, or wealth. So too do many other assets (eg land, buildings, art treasures, bank deposit accounts and index linked securities).

Not all assets which act as a store of value will be included in a definition of money. Money is more properly described as acting as a *liquid* store of value. This definition has two parts to it.

(a)   Money is a store of value or wealth. A person can hold money in the *certainty* that its value does not fall and that it will have the same exchange value in the future that it does now, in 'normal' terms at least - ignoring inflation.

(b)   Money is a liquid asset.

1.11 The erosion of the value of money due to inflation provides one good reason why someone with wealth to store should hold assets which are *not* cash.

Can inflation ever be acceptable?

1.12 For the reasons explained above it is recognised that inflation is a serious economic problem, which the government should tackle. Yet, when the cost of reducing or controlling inflation is higher unemployment it is reasonable to ask whether the benefits of counter-inflation policy outweighs its costs.

1.13 Could we not live happily with a particular rate of inflation? If the inflation rate was positive but unchanging, this rate could be built in to all economic decision making. (Some commentators take the view that an inflation rate of 2% per year is to be expected in any case as a reflection of improvements to products, so we are thinking here of an inflation rate above this level.) But the danger is that inflation may accelerate, and if this raises *expectations* of still higher inflation, wage demands may escalate and there could be a 'wage-price spiral'. It is very easy for governments to lose control of inflation rates, particularly if they take a short term view.

The causes of inflation

1.14 As already indicated, different schools of economic thought take different approaches to identifying the causes of inflation.

1.15 As we have already seen, Keynesian analysis demonstrated that inflation is a result of too much demand in the economy.

Figure 1
Inflationary gap

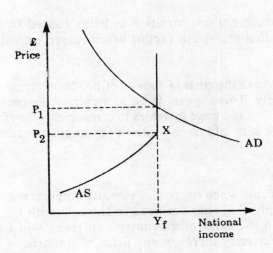

(a) At the full employment level of national income, the AS curve rises vertically, because real output levels are at a maximum, and any increase in demand will result in higher prices, but no more output.

(b) Equilibrium national income might be at the full employment level of national income, but with aggregate demand so strong that price levels are higher than they ought to be. This is shown in Figure 1, where price levels are at P_1 but could be lower at P_2.

(c) According to Keynesian economists, inflation can be virtually eliminated by achieving a downward shift in to the left in the AD curve.

(d) An inflationary gap is the amount by which aggregate demand must be reduced to squeeze inflation out of the economy. This could be done by shifting AD so that it passes through point X in Figure 1.

1.16 A number of factors have been recognised as general causes of inflation:

(a) Demand-pull factors;
(b) Cost-push factors;
(c) Import-cost factors;
(d) Expectations.

1.17 *Demand-pull inflation* occurs when the economy is buoyant and there is high aggregate demand which is in excess of the economy's ability to supply.

(a) Because aggregate demand exceeds supply, prices rise.

(b) Since supply needs to be raised to meet the higher demand, there will be an increase in demand for factors of production, and so factor rewards (wages, interest rates, and so on) will also rise.

(c) Since aggregate demand exceeds the output capability of the economy, it should follow that demand-pull inflation can only exist when unemployment is low. A feature of inflation in the UK in the 1970s and early 1980s, however, was high inflation coupled with high unemployment.

Traditionally Keynesian economists saw inflation as being caused by demand-pull factors. However, they now accept that cost-push factors are involved as well.

1.18 *Cost-push inflation* occurs where the costs of factors of production rise regardless of whether or not they are in short supply. This appears to be particularly the case with wages: workers anticipate inflation rates and demand wage increases to compensate, thus initiating a wage-price spiral. Interest rate rises can also add to the rate of inflation, because mortgage costs will rise.

1.19 *Import cost-push inflation* occurs when the cost of essential imports rise regardless of whether or not they are in short supply. This has occurred in the past with the oil price rises of the 1970s. Additionally, a fall in the value of a country's currency will have import cost-push effects since a weakening currency increases the price of imports.

1.20 A further problem is that once the rate of inflation has begun to increase, the serious danger of *'expectational inflation'* will arise. Regardless of whether the factors that have caused inflation are still persistent or not, there can arise a generally held view of what inflation is likely to be. To protect future income, wages and prices will be raised now by the expected amount of future inflation, leading to a 'wage-price spiral', in which inflation becomes a relatively permanent feature because of people's expectations that it will occur.

1.21 Monetarists argue that inflation is caused by *increases in the supply of money*. There is considerable debate as to whether increases in the money supply are a *cause* of inflation or whether increases in the money supply are a *symptom* of inflation. The monetarists argue that since inflation is caused by an increase in the money supply, inflation can be brought under control by reducing the rate of growth of the money supply.

1.22 The monetarist school of thought believes that inflation can only ever have one cause - an excessively rapid increase in the money supply. Inflation occurs when the government allows the amount of purchasing power in the economy to expand faster than economic output is increasing. Based on the quantity theory of money, any changes in M and V which are not compensated for by T must result in changes in the price level. Remember that:

$$MV = PT$$

1.23 Friedman recognises that there are a number of factors which can cause pressure on the money supply, including demand pull and cost push factors. However, as he points out, consumers always want more goods and workers always want higher wages, and business is also recognised in economic theory as seeking to maximise its profits. The question is why does this on some occasions lead to inflation and on other occasions not. Monetarists are clear that inflation only occurs if the government allows the money supply to grow. Therefore inflation always has a monetary cause.

Control of inflation

1.24 Over the years, different governments have resorted to a variety of anti-inflation policies. Their choice has been mainly influenced by their analysis of the main causes of inflation. In the 1960s and 1970s, prices and incomes policies of various sorts were tried in the UK. After 1979, the government mainly sought to reduce money supply growth, as government economic thinking has favoured Friedman's view of the economy over the demand management policies advocated by Keynes.

ANTI-INFLATION POLICIES

Perceived cause of inflation	*Policy to control inflation*
• Demand-pull - ie high consumer demand	• Take steps to reduce demand in the economy, perhaps by
	o Higher taxation, to cut consumer income and spending
	o Lower government expenditure (and lower government borrowing to finance its expenditure)
	o Higher interest rates
• Cost-push factors - ie higher wage costs and other costs working through to higher prices	• Take steps to reduce production costs and price rises
	o Encourage greater productivity in industry
	o Apply controls over wage and price rises (prices and incomes policy)
• Import-cost-push factors	• Take steps to reduce the quantities or the price of imports. Such a policy might involve trying to achieve either an appreciation or depreciation of the domestic currency
• Excessively fast growth in the money supply	• Take steps to try to reduce the rate of money supply growth, perhaps by
	o Cutting the Public Sector Borrowing Requirement
	o Funding the PSBR by borrowing from the non-bank private sector
	o Trying to control or reduce bank lending
	o Trying to achieve a balance of trade surplus
	o Maintaining interest rates at a level that might deter money supply growth
• Expectations of inflation	• Pursue clear policies which indicate the government's determination to reduce the rate of inflation

High interest rates and inflation

1.25 A government may adopt a policy of high interest rates to try to reduce the rate of inflation, when inflation is being caused by a boom in consumer demand (ie with demand rising faster than the ability of industry to increase its output to meet the demand).

    (a) When mortgage rates go up, there will be an initial increase in the rate of inflation as measured by the Retail Prices Index, because mortgage interest payments are included in the RPI.

    (b) If interest rates are high enough, there should eventually be a reduction in the rate of growth in consumer spending. This reduction should occur because:

        (i) people who borrow must pay more in interest out of their income. This will leave them less income, after paying the interest, to spend on other things. (The government would not want wages to rise, though, because if people build up their income again with high wage settlements, the consumer spending boom could continue);

        (ii) high interest rates might deter people from borrowing, and so there would be less spending with borrowed funds;

        (iii) high interest rates should encourage more saving, with individuals therefore spending less of their income on consumption;

        (iv) high interest rates will tend to depress the values of non-monetary assets, such as houses, and the reduction in people's perceived wealth may make people feel 'poorer' and consequently reduce the amounts they spend on consumer goods.

1.26 From 1988, when a high interest rate policy became the UK government's main monetary policy weapon, to 1990, the Chancellors of the Exchequer repeatedly stated that interest rates would have to remain as high as was necessary for as long as necessary to control inflation.

Prices and incomes policy

1.27 The first prices and incomes policy was introduced in Britain by the then prime minister, Harold Macmillan, in 1962. There have been several attempts to find a successful policy since then, the last being the 'social contract' of the late 1980s under the Labour government of James Callaghan.

1.28 If prices but not wages are controlled the results would be:

    (a) a profit squeeze; and/or
    (b) a rise in unemployment, with firms shedding labour in order to remain profitable.

This suggests that wages ought to be kept under control as well as prices. This would be particularly important if wage rises are a major cause of cost-push inflation.

1.29 A prices and incomes policy is likely to be treated as a temporary policy. Once it has succeeded in reducing the rate of inflation, it will be eased or removed entirely. There are some economists however who believe that some form of prices and incomes control ought to be applied permanently. In the past, prices and incomes policies have put a lid on price pressure, but have not tackled the underlying causes. When the policies have been relaxed, there has tended to be an explosion of pent-up price rises and wage demands. A further difficulty with a prices and incomes policy is that of enforcement.

Deflationary policies

1.30 The alternative range of deflationary demand-reducing policies advocated by Keynes have the high social cost of unemployment attached to them. High levels of unemployment may also have a high political cost in that they make the political party in power unpopular.

2. UNEMPLOYMENT

Unemployment and its consequences

2.1 Unemployment can be defined as the number of people able and willing to work who cannot find full-time employment.

    (a) Over recent years government has made a number of modifications to the calculation of the unemployment statistics, making it difficult to confirm the precise trend of unemployment over the last decade.

    (b) The official unemployment figures are understated because of people wanting to work, but for some reason ineligible to register, for example, those working part-time but willing to work full-time.

    (c) On the other hand figures are overstated by those registering as unemployed, but who are working in the black or shadow economy and therefore not declaring their earnings.

2.2 Unemployment results in the following.

    (a) *Loss of output:* if labour is unemployed, the economy is not producing as much output as it could. Thus, total national income is less than it could be.

    (b) *Loss of 'human capital' - ie labour skills:* labour skills are sometimes called 'human capital'. If there is unemployment, the unemployed labour will gradually lose its skills, because skills can only be maintained by working. The country's stock of human capital will be depleted.

    (c) *Increasing inequalities in the distribution of income:* unemployed people earn less than employed people, and so when unemployment is increasing, the poor get poorer.

    (d) *Social costs:* unemployment brings social problems of personal suffering and distress, and possibly also increases in crime such as theft and vandalism.

There will always be at least a certain *natural rate of unemployment,* which is the minimum level of unemployment that an economy can expect to achieve. A major aim of government policy could be to reduce unemployment to this minimum natural rate, and so get as close as possible to the goal of 'full' employment.

Causes and cures for unemployment

2.3 There is no single cause for unemployment and policies may have to be developed to tackle the variety of types of unemployment:

    (a) cyclical unemployment
    (b) structural unemployment
    (c) frictional unemployment
    (d) seasonal unemployment
    (e) technological unemployment.

2.4 *Cyclical unemployment*
This was the unemployment which Keynes identified as being caused by the fluctuations in economic activity associated with the trade cycle. Resulting from a deflationary gap, policies to reflate or add demand to the economy could be used to tackle such unemployment.

Figure 2
Deflationary gap

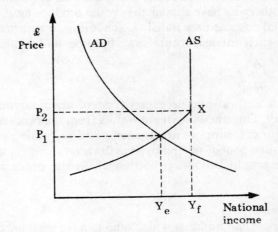

(a) Equilibrium national income might be at a level of national income which is below the full employment level of national income Y_f. This is shown as output/national income level Y_e in Figure 2. There will be unemployed resources in the economy to the extent that Y_e is less than Y_f.

(b) According to Keynesian economists, unemployment can be reduced by giving a boost to aggregate demand, so that the AD curve shifts to the right.

(c) If AD can be shifted to the right so that it goes through point X, full employment national income can be achieved. A deflationary gap is the amount by which aggregate demand must be increased to produce the full employment level of national income.

(d) In order to close the deflationary gap, so as to achieve full employment national income, there will have to be some increase in price levels - ie inflation - from P_1 to P_2.

2.5 *Structural unemployment*
Structural unemployment is the result of a decrease in the demand for an industry's output. This may be the result of new products having been produced to replace the good, or as a result of increased competition for other producing nations, as in the cases of shipbuilding and textiles in the UK. As demand for the goods decreases, so demand for those employed in their production decreases, leaving 'pockets' of a population unemployed. If firms in the same industry had tended to locate in the same area attracted by the economic advantages of the location or the

external economies of scale available, so these pockets of unemployed are concentrated geographically, resulting in regional unemployment. The effect of the decline of the traditional labour-intensive industries of Britain were intensified by a local multiplier effect. If the local factory closes down, so the local shops and pubs will suffer reduced sales and in turn lay people off.

2.6 Government tackles structural unemployment through its regional economic policy. There are really only two alternatives:

(a) take work to the people, through subsidies and incentives to attract new industry and employment opportunities to an area;

(b) assist people in moving to where the work is.

2.7 The first option involves economic costs, because firms are being encouraged to operate in an area they would not otherwise have chosen: they could produce more cheaply elsewhere. The second option involves social costs as new housing, schooling, transport etc has to be provided in the growth area whilst such infrastructure may become under-utilised in depressed areas.

2.8 *Frictional unemployment*
This may be seen as a 'natural' and necessary form of unemployment and essential to a dynamic and growing economy. This unemployment results from the process of people changing work and location. Government can support job agencies and retraining programmes to speed up such transitions, but without a pool of unemployed to draw on firms cannot grow and expand. A lack of available workforce would become a bottleneck in the process of economic growth.

2.9 *Seasonal unemployment*
In industries like tourism and building which tend to have seasonal demand patterns, employment also tends to be seasonal. Developing new industry with complementary demand patterns is the only real policy which can be adopted externally to tackle this unemployment. However within the firms or industry, marketing techniques might be used to spread demand and so even out employment trends.

2.10 *Technological unemployment*
This is unemployment which is caused when labour is replaced by capital, usually as a result of technological development. This has been a major reason for unemployment since the Industrial Revolution and it still causes the same short term dislocation of work opportunities in a sector as it did in earlier times. A relatively recent example is the impact of new technology on the newspaper industry.

2.11 Technological development increases output, so the total goods available to the community is greater. The difficulty arises from ensuring that everyone gets a share of those goods. Skill shortages may arise as new technologies require a more highly skilled workforce. If the new technology eventually results in *everyone* working less, more holidays, a shorter working week and earlier retirement, then we would want to say that there is an improved standard of living.

2.12 In essence, we have redefined full employment. Fifty years ago in the UK full time work meant 50 working weeks a year, 45 hours a week and starting work at 14 years old. Now a working life is from age 16 to 65, 45 weeks per year, and around 38 hours a week. These changes take time, but do represent a long run way of dealing with fundamental shifts in employment opportunities.

Note also that new technologies have in the past generated new job opportunities themselves, such as the expansion of the computer services industry as a result of the 'microchip revolution'.

2.13 In conclusion, governments need to develop a package of policies to tackle the complex causes of unemployment in a developed economy.

3. INFLATION AND UNEMPLOYMENT: THE PHILLIPS CURVE

3.1 As we have already seen, inflation and unemployment appear to be problems which cannot easily be solved simultaneously. Policies to solve one often aggravate the other and in the past governments have tended to make a choice between them based on their political and economic priorities.

The Phillips curve

3.2 A W Phillips discovered (1958) a statistical relationship between unemployment and the rate of wage inflation which implied that, in general, the rate of inflation fell as unemployment rose and vice versa. A curve, known as a Phillips curve, can be drawn linking inflation and unemployment.

Figure 3
Phillips curve

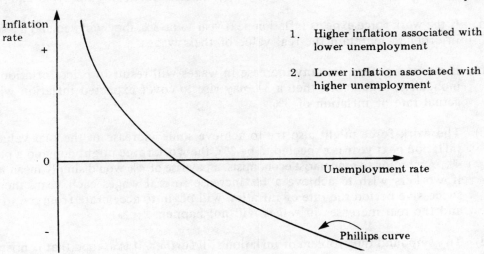

1. Higher inflation associated with lower unemployment

2. Lower inflation associated with higher unemployment

3.3 You should be able to draw and explain this curve. Two points should be noted about the Phillips curve.

(a) The curve crosses the horizontal axis at a positive value for the unemployment rate. This means that zero inflation will be associated with some unemployment; it is not possible to achieve zero inflation and zero unemployment at the same time.

(b) The shape of the curve (concave) means that the lower the level of unemployment, the higher the rate of increase in inflation.

3.4 The existence of a relationship between inflation and unemployment of the type indicated by the Phillips curve suggests that the government should be able to choose some point on the curve, according to its preference, and use demand management policies to take the economy to that point - ie to 'strike a balance' between acceptable levels of inflation and unemployment.

This re-emphasises the argument of Keynesian economists that in order to achieve full employment, some inflation is unavoidable. If achieving full employment is an economic policy objective, a government must therefore be prepared to accept a certain level of inflation as a necessary 'evil'.

3.5 However, the Phillips curve relationship between inflation and unemployment broke down at the end of the 1960s when Britain began to experience rising inflation at the same time as rising unemployment. In other words, the new curve seemed to be *upward* sloping.

Inflationary expectations: refinements to the Phillips curve

3.6 An explanation of rising inflation rates combined with rising unemployment was put forward based on inflationary expectations. This 'natural rate hypothesis' is supported by monetarist economists.

3.7 Inflationary expectations involve the rates of inflation that is expected in the future. The inflationary expectations of the work force will be reflected in the level of wage rises that is demanded in the annual round of pay negotiations between employers and workers.

(a) If the work force expects inflation next year to be 3%, they will demand a 3% wage increase in order to maintain the real value of their wages.

(b) If we now accept that any increase in wages will result in price inflation (which is the monetarist argument), then a 3% pay rise to cover expected inflation will result in an actual rate of inflation of 3%.

(c) The work force might also try to achieve some increase in the real value of wages. If inflation next year is expected to be 3%, the work force might demand a pay rise of, say, 4%. According to monetarist economists, a pay rise of 4% would simply mean inflation of 4%. If workers wish to achieve a 1% increase in real wages each year, then during each successive period the rate of inflation will begin to accelerate from 5% to 6% to 7% etc, and the real increases in wages will not happen.

(d) To compound the problem of inflation still further, it is argued that if mistakes are made over expectations, then money wages will be adjusted upwards next period in order to rectify the mistake made last period.

(i) For example, in one year the work force might expect inflation to be 3%, and so demand a 3% increase in wages. If this is achieved, but the actual rate of inflation during the year is 5%, the work force will try to put things right. They will demand a 2% pay increase, just to cover the 'lost ground' last year, as well as an increase to cover expected inflation next year.

(ii)   It follows that if expected inflation next year is 5%, the pay demand will be 7% (plus any demand for an increase in the value of wages). If a 7% pay rise is granted, inflation will go up to 7% pa.

(e)   Any 'external' factor (such as increases in the prices of imported goods, or higher indirect taxes) which may lead wage earners to expect higher prices in the near future will of course result in even higher wage claims.

Many economists believe that events in the UK from about 1967 well into the 1970s followed a sequence of events not unlike that described above.

The natural rate hypothesis

3.8   The natural rate hypothesis incorporates these views on inflationary expectations, to produce a refinement of the Phillips curve.

3.9   Suppose that the economy is characterised by the Phillips curve PC₁ in Figure 4. Initially say, that is an unemployment rate of 4% and zero price and wage inflation.

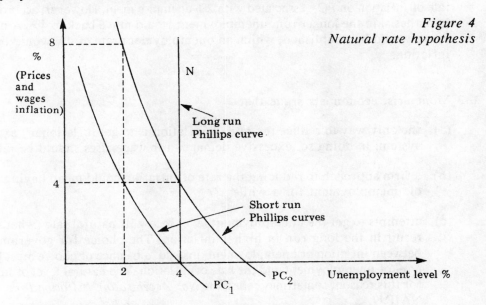

Figure 4
Natural rate hypothesis

(a)   Suppose now that the government expands aggregate demand so as to reduce unemployment to, say, 2% of the labour force. There is a movement along the Phillips curve, and the new unemployment level turns out to be associated with 4% inflation.

(b)   As employers realise that they are paying higher wages as well as receiving higher prices, and as workers realise that the real value of their wages has not risen, the unemployment rate rises to 4% again.

(c)   But in the meantime the period of positive inflation has generated inflationary expectations and 4% unemployment is now associated with 4% inflation, because the Phillips curve has shifted from PC₁ to PC₂.

3.10 In effect, the *short-run* Phillips curve has shifted outwards from PC_1 to PC_2 in Figure 4.

Monetarist economists state that the *long-run* Phillips curve is vertical at the *natural rate of unemployment.*

In our example, monetarists would claim that the long-run Phillips curve is NN in Figure 4 so that there is a natural unemployment rate of 4%. (*Note:* this figure of 4% is hypothetical only.)

3.11 In the long run, unemployment will revert towards its natural level. The rate of inflation, however, will be determined by the short run Phillips curve, which will shift upwards as inflationary expectations increase.

The distinction between short and long-run Phillips curves can help explain the observation that in Britain unemployment and inflation have often both risen at the same time.

3.12 To check whether you understand this point, suppose that the short run Phillips curve is now PC_2 in Figure 4, with unemployment at 4% and inflation 4% pa. What would happen if the government now took measures to reduce unemployment to 2%? Inflation would rise to about 8%, which is the rate of inflation on PC_2 associated with 2% unemployment. However, according to the natural rate hypothesis, in the longer run, unemployment would move back to 4%. A new short run Phillips curve would be established, which an unemployment rate of 4% would be associated with 8% inflation.

3.13 Monetarist economists argue that:

(a) the only way to reduce the rate of inflation is to get inflationary expectations out of the system. In doing so, excessive demands for wage rises should be resisted by employers;

(b) a firm approach to reducing the rate of inflation could mean having to accept high levels of unemployment for a while;

(c) attempts to get the unemployment level below its natural rate (whatever this is) will only result in the long run in higher inflation. The choice for government is therefore *not* between inflation or unemployment; instead, a balance or choice must be made between the *level* of unemployment and the *rate* of inflation. The natural level of unemployment is now, for this reason, sometimes called the *Non Accelerating Inflation Rate of Unemployment* or NAIRU.

4. ECONOMIC GROWTH

What is economic growth?

4.1 Economic growth may be measured by increases in the 'real' Gross National Product per head of the population.

(a) Measuring 'real' GNP removes increases in GNP caused solely by price inflation.

(b) Increases in the average standard of living of a population could be measured by GNP per head of population. If a country's GNP is rising by, say, 3% pa but the population is also increasing by 3% pa, it would be concluded that the increase in living standards in the country is really zero.

(c) Remember, though, that national income statistics are not altogether reliable, for reasons described in the earlier chapter on national income.

4.2 However, it is not unusual to find economic growth measured simply as increases in total GNP, regardless of inflation and changes in population size.

4.3 Economic growth may be:

(a) *balanced:* ie all sectors of the economy expand together; or

(b) *unbalanced:* eg there may be a specialisation in areas of the economy where there is a comparative advantage so that some sectors of the economy grow faster than others.

4.4 Less developed countries (LDCs) in particular find it difficult to achieve economic growth, because many of the factors necessary for growth are absent in these countries.

Factors needed for economic growth

4.5 *Sustained* economic growth depends heavily on an adequate level of new investment.

4.6 Investment is undertaken if there are *expectations* of future growth in demand. Investment is an injection to the circular flow of income. After investment has taken place on the basis of expectations, the level of income will increase by a multiple of that investment (ie with the operation of the multiplier). But there is no reason why the actual level of income should end up increasing as much as the investing business person thought it would. If business people expect a 10% increase in national income (ie an expected growth rate of 10%) and they invest accordingly, and the actual rate of growth turns out to be 15% (or 5%) then it would follow that they had either invested too little (or too much).

It follows that investment, a factor in growth, is dependent on *business confidence* in the future, which is reflected in expectations of growth in consumption.

Natural resources

4.7 The rate of extraction of natural resources will impose a limit on the rate of growth. The problem is analogous to that of labour supply bottlenecks, except that natural resources are *non-renewable*. Production which uses up a country's natural resources, such as oil, coal and other minerals, depletes the stock of available resources; it is therefore in a sense *disinvestment*.

This suggests that the desirable rate of growth is in fact quite low, unless there is technical progress which reduces the use of non-renewable resources or replaces them. For example, if energy needs could only be supplied by oil and coal there would be a strong case for limiting energy use severely; but developments in nuclear and solar technology may be able to provide alternative energy sources.

10: EMPLOYMENT, INFLATION AND GROWTH

Technological progress

4.8 This is a very important source of faster economic growth. Technological progress means that:

(a) the same amounts of the factors of production can produce a higher output;

(b) new products will be developed, thus adding to output growth.

The Industrial Revolution in the West was a period of concentrated technological developments leading to an astounding increase in the rate of growth, which eventually benefited the whole population in the industrialised countries. There are more recent, though less dramatic, examples. Transistors replaced valves, saving energy and materials. We are now seeing the widespread use of microtechnology - the 'microchip revolution'.

4.9 Technological progress provides the means of escaping the physical resource constraints on growth.

There can also be 'technical progress' in the labour force. If workers are better educated and better trained they will be able to produce more. For example, if there is a fault in the production process, a skilled worker will be able to deal with it quickly, whereas an unskilled one might have to call for a superior instead.

4.10 Technological progress has contributed immensely to economic growth and hence to the rise in general living standards.

Technological progress can be divided into three types:

(a) *capital saving:* technical advance that uses less capital and the same amount of labour per unit of output;

(b) *neutral:* technical advances that required labour and capital in the same proportions as before, using less of each unit per output;

(c) *labour-saving:* technical advance that uses less labour and the same amount of capital per unit of output.

4.11 If technological progress is of type (c), then unemployment will rise unless there is either:

(a) a simultaneous expansion of demand; or

(b) a reduction in hours worked by each person, in which case there is no productivity increase associated with the technological progress. It seems likely that policy makers will soon have to face this dilemma, since the growth of world demand is low and high demand would anyway prove impossible because of energy shortages and food shortages.

4.12 Technological progress may therefore stimulate growth, but at the same time create technological unemployment, as we have already seen. A further consequence of this could be that those people in work would benefit from economic growth in the form of higher wages, but those people put out of work by the new technology would be left with a lower income. There is thus a danger that the rich will get richer and the poor will get poorer in spite of economic growth, and this would be regarded by many people as an undesirable development.

4.13 Productivity and technological progress together are two major contributing factors to *economies of scale*, and the development of *mass production industry* has been a feature of much economic growth in the past.

External trade influences on economic growth

4.14 An improvement in the *terms of trade* - the quantity of imports that can be bought in exchange for a given quantity of exports - means that more imports can be bought, or, alternatively, a given volume of exports will earn higher profits. This will boost investment and hence growth.

4.15 The rate of growth of the rest of the world is important for an economy that has a large foreign trade sector. If trading partners have slow growth, the amount of exports a country can sell to them will grow only slowly, and this limits the country's own opportunities for investment and growth.

What other factors promote economic growth?

4.16 For economic growth to occur, there must be a sufficient availability of *factors of production* (of the right quality) and sufficient demand in the market.

   (a) There must be sufficient *labour* skilled in the techniques and technologies of production. The population must therefore be skilled and educated, or at least in a position where they are capable of being trained and willing to learn new skills. There should be sufficient mobility of labour to ensure that available skilled labour will move to the regions where there is a demand for their work.

   (b) There must be sufficient *capital*. The purchase of new capital equipment requires finance, which must be available from retained profits of firms or a well-organised capital market (or, in the case of government investment, from taxation). The rate of interest - the cost of capital - can help to attract or deter business investment.

   (c) *Land* must be available, and there must also be a suitable infrastructure (roads, railways, communications network etc) to support commercial activity.

   (d) The *government's policy* should be to achieve economic growth, because if there is an alternative economic objective (eg restoring a balance of payments equilibrium) government policy might suppress growth.

   (e) *International trade* should be encouraged as a means to growth. This is because international trade opens up markets for exporters, and at the same time allows firms to benefit from economies of scale by supplying to larger markets than they could by selling to domestic customers only.

Advantages and disadvantages of economic growth

4.17 Economic growth should mean that the population as a whole will be able to raise its standard of living in material terms, and that there should also be an improvement in economic welfare. A country with economic growth is more easily able to provide a welfare state service without creating intolerable tax burdens on the community.

4.18 There are possible disadvantages to growth, however.

(a) Growth implies the faster use of the earth's natural resources. Without growth, these resources would last longer.

(b) Much economic activity tends to create pollution (eg acid rain, nuclear waste). It leads to CO_2 emissions which threaten to produce disruptive climatic changes through an increase in the 'greenhouse effect'. It results in more roads, cultivated farmland, new and larger towns, and less unspoilt countryside.

(c) There is a danger that some sections of the population, unable to adapt to the demands for new skills and more training, will not find jobs in the developing economy. This structural unemployment might create a large section of the community which gains no benefit from the increase in national income.

(d) Governments being too ambitious in their growth targets may force the economy into inflation and balance of payments problems. An 'overheated' economy may encounter problems of recession in later years.

How does controlling inflation help the economy to grow?

4.19 Monetarists argue that monetary control will put the brake on inflation, but how does this help the economy? The main reasons are that:

(a) high inflation increases economic uncertainty. Bringing inflation under control will restore business confidence and help international trade by stabilising the exchange rate;

(b) a resurgence of business confidence through lower interest rates (due to less uncertainty and lower inflation) will stimulate investment and real output;

(c) A *controlled* growth in the money supply will provide higher incomes for individuals to purchase the higher output.

5. DEMAND MANAGEMENT AND SUPPLY SIDE ECONOMICS

5.1 It is worth summarising here the Keynesian and monetarist positions.

5.2 Keynesians believe that a depressed economy can be revived by increases in public expenditure (ie through fiscal policy).

By increasing investment, an initial stimulus to expenditure, through the multiplier-accelerator effect, will result in an even bigger increase in national income. If this increased expenditure must be financed by borrowing there will be an increase in the PSBR. Keynesians consider this unimportant:

(a) because the size of the PSBR, they argue, has no effect on interest rates;

(b) because, although it is possible that the PSBR may be responsible for the growth of the money supply, it is not at all certain that an increase in the money supply will lead to higher inflation.

5.3 Monetarists disagree. They believe that a depressed economy cannot be successfully revived by an increase in public expenditure, since any increase in expenditure will normally have to be financed by increased borrowing which will:

(a) further depress the economy through the crowding out effect, and higher interest rates;

(b) increase the money supply and thus cause more inflation.

5.4 The priority, rather, must be to create the conditions for confidence in the economy and incentives for enterprise. One of the key barriers to confidence is seen as inflation. To achieve a reduction in the rate of inflation, it is necessary to:

(a) control the growth in the money supply; and

(b) reduce inflationary expectations.

Supply side economics

5.5 A set of policies formulated by the monetarists which has gained favour in the USA and UK is that known as supply side economics. The use of fiscal and monetary policies by government to reach their macroeconomic policy objectives is termed *demand management*. Demand management relies upon the proposition that the level of aggregate demand determines the level of national income and prices, ie that demand creates supply.

5.6 Supply side economics, on the other hand, focuses policy upon the conditions of aggregate supply, taking the view that the availability, quality, and cost of resources are the long term determinants of national income and prices. Supply-siders argue that by putting resources to work, an economy will automatically generate the additional incomes necessary to purchase the higher outputs, ie *supply creates its own demand* (a proportion sometimes termed 'Say's Law' after the eighteenth century French economic Jean Baptiste Say).

5.7 Supply side economics is characterised by the following propositions.

(a) The predominant long-term influence upon output, prices, and unemployment are the conditions of aggregate supply.

(b) Left to itself, the free market will automatically generate the highest level of national income and employment available to the economy.

(c) Inflexibility in the labour market through the existence of trade unions and other restrictive practices retain wages at uncompetitively high levels. This creates unemployment and restricts aggregate supply.

(d) The rates of direct taxation have a major influence upon aggregate supply through their effects upon the incentive to work.

(e) There is only a limited role for government in the economic system. Demand management can only influence output and employment 'artificially' in the short-run, creating inflation and hampering growth in the long-run. State-owned industries are likely to be uncompetitive and accordingly restrict aggregate supply.

5.8 The importance of aggregate supply is demonstrated in Figures 5(a) and (b).

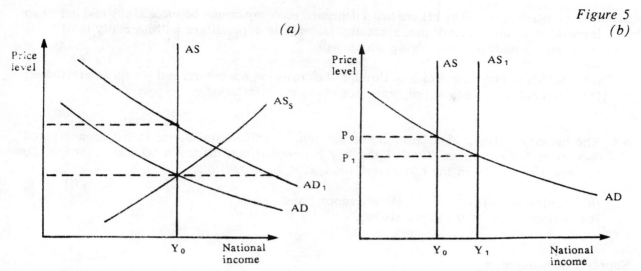

Figure 5
(a)
(b)

Figure 5(a) demonstrates the effect of a rise in aggregate demand (perhaps as the result of expansionary demand management policies) as a shift in the aggregate demand schedule from AD to AD_1, but in the long run national income remains at Y_0. The effect of the rise in aggregate demand is due to an increase in prices from P_0 to P_1. Supply-side theorists accept that in the short-run, national income may rise along the short-run aggregate supply curve AS_s but contend that ultimately national income will fall to its long-run level of Y_0. Consequently aggregate demand is powerless to increase long-run output or employment.

Figure 5(b) illustrates a rise in aggregate supply from AS to AS_1. The income generated from the higher employment causes aggregate demand to extend and consequently national income rises from Y_0 to Y_1. This demonstrates the supply-side view that only changes in the conditions of aggregate supply can lead to a sustained increase in output and employment. The fall in the price level from P_0 to P_1 will be discussed below.

5.9   The economy will self-regulate through the actions of the price mechanism in each market. Flexible prices in goods and factor markets will ensure that at the microeconomic level each market tends towards a market-clearing equilibrium. At the macroeconomic level the maximum attainable level of national income is at the level of full-employment determined by the position of the long-run Phillips curve. The exponent of supply-side economics argues that flexible wages will ensure the economy reaches this point.

5.10 The importance of flexible wages is shown in Figure 6.

Figure 6

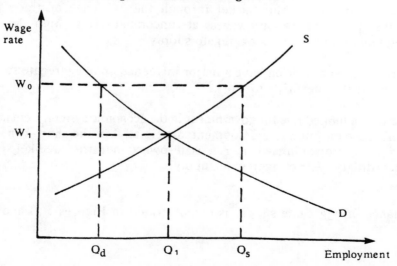

When the wage rate is at W_0 the demand for labour is Q_d whilst the total supply of labour stands at Q_s. This creates involuntary unemployment of Q_s-Q_d at the prevailing wage rate. By accepting lower wages workers can 'price themselves back into jobs' and consequently unemployment falls. If wages were perfectly flexible downwards then the market would restore full-employment at wage rate W_1. This would leave unemployment at its 'natural rate'.

5.11 High taxation is claimed to act as a disincentive to work because if marginal tax rates (ie the proportion of additional income taken as tax) are high, the individual is likely to behave in one of two ways:

(a) to forgo opportunities to increase income through additional effort on the basis that the increase in net income does not adequately reward the effort or risk;

(b) to resort to working in the parallel economy to avoid paying the tax.

5.12 The Laffer Curve (named after Professor Arthur Laffer) illustrates the effect of tax rates upon government revenue and national income.

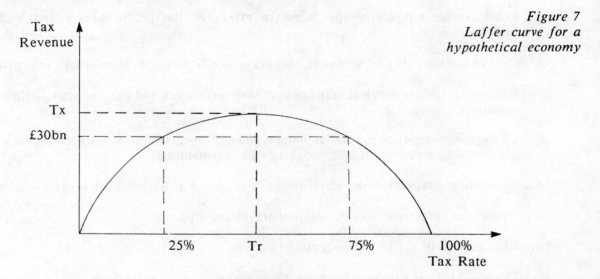

Figure 7
Laffer curve for a
hypothetical economy

In the hypothetical economy depicted in Figure 7 a tax rate of 0% results in the government receiving no tax revenue irrespective of the level of national income. If the rate is 100% then nobody will work because they keep none of their earnings and so once again total tax revenue is zero. At 25% tax rates the government will achieve a total tax take of £30bn; the same as they revenue they enjoy at rates of 75%. By deduction the level of national income when taxes are 25% must be £120bn compared with only £40bn if taxes are 75%. High taxation appears to operate as a disincentive.

5.13 Three consequences flow from this Laffer curve analysis.

(a) High rates of taxation act as a disincentive to work and accordingly reduce output and employment.

(b) Governments cannot always expect to increase tax revenue by increasing tax rates. There appears to be a crucial tax rate beyond which the fall in national income resulting from the erosion of incentives and effort outweighs the increased tax rate. In Figure 7 the maximum tax revenue is at Tx with an average tax rate Tr. If tax rates are above Tr the government can increase tax revenues by cutting tax rates.

(c) There will always be two tax rates available which can yield the same total tax revenue, one associated with a high level of national income and another associated with a lower level. In consequence governments committed to high government expenditure need not always be associated with high rates of tax.

5.14 Supply side economists advise against state involvement in the economy at both the microeconomic and macroeconomic levels. Microeconomic involvement is disliked for the following reasons.

(a) Price regulation distorts the signalling function essential for markets to reach optimal equilibrium.

(b) Wage regulation distorts the labour market's ability to ensure full employment.

(c) Public ownership blunts the incentive effect of the profit motive and leads to inefficiency.

(d) Government grants and subsidies encourage inefficient and 'lame-duck' industries.

(e) Public provision of services may not encourage efficiency and can limit the discipline of consumer choice.

(f) Employment legislation such as employment protection limits market flexibility by discouraging recruitment and encouraging over-manning.

Macroeconomic intervention by government is regarded as harmful for several reasons.

(a) Demand management will be inflationary in the long-run.

(b) High taxes will act as a disincentive.

(c) The possibility of politically motivated policy changes will create damaging uncertainty in the economy. This will discourage long-term investment.

5.15 Although most would accept the need for expansion of the money stock by government to accommodate increases in aggregate demand, some supply-siders have denied even this role to the government.

5.16 Where aggregate supply increases and the nominal money stock is held constant the resulting excess supply of outputs will force the general price level down (providing nominal wages also fall) thereby increasing the real money stock to accommodate the higher aggregate demand. This is illustrated in Figure 4(b) above.

5.17 Supply side economics is commonly associated with a number of policy propositions.

(a) Reduction in the role of government through elimination of budget deficits and reduction in the proportion of total expenditure attributable to governments.

(b) Elimination of restrictive trade practices in the goods market through deregulation and liberalisation.

(c) Reduction of labour market imperfections through legislation to weaken collective bargaining. This is often accompanied by the adoption of a tougher line by government towards unions in the public sector.

(d) Reduction in the size of the public sector through privatisation of nationalised industries and disposal of public assets. This can also include a greater reliance upon the private sector for the provision of public services.

(e) Reduction in the rates of direct taxation through constraints on government expenditure and a shift towards indirect taxation.

5.18 The policies of Thatcherism in the UK during the 1980s were particularly influenced by supply side economic views.

6.   CONCLUSION

6.1   The key points in this chapter are as follows:

(a) Demand management uses fiscal policy to influence the economy by altering aggregate demand and so raise or lower the equilibrium national income level, in order to close an inflationary or deflationary gap. However, there appears to be a connection between the rate of inflation and unemployment. The Phillips curve has been used to show that when there is zero inflation, there will be some unemployment.

(b) Monetarist economists would argue that a Keynesian government policy to boost demand in the economy is likely to be inflationary and that inflation will create more unemployment. They prefer to concentrate on the 'supply side' of the economy - ie pursue policies which will affect supply and the costs of production, rather than policies for influencing demand.

(c) A conclusion from the link between unemployment and inflation is that if the government wants to reduce unemployment, it must accept a faster rate of inflation in the economy. Trying to reduce inflation in order to stimulate economic growth and more employment in the longer term may result in higher unemployment in the short term.

(d) Efforts to control inflation might be directed at high taxes or high interest rates to reduce consumer demand, exchange rate policies to control the cost of imported goods, control of the money supply, or direct controls over price and wage increases.

(e) Macroeconomic policy aims cannot necessarily all be sustained together for a long period of time; attempts to achieve one objective will often have adverse effects on others, sooner or later.

(f) There are some significant differences of opinion about appropriate economic policy between the monetarists, who advocate supply side policies, and the Keynesian advocates of demand management. The implications of these differences need to be understood by business people.

TEST YOUR KNOWLEDGE
The numbers in brackets refer to paragraphs of this chapter

1 Why is inflation considered to be a serious economic problem? (1.3)

2 How does inflation affect money's ability to perform its functions? (1.4)

3 What is the monetarist view of the cause of inflation? (1.21-1.23)

4 List the various types of unemployment. (2.3)

5 In what way is technological unemployment different from other causes of unemployment? (2.10-2.13)

6 What is the Phillips Curve? (3.2)

7 Illustrate how the expectation of inflation affects the Phillips curve. (3.9)

8 How can we define economic growth? (4.1)

9 What are the possible disadvantages to economic growth? (4.18)

10 What is supply side economics? (5.4-5.6)

11 Illustrate a Laffer curve and explain the consequences of Laffer curve analysis. (5.12, 5.13)

Now try illustrative questions 19 and 20 at the end of the text

PART D
THE INTERNATIONAL DIMENSION

Chapter 11

INTERNATIONAL TRADE

This chapter covers the following topics.

1. Reasons for international trade
2. Protectionism and free trade
3. The importance of international trade to the marketer

---

1. REASONS FOR INTERNATIONAL TRADE

1.1 Trade between two countries is not in essence much different from trade and exchange between two people. Trade will only take place if both parties benefit.

1.2 There are a number of reasons why international trade can be beneficial.

(a) It increases total utility. If one country produces oranges and another produces apples, the total utility derived from apples and oranges can be increased by trade.
Consuming an additional orange in a country with only oranges available will provide limited additional utility (by the law of diminishing marginal utility), but the same orange will provide much greater benefit to an individual whose choice has been limited to apples.

(b) Trade allows countries access to raw materials and products which they do not have or could not produce for themselves, because of their climate, limited natural resources or lack of technical expertise. In these instances, trade will occur when countries have a surplus or a deficit of raw materials which can be sold and bought internationally. For example, Zambia has a surplus of copper and many developed Western countries have a deficit of oil.

(c) Trade increases competition and the efficiency of production:

(i) through the transfer of new technology and methods of production; and
(ii) possible economies of scale resulting from the potential market size.

(d) Trade is an essential ingredient in the recipe for economic growth. It has been described as the 'engine of growth' and the opportunities afforded by trade are widely seen as beneficial to an economy.

(e) Trade can reduce international tensions. It serves to develop political links and a degree of economic interdependency which may reduce the likelihood of war.

(f) Trade enables countries to specialise in producing what they are best at. In this way more output can be generated from the same resources: trade makes scarce economic resources go further.

1.3 The benefit of international trade can be demonstrated by two 'laws':

(a) the law of absolute advantage;
(b) the law of comparative advantage.

The law of absolute advantage

1.4 Some countries will be more efficient than others in producing certain goods and services, perhaps because they have a more highly-skilled and educated workforce, or a better commercial and economic environment. When one country has the potential to produce a good more efficiently than another country, it is said to have an *absolute advantage* over the other country in the production of that good.

1.5 In the following example we can see how many cars or tons of wheat one unit of productive resource can produce in each of two countries, Agraria and Industria.

	Output per unit of production Cars	Output per unit of production Wheat Tons
Industria	10	5
Agraria	5	10

1.6 This shows that Industria is absolutely better at producing cars, and is able to produce twice as many from the same resources. Agraria on the other hand is absolutely better at producing wheat.

1.7 Comparing production costs between two countries like this has to be done in terms of opportunity cost.

In Industria the cost of one car is the lost production of $\frac{1}{2}$ ton of wheat.
In Agraria a car costs two tons of wheat, but one ton of wheat only costs $\frac{1}{2}$ a car.

1.8 If each country had 100 units of production divided equally between the two sectors and there was no trade we can see that total output would be:

	50 units of production Cars	50 unit of production Wheat Tons
Industria	500	250
Agraria	250	500
Total output without trade	750	750

1.9 If the two countries were to agree to trade and specialise in their areas of absolute advantage, each could concentrate all 100 units of production in their 'best' activity.

	Cars	Wheat Tons
Industria	1,000	-
Agraria	-	1,000
Total output with trade	1,000	1,000

1.10 You can see that with specialisation the total output of both cars and wheat has increased from the same 200 units of production. This clearly represents a better use of scarce resources.

1.11 Trade will now need to take place between the two countries and because in this simple example the opportunity cost ratios are the same for each country the balance of negotiating power is the same. An exchange rate of one car for one ton of wheat would allow both countries to be better off in terms of both cars and wheat.

	Cars	Wheat Tons
Industria	600	400
Agraria	400	600

1.12 Both countries are better off in terms of cars and wheat after trade.

1.13 Now suppose that a country with a well-developed economy is so efficient in production that it can produce all goods and services with fewer resources and more cheaply than any other country. The country would then have an absolute advantage in production over every other country in the world. That being so, it might seem logical that the country should produce everything that it needs for itself, and should not buy any goods from other countries at all.

1.14 Is there any reason why a country that has an absolute advantage over others in production should bother to trade internationally with those other countries?

1.15 The answer is 'yes', as we shall see below, and the answer is to do with *comparative advantage* as distinct from absolute advantage.

The law of comparative advantage

1.16 As we have seen, the cost of producing goods can be measured as an *opportunity cost* of not being able to produce alternative goods with the resources that are used up. Thus, if country A can use one unit of production resource to make either two units of product X or four units of product Y, we can say that the cost of making one unit of X is the opportunity cost of not being able to make 2(4 ÷ 2) units of Y. Similarly, the cost of making one unit of Y is the opportunity cost of not being able to make ½(2 ÷ 4) unit of X.

1.17 One country has *comparative advantage* over another in making a particular product if it has a lower opportunity cost of production, measured as production forgone of another product. This can be seen in the example below.

	One unit of production Tractors	One unit of production Rice Tons
Ruritania	4	8
Utopia	10	10

1.18 In this example you can see that Utopia is absolutely better at both producing rice and tractors. However a comparison of their relative opportunity costs shows that:

	Utopia	Ruritania
The cost of a tractor	1 ton rice	2 tons rice
The cost of one ton rice	1 tractor	$\frac{1}{2}$ tractor

1.19 Although Utopia is absolutely better at producing tractors and rice, Ruritania is comparatively better at producing rice.

1.20 If we again assume that each country has 100 units of production equally divided between the two sectors we can see what the position in each country would be without trade.

	50 units of production Tractors	50 units of production Rice Tons
Ruritania	200	400
Utopia	500	500
Total output without trade	700	900

1.21 If Ruritania was to specialise in its area of comparative advantage and Utopia to concentrate, but not specialise, in the other area, we can see how total production of tractors and rice might increase.

	Tractors	Rice Tons
Ruritania	-	800
Utopia	800	200
	800	1,000

Output of tractors and rice has increased.

1.22 The basis of the exchange price between the two countries will be influenced by a number of factors, but will be constrained by the opportunity cost ratios and the requirement that both countries needs to be able to benefit from trade.

1.23 In this example the price of a tractor cannot be more than two tons of rice, or Ruritania could provide its own tractors more cheaply. Likewise the price has to be greater than one ton of rice or Utopia makes no gains from trade. Somewhere between these two levels of price, a mutually beneficial exchange price will be agreed. If we assume it is set at $1\frac{1}{2}$ tons of rice for one tractor, we can again see that both countries can have benefited from trade. After trading 350 tons of rice for 233.3 tractors, we have:

	Tractors	Rice Tons
Ruritania	233	450
Utopia	567	200 (produces itself)
		350 (trades)
	800	1,000

After trade both countries have more of both products than they would have without trade. (Look back to paragraph 1.20 to check for yourself.)

1.24 Although in these simple illustrations of the laws of comparative and absolute advantage we have dealt with just two countries and two products, the basic principles apply in the case of many countries also.

1.25 There are, however, there are certain limitations to specialisation and international trade.

    (a) *Free trade does not always exist.* Some countries take action to protect domestic industries and discourage imports. This means that a country might continue to produce goods in which it does not have a comparative advantage.

    (b) *Transport costs can be very high in international trade* so that it is cheaper to produce goods in the home country rather than to import them.

Free trade and its advantages: summary

1.26 The law of comparative advantage states perhaps the major advantage of international trade. However, there are other advantages to the countries of the world from encouraging international trade. These are as follows:

    (a) Some countries have a surplus of raw materials to their needs, and others have a deficit. A country with a surplus (eg of oil) can take advantage of its resources to export them.

    A country with a deficit of raw material must either import it, or accept restrictions on its economic prosperity and standard of living.

    (b) International trade helps to increase competition among suppliers in world markets.

    Greater competition reduces the likelihood of a market for a good in a country being dominated by a monopolist. The greater competition will increase the pressures on firms to be efficient, and also perhaps to produce goods of a high quality.

(c) International trade creates larger markets for a firm's output, and so many firms can benefit from *economies of scale* by engaging in export activities.

Economies of scale improve the efficiency of the use of resources, reduce the output costs and also increase the likelihood of output being sold to the consumer at lower prices than if international trade did not exist.

(d) There are political advantages to international trade, because the development of trading links provides a foundation for closer political links.

An example of the development of political links based primarily on trade is the European Community (EC).

Free movement of capital

1.27 Free trade is associated with the free movement of goods (and services) between countries. Another important aspect of international trade is the free movement of capital.

For example, if a UK company or investor wishes to set up a business in a different country, or to take over a company in another country, how easily can it transfer capital from the UK to the country in question, to pay for the investment?

1.28 Some countries (including the UK in recent years) have allowed a fairly free flow of capital into and out of the country. Other countries have been more cautious, mainly for one of two reasons.

(a) The free inflow of foreign capital will make it easier for foreign companies to take over domestic companies. There is often a belief that certain 'key' industries should be owned by residents of the country. Even in the UK, for example, there are restrictions on the total foreign ownership of shares in companies such as British Gas and British Telecom.

(b) Less developed countries especially, but other more advanced economies too, are reluctant to allow the free flow of capital *out* of the country. After all, they need capital to stay in the country to develop the domestic economy.

1.29 The free flow of capital between countries in the European Community is one of the principles of the 'Single European Market'.

1.30 For countries with a large and continuing balance of trade deficit, such as the UK and the USA, it is *essential* that capital should come into the country to help finance the deficit.

The balance of payments is discussed in the next chapter.

2. PROTECTIONISM AND FREE TRADE

2.1 Free trade exists where there is no restriction on imports from other countries or exports to other countries. In practice, however, many barriers to free trade exist because governments wish to protect home industries against foreign competition (although within the EC, most trade barriers between member countries were removed at the end of 1992 with the creation of a 'Single European Market').

2.2 Protectionist measures may be implemented by a government, but popular demand for protectionism commonly exceeds what governments are prepared to allow. In the UK, for example, some protectionist measures have been taken against Japanese imports (eg a voluntary restriction on car imports by Japanese manufacturers) although more severe measures are called from time to time by popular demand or lobbying interests.

2.3 Protection can be applied by a government in several ways.

(a) tariffs or customs duties;
(b) import quotas;
(c) embargoes;
(d) hidden subsidies for exporters and domestic producers;
(e) import restrictions;
(f) government action to devalue the nation's currency against other currencies.

Tariffs or customs duties

2.4 Tariffs or customs duties are taxes on imported goods. The effect of a tariff is to raise the price paid for the imported goods by domestic consumers, while leaving the price paid to foreign producers the same. The difference goes to the government.

For example, if goods imported to the UK are bought for £100 per unit, which is paid to the foreign supplier, and a tariff of £20 is imposed, the full cost to the UK buyer will be £120, with £20 going to the government.

Figure 1
Effect of tariffs on prices and output

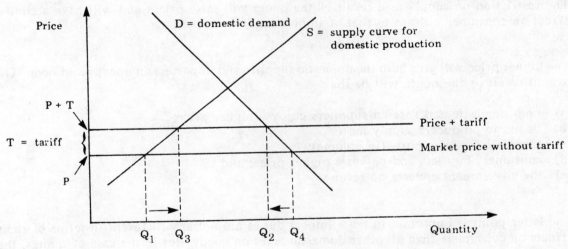

2.5 In Figure 1 the market purchase price of the good is P. At that price, *domestic suppliers* are willing to supply Q_1 but consumers are willing to buy Q_4. The difference $Q_1 - Q_4$ is then the amount of imports.

An import tariff will raise the price to the consumer to P + T. The domestic suppliers need not, of course, raise their prices, but at the higher price, consumers demand Q_2.

If the domestic producers were to raise their prices to P + T then they would expand their output to Q_3. Imports would fall from $(Q_4 - Q_1)$ to $(Q_2 - Q_3)$.

2.6 The end result of imposing the tariff is that:

(a) domestic consumers buy fewer units;
(b) domestic producers supply more to the market;
(c) foreign suppliers provide less to the market;
(d) the government earns some tax revenue $(Q_2 - Q_3) \times T$.

In such cases, import duties benefit the domestic producers and the government, but they harm the consumer.

The government raises revenue and domestic producers expand their sales, but consumers either pay higher prices if they buy imported goods, or are forced to buy domestic goods. In the latter case there must be some loss of welfare because previously consumers were not buying domestically produced goods at the world price, P. Now they are forced to because of the higher prices, $P + T$.

2.7 Note that the price elasticity of the demand and supply functions may be important in determining by how much a tariff will reduce imports. If demand and supply are price inelastic, a tariff will have a fairly small effect on import volumes.

Import quotas

2.8 Import quotas are restrictions on the *quantity* of a product that is allowed to be imported into the country.

2.9 The restriction on supply as a result of the quota will raise prices and will have a similar effect on consumer welfare to that of import tariffs.

2.10 The higher price will give both the domestic supplier and importers an unexpected boon. The overall result of the quota will be that:

(a) both domestic and foreign suppliers enjoy a higher price;
(b) domestic producers supply more;
(c) there are fewer imports (in volume);
(d) consumers buy less and pay at a higher price; and
(e) the government collects no revenue.

2.11 The latter point is important to note. Import duties are not any different in terms of their effects on consumers than all other domestic taxes on goods. But in the case of quotas, the government does not even raise revenue.

Embargoes on imports

2.12 An embargo on imports from one particular country is a total ban - effectively a zero quota. An embargo may have a political reason, and may deprive consumers at home of the supply of an important product. Embargoes are often difficult to enforce and if unexpected can cause sudden hardship to exporting companies.

Hidden export subsidies and import restrictions

2.13 An enormous range of government subsidies and assistance for exports and deterrents against imports have been practised, such as:

(a) *for exports* - export credit guarantees (ie government-backed insurance against bad debts for overseas sales), financial help (such as government grants): the substantial subsidies given to European agriculture through the EC's Common Agricultural Policy (CAP) are an important and controversial example of protectionist measures;

(b) *for imports* - complex import regulations and documentation, or special safety standards demanded for imported goods making product modifications to meet standards prohibitively expensive, or ensuring documentation is very time consuming.

Government action to devalue or depreciate the currency

2.14 If a government allows its currency to fall in value, imports will become more expensive to buy.

This will reduce imports by means of the price mechanism, especially if the demand and supply curves for the products are *price elastic*. For example, if the exchange rate between sterling and the US dollar is £1 = $1.60, a good imported from the USA to the UK at a cost of $8,000 would cost the UK buyer £5,000. Now if the government takes action to reduce interest rates, say, which has the effect of weakening the value of sterling, the exchange rate might change to £1 = $1.50. The same good costing $8,000 will now cost a UK buyer £5,333 - ie £333 more than before. At this higher price, the total UK demand for the US good will probably fall.

The extent of the fall in imports will depend on the price elasticity of demand in the UK for the US good. Exchange rates will be covered in more detail in the next chapter.

Arguments for and against protection

2.15 Arguments for protection are as follows.

(a) Protectionist measures can be taken against imports of cheap goods that compete with higher-priced domestically produced goods, and so preserve output and employment in domestic industries.

In the UK, advocates of protection have argued that UK industries are declining because of competition from overseas, especially the Far East, and the advantages of more employment at a reasonably high wage for UK labour are greater than the disadvantages that protectionist measures would bring.

(b) Measures might be necessary to counter 'dumping' of surplus production by other countries at an uneconomically low price.

For example, if the EC were to over-produce quantities of steel, wine, beef or butter, it might decide to dump the surpluses on other countries. The 'losses' from overproduction would in effect be subsidised by the EC governments, and so the domestic industries of countries receiving dumped goods would be facing unfair competition from abroad. Although dumping has short-term benefits for the countries receiving the cheap goods, the longer term consequences would be a reduction in domestic output and employment, even when domestic industries in the longer term might be more efficient.

(c) Protectionist measures by one country are often implemented in retaliation against measures taken by another country that are thought to be unfair.

This is why protection tends to spiral once it has begun. Any country that does not take protectionist measures when other countries are doing so is likely to find that it suffers all of the disadvantages and none of the advantages of protection.

(d) There is an argument that protectionism is necessary, at least in the short term, to protect a country's *'infant industries'* that have not yet developed to the size where they can compete in international markets.

Less developed countries in particular might need to protect industries against competition from advanced or developing countries, who are already enjoying economies of scale.

(e) Protection might also help a country in the short term to deal with the problems of a declining industry.

Without protection, an industry might quickly collapse and there could be problems of sudden mass unemployment amongst workers in the industry. By imposing some protectionist measures, the decline in the industry might be slowed down, and so the task of switching resources to new industries could be undertaken over a longer period of time.

(f) Protection is often seen as a means for a country to reduce its balance of trade deficit, by imposing tariffs or quotas on imports.

However, because of retaliation by other countries, the success of such measures by one country would depend on the demand by other countries for its exports being inelastic with regard to price and its demand for imports being fairly elastic.

(g) Protection may be necessary to ensure self sufficiency in key industries.

There is an argument that countries should retain some capability in certain key industries and sectors, for example on the grounds of national security. To achieve this some protectionism of industries like agriculture, defence and iron and steel may be advocated.

2.16 Arguments against protection are as follows.

(a) Because protectionist measures taken by one country will almost inevitably provoke retaliation by others, protection will reduce the volume of international trade. This means that the benefits of international trade will be reduced. As we have seen, these benefits are:

(i) *specialisation:* the law of comparative advantage states that countries will specialise in the production of goods which they can make with greater efficiency, and specialisation will increase total output and increase the economic wealth of the countries of the world as a whole;

(ii) *greater competition* (and so greater efficiency amongst producers);

(iii) *economies of scale* amongst producers who need world markets to achieve their economies and so produce at lower costs.

(b) Because of retaliation by other countries, protectionist measures to reverse a balance of trade deficit are unlikely to succeed. Imports might be reduced, but so too would exports.

(c) Protection creates political ill-will amongst countries of the world and so there are political disadvantages in a policy of protection.

2.17 It is generally argued that widespread protection will damage the prospects for economic growth amongst the countries of the world, and protectionist measures ought to be restricted to 'special cases' which might be discussed and negotiated with other countries.

2.18 As an alternative to protection, a country might try to stimulate its export competitiveness by making efforts to improve the productivity, improve its international marketing and lower the costs of domestic industries, thus making them more competitive against foreign producers. Hidden subsidies and exchange rate devaluation or depreciation are arguably examples of indirect protectionist measures, but other measures, such as funding industrial training schemes and educational policies, could in the longer term result in improvements in domestic productivity.

General Agreement on Tariffs and Trade (GATT)

2.19 It is apparent from what we have said so far that reducing the level of trade protection internationally is to the collective benefit of the trading nations involved. However, to prevent individual countries from taking advantage of the benefits of imposing protectionism unilaterally, there is a need for agreement among the trading nations to secure free trade. The General Agreement on Tariffs and Trade (GATT) is such an agreement.

2.20 The agreement was originally signed by 23 countries in 1947. The aims of GATT are:

(a) to reduce existing barriers to free trade;

(b) to eliminate discrimination in international trade;

(c) to prevent the growth of protection by getting member countries to consult with others before taking any protectionist measures.

2.21 The 'most-favoured nation' principle applies whereby one country (which is a member of GATT) which offers a reduction in tariffs to another country must offer the same reduction to all other member countries of GATT.

2.22 GATT now consists of about 100 members.

GATT has succeeded in reducing world tariffs, but there are serious problems which can arise:

(a) a country wishing to join GATT must consider the effect of reducing tariffs on its balance of payments and domestic economy;

(b) special circumstances (eg economic crises, the protection of an infant industry, the rules of the EC) may be admitted whereby protection or special low tariffs between a group of countries are allowed;

(c) a country in GATT may prefer not to offer a tariff reduction to another country because it would have to offer the same reduction to all other GATT members;

(d) protectionist measures (and the threat of further protection) are widespread, and GATT has serious difficulties in persuading member countries to remove them. A sticking point in the most recent GATT talks at the time of writing has been the subsidies protecting agriculture in the European Community.

3. THE IMPORTANCE OF INTERNATIONAL TRADE TO THE MARKETER

3.1 International trade opens up new market opportunities which often have significant strategic implications for companies and therefore for marketing.

3.2 Overseas markets at different stages of technological development and with different needs can present the opportunities for extending the life cycle of mature products. Greater returns and profits from mature 'cash cow' products provides funds for research and development and further innovation.

3.3 But government actions, for example the imposition of restrictions on trade with a particular country for political reasons, or the beginning of a 'trade war' resulting from protectionist actions, can cause sudden and unexpected changes in export market opportunities and as a result make developing international markets more risky than home markets.

3.4 Markets in general are without doubt becoming increasingly global and a number of trends and developments are likely to reinforce the importance of international trade over the next decade or so:

(a) the impact of the single European market (by the end of 1992), freeing up trade within Europe;

(b) the development of trade links and opportunities with the Eastern bloc countries whose command economies are gradually being dismantled;

(c) improved standards of living in India and China and therefore increased demand from these relatively untapped and massive consumer markets;

(d) the increased growth of multinational companies and expansion of global brands.

> One of the optional papers at CIM Diploma level is *International Marketing*. Students need to have a grasp of the economics of trade for this paper and to help them develop international marketing strategies. In the next chapter we consider exchange rates, including their impact on setting prices in international markets.

4. CONCLUSION

4.1 The key points in this chapter are as follows.

(a) World output of goods and services will increase if countries specialise in the production of goods/services in which they have comparative advantage.

(b)   There are various advantages and disadvantages of trade protection for an individual country, although free trade will generally be of advantage to the trading nations taken together. Even so, in recent years there has been a growing threat of protection:

(i)   In the USA, which has had a very large balance of trade deficit, there is a body of opinion which favours protectionist measures against other countries, such as Japan, which supply goods in large volumes to the USA.

(ii)   Free trade unions which are developing, such as the EC, threaten to 'lock out' other countries from their free trade union, making it more difficult to export goods to them. Countries such as the USA and Japan, for example, have been concerned that the new rules on trade within the EC applying from the end of 1992 could act as protectionist measures against them, and the EC's agricultural subsidies have held up progress in recent GATT trade liberalisation talks.

TEST YOUR KNOWLEDGE
The numbers in brackets refer to paragraphs of this chapter

1   What reasons are there for claiming that international trade is beneficial? (1.2)

2   What is meant by saying that one country has an absolute advantage in the production of a good? (1.4)

3   In what ways can a government apply protectionist measures? (2.3)

4   What is likely to be the end result of imposing a tariff? (2.6)

5   What is the effect of imposing a tariff on a product with price inelastic demand? (2.7)

6   What might be the reason for an import embargo? (2.12)

7   What are the main arguments for imposing protectionist measures? (2.15)

8   If free trade is beneficial, why should free trade agreements be necessary? (2.19)

Now try illustrative question 21 at the end of the text

Chapter 12

THE BALANCE OF PAYMENTS

This chapter covers the following topics.

1. The balance of payments
2. Trade deficits and surpluses
3. The terms of trade
4. External debt and the balance of payments

---

1. THE BALANCE OF PAYMENTS

The nature of the balance of payments

1.1 The balance of payments is a statistical 'accounting' record of a country's international trade transactions and capital transactions with other countries during a period of time.

1.2 Under the current method of presentation of the UK balance of payments statistics and the broad classifications of transactions are:

(a) current account transactions sub-divided into:

(i) transactions in 'visibles' - ie goods;
(ii) transactions in 'invisibles' - eg services;

The current account is therefore the record of a country's trading in exports and imports of goods and services.

(b) changes in the UK's external assets and liabilities, sub-divided into:

(i) changes in the UK's external assets. External assets include:

(1) holdings of foreign currency by anyone resident in the UK;

(2) holdings of shares or other investments in overseas companies by anyone resident in the UK (including UK firms);

(3) loans to anyone overseas by UK banks;

(ii)   changes in the UK's external liabilities.

External liabilities include:

(1)   investments in the UK, eg in UK government stocks or shares of UK firms, by overseas residents (such as overseas firms);

(2)   borrowing from abroad by anyone in the UK.

The sum of the balance of payments accounts is zero

1.3   The sum of the balance of payments accounts must always be zero (ignoring statistical errors in collecting the figures).

This is because every transaction in international trade has a double aspect (in much the same way that accountants regard all business transactions as having matching 'debit' and 'credit' items). In the balance of payments, every 'plus' item should have a matching 'minus' item.

1.4   You do not need to worry too much about the detail of the matching pluses and minuses in the balance of payments, but some examples might help you to appreciate how they occur.

1.5   We shall now look at balance of payments items in a bit more detail, using UK statistics to illustrate principles which apply equally to the balance of payments of every other country too.

The UK balance of payments accounts

1.6   The method used in the UK to present balance of payments figures is illustrated below.

Table 1
UK BALANCE OF PAYMENTS

	19X0	
Current account	£bn	£bn
Exports		102.0
Imports		120.7
Visible balance		(18.7)
Invisibles		
Services	5.2	
Interest, profits, dividends	4.0	
Transfers	(4.9)	
		4.3
Current balance		(14.4)
UK external assets and liabilities: net (see *Table 2*)		12.1
Balancing item		2.3
		14.4

Table 2

TRANSACTIONS IN EXTERNAL ASSETS AND LIABILITIES

	19X0	
	£bn	£bn
Investments overseas by UK residents		
Direct	(11.7)	
Portfolio	(12.6)	
		(24.3)
Investments in the UK by overseas residents		
Direct	19.0	
Portfolio	5.1	
		24.1
Foreign currency lending abroad by UK banks		(33.3)
Foreign currency borrowing abroad by UK banks		34.0
Sterling lending abroad by UK banks		(3.9)
Sterling borrowing and deposit liabilities		
abroad of UK banks		12.2
UK non-bank private sector:		
Deposits with and lending to banks abroad	(5.7)	
Borrowing from banks abroad	7.3	
		1.6
Official reserves (additions to = -/reductions = +)*		(0.1)
Other external assets of UK non-banks		(5.0)
Other external liabilities of non-banks		6.8
Net transactions in assets and liabilities (see *Table 1*)		12.1

* An increase in UK assets, and so a minus value in the balance of payments.

Notes

(a) A transaction in external assets (eg an overseas investment of a UK resident) is 'minus' when an investment abroad is *increased*. A disinvestment is a 'plus'.

(b) Similarly, a transaction in external liabilities (eg an investment in the UK by an overseas resident) is a 'plus' when an investment in the UK is *increased*. A disinvestment is a 'minus'.

(c) A *portfolio investment* is an investment where the investor doesn't have a voice in the management of the enterprise. It is often a *short-term* investment.

(d) A *direct investment* is a transaction between companies which are affiliated, but in different countries - eg a head office company in the USA or France, acquiring control of a UK company, which becomes a subsidiary of the head office company.

1.7 If the balance of payments in principle sums to zero, you may wonder what is meant by a surplus or deficit on the balance of payments. When journalists or economists speak of the balance of payments they are usually referring to the deficit or surplus on the *current account*, or possibly to the surplus or deficit on visibles only (this is also known as the 'balance of trade').

1.8 We shall now consider the components of the balance of payments in more detail, starting with the current account.

12: THE BALANCE OF PAYMENTS

The visible balance

1.9 The visible balance is sometimes referred to as the 'balance of trade'. The visible balance is the difference between the value of exported *goods* from the country and the value of *goods* imported into the country.

The invisible balance

1.10 The invisible balance consists of services, interest, profit and dividends, and transfers.

(a) *Services*. Exported services are simply services sold to other countries, including international transport services, banking services and other financial services, and earnings from tourism.

(b) *Interest, profits and dividends (IPD) as an item of invisible trade*. These consist of items such as:

   (i) direct investment earnings. These are the share of profits in overseas branches, overseas subsidiary companies and overseas associated companies. Direct investment earnings might bring income into the country (domestic firms investing overseas) or cause outflows (profits of overseas firms investing in the country);

   (ii) portfolio investment earnings - ie the payment of interest and dividends on stocks and shares held in securities overseas;

   (iii) interest on borrowing and lending abroad by banks.

   IPD are an important item of invisible trade. When a country's residents invest heavily in foreign countries, there will initially be an outflow of capital investment from that country, but eventually there will be an outflow of interest and dividends on those investments.

(c) *Transfers as an item of invisible trade*. Transfers are the transfer of funds to other countries, or the receipt of funds from other countries, for non-trading and non-commercial transactions. They include:

   (i) general government transfers which are grants to overseas countries, eg the payment of cash grants to a developing country;

   (ii) subscriptions and contributions to international organisations, such as the United Nations; and

   (iii) other transfers by the government overseas or to the government from overseas, eg, in the case of the UK, transfers to the EC or rebates from the EC.

   (iv) *Private transfers which* include gifts of goods sent by parcel post, payments by UK residents to dependents overseas, transfers of sums by relief organisations and missionary societies, and the payment of legacies.

UK external assets and liabilities

1.11 Transactions in UK external assets and liabilities record the increases or decreases in:

(a) the assets of other countries, including foreign currency, that are held by UK residents (including the UK government);

(b) the liabilities of the UK to residents of other countries. These are increases or decreases in UK assets, including sterling, that are held by individuals, firms or governments in other countries.

1.12 Assets, remember, are items that are owned. They include money (foreign currency), loans to residents of other countries, and holding stocks and shares of firms in other countries.

1.13 Liabilities are debts or 'obligations' owed. Whenever a firm issues shares or debt capital, or incurs a trade debt, these are liabilities. If the liabilities of UK firms are owed to residents of other countries, they will become balance of payments items. The same applies to liabilities incurred by the UK government, or by individuals resident in the UK.

1.14 The balance of payments records only 'new' transactions in assets and liabilities during the course of the period. It is not a record of the grand total of external assets or liabilities that have built up over time.

1.15 You should look at the items in Table 2 carefully, to see what types of transaction are included as:

(a) transactions in assets; and
(b) transactions in liabilities.

1.16 Notice too that an increase in external assets held by UK residents is given a minus value in the balance of payments, and any increase in external liabilities is given a plus value.

Transactions in official reserves (official financing)

1.17 An item under the heading of transactions in assets in the balance of payments consists of drawings on or additions to the official reserves (Table 2).

1.18 The official reserves consist of mainly gold and convertible foreign currencies, held in the government's Exchange Equalisation account with the Bank of England. (Other countries similarly have official reserves, which are kept and managed on behalf of the government by the central bank.)

1.19 In years past, movements on the official reserves were given greater prominence in the UK balance of payments statistics, but other international capital transactions are so large that they now 'dwarf' any changes in official reserves, and so changes in the official reserves are no longer given the same prominence as before. Instead, they are included as an item in the assets section of the balance of payments accounts.

12: THE BALANCE OF PAYMENTS

Balancing item

1.20 There is one final figure in the balance of payments accounts. This is a balancing item, which arises because of errors and omissions in collecting statistics for the accounts (eg sampling errors for items such as foreign investment and tourist expenditure and omissions in the data gathered about exports or imports). The size of the balancing item, as you can see from the figures in Table 1, can be very large, indicating that the other balance of payments figures must contain significant inaccuracies.

Trends in the UK balance of payments

1.21 The most significant aspect of the UK balance of payments in recent years has been heavy deficit in the balance of trade (the current balance), as can be seen from the data below.

£ million

	1983	1984	1985	1986	1987	1988	1989	1990	1991	1992
Current account										
Visible trade										
Exports (fob)	60 700	70 265	77 991	72 627	79 153	80 346	92 154	101 718	103 413	106 375
Imports (fob)	62 237	75 601	81 336	82 186	90 735	101 826	116 837	120 527	113 703	120 546
Visible balance	-1 537	-5 336	-3 345	-9 559	-11 582	-21 480	-24 683	-18 809	-10 290	-13 771
Services balance	4 064	4 519	6 687	6 808	6 745	4 397	4 039	4 581	4 750	3 730
IPD balance	2 831	4 345	2 560	4 974	3 754	4 423	3 495	2 094	500	3 200
Transfers balance	-1 593	-1 730	-3 111	-2 157	-3 400	-3 518	-4 578	-4 897	-1 345	-5 073
Invisibles balance	5 302	7 134	6 136	9 625	7 099	5 302	2 956	1 778	3 905	1 857
Current balance	3 765	1 798	2 790	66	-4 482	-16 179	-21 726	-17 029	- 6 382	-11 916

Note. IPD refers to interest, profits and dividends.

1.22 Significant changes in the *visibles section* of the UK balance of payments in recent years have included:

(a) a steady decline in the balance of trade in manufactured goods.

(b) a boom in consumer spending on imports in the late 1980s in the UK. UK manufacturers have been unable to increase their output sufficiently to meet demand, so that there was a surge in imports of consumer goods, until the recession of 1990 to 1992 brought dampened consumer demand;

(c) a decline in the export revenues from North Sea Oil. By the end of 1984, Britain was the fourth-largest oil producer in the world. Export revenues have fallen since then, because of:

(i) a decline in the annual volume of oil output from the North Sea; and
(ii) a fall in oil prices since 1984/85.

1.23 Significant features of the *invisibles section* of the UK balance of payments in recent years have included:

(a) a large surplus on services, achieved mainly by the high earnings from financial institutions (including those in the 'City');

(b) a large surplus on the balance on interest, profits and dividends, reflecting the high volume of investments abroad in the 1980s. However, IPD payments to foreign investors are also rising, which is indicative of the increasing 'globalisation' of the capital markets and investments;

(c) the development of tourism as a service, both earning income for the UK (from tourists to the UK) and incurring overseas payments (by UK travellers abroad);

(d) large net payments by the UK to the EC.

1.24 Britain's membership of the EC has continued to be an important influence on external trade, in both visibles and invisibles, with a large proportion of the UK's external trade (over 40%) now being with other EC countries. The UK has been in deficit on current account trade with the rest of the EC.

1.25 *Transactions in external assets and liabilities* are an important element in the balance of payments, with several significant developments in recent years.

(a) In 1979, exchange control regulations in the UK were removed and capital was allowed to move freely into and out of the country. One consequence was that a substantial amount of investment overseas by UK residents has taken place. The volume of capital transactions is high, both for inflows and outflows of capital.

The benefits of investments abroad are reflected in the increase in the payments of dividends and interest into the country (adding to income on current account). Eventually, if the investments abroad are realised, there will be a substantial inflow of capital back into the UK.

(b) The large volume of investments abroad by UK firms and investments in the UK by overseas firms explains the growth in the size of interest, profits and dividends (IPD) in the invisibles section of the balance of payments current account.

(c) The large deficit in the UK's current account balance has generally been 'financed' externally, by capital inflows to the UK - ie by borrowing from abroad, or by selling off foreign assets.

Foreign currency and international trade

1.26 Whenever there is international trade, there is a need for foreign currency by at least one of the traders, the buyer or the seller. For example:

(a) if a UK exporter sells goods to a US buyer, and charges the buyer £20,000, the US buyer must somehow obtain the sterling - to him, this is foreign currency - in order to pay the UK supplier. The US buyer will do this by using some of his US dollars to buy the £20,000 sterling, probably from a bank in the USA;

(b) if a UK importer buys goods from Germany, he might be invoiced in deutschmarks, say DM100,000. He must obtain this foreign currency to pay his debt, and he will do so by purchasing the deutschmarks from a UK bank in exchange for sterling;

(c) if a UK investor wishes to invest in US capital bonds, he would have to pay for them in US dollars, and so he would have to sell sterling to obtain the dollars. Thus *capital outflows*, such as investing overseas, not just payments for imports, cause a demand to sell the domestic currency and buy foreign currencies. On the other hand, exports and capital inflows to a country cause a demand to buy the domestic currency in exchange for foreign currencies.

1.27 Significant movements in the exchange rate of a country's currency can have implications for the country's balance of payments, depending upon the elasticities of demand for imports and exports. This effect is discussed in the next section of this chapter.

Interest rates and the balance of payments

1.28 The UK government has recently employed a policy of high interest rates. High interest rates, such as those which prevailed in the UK from 1988 to 1990 have several consequences for the balance of payments.

(a) They attract foreign investment into the UK.

(b) Foreign investors have to buy sterling to pay for their investment. An inflow of foreign capital to the UK therefore helps to support the exchange rate of sterling (When demand for sterling has been very strong, the Bank of England has been able to intervene in the foreign exchange markets, selling sterling in exchange for foreign currencies, and building up the official reserves).

(c) The relatively high exchange rate makes it more difficult for UK exporters to sell goods and services abroad. Exports from the UK are usually priced in £, and when sterling is stronger, exports are relatively more expensive to foreign buyers.

(d) A high exchange rate makes imports relatively cheap. Purchases of imports into the UK are likely to be higher when sterling is strong.

Equilibrium in the balance of payments

1.29 A balance of payments in equilibrium should perhaps be defined as follows.

A balance of payments is *in equilibrium* if, on balance over a period of years:

(a) the exchange rate remains stable; and

(b) autonomous 'credits' and 'debits' are equal in value (ie visible and invisible exports on the current account are equal, with any minor differences accounted for entirely by additions to or drawings on official reserves); and

(c) to achieve this situation, the government is not required to introduce measures which:

    (i)   create unemployment or higher prices;

    (ii) sacrifice economic growth; or

    (iii) impose trade barriers (eg import tariffs and import quotas).

2. TRADE DEFICITS AND SURPLUSES

A continual surplus or deficit in the balance of payments

2.1 A problem arises for a country's balance of payments when the country has a continual deficit year after year on its current account, although there can be problems too for a country which enjoys a continual current account surplus.

2.2 The problems of a *deficit* on the current account are probably much more obvious to you. When a country is continually in deficit, it is importing more goods and services that it is exporting, and so:

(a) it must either borrow more and more from abroad, to build up external liabilities which match the deficit on current account, eg encourage foreign investors to lend more by purchasing the government's gilt edged securities; or

(b) it must sell more and more of its external assets. This has been happening recently in the USA, for example, where a large deficit on the US current account has resulted in large purchases of shares in US companies by foreign firms.

2.3 Even so, the demand to buy the country's currency in the foreign exchange markets will be weaker than the supply of the country's currency for sale. As a consequence, there will be pressure on the exchange rate to depreciate in value.

2.4 The problems of a continual *surplus* on current account are not so obvious, but they might nevertheless exist.

2.5 If a country has a surplus on its current account year after year, it might invest the surplus abroad or add it to official reserves. The balance of payments position would be strong. There is the problem, however, that if one country which is a major trading nation (eg Japan) has a continuous surplus on its balance of payments current account, other countries must be in continual deficit. These other countries can run down their official reserves, perhaps to nothing, and borrow as much as they can to meet the payments overseas, but eventually, they will run out of money entirely and be unable even to pay their debts.

2.6 Political pressure might therefore build up within the importing countries to impose tariffs or import quotas.

2.7 Every country must have a reasonably sound balance of payments position if international trade is to prosper. It might therefore be argued that a country has a good balance of payments position if, in the long run, it has neither surplus nor deficit on its current account, or at least if in the long run, its current account deficit is matched by inflows of direct investment (ie long term) capital.

12: THE BALANCE OF PAYMENTS

Does the UK's balance of payments deficit matter?

2.8   The UK's balance of payment statistics have shown substantial deficits in the years 1988 to 1990 and attention has consequently been drawn to the UK balance of payments position. There is no problem with a small deficit, or a short term deficit, in the balance of payments on current account. But the UK's balance of payments position was suggesting a *large* and potentially *long term* deficit. This is clearly a serious threat: no country can finance a large balance of payments deficit on current account for a long time (not even the USA, which also has a serious balance of trade problem).

2.9   A former Chancellor of the Exchequer Mr Nigel Lawson took a surprisingly 'relaxed' view of the situation.

        He argued that the balance of trade deficit was not as bad as it might seem, for two broad reasons:

        (a)   the causes of the deficit;
        (b)   the way in which the deficit is funded.

2.10   There are two broad causes of deficit.

        (a)   The UK economy was growing faster than many other industrial countries. A fast-growing economy means a fast growth in consumer demand, and the consumer boom sucked in imports to the UK.

                The UK economy would eventually slow down relative to other countries and so the Chancellor argued that the large influx of consumer goods imports would not continue for long.

        (b)   A large part of the deficit has been caused by an investment boom by UK companies, which have been purchasing capital equipment from abroad. When this new output capacity comes on stream, it is argued, UK output will increase:

                (i)   stemming the flow of imports, because of extra competition from UK-produced goods; and

                (ii)   making UK exports more competitive.

2.11   *Funding of the deficit*. The UK's balance of payments deficit is being financed by private sector borrowing, ie by 'commercial' borrowing decisions. The government does not have a budget deficit, and so the public sector finances have been brought under control. This should put the UK in a good position to resolve its balance of payments position through the workings of 'market forces' - unlike the USA, in contrast, which has had both a large external payments deficit and also a very large public sector deficit.

2.12   The Chancellor's argument about funding the deficit was reinforced by two further factors:

        (a)   the size of the official reserves, which reached over £50 billion for the first time in July 1988;

    (b)   the substantial external assets that the UK *private sector* has acquired in recent years. If the UK private sector needs to finance its exports, it still has a lot of assets to draw on.

Practical ways of rectifying a current account deficit

2.13   The government of a country with a current account deficit will usually be expected to take measures to reduce or eliminate the deficit.

A deficit on current account may be rectified by one or more of the following measures:

(a)   a depreciation or devaluation of the currency;

(b)   direct measures to restrict imports, such as tariffs or import quotas or exchange control regulations;

(c)   domestic 'deflation' to reduce aggregate demand in the domestic economy.

Can the balance of payments position be rectified by a change in the exchange rate?

2.14   In theory, a balance of payments deficit on the current account can be rectified by allowing the domestic currency's exchange rate to fall.

2.15   For simplicity, we shall begin by ignoring capital transactions on external assets and liabilities. For example, if the UK has an adverse balance of payments on current account, and the value of sterling fell against other currencies, UK exports would become relatively cheaper in overseas markets, and foreign imports relatively more expensive in UK markets.

A change in the volume of overseas trade would result, with exports increasing and imports falling, and, in theory at least, the balance of payments would stabilise at a new level where the current account deficit is wiped out.

If the government allows its domestic currency to find its own value in the market, there will be no requirement to use up foreign exchange from the official reserves to support its value.

2.16   In practice, a correction of the balance of payments position by means of 'market' adjustments to the exchange rate will not work on its own. We should note however that in the case of the UK, the government's ability to allow a depreciation of sterling was limited by the rules of the European Exchange Rate Mechanism (ERM), from the time of the UK's entry in October 1990 until its suspension in September 1992.

2.17   A fall in the exchange rate makes imports more expensive. If a country is heavily dependent on imports (and the UK is in this position) a large depreciation of the domestic currency would *increase the rate of inflation.*

2.18   One cause of inflation in the UK might be 'import-cost-push', meaning the rising cost of imports as sterling falls in value against other currencies. Higher inflation in turn would make exports more expensive and so less competitive, and so the improvement in export competitiveness from a fall in the exchange rate might be offset (partially at least) by domestic inflation. Domestic inflation in turn might have damaging effects on the national economy (eg on output, employment and domestic demand).

2.19 Following a depreciation (or 'devaluation') of the currency, exports will become relatively cheaper to foreign buyers, and so the demand for exports will rise. The extent of the increase in *export revenue* would depend on:

(a) the *price elasticity of demand for the goods in export markets;*

(b) the extent to which industry is able to respond to the export opportunities by either producing more goods, or switching from domestic to export markets; and

(c) perhaps also the price elasticity of supply. With greater demand for their goods, producers should be able to achieve some increase in prices (according to the law of supply and demand), and the willingness of suppliers to produce more would then depend on the price elasticity of supply.

2.20 The cost of *imports* would also rise because more domestic currency would be needed to obtain the foreign currency to pay for imported goods.

The volume of imports would fall, although whether or not the total value of imports fell too would depend on the *elasticity of demand for imports:*

(a) if demand for imports is inelastic, the volume of demand would fall by less than their cost goes up, so that the total value of imports would rise;

(b) if demand for imports is elastic, the total value of imports would fall since the fall in volume would outweigh the increase in unit costs.

2.21 If a country imports raw materials and exports manufactured goods which are made with those materials, the cost of imported raw materials will rise, and so producers will have to put up their prices to cover their higher costs. There will be a net fall in export prices, as explained above, but perhaps not by much.

2.22 Because the effect of depreciation or devaluation depends on price elasticities of demand in this way, it might be the case that depreciation of the currency on its own would be insufficient to rectify the balance of payments deficit, unless an extremely large depreciation took place.

2.23 We can now summarise some of the points made so far by considering what would happen to the UK current account balance if there is a fall in the value of sterling.

(a) The immediate effects will depend on the elasticity of demand for imports. In the short run, demand is likely to be fairly inelastic and so total expenditure on imports will rise.

(b) Exports will be cheaper in overseas markets (in foreign currency) but in the short run, UK exporters might be unable to increase their output to meet the higher demand.

(c) Until UK industry adjusts to the change and increases its output of:

    (i) exported goods; and

    (ii) home-produced substitutes for imported goods;

there will be a deterioration in the current account of the balance of payments.

(d) After a time lag, production of exports and import substitutes will rise, so that:

    (i) the volume of exports will rise, thereby increasing the sterling value of exports (regardless of sterling's lower exchange rate);

    (ii) the volume of imports will fall further. This will improve the current account balance.

The extent of this improvement will depend on the price elasticity of demand for UK exports abroad and the price elasticity of demand for foreign imports in the UK.

(e) The improvement in the balance of payments will have some limit, and the current balance should eventually level off. The effect of the falling exchange rate on the current balance might therefore be described by a 'J' curve (Figure 1).

Figure 1
J curve

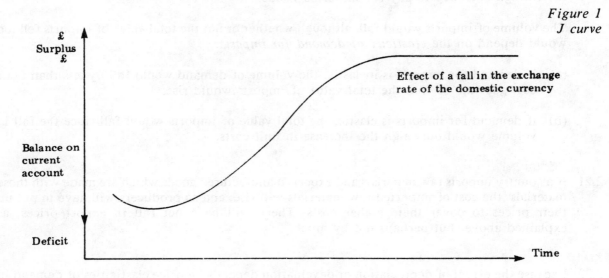

Protectionist measures

2.24 Another way of attempting to rectify a balance of payments deficit is to take direct protectionist measures to reduce the volume of imports. These measures might consist of:

(a) import tariffs;

(b) import quotas;

(c) a total ban or embargo on imports from a certain country;

(d) placing administrative burdens on importers (eg increasing the documentation required or safety standards that imported goods must comply with);

(e) *exchange control regulations* which make it difficult for importers to obtain foreign currency to buy goods from abroad;

(f) providing export subsidies to encourage exports, and other measures of financial support to exporters.

2.25 Import restrictions and export subsidies give rise to counter-measures by other countries. They are therefore dangerous measures for a country whose economy relies heavily on external trade. Exchange control regulations might be essential, however, for a country with a balance of payments deficit, low official reserves and which has great difficulty in borrowing capital from abroad.

Domestic deflation

2.26 The term 'deflation' might make you think of falling prices - ie the opposite of inflation. It means, however, rather more than this. When the total volume of expenditure and demand for goods in a country's economy is too high, the government can take steps to reduce it, by reducing its own expenditure, raising interest rates to deter borrowing, and cutting private consumption by raising taxes. This fall in demand should lead to a fall in prices or at least to a reduction in the rate of domestic inflation. Unfortunately, it might also lead, in the short term at least, to a reduction in industrial output and a loss of jobs in the country's economy. Certainly, the country must accept a lowering of its standard of living if severe deflationary measures are taken. The effect of deflation is not only to dampen domestic inflation rates, but to force domestic manufacturers, who will be faced with lower domestic demand for their goods, to switch more effort into selling to export markets.

2.27 Deflationary measures include cutting government spending, increasing taxation and raising interest rates. The purposes of deflationary measures would be:

(a) to reduce the demand for goods and services at home, and so to *reduce imports;*

(b) to *encourage industry to switch to export markets,* because of the fall in domestic demand;

(c) to *tackle domestic inflation,* which might be undermining the beneficial effect for exports of a depreciating domestic currency by raising the prices of exported goods in terms of the domestic currency.

2.28 Sometimes, a government's domestic economic policies are not deflationary, despite a balance of payments deficit, and on the contrary, the government's economic policies might encourage increasing demand, which will both boost demand for imports, and cause more inflation and a falling exchange rate. Economic policies which boost demand in the economy in spite of a balance of payments deficit will worsen, rather than improve, the deficit.

The balance of payments and the domestic economy

2.29 You should also try to view any country's balance of payments position in the context of its domestic economy.

(a) When a country's exports exceed its imports, or vice versa, there may be a lack of equilibrium between:

(i)   withdrawals from the circular flow of income in the domestic economy (remember that these withdrawals include imports); and

(ii)   injections into the circular flow of income (which include exports).

Equilibrium in the balance of payments (ie 'external equilibrium') will also help a country to achieve equilibrium in its circular flow of income (ie 'internal equilibrium').

(b)   If a country's international trade is only small in size compared with its domestic economy, problems with any balance of payments deficit will be much less than for a country which relies heavily on international trade.

3.   THE TERMS OF TRADE

Defining the terms of trade

3.1   The balance of trade for any country depends on two things:

(a)   the volume of goods exported and imported; and
(b)   the relative prices of exports and imports.

3.2   The *terms of trade* can be defined as the quantities of domestic goods that a country must give up to obtain a unit of imported goods. For example, if country X must produce 1.2 units of domestically-produced goods to obtain 1 unit of goods from country Y, the terms of trade could be described as 1.2 units of X goods: 1 unit of Y goods. In effect, the terms of trade are an export : import price ratio, which measures the relative prices of a country's exports to the prices paid for its imports. The terms of trade for a country continually change as export prices and import prices change.

(a)   If circumstances change so that X must produce and export 1.5 units of its goods to obtain 1 unit of goods from Y, the terms of trade will have shifted against X and in favour of Y.

(b)   If circumstances change so that X must produce and export only 1 unit of its goods to obtain 1 unit of goods from Y, the terms of trade will have shifted in favour of X and against Y.

3.3   The ratio of export to import prices – the terms of trade – determines the volume of exports necessary to pay for a given volume of imports or, meaning the same thing, the volume of imports that can be purchased with the proceeds of a given volume of exports.

3.4   Other things being equal, if the price of exports falls relative to that of imports (a fall in the terms of trade) the trade balance will deteriorate, or vice versa.

Note: the trade balance depends not just on the physical volume of exports and imports, but also on the prices at which they are traded.

Measuring the terms of trade

3.5   The terms of trade are measured as:

$$\frac{\text{unit value of exports}}{\text{unit value of imports}}$$

Some recent terms of trade figures for the UK are set out below.

Table 3
TERMS OF TRADE (VISIBLE TRADE) FOR THE UK

(Index values 1985 = 100)

	Unit value of exports (A)	Unit value of imports (B)	Terms of trade (A ÷ B)
1980	70.0	68.5	102.2
1985	100.0	100.0	100.0
1987	94.3	98.5	95.7
1989	101.2	103.8	97.5

3.6   In practice economists are usually concerned not with a measurable value for the terms of trade but with a measure of *changes* in the terms of trade, (eg from one year to the next).

Using indices for the average prices of imports and exports, the movement in the terms of trade between 1993 and 1992 would be computed as:

$$\frac{\text{Price of exports 1993/price of exports 1992}}{\text{Price of imports 1993/price of imports 1992}}$$

Changes in the terms of trade

3.7   Change in a country's terms of trade occur because of:

(a)   a change in the composition of exports or imports - eg in the UK two main things:

   (i)   fewer oil exports; and

   (ii) manufacturers trading up to higher-price products for export;
         have improved the UK's terms;

(b)   lower or higher prices of imports/exports - eg the oil price collapse in 1985, which worsened the terms of trade for the UK.

3.8   A government has limited 'powers' to influence its country's terms of trade, since it cannot directly influence the composition nor the prices of imports and exports - although it *can* affect the terms of trade through a revaluation or devaluation of the currency which would alter relative import/export prices.

3.9 If a country's terms of trade *worsen*, the unit value of its imports will rise by a bigger percentage than the unit value of its exports. The terms of trade will worsen when the exchange rate of the currency depreciates in value against other currencies.

3.10 If a country's terms of trade *improve*, the unit value of its exports will rise by a bigger percentage than the unit value of its imports. The terms of trade will improve when the exchange rate of the country's currency appreciates in value against other currencies.

3.11 It would seem logical to assume that an improving terms of trade is 'good' for a country and a worsening terms of trade is 'bad'. But this is not necessarily the case.

3.12 What is the effect of a change in the terms of trade? This should be considered in the context of the country's balance of payments. If the terms of trade worsen for a country, the country will be unable to afford the same volume of imports, or else its balance of payment position will deteriorate. In contrast, a country with improving terms of trade will be able to afford more imports or will improve its balance of payments.

3.13 Changes in the terms of trade affect a country's balance of payments via the price elasticity of demand for the goods traded. If a country's terms of trade improve, so that the price of its exported goods rises relative to the price of its imported goods, there will be a relative fall in the volume of goods exported and a rise in the volume of imports. The size of this fall in exports and increase in imports will depend on the price elasticities of demand for exported goods in foreign markets and imported goods in the country's domestic markets.

(a) If the demand for exported goods is inelastic the total *value* of exports will rise if their price goes up.

(b) If the demand for imported goods is inelastic the total value of imports will fall if their price falls.

(You need to remember the significance of price elasticities of demand for price changes and the consequence for total revenue.)

3.14 Provided that price elasticity of demand for both exports and imports is inelastic, an improvement in the terms of trade will result in an improvement in the current balance of trade.

3.15 On the other hand if the price elasticity of demand for both exports and imports is elastic, an improvement in the terms of trade will lead to a worsening current balance of trade, because:

(a) a rise in export prices would reduce total export revenue, and
(b) a fall in import prices would increase total payments for imports.

3.16 An improvement in the terms of trade might therefore result in a better or a worse balance of payments position. The same applies to a worsening terms of trade.

4. EXTERNAL DEBT AND THE BALANCE OF PAYMENTS

External debt

4.1 A country's external debt is the total amount that the country owes to foreign creditors. External debt includes debts of both the government and the private sector of the economy to foreign investors and lenders.

4.2 The external debt of a country might include:

    (a) loans from specialist international lending organisations, in particular the International Monetary Fund and the World Bank.

    (b) loans from foreign governments;

    (c) loans from private foreign investors, in particular foreign *banks*.

4.3 *Borrowing* therefore includes both:

    (a) borrowing by firms from overseas lenders (or investors); and

    (b) borrowing by governments, from overseas lenders (or investors) especially banks, or from international institutions which specialise in international lending, notably the International Monetary Fund (IMF) and the World Bank.

External debt and the balance of payments

4.4 A country's external debt increases whenever it has a balance of payments deficit on current account.

    (a) A deficit on current account must be balanced (ie equalled) by a matching surplus in transactions in external assets and liabilities, in other words, by:

        (i) borrowing from abroad; or
        (ii) selling assets that are owned abroad.

    (b) If a country's balance of trade deficit is very high, it must borrow heavily from abroad. Borrowing could be:

        (i) borrowing by the government;

        (ii) borrowing by the private sector;

        (iii) increasing investments in the country's private sector by foreign firms - eg takeovers of domestic companies by foreign companies.

    (c) There would be fears of a depreciation in the exchange rate of the country's currency, as a consequence of the balance of trade deficit. How can a country succeed in attracting foreign investors if they fear that the value of their investment might fall because of a currency depreciation?

Interest rates will probably have to remain high to compensate foreign investors for this risk.

(d) If the country's external debt becomes very high, the cost of servicing the debt - ie meeting interest payment schedules - could become a severe burden on the country's economy.

4.5 A significant feature of the world economy during the 1980s was the external debt problems of many developing countries, especially in South and Central America, and Africa.

The International Monetary Fund

4.6 The IMF was established in 1944. The three broad aims of the IMF are:

(a) to promote international monetary co-operation, and to establish a code of conduct for making international payments;

(b) to provide financial support to countries with temporary balance of payments deficits;

(c) to provide for the orderly growth of international liquidity, through its SDR scheme (launched in 1970). SDRs are a form of international currency, whose use is restricted.

4.7 Most countries of the world have membership of the IMF. The Soviet Union has not been a full member. However, during 1990 the influential USA permitted the Soviet Union to use IMF credit facilities as if it were a full member.

The IMF and financial support for countries with balance of payment difficulties

4.8 If a country has a balance of payments deficit on current account, it must either:

(a) borrow capital; or
(b) use up official reserves

to offset this deficit. Since a country's official reserves will be insufficient to support a balance of payments deficit on current account for very long, it must borrow to offset the deficit.

4.9 Until the 'eurocurrency' international lending markets emerged in the 1970s, international lending was mainly carried out by means of lending to governments by the IMF and World Bank, and the problem was seen mainly as one of providing governments with funds to top up their official reserves, to help them to overcome a short term balance of payments problem.

4.10 The IMF can provide financial support to member countries with *temporary* balance of payments difficulties. Most IMF loans are repayable in 3 to 5 years.

Of course, to lend money, the IMF must also have funds. Funds are made available from subscriptions or 'quotas' of member countries.

The IMF uses these subscriptions to lend foreign currencies to countries with a balance of payments deficit which apply to the IMF for help.

IMF loan conditions

4.11 The pre-conditions that the IMF places on its loans to debtor countries vary according to the individual situation of each country, but in general terms:

(a) the IMF regards its lending as fairly short-term in nature; this means that countries which borrow from the IMF should get into a position to start repaying the loans fairly quickly;

(b) to do this, the countries must take effective action to improve their balance of payments position;

(c) to do this, the IMF generally believes that a country should take action to reduce the demand for goods and services in the economy (eg by increasing taxes and cutting government spending). This will reduce imports and help to put a brake on any price rises. The country's industries should then also be able to divert more resources into export markets;

(d) with 'deflationary' measures along these lines, standards of living will fall (at least in the short term) and unemployment may rise. The IMF regards these short term hardships to be necessary if a country is to succeed in sorting out its balance of payments and international debt problems.

5. CONCLUSION

5.1 The key points in this chapter are as follows.

(a) The balance of payments accounts consist of a current account and transactions in capital (external assets and liabilities including official financing). The sum of the balances on these accounts must be zero, although in practice there is a balancing figure for measurement errors.

(b) A surplus or deficit on the balance of payments usually means a surplus or deficit on the current account. It is possible for countries to try to finance a deficit on the current account from a surplus on capital account, temporarily at least. However, to do so, the country must be able to attract finance (eg investment capital) from abroad, and so the country needs to remain 'creditworthy', with investors having confidence in the stability of the exchange rate for the country's currency. (A depreciation in the currency would create a capital loss for foreign investors.)

(c) A country can rectify a balance of payments deficit by:

(i) allowing its currency to depreciate or devalue in foreign exchange value;

(ii) imposing protectionist measures or exchange control regulations;

(iii) deflationary economic measures in the domestic economy. These are usually a precondition of any IMF financial assistance to countries in balance of payments difficulties.

(d) The success of measures to rectify a balance of payments deficit will depend on retaliatory measures by other countries, and also the price elasticity of demand for imports and exports. The effects of a fall in the exchange rate on the balance of payments were discussed in terms of elasticity of demand.

(e)   The balance of trade depends not only on the volumes of goods traded, but on the relative *prices* of exports and imports (ie on the terms of trade).

(f)   There are significant imbalances in international trade. Some countries, such as the UK, have large trade deficits, whereas others such as Japan have large surpluses. In the early 1980s, until the sovereign debt crisis emerged, developing countries such as Brazil and Mexico also financed a large trade deficit by borrowing from abroad. It remains to be seen how or whether these large trade imbalances will be fully rectified over time.

TEST YOUR KNOWLEDGE
The numbers in brackets refer to paragraphs of this chapter

1   What is the balance of payments? (1.1)

2   What is meant by the 'balance of trade? (1.7)

3   Why might a current account deficit matter? (2.2)

4   By which methods may a government try to reduce or eliminate a current account deficit? (2.13)

5   What are the 'terms of trade'? (3.2)

Now try illustrative question 22 at the end of the text

Chapter 13

EXCHANGE RATES

This chapter covers the following topics.

1. Exchanging currencies
2. Influences on exchange rates
3. Exchange rate policies and international cooperation
4. European monetary cooperation
5. Exchange controls

---

1. EXCHANGING CURRENCIES

Rates of exchange

1.1 An exchange rate is the rate at which one country's currency can be traded in exchange for another country's currency. If an exporter in the UK sells goods to a buyer in Germany, the invoice price might be £1,000. The German buyer would have to get the sterling to pay the invoice, and he would usually ask a bank to sell the sterling to him in exchange for deutschmarks. If the exchange rate is £1 = 3DM, the German buyer will pay his bank DM3000 for the sterling. The German bank, to obtain sterling to sell to its customers, would buy the sterling on one of the world's foreign exchange markets.

1.2 Although it is convenient to refer to the 'exchange rate' for currency - eg the exchange rate for sterling - every traded currency in fact has many exchange rates. There is an exchange rate with every other traded currency on the foreign exchange markets, so that there is an exchange rate for sterling with the US dollar, the Canadian dollar, the yen, the deutschmark, the French franc, and so on.

1.3 Foreign exchange dealers make their profit by buying currency for less than they pay for it, and so there are really 2 exchange rates, a selling rate and a buying rate; eg

	Bank's selling rate	*Bank's buying rate*
£/US dollar exchange rate	$1.5020	$1.5080

1.4 When exchange rates are quoted in the press, the 'middle rate' between the selling and buying rates would be used. In the example above, the sterling/US dollar exchange rate would be midway between $1.5020 and $1.5080 - ie $1.5050 to £1.

13: EXCHANGE RATES

Spot rates and forward rates

1.5 Broadly speaking, there are two ways in which foreign currency is bought and sold:

(a) *spot* - ie for immediate 'delivery';
(b) *forward* - ie for delivery at a date in the future.

1.6 Thus, a UK firm might receive US$100,000 from a US customer, and sell it 'spot' to a bank, to receive sterling immediately (in practice three days after the contract is made). If the exchange rate is $1.8000 to £1, the UK firm would receive £55,555.56.

1.7 If a firm knows that it is going to receive some foreign currency in the near future, which it will want to sell in exchange for domestic currency, it can make a forward exchange contract with a bank, at an exchange rate that is specified in the contract. Thus, if a firm knows that it is going to receive US$100,000 in three months' time, it can make a forward exchange contract 'now' to sell the US dollars in three months' time at a specified exchange rate. If the 'spot' rate is $1.8000 to £1, the 'forward' rate may be higher or lower than $1.8000 (depending on comparative interest rates in the USA and the UK).

The foreign exchange (FX) markets

1.8 Since foreign exchange rates are *not* fixed, but are allowed to vary ('float') according to market conditions, rates are continually changing, and each bank will offer new rates for new customer enquiries according to how its dealers judge the market situation. Dealers are kept continually informed of rates at which deals are currently being made, by means of computerised information services.

1.9 Although exchange rates are determined in the market by the forces of supply and demand, a government's policy on the exchange rate for its currency can have an important influence on how the exchange rate is determined in the FX markets.

1.10 International trade thus involves foreign currency, for either the buyer, the seller, or both (eg a Saudi Arabian firm might sell goods to a UK buyer and invoice for the goods in US dollars). As a consequence, it is quite likely that exporters might want to sell foreign currency earnings to a bank in exchange for domestic currency, and that importers might want to buy foreign currency from a bank in order to pay a foreign supplier.

1.11 The foreign exchange market is worldwide, and the main dealers are banks.

(a) Banks buy currency from customers and sell currency to customers - typically, exporting and importing firms.

(b) Banks may buy currency from the government or sell currency to the government - this is how a government builds up its official reserves.

(c) Banks also buy and sell currency between themselves.

1.12 Although the demand to buy and sell foreign currencies arises from the demand of individuals (eg tourists going abroad) firms (eg importers, exporters, firms investing overseas and governments) the bulk buying and selling of foreign currencies, as mentioned, is done mainly by banks in the foreign exchange markets of the world, such as London.

Measuring changes in a currency's exchange rates

1.13 When exchange rates fluctuate all the time, day by day, on the FX markets, it is obviously not possible to measure the exchange rate for any individual currency against a fixed standard. Sterling for example, changes in value continually against the US dollar, the deutschmark, the yen, the French franc, the Swiss franc, the Belgian franc, the lira, the Canadian dollar and so on.

1.14 How, then, can a currency's exchange rate trend be reported?

For any currency, there are two common methods of reporting exchange rates (assuming that exchange rates are not 'fixed' by international agreement):

(a) reporting the exchange rate for a currency against the foreign currency in which most foreign exchange deals are made;

(b) reporting the exchange rate against a 'basket' of other currencies on a trade-weighted basis.

1.15 In the case of sterling, the exchange rate is commonly reported:

(a) against the US dollar, because most foreign exchange deals in sterling are made in US dollars;

(b) against the deutschmark, because of the deutschmark's importance in Europe;

(c) against a basket of other currencies on a trade-weighted basis, as with the Exchange Rate Index (ERI).

2. INFLUENCES ON EXCHANGE RATES

Factors influencing the exchange rate for a currency

2.1 The exchange rate between two currencies - ie the buying and selling rates, both 'spot' and forward - is determined primarily by supply and demand in the foreign exchange markets. Demand comes from individuals, firms and governments who want to buy a currency and supply comes from those who want to sell it.

2.2 Supply and demand in turn are influenced by:

(a) the rate of inflation, compared with the rate of inflation in other countries;
(b) interest rates, compared with interest rates in other countries;
(c) the balance of payments;
(d) speculation;
(e) government policy on intervention to influence the exchange rate.

2.3   Other factors influence the exchange rate through their relationship with the items identified above. For example:

    (a)   total income and expenditure (demand) in the domestic economy determines the demand for goods, including:

        (i)   imported goods;
        (ii)   goods produced in the country which would otherwise be exported if demand for them did not exist in the home markets;

    (b)   output capacity and the level of employment in the domestic economy might influence the balance of payments, because if the domestic economy has full employment already, it will be unable to increase its volume of production for exports;

    (c)   the growth in the money supply influences interest rates and domestic inflation.

Purchasing power parity theory

2.4   If the rate of inflation is higher in one country than in another country, the value of its currency will tend to weaken against the other country's currency.

2.5   *Purchasing power parity theory*, which developed in the 1920s, attempted to explain changes in the exchange rate exclusively by the rate of inflation in different countries. The theory predicts that the exchange value of a foreign currency depends on the relative purchasing power of each currency in its own country. As a simple example, suppose that there is only one commodity, which costs £110 in the UK and 880 francs in France. The exchange rate would be £1 = 8 francs. If, as a result of inflation, the cost of the commodity in the UK rises to £120, the exchange rate would adjust to:

$$(8 \times \frac{110}{120}) \times £1 = 7.33 \text{ francs.}$$

If the exchange rate remained at £1 = 8 francs, it would be cheaper to import more of the commodity from France for £110 and the UK would have a balance of trade deficit. This would only be corrected by an alteration in the exchange rate, with the £ weakening against the franc.

2.6   Purchasing power parity theory states that an exchange rate varies according to relative price changes, so that

'Old' exchange rate $\times \dfrac{\text{Price level in country A}}{\text{Price level in country B}} = $ 'New' exchange rate

2.7   The theory has been found to be inadequate to explain movements in exchange rates in the short term, mainly because it ignores payments between countries (ie demand and supply transactions) and the influence of supply and demand for currency on exchange rates.

2.8 The demand and supply for goods and services between countries (ie the current account in the balance of payments) will obviously influence the demand and supply of currencies, and so the exchange rate.

Interest rates and the exchange rate

2.9 It would seem logical to assume that if one country raises its interest rates, it will become more profitable to invest in that country, and so an increase in (mainly short-term) investment from overseas will push up the exchange rate because of the extra demand for the currency from overseas investors.

2.10 This is true, but there is a limit to the amount of investment capital that will flow into a country because of higher interest rates. A major reason this is that investors may expect a 'risk premium' for investing in a high interest rate currency if they fear that the currency will depreciate in value. This seems to have been the case in the months following sterling's entry into the European Exchange Rate Mechanism (ERM) in October 1990. In spite of high interest rates in the UK, relative to other European currencies, sterling remained weak within the ERM, probably because investors feared that the UK government might seek a devaluation of the currency.

The balance of payments and the exchange rate

2.11 Purchasing power parity theory is more likely to have some validity in the long run, and it is certainly true that the currency of a country which has a much higher rate of inflation than other countries will weaken on the foreign exchange market. In other words, the rate of inflation relative to other countries is certainly a factor which influences the exchange rate.

Although this influence is obvious, it is not predominant. This is apparent from the fact that if exchange rates did respond to demand and supply for current account items, then the balance of payments on the current account of all countries would tend towards equilibrium. This is not so, and in practice other factors influence exchange rates more strongly.

2.12 Demand for currency to invest in overseas capital investments and supply of currency from firms disinvesting in an overseas currency have more influence on the exchange rate, in the *short term* at least, than the demand and supply of goods and services.

2.13 The effect of a surplus or deficit in the balance of payments on the exchange rate, in the absence of government intervention to 'manage' it, was described in the previous chapter of this book. However, you should note that if a country has a continual deficit in its balance of payments current account, international confidence in that country's currency will eventually be eroded, and in the long term, its exchange rate will fall as capital inflows are no longer sufficient to counterbalance the country's trade deficit.

Speculation and the exchange rate

2.14 Speculators in foreign exchange are investors who buy or sell assets in a foreign currency, in the expectation of a rise of fall in the exchange rate, from which they seek to make a profit.

(a) Speculation could be a stabilising influence. For example, if a country has a deficit on its current account in the balance of payments, there will be pressure on its currency to weaken. However, if speculators take the view that the deficit is only temporary, they might purchase assets in the currency when there is a balance of payments deficit and sell them, perhaps at a small profit, when the balance returns to surplus later.

(b) However, speculation is more likely to be destabilising by creating such a high volume of demand to buy or sell a particular currency that the exchange rate moves to a level where it is overvalued or under-valued in terms of what 'hard economic facts' suggest it should be.

If a currency does become undervalued by heavy speculative selling, investors can make a further profit by purchasing it at the undervalued price and selling it later when its price rises.

2.15 Much speculation occurred around the time of sterling's suspension from the European exchange rate mechanism in September 1992. Speculators were effectively 'betting' that sterling would have to leave the ERM and would fall in value as a result, and they were proved correct.

Other factors influencing the exchange rate

2.16 Before we consider government *intervention* as an influence on exchange rates, there are a number of other factors to note which influence the exchange rate of a currency because they affect the trade in goods and services and capital investments. These are as follows:

(a) The *natural resources of the country*. A country which is rich in natural resources should benefit not only from a net surplus on its current account (exports less payments of interest and dividends) but also from long term capital investment from overseas investors wanting to invest in the future exploitation of the resources. The country's currency should therefore be strong in the foreign exchange market.

(b) The *political stability of the country*. A country with an uncertain political or economic future is likely to suffer from disinvestment and speculation against its currency.

(c) Government intervention might take the form of *exchange controls, import controls* or *import tariffs*. If there is no retaliation by other countries against such measures, their effect should be to strengthen the exchange rate.

(d) Some currencies (especially the US dollar but also the yen and deutschmark, for example) are held as *reserve currencies* by other countries. (A reserve currency is a currency used as part of the official reserves of another country). Trading in a reserve currency by the governments of these other countries will influence the exchange rate of the currency.

(e) *Speculation* in a currency might be carried out *by traders* as well as investors of capital. When a currency is expected to devalue or depreciate, debtors who owe money in that currency will pay their debts more slowly, hoping that the currency will become cheaper by the time they have to pay. Debtors owing money in a currency which is expected to appreciate will pay more quickly, before the currency becomes more expensive. Quicker payments temporarily increase the demand for the currency in the foreign exchange market and slower payments temporarily reduce demand for a currency. These *leads and lags* add to the speculative pressure on currencies by altering supply and demand.

Government intervention

2.17 The government can intervene in the foreign exchange markets:

(a) to sell its own domestic currency in exchange for foreign currencies, when it wants to keep down the exchange rate of its domestic currency. The foreign currencies it buys can be added to the official reserves;

(b) to buy its own domestic currency and pay for it with the foreign currencies in its official reserves. It will do this when it wants to keep up the exchange rate when market forces are pushing it down.

2.18 The government can also intervene indirectly, by changing domestic interest rates, and so either attracting or discouraging investors in financial investments which are denominated in the domestic currency. Purchases and sales of foreign investments create a demand and supply of the currency in the FX markets, and so changes in domestic interest rates are likely to cause a change in the exchange rate.

2.19 By managing the exchange rate for its currency, a government does not stop all fluctuations in the exchange rate, but it tries to keep the fluctuations within certain limits. These limits might be:

(a) 'unofficial' - a government might intervene in the foreign exchange markets and sell foreign currency from its official reserves to buy the domestic currency, and so support its exchange rate, even though there is no officially declared exchange rate that it is trying to support; or

(b) official - eg countries in the European Exchange Rate Mechanism, allow their domestic currency to fluctuate against each other's currency only within specified limits. (Devaluation or revaluation beyond those limits is only permitted following a 'realignment' of ERM currencies.)

Consequences of an exchange rate policy

2.20 Reasons for a policy of controlling the exchange rate may be to:

(a) rectify a balance of trade deficit, by trying to bring about a fall in the exchange rate;

(b) prevent a balance of trade surplus from getting too large, by trying to bring about a limited rise in the exchange rate. Japan has been under international pressure to do this in recent years, and the Japanese government has attempted to 'manage' an appreciation of the yen to a level consistent with its general economic policy;

(c) emulate economic conditions in other countries. The UK's membership of the ERM (discussed later) has as one of its aims that of emulating the conditions of lower inflation which exist in other ERM member countries.

13: EXCHANGE RATES

Stabilising the exchange rate

2.21 A country's government might have a policy of wanting to *stabilise* the exchange rate of its currency. A stable currency increases confidence in the currency and promotes international trade.

(a) Exporters do not want their profit on trading to be wiped out by an adverse movement in exchange rates, which means that their foreign currency earnings are worth less in domestic currency than they anticipated when the export sale was made.

(b) Similarly, importers do not want to find that the cost of imported goods rises unexpectedly because of an adverse exchange rate movement, which means that they must spend more domestic currency to buy the foreign currency to pay their overseas suppliers.

UK balance of trade effects

2.22 You will remember from the previous chapter that the balance of trade will improve after a fall in the exchange rate if:

(a) the elasticity of demand for exports is high, (and the country's producers are able to gear up production to a higher volume of foreign demand);

(b) the elasticity of demand for imports is high.

The improvement will take time to occur, because of the J curve effect (see Figure 1 in Chapter 12).

2.23 In the UK, the demand for imports appears to be relatively price inelastic, and so a fall in the value of sterling would not reduce the value of imports significantly, if at all.

Exchange rate policy and inflation

2.24 Suppose sterling was devalued. What would happen?

(a) We have seen that *exports*, priced mainly in sterling, would become cheaper to foreign buyers. The volume and value of exports would rise.

(b) We have also seen that *imports*, priced mainly in foreign currencies, would become more expensive to UK buyers. However, since demand for imports is price inelastic, UK buyers continue to buy imports in large quantities, even at higher prices. For a country such as the UK, which depends heavily on imports, these higher import prices could add to the rate of inflation.

(c) *Inflation.* There could be an increase in the rate of inflation, because of:

(i) higher import prices;
(ii) higher wage settlements by UK firms.

If UK firms export goods abroad, a depreciation in sterling would help to boost their export sales and profits. This could encourage them to agree to higher wage settlements for employees, which could also be inflationary.

(d) *Balance of trade.* As a result of a depreciation in sterling, exports would rise, but so too would imports (due to inelastic demand). The balance of trade *might* improve, but not necessarily by much.

(e) *Capital transactions.* As a result of a depreciation in sterling, or a threatened depreciation, investors would switch capital out of sterling and into other currencies. These capital movements would result in sales of sterling on the FX markets, and create pressures for further depreciation.

2.25 In summary, a depreciation in sterling:

(a) could be inflationary;
(b) could create further problems for the UK balance of payments.

3. EXCHANGE RATE POLICIES AND INTERNATIONAL COOPERATION

Exchange rate policies of governments

3.1 We shall now go on to consider in more detail the different exchange rate policies which are open to governments. These may be categorised as:

(a) fixed exchange rates;
(b) free floating exchange rates;
(c) margins around a moveable peg;
(d) managed floating.

Fixed exchange rates

3.2 A policy of rigidly fixed exchange rates means that the government of every country in the international monetary system must use its official reserves to create an exact match between supply and demand for its currency in the FX markets, in order to keep the exchange rate unchanged. Using the official reserves will therefore cancel out a surplus or deficit on the current account and non-official capital transactions in their balance of payments. A balance of payments surplus would call for an addition to the official reserves, and a deficit calls for drawings on official reserves.

3.3 The official reserves could in theory consist of any foreign currency (or gold) within the fixed exchange rate agreement. The exchange rates of the various currencies in the system might all be fixed against each other. However, for simplicity and convenience, it is more appropriate to fix the exchange rate for every currency against a standard. The standard might be:

(a) gold. If every currency is valued in terms of gold, official reserves would consist mainly, or even entirely, of gold;

(b) a major currency, such as the US dollar. If every currency is valued in terms of the dollar, the fixed exchange rate between currencies is easily calculated. The dollars would then be the major reserve currency;

(c) a 'basket' of major trading currencies.

Floating exchange rates

3.4   Free floating exchange rates are at the opposite end of the spectrum to rigidly fixed rates. Exchange rates are left to the free play of market forces and there is no official financing at all. There is no need for the government to hold any official reserves, because it will not want to use them.

3.5   Floating exchange rates (free floating and managed floating) have been criticised in the past because they allow wide fluctuations in exchange rates. Certainly, in the foreign exchange markets today, there are large fluctuations which are unsettling for international trade. However, the (then) Governor of the Bank of England said in a speech (September 1981) that 'wide fluctuations in exchange rates are not a reason for criticising floating rate policies, since the underlying economic turbulence would have made a fixed rate system difficult, if not impossible, to work.'

3.6   Floating exchange rates are the only option available to governments when other systems break down and fail. Professor Friedman remarked (1967) 'Floating exchange rates have often been adopted by countries experiencing financial crises when all other devices have failed. That is a major reason why they have such a bad reputation.' In practice, countries would operate 'managed floating' of their currency and a policy of allowing a currency to float freely is rare.

Fixed versus floating rates: summary

3.7   A brief summary of the advantages and disadvantages of a system of fixed exchange rates compared with a system of floating exchange rates is given below.

Fixed rates: advantages

(a)   Removes exchange rate uncertainty and risk for importers and exporters and so encourages international trade.

(b)   Imposes economic disciplines on governments. The European ERM has been seen to help member countries reduce inflation to rates of other member countries. Devaluation is no longer an option if exchange rates are fully fixed.

Floating rates: advantages

(a)   Continuous adjustment of exchange rates.

(b)   Independence of domestic economic policies.

(c)   No need for large official reserves. (With free floating, no need for any official reserves).

(d)   A 'fall-back' system. If a fixed exchange rate system breaks down, exchange rates would 'naturally' float.

(e)   There is no imported inflation. Higher prices of imported goods are cancelled out by an appreciation in the domestic currency's exchange rate.

13: EXCHANGE RATES

Fixed rates: disadvantages

(a) Need for official reserves, eg US$ or gold. Reserves are not limitless, and the size of capital flows is extremely large.

(b) When a currency is clearly under- or over-valued, there will be speculation.

(c) Widely differing rates of inflation from one country to another make fixed rates impossible to maintain for more than a short period of time.

(d) Governments are reluctant to subordinate domestic economic interests for the sake of a fixed exchange rate. For example, a government's interest rate policy will need to be consistent with the exchange rate which must be maintained under a fixed rate system. This could conflict at times with government policy aims, such as reducing inflation or simulating economic growth.

(e) It is sometimes necessary to recognise a fundamental disequilibrium in a country's balance of payments devalue/revalue a domestic currency without trying to support an unrealistic exchange rate.

Floating rates: disadvantages

(a) Where imports are a large part of a country's economy (as in the UK) the exchange rate is too important for the government to ignore. In the absence of fixed exchange rates, there should at least be managed floating.

(b) There is a danger with managed floating that governments will pursue aggressive economic policies and provoke retaliation.

(c) The adjustment process to bring the balance of payments back into equilibrium does not necessarily work. Much depends on elasticities of demand for imports and exports and elasticities of supply.

(d) A failure to control domestic inflation will wipe out the competitive advantage of a depreciation of the currency, and so provoke further depreciation. With higher import and prices, higher wages and higher prices, there might be a price-wage spiral unless the government takes steps to control the economy firmly, including its exchange rate.

(e) With managed floating there is still a need for official reserves. Governments may be unable to prevent speculation because reserves are not enough.

A moveable peg or adjustable peg system

3.8 A moveable or adjustable peg system is a system of fixed exchange rates, but with a provision for:

(a) the devaluation of a currency, eg when the country has a fundamental balance of payments deficit;

(b) the revaluation of a currency, eg when the country has a fundamental balance of payments surplus.

3.9 A moveable peg system provides some flexibility. Exchange rates, although fixed, are not rigidly fixed, because adjustments are permitted. Even so, it is still fairly inflexible, because governments only have the choice between a revaluation/devaluation or holding the exchange rate steady. A more flexible system would allow some minor variations in exchange rates. For example, the exchange rate between sterling and the US dollar might be fixed at $2 to £1, but governments might only be required to maintain the exchange rate within a margin of, say, 2% on either side of this rate. If this were the case, the UK government would undertake to keep the exchange rate for sterling between $1.96 and $2.04 to £1.

3.10 The current European Exchange Rate Mechanism (ERM) is an adjustable peg system. The advantages and disadvantages of an adjustable peg system will however be discussed firstly below within the context of the Bretton Woods agreement.

The Bretton Woods agreement 1944-1971

3.11 The Bretton Woods agreement was formulated in 1944 near the end of the Second World War but it was adopted only gradually as national economies recovered from the devastations of war. The terms of the international monetary system created by the agreement, which was eventually adopted by most advanced Western countries, were as follows.

(a) There was agreement on fixed exchange rates, but with:

(i) an adjustable peg. Countries were permitted to devalue or revalue their currency when their balance of payments was in 'fundamental disequilibrium'. The exchange rates were fixed ('pegged') against gold, but it became common practice to express exchange rates against the US dollar;

(ii) a margin on either side of the pegged rate was permitted. The monetary authorities of each country undertook to use their official reserves to keep their currency's exchange value within plus or minus 1% of the par value. (The margins for fluctuation were quite narrow, at only 1%).

(b) The US dollar was pegged to gold at the rate of $35 per ounce. The US authorities were prepared to buy and sell dollars for gold at this rate, with any other central bank in the system.

3.12 The system succeeded for a while in achieving its main aim. Exchange rate stability did appear to improve business confidence, and in the 1960s, international trade expanded at an unprecedented rate. Most national economies had high rates of growth, output and employment.

3.13 Eventually, however, problems crept into the system and it collapsed in 1971.

(a) The system depended on exchange rates remaining fixed for long periods of time, but for a devaluation or revaluation to be made as soon as a fundamental disequilibrium in a country's balance of payments became apparent.

(i) Countries with a balance of payments surplus did not want to revalue their currency and pursue inflationary policies.

(ii) Deficit countries were reluctant to recognise a fundamental disequilibrium in their balance of payments.

(b) Fixing the nominal value of exchange rates did not protect real values, because the rate of inflation differed from one country to another. The problem of inflation meant that exchange rates would need to be adjusted more frequently, thereby removing a major reason for having a fixed exchange rate/adjustable peg system.

(c) Speculation could put excessive pressure on a currency, and force a devaluation.

(d) International liquidity also became a problem because of loss of confidence in the US dollar.

Managed floating

3.14 By 1973, most major currencies had abandoned official par rates and were allowed to float. Floating was adopted because the alternatives had failed, and not for any more positive reason. A major problem with floating exchange rates in the 1980s was the wide fluctuations in foreign exchange rates for the leading international currencies.

3.15 Short term variability is inconvenient to traders and travellers abroad, but traders can protect themselves by using the forward exchange markets. *Long term volatility* is more of a problem because:

(a) a long term under-valuation of a currency affects the competitiveness of its exports and makes the country more receptive to imports;

(b) a long term under-valuation of a currency makes some investments seem worthwhile that might later turn out to be unprofitable if more 'realistic' exchange rates are re-established;

(c) it discourages long term investment.

3.16 Concern about the volatility of exchange rates led to some efforts of the authorities of the major Western countries to give the markets a lead, and make a more conscious attempt at managed floating of exchange rates.

3.17 Two international agreements were reached.

(a) the Plaza agreement in September 1985;
(b) the Louvre accord (or Paris agreement) in February 1987.

The Plaza agreement 1985

3.18 The Plaza agreement was an agreement by the authorities of the five major countries * to co-operate in securing an orderly fall in the value of the US dollar, which they thought had become seriously over-valued.

(* The Group of Five - ie the USA, Japan, West Germany, France and the UK.)

3.19 There was a general belief that:

    (a)   the gyrations in exchange rates in the foreign exchange markets had become excessive and were damaging international trade and investment;

    (b)   there was an immediate problem of an over-valued US dollar;

    (c)   it was time for the authorities of the major countries to give the markets a lead, to indicate what they thought exchange rates ought to be.

3.20 The outcome of the Plaza agreement was a steady fall in the value of the US dollar over the next fifteen months, encouraged by a policy of managed floating from the governments of all five countries concerned.

The Louvre accord, 1987

3.21 By early 1987, the authorities of the countries involved believed that the US dollar had fallen far enough. However, it was agreed that international co-operation on exchange rates should continue, with managed floating of exchange rates, but that current exchange rates were more or less 'correct'. The Louvre accord between the 'Group of Seven' (G7) countries, ie the USA, West Germany, Japan, the UK, France, Canada and Italy - was a further agreement at international co-operation on managing exchange rates with the aim of securing greater stability in exchange rates.

3.22 Initially the accord appears to have been an agreement to try to keep exchange rates at about their current levels, with central banks intervening in the foreign exchange markets or perhaps adjusting domestic interest rates to prevent excessive changes in the rates. Some fluctuations in rates within tolerable margins would be permitted, but currencies should not rise or fall in value beyond these margins.

3.23 Apart from statements that the Louvre accord was very flexible, there were no public details on just what the accord was!

It involved two main ingredients however:

    (a)   a willingness by the central banks of the countries involved to intervene directly in the foreign exchange markets on a large scale;

    (b)   an apparent willingness for the countries involved to co-ordinate their monetary and fiscal policies, so as to achieve the essential requirements for exchange rate stability.

How was international co-operation on managed floating made possible?

3.24 There appear to have been two main reasons why the authorities of the major countries have been able to agree on a policy of co-operating over managed floating of exchange rates.

    (a)   Inflation rates were reduced to low levels, and so authorities did not have to give such pre-eminence in their monetary policies to reducing the rate of inflation.

(b) The authorities of the major countries have achieved a broad consensus about their approach to economic policy based on firm fiscal and monetary measures. This has made it easier for the countries to agree on what the exchange rates of their currencies ought to be.

'What made the Plaza and Louvre agreements possible was that the countries participating were, and remain, in effect, members of an anti-inflationary club, with a clear commitment to taking whatever steps are necessary to curb their own inflation. It is vital that the commitment continues, individually and collectively.' *(The Chancellor of the Exchequer, September 1987)*

Has international co-operation on managed floating been successful?

3.25 International co-operation at managed floating had some success:

(a) there was a successful depreciation of the dollar in 1986;

(b) there was a period of several months in 1987 when exchange rates remained more or less stable, and within what was believed to be the (undisclosed) limits set by the Louvre accord. However, the value of the dollar was kept up to some extent by large-scale intervention in the foreign exchange markets by the central banks of the G7 countries (particularly West Germany, Japan and the UK), to buy US dollars in exchange for their own domestic currencies.

Recent G7 actions on exchange rates

3.26 In September 1989, the finance ministers and central bank governors from the Group of Seven (G7) countries - the USA, Japan, West Germany, France, Britain, Canada and Italy - issued a joint statement that a 'rise of the dollar above current levels, or an excessive decline, could affect prospects for the world economy'.

They pledged to continue to co-operate closely in the foreign exchange markets, which at that time meant agreement to intervene in the markets to try to keep *down* the US dollar's value.

3.27 There have also been subsequent instances of concerted intervention by the G7 group, for example in February 1991, indicating that international monetary cooperation is not yet dead. The intervention in February 1991 involved the buying of dollars by the central banks of all the G7 countries except Japan. This was designed to halt the steep fall in the US dollar. This fall had been caused by a widening of interest rate differentials between the US, which was cutting rates to alleviate recession, and Germany, which had applied upward pressure on rates to dampen possible inflationary tendencies following German reunification.

3.28 In general, it appears that G7 statements on exchange rates have been designed to reduce fluctuations in the US dollar exchange rate rather than to aim for any particular exchange rate which might be perceived as the 'optimal' rate.

The need for international agreements on exchange rates

3.29 The 'globalisation' of capital markets has been a major reason for the desire of Western governments to co-ordinate their monetary and fiscal policies. Within Europe, monetary and economic convergence has been fostered within the European Monetary System. This is discussed in the next section of this chapter.

4. EUROPEAN MONETARY COOPERATION

The European Monetary System (EMS)

4.1 The European Community opted for a 'local' international agreement on exchange rates, originally known as the European Snake but amended in 1979 to the EMS system. In the EMS:

(a) there is a scheme of margins around a central peg for exchange rates between the currencies of the countries in the EMS; but

(b) a policy of managed floating between their currencies and the currencies of countries outside the system.

4.2 The Exchange Rate Mechanism (ERM) is the exchange rate agreement of the European Monetary System, formed on 13 March 1979. The United Kingdom has been a member of the EMS since then, but did not join the exchange rate mechanism of the EMS until October 1990, suspending its membership in September 1992. Italy left the ERM in the same month. The ERM member nations (at the time of writing) are the nations of the European Community, excluding Greece, Italy and the UK. Belgium and Luxembourg are in a monetary union. The currencies within the ERM are the following:

(a) Belgian franc;
(b) Danish krone;
(c) German mark;
(d) French franc;
(e) Dutch guilder;
(f) Irish punt;
(g) Spanish peseta;
(h) Portuguese escudo.

4.3 The purposes of the EMS are:

(a) in the long term, to develop European economic and monetary union (EMU);

(b) in the shorter term, to promote economic convergence in Europe, pushing inflation rates down by forcing economic policies on partner governments similar to the policies of the more successful members (eg Germany);

(c) in the immediate term, to stabilise exchange rates between the currencies of the member countries.

4.4 The main features of the EMS are as follows.

(a) It provides for the system of exchange rates for member currencies commonly known as the 'ERM'. Each currency has a 'central parity' rate against the ecu (see (b)).

(b) The EMS created the new currency, the *European Currency Unit or ecu*. An ecu is a unit of currency based on a 'basket' of the currencies of the participating countries. The value of the ecu therefore depends on the weightings given to each individual currency in the basket, and these weightings were based on the relative importance of each currency in European Community trade at the time the ecu was devised.

(c) Until mid-1993, within the ERM the exchange rate of the currency of each member country was permitted to vary within a margin of plus or minus $2\frac{1}{4}$% against its central parity, except for the Spanish peseta, the UK pound (when it was a member) and the Portuguese escudo which have been allowed a 6% margin. Each currency must also keep within the same limit ($2\frac{1}{4}$% or 6% as applicable) of each other currency within the system. However, the limits for most of the ERM currencies were raised to 15% in August 1993.

(d) The exchange rate of each currency is therefore pegged against the ecu and also against every other ERM member currency.

(e) In addition, there are limits on the ecu equivalents of currencies' values, narrower than the margins mentioned in (c) above, which act as an early warning system. When these limits (or 'divergence thresholds') are reached it is presumed that the central bank of the countries concerned will intervene, using its official reserves and acting to buy or sell its currency in the foreign exchange markets. If central bank intervention in the FX markets is not sufficient, a government might have to change interest rates in order to make its currency more or less attractive to hold.

(f) As the ERM is a 'moveable peg' system, occasional revaluations or devaluations of the central parity rates can occur, but only as a last resort measure. These are called *realignments*. There were four realignments between March 1983 and January 1987, but none from January 1987 up to September 1992, when the Italian lira and the Spanish peseta were devalued.

The raising of the permitted margins to 15%, following significant downward pressure in the value of the French franc in mid-1993, has made the ERM so flexible as to be largely ineffectual. The major European currencies are therefore effectively floating against each other again.

Sterling's membership of the ERM

4.5 On sterling's entry into the ERM in October 1990, a central 'parity' rate equivalent to DM 2.95 per pound was set and sterling was allocated its 6% margins within the system. The initially wide margin for sterling was intended to allow the financial markets time to adjust to ERM membership. The rules of the ERM already outlined provide that with its 6% margins, sterling could not fall 6% below the strongest currency in the ERM (nor 6% above the weakest) at any particular time.

4.6 The central parity rate of DM 2.95 was seen by some as being too high. A high exchange rate for sterling has the effect of 'squeezing' exporters who have to cut costs in order to remain competitive: it was argued by some that this would encourage wage restraint because these exporters would be encouraged to resist large wage increases.

4.7 However, membership of the ERM should enable UK exporters, and foreign investors in the UK, to plan ahead with more certainty on pricing and profit margins. There is less risk that a decline in sterling will lead to fluctuations in the prices of imported components. Manufacturers, it is hoped, will control their costs and improve productivity, knowing that devaluation of the currency is not available as an option if they should price themselves out of their markets. So, instead of interest rates, the main weapon against inflation becomes the knowledge that it will not be possible to pass on cost increases, particularly wage cost increases, in international markets and in internationally competitive domestic markets.

4.8 Exchange rate stability within an exchange rate regime such as the ERM prevents a government from allowing the currency to drift downwards in value to compensate for inflation. At the same time, it means that interest rate policy must be consistent with keeping the currency stable. If interest rates are too high, foreign investors will buy sterling, leading to capital inflows, much of which may be of short term 'hot money', and there will be upward pressure on the currency. If interest rates are too low, there will conversely be downward pressure on the currency.

4.9 Another consequence of stabilisation within an exchange rate system is that there may be effects on people's expectations and on the perceived risk of exchange rate movements between member currencies. As well as allowing firms to plan and forecast with greater certainty, exchange rate stability ought to make a currency less risky to hold.

Sterling's suspension from the ERM - September 1992

4.10 The stability of sterling within the ERM relied on market confidence that no such devaluation is likely to take place. Statements by the Chancellor the Exchequer Norman Lamont could often be seen as designed to bolster that confidence. For example, on 27 November 1991 Mr Lamont stated: 'Come what may, we intend to stick within our bounds of the ERM. We have no intention whatsoever of altering our parity'.

4.11 During September 1992, the UK government was forced to leave the ERM following a relatively short period of turmoil on the European foreign exchange markets. Interest rates in Germany remained relatively high, largely because of the need to finance economic development in the Eastern half of that country. There was also growing uncertainty about the political climate surrounding moves to European Economic and Monetary Union. Turbulence in the foreign exchange markets led to the devaluation of the Italian lira and its departure from the ERM, and the devaluation of the Spanish peseta.

4.12 Huge flows of speculative money switched out of sterling into other currencies (eg the US dollar and the deutschmark) and the Bank of England was forced to intervene heavily, spending a total of £10 billion in foreign exchange reserves to buy sterling. Sterling's value continued to fall in spite of this, and in spite of a final move by the UK government to raise base interest rates from 10% to 15% in a single day. Hours later, the suspension of sterling from the ERM was announced; interest rates were brought back to 10% and sterling was floated on the foreign exchange markets.

Has the EMS been successful?

4.13 The shorter term aims of consistent economic policies and exchange rate stability have had mixed success.

4.14 The successes of the EMS have been:

(a) the relative stability of the value of the ecu against other world currencies, and the slowly developing use of the ecu in international commerce;

(b) member countries beginning to accept the need for broadly similar economic policies;

(c) it has survived since 1979, although, as already mentioned, in a rather ineffectual form following the raising of the ERM margins to 15% in August 1993.

4.15 The failures of the EMS have been:

(a) the slowness of progress towards European monetary union;

(b) frequent realignment of currency values, which has often undermined the stability of exchange rates that was being sought;

(c) the fact that the government of an individual member state might refuse to adapt its economic policies to the needs of a stable EMS. For example in the early years of the presidency of M Mitterrand, France adopted an independent (but eventually unsuccessful) economic policy.

Steps towards European EMU (Economic and Monetary Union)

4.16 One of the aims behind the EMS is European Economic and Monetary Union (EMU). This is a long-standing objective of the EC, reaffirmed in the Single European Act of 1985.

(a) *Monetary union* can be defined as a single currency area, which would require a monetary policy for the area as a whole.

(b) *Economic union* can be described as an unrestricted common market for trade, with some economic policy co-ordination between different regions in the union.

4.17 Although the whole package of measures included in EMU is not paralleled anywhere else in the world, there have been many international monetary unions. For example, Belgium and Luxembourg are in a monetary union as mentioned earlier, and the UK and the Republic of Ireland were in currency union until the 1970s. There are three main aspects to full European monetary union.

(a) A *common currency*. By this, we mean that instead of using sterling in the UK, deutschmarks in Germany and francs in France, a common currency will be used for normal everyday money transactions by everyone in the monetary union.

(b) A *European central bank*. A European central bank would have the role of:

(i) issuing the common currency;
(ii) conducting monetary policy on behalf of the central government authorities;

      (iii) acting as lender of last resort to all European banks;

      (iv) managing the exchange rate for the common currency.

(c)   A *centralised monetary policy* for all the countries within the union. This would involve the surrender of control over aspects of economic policy and therefore surrender of some political sovereignty by the government of each member state to the central government body of the union.

4.18 Advantages of having a single European currency are as follows.

(a)   For organisations trading within the single currency area, uncertainty about exchange rate movements would be eliminated. Business confidence would be improved. The need to 'hedge' against foreign exchange risks would be removed. There would also be savings in the transactions costs (bank commission etc) involved in exchanging currencies.

(b)   Without transactions costs and the costs of hedging against foreign exchange risks (eg having to arrange forward exchange contracts) trade between countries in the currency area would become easier and the volume of trade should increase.

4.19 The disadvantages of a single European currency are a bit more difficult to assess.

(a)   The main problem is that each member state's government loses its autonomy over its domestic monetary policy.

(b)   In particular, a government cannot use changes in the exchange rate for its currency as a policy weapon to influence the national economy.

Recent developments

4.20 During 1991 further talks took place on the formulation of a new treaty on European economic and monetary union (EMU), culminating in the signing at the December 1991 Maastricht summit of a Treaty agreement. The agreement remains unratified at the time of writing. A referendum in Denmark has turned out against the agreement, while a referendum in France has been narrowly in favour.

4.21 Early in 1991, it seemed as though opposition in the UK to a single European currency stood as the main obstacle to EMU. However, other events have served to highlight that establishing EMU could be complex and problematic for other reasons.

(a)   One such event is German unification which has had far greater economic consequences for that country, such as a budget deficit and a need for higher interest rates, than were envisaged earlier.

(b)   Another is the rapid and widespread political change in the former command economies of Eastern Europe: at the same time as the European Community (EC) is considering *strengthening* the Community (for example through the proposed creation of a single currency), the new issue of *widening* EC membership to include a number of new member states is coming to the fore. The emergent market economies of the former communist bloc would not be able to 'converge' economically with the existing EC countries in terms of inflation, public finances and external accounts for some time to come, raising questions about whether the EC might require a 'two-tier' structure to accommodate some of the aspiring new members.

(c) Finally, the Maastricht Treaty encompassing EMU could collapse if individual countries fail to agree on its implementation.

4.22 In the remainder of this section, we discuss plans for the ambitious venture of EMU as envisaged in the Maastricht Treaty.

EMU Stage 1

4.23 The Maastricht proposals envisage the completion of Stage 1 of EMU by the beginning of 1994. In this stage EC member states are to take appropriate steps to ensure economic convergence, particularly with regard to price stability and public finances.

EMU Stage 2

4.24 Stage 2 of EMU is to begin in January 1994. This stage is to include the creation of a European Monetary Institute (EMI) which will coordinate monetary policy among the twelve current EC members and will also be concerned with issues of banking supervision. The establishment of a European Central Bank which was proposed under the original 'Delors plan' is delayed until Stage 3 when the creation of a single European currency would require such an institution. In Stage 2, monetary policy in EC member states will remain under the control of each state's monetary authorities (ie the government and the Bank of England in the UK).

4.25 During Stage 2, member states will be expected to avoid excessive government deficits, and to begin to make their own central banks independent.

4.26 The most important decisions on the creation of a full monetary union are due to be made by the end of 1996. By this time, the European Commission and the EMI will report to the European Council of Ministers on the progress made by EC member states towards EMU. Central to this is the degree of economic 'convergence' achieved by the member states with regard to inflation, interest rates, government debt and budget deficits, and exchange rate stability.

4.27 Four convergence criteria have been formulated for individual member countries to meet:

(a) an individual nation's inflation rate of consumer prices should be within $1\frac{1}{2}$ percentage points of the three lowest national rates, and price performance should be 'sustainable';

(b) a nation's long-term interest rate should be within 2 percentage points of the same three nations;

(c) a nation's general budget deficit should not exceed 3 per cent of gross domestic product *or* a gross public debt to GDP ratio of 60 per cent, unless it is falling 'at a satisfactory pace'.

(d) there should be no devaluation within the ERM in the previous two years.

4.28 Many of the potential new entrants to the EC, such as Austria, Norway, Switzerland, Sweden and Finland could find it easier to comply with the convergence criteria than some of the current member states.

EMU Stage 3

4.29 On the basis of the European Commission's and the EMI's reports, the Council of Ministers will decide whether to move to Stage 3 of EMU and, if so, when this should start. If this is agreed, in Stage 3 exchange rates will be fixed irrevocably and a European central bank will take over the functions of the EMI.

4.30 By 1998, if a single currency has not been introduced earlier, the Council of Ministers will assess which member states meet the conditions for joining a full economic and monetary union. These states will go ahead to the final stage of EMU – and a single European currency – by 1 January 1999 at the latest. Other states may join later when they meet the convergence criteria.

The UK and EMU

4.31 The following special 'opt-out clause' for the UK appears in the Maastricht Treaty:

'The United Kingdom shall not be obliged or committed to move to the third stage of economic and monetary union without a separate decision to do so by its government and Parliament.'

5. EXCHANGE CONTROLS

5.1 A government can seek to regulate imports and at the same time manage the exchange rate for its currency by controlling foreign exchange transactions.

5.2 For example:

(a) exporters might be required to sell all their foreign currency from sales abroad to authorised exchange dealers at a fixed rate of exchange;

(b) importers might be required to obtain currency for foreign payments by buying from the authorised dealers at a fixed rate. The supply of available foreign exchange to importers might be rationed out by further government control;

(c) restrictions might be placed on the export of capital or cash (the nation's currency) so as to restrict the supply of the currency and thereby maintain its value.

5.3 The types of exchange control vary from country to country. The more common ones are as follows.

    (a) *Controls over inflows:*

        (i)   suspension of the convertibility of foreign currency into the domestic currency;

        (ii)   outright prohibition of the taking by banks of additional deposits from non-residents;

        (iii) instructions to banks to place a proportion of their non-resident deposits with the central bank interest-free; this device reduces the yield to the banks from their investment of the deposit received from abroad.

    (b) *Controls over outflows:*

        (i)   requirements that organisations or individuals wishing to transfer cash abroad must buy the necessary foreign currency from the central bank, which examines the transactions before agreeing to provide the currency;

        (ii)   rules as to the transactions for which cash may be transferred abroad – for example, all business transactions might be allowed, but personal transactions restricted;

        (iii) currency required for certain non-business transactions to be purchased at a price different from that for business deals – perhaps through a two-tier system of exchange rates, or a separate pool of investment currency;

        (iv) prohibition of the holding by residents of any foreign currency, even that which arises as a result of international trading.

5.4   In the United Kingdom, all four of the above controls over outflows were in operation for capital transactions until removed by the government in 1979. Exchange controls remain common in less developed countries.

5.5   Europe's 'single market' programme requires the removal of all capital controls between EC countries. Nevertheless, such controls were reintroduced by Spain in September 1992 to try to protect the value of the peseta within the ERM.

5.6   Controls over capital *inflows* tend to be short-lived crisis measures since by and large countries welcome inflows of foreign currency to bolster the national convertible currency reserves. Increased reserves provide extra means of supporting the exchange rate, should there be net capital outflows in the future. Controls over capital outflows, however, are usually permanent. In part, this is to protect the reserves so that there are funds available to support a weak exchange rate, when the government is operating a managed float policy.

5.7   The stringency of the controls over *outflows* depends upon the particular circumstances of the country concerned. As a general rule, it can be stated that the controls in the least developed countries tend to be the tightest, since capital is desperately needed to finance domestic industrialisation. As economies become more sophisticated, the controls tend to be progressively relaxed.

6. CONCLUSION

6.1 Factors influencing the exchange rate are the comparative rates of inflation in different countries, comparative interest rates in different countries, the underlying balance of payments, speculation and government policy on managing or fixing exchange rates.

6.2 The traditional view that exchange rates will depend in the long run on the country's balance of trade (more exactly, on its current account surplus or deficit) is still valid.

6.3 However, *capital transactions* can influence the exchange rate significantly, especially in the short term.

6.4 Exchange rates are essentially determined by supply and demand, but governments can intervene to influence the exchange rate. Government policies on exchange rates might be fixed exchange rates or free floating exchange rates as two extreme policies. In practice, 'in-between' schemes have been:

(a) fixed rates, but with provision for devaluations or revaluations of currencies from time to time ('adjustable pegs') and also some fluctuations ('margins') around the fixed exchange value permitted - eg Bretton Woods, the ERM;

(b) managed floating - eg the US dollar, the yen.

6.5 Exchange controls can be another policy for protecting a domestic currency, as well as protecting domestic industry against foreign imports.

TEST YOUR KNOWLEDGE
The numbers in brackets refer to paragraphs of this chapter

1 What are spot and forward exchange rates? (1.5)

2 What does the theory of purchasing power parity say? (2.5-2.6)

3 How may the government intervene in the foreign exchange markets? (2.17)

4 What are the advantages and disadvantages of fixed exchange rates? (3.7)

5 What are the advantages and disadvantages of floating exchange rates? (3.7)

6 What are the purposes of the European Monetary System? (4.3)

7 What is the European Currency Unit? (4.4)

8 What is meant by EMU? (4.16)

Now try illustrative questions 23 and 24 at the end of the text

Accelerator principle	The theory that new investment increases in response to a change in output.
Aggregate demand	The total of planned expenditure on goods and services in an economy.
Autonomous investment	Expenditure on investment which is not induced by changes in income levels. Infrastructure investment by government and investment by firms on new plant to exploit an invention are examples.
Balance of payments	The statistical accounting record of all of a country's external transactions in a given period.
Business cycle (or trade cycle)	The periodic fluctuation of levels of economic activity, for example output and employment.
Cartel	An association of supplier for the purpose of cooperating on the fixing of variables such as price and output levels.
Central bank	The institution which has the job of controlling the monetary and banking system, acts as banker to the banks, and as lender of last resort. Most are established as public bodies, but the degree of independence varies between countries, as do the precise functions of the central bank.
Central planning	An economic system in which the government makes all major economic decisions.
Ceteris paribus	A Latin term, meaning 'other things being equal' or 'other things remaining unchanged'.
Comparative advantage	The principle that economic agents are best employed in activities which they carry out relatively better than in other activities. A country has a comparative advantage in producing good X over good Y if it can produce good X at a low opportunity cost relative to good Y. Applied to international trade, a country will gain from specialising in producing goods in which it has a comparative advantage.
Complements	Two goods are complements of each other if changes in the demand for one will have a complementary effect on the demand for the other, eg compact disc players and compact discs; cars and petrol.
Consumption	The use of goods and services to satisfy current wants.
Cost-push inflation	Inflation resulting from an increase in the costs of production of goods and services, eg through escalating prices of imported raw materials or from wage increases.
Credit	A wide term, broadly referring to the financing of the expenditure of others against future repayment to enable them to purchase goods and services out of future income.

GLOSSARY

Cross elasticity of demand   A measure of the responsiveness of demand for one good to changes in the price of another: the percentage change in the quantity demanded of one good divided by the percentage change in the price of the other good.

Demand management   An approach to economic policy making which seeks to control the level of aggregate demand through fiscal policy and/or monetary policy.

Demand-pull inflation   Inflation resulting from a persistent excess of aggregate demand over aggregate supply. Supply reaches a limit on capacity at the full employment level.

Devaluation   A reduction in the fixed or pegged exchange rate between one currency and other currencies.

Diminishing returns   The law of diminishing returns (or law of variable proportions) states that as additional units of a factor or production are employed, while others are held constant, the additional output thereby generated (its marginal physical product) will eventually diminish.

Direct taxation   Tax levied directly on individuals or firms, such as income tax, corporation tax, and capital gains tax.

Economic rent   Payment received for the services of a factor of production in excess of its transfer earnings or opportunity cost.

Economies of scale   Reductions in the average cost of producing a commodity in the long run as the output of the commodity increases.

Entrepreneur   An economic agent who organises the exploitation of factors of production in a firm.

Eurocurrency   Currency which is held by individuals and institutions outside the country of issue of the currency.

Exchange rate   The price of a currency expressed in terms of another currency.

Externality   Positive or negative external effects on third parties resulting from production and consumption activities.

Factor of production   The resources or inputs used in production. The main categories of the factors of production are land, labour and capital, with entrepreneurship sometimes treated as a fourth.

Fine tuning   A term referring to government policies which are designed to influence employment, national income and price levels by making small changes in taxation and expenditure.

Fiscal policy   The regulation of the economy through taxation and government expenditure.

Floating exchange rates   Exchange rates which are allowed to fluctuate according to demand and supply conditions in the foreign exchange markets.

GLOSSARY

Giffen good	A commodity for which demand increases with a rise in price and falls with a lowering of price, because the income effect outweighs the substitutions effect.
Gross domestic product (GDP)	A measure of the value of the goods and services produced by an economy in a given period.
Gross national product (GNP)	GDP plus the income accruing to domestic residents from investments abroad less income accruing to foreign residents from investments in the domestic market.
Horizontal integration	The merging of firms producing similar products.
Imperfect market	A market in which the assumptions of perfect competition do not hold (see *Perfect market*), and the forces which create the conditions of productive and allocative efficiency are hindered as a result.
Income effect	The effect on the level of consumption of a good of a change in real income caused by a change in its price.
Income elasticity of demand	A measure of the responsiveness of demand to changes in income: the percentage change in the quantity of a good demanded, divided by the percentage change in the income of consumers, with prices held constant.
Indirect taxation	Tax on the sale of goods and services, such as value added tax.
Inferior good	A good for which demand falls as consumers' incomes rise.
Inflation	A sustained rise in the general level of prices.
Interest rate	The percentage of a sum lent which the borrower pays to the lender: in other words, the price of money.
Investment	The production or maintenance of the real capital stock (eg machinery, buildings) which will allow the production of goods and services for future consumption.
Invisible trade	The exporting and importing of services (as distinct from physically visible goods).
Laffer curve	A curve depicting the relationship between tax revenue and the average tax rate, designed to illustrate the thesis that there is an optimal tax rate at which tax revenues are maximised.
Long run	The period of time over which all factors of production can be varied.

GLOSSARY

Macroeconomics	The study of the economy as a whole.
Marginal cost	The additional cost of producing an additional unit of output.
Marginal rate of taxation	The rate of tax on an additional unit of income earned.
Marginal utility	The additional satisfaction derived from a commodity by an individual from the consumption of one extra unit of the commodity.
Market	A situation in which potential buyers and potential sellers of a good or service come together for the purpose of exchange.
Market economy	An economy in which economic decisions are made by consumers, producers and owners of factors of production.
Market failure	A situation in which the market mechanism fails to result in economic efficiency, and therefore the outcome is sub-optimal.
Microeconomics	The study of the behaviour of individual economic units, particularly consumers and firms.
Mixed economy	An economy in which both public and private enterprise engage in economic activity. All contemporary economic systems are mixed to some extent.
Monetarism	A school of thought in economics which takes the view that instability in the economy is largely caused by factors within the monetary sector.
Monetary policy	The regulation of the economy through control of the monetary system by operating on such variables as the money supply, the level of interest rates and the conditions for availability of credit.
Money	Something which is generally acceptable in settling debts, or in exchanging for goods.
Money markets	The markets for lending and borrowing largely short-term capital, including for example the discount market (the market for bills), the interbank market, the market in Certificates of Deposit, the local authority market and the commercial paper market.
Money supply	The amount or stock of money in an economy.
Monopolistic competition	A market structure in which a large number of competing suppliers each sell a differentiated product.
Monopoly	A market with only one supplier of a product.
Multiplier	The ratio of the change in income to the change in expenditure which caused it.

GLOSSARY

National debt

The total outstanding debt obligations of central government, comprising both marketable debt (eg securities) and non-marketable debt (eg national savings certificates).

National income

A measure of the value of goods and services available to the people in an economy in a given period.

Negative income tax

A scheme in which payments are made to individuals or households whose income falls below a specific level.

Non-price competition

The use of means other than lower prices to seek to attract business from competitors. Product differentiation and special offers are examples.

Normal profit

The minimum profit which a firm must earn in order to induce it to stay in production. At this level of profit, the opportunity costs of the entrepreneur retaining capital in the business are just covered by total revenue.

Oligopoly

A market dominated by a few suppliers.

Opportunity cost

It is fundamental to economics that the opportunity cost of an action is the value of the alternative action which is forgone by doing it.

Optimum

A situation in which the objective of an economic unit is being served in the most effective way possible, given the constraints which apply.

Perfect market

A perfectly competitive market is one in which there is a large number of firms, each with a very small share of the market, producing a homogeneous product, with firms and consumer possessing perfect information, and with free entry to and exit from the industry.

Phillips curve

A curve depicting a relationship between the level of unemployment and inflation in prices or wages.

Positive economics

The part of economics which is concerned with statements which are verifiable by reference to facts.

Price discrimination

The practice of charging different prices for a product to different groups of consumers, or to the same consumer for different units of the product. For price discrimination to succeed, segmentation of the market and prevention of resale between segments must both be possible.

Price elasticity of demand

A measure of the responsiveness of demand to changes in price: the percentage change in the quantity of a good demanded, divided by the percentage change in its price.

Price elasticity of supply

A measure of the responsiveness of the quantity supplied of a good to changes in its price: the percentage change in the quantity supplied divided by the percentage change in price.

Price mechanism	The way in which prices act as signals which coordinate the actions of economic agents in a free market economic system.
Prices and incomes policy	A policy which aims to restrain both prices and incomes.
Privatisation	Policy to transfer economic activities to private ownership and control, including the sale of shares in previous nationalised industries to private individuals and institutions, contracting out of publicly funded services to private companies, and the sale of public housing.
Production efficiency	Production of a good is efficient in an economy if, for a given level of output of all other goods, and given the resources and technology available, the maximum possible quantity of the good is produced. The economy is then producing on the production possibility frontier.
Production possibility frontier	A curve showing the limits of the quantities of two commodities, or groups of commodities, which may be produced given limited resources. The axes of the diagram represent the quantities of goods X and Y respectively.
Public good	A good whose benefits cannot be restricted to particular consumers. Consumption of a public good is non-rivalrous, meaning that consumption by one person does not deprive others of the good.
Purchasing power parity	The theory that, in the long run at least, the equilibrium exchange rate between two currencies is that which equates the domestic purchasing power of each. For example, UK$2 = £1 will represent equilibrium if $2 will buy the same amount of goods in the US as £1 will buy in the UK.
Quantity theory of money	The theory which holds that changes in the level of prices are caused predominantly by changes in the supply of money. This derives from the Fisher equation, $MV = PT$, assuming that the velocity of circulation V and the number of transactions T are stable.
Saving	Income which is not spent on current consumption.
Short run	The period of time over which the supply of at least one factor of production is fixed, thus constraining the productive capacity of a firm. However, the degree of utilisation of variable factors can be changed in the short run.
Social cost	The total cost of an economic activity to society. Social costs may diverge from private costs, as in the case of pollution. Taxation policy may aim to reflect social costs so that market prices reflect social costs (eg 'polluter pays' policies).
Substitute	A good which can be substituted for another good, or an input which can be substituted for another input.

GLOSSARY

Substitution effect	The effect on the level of consumption of a good of a change in its price relative to other goods.
Sunk costs	Costs which have already been incurred irretrievably, and which are therefore irrelevant to current decisions.
Supernormal profits	Profit in excess of the opportunity cost of capital (*see Normal profit*).
Supply side economics	An approach to economic policy making which advocates measures to improve the supply of goods and services (eg through deregulation) rather than measures to affect aggregate demand.
Tariff	A tax on an imported good.
Terms of trade	The ratio of export prices to import prices.
Transfer earnings	The minimum payment needed to prevent a factor of production from moving to other employment. For example, the transfer earnings of a person who earns £30,000 and whose next best alternative employment is a job paying £25,000 are £25,000.
Transfer payments	Payments which are not paid in return for goods or services. Student grants and social security payments are examples.
Utility	The satisfaction derived by an individual from a particular situation or from the consumption of goods or services.
Variable costs	Costs which vary with the level of output produced by a firm.
Velocity of circulation	The average frequency with which money is passed between one economic agent and another.
Vertical integration	The extension of a firm's activities into earlier (backward integration) or later (forward integration) stages of production of its goods or services.
Visible trade	The exporting and importing of physical goods.
X-inefficiency	A failure to maximise technical efficiency, frequently resulting from a lack of competitive pressure, as for example in the case of a monopolist.

JUNE 1992
EXAMINATION PAPER

CERTIFICATE IN MARKETING:

(02) Economics

Read all the questions carefully. Then answer any *five* questions. Define your terms and give factual reasons to support your statements. *Do not* repeat the question in your answer.

All questions carry equal marks

Time allowed: 3 hours

1 (a) What do you understand by the concept of price elasticity of demand and explain briefly why it is important to the marketer. (12 marks)

   (b) How might you expect the value of price elasticity to vary across the product life cycle of an innovative new sound system for the home? (8 marks)

2 (a) A firm faces a similar economic problem to that faced by an individual or a nation. Explain what this problem is and how the firm can go about resolving it. (12 marks)

   (b) In what way can a marketing orientation to business be seen as a mechanism for helping the firm to resolve its economic problem? (8 marks)

3 (a) How and why might a firm's costs change in the long run? (14 marks)

   (b) What effect might promotional expenditure have on long run average costs? (6 marks)

4 (a) What is meant by market demand? (10 marks)

   (b) Illustrate how and why the marketing activity tries to change this demand. (10 marks)

5 (a) Explain briefly what a cartel is and how it operates. (8 marks)

   (b) What form would you expect competitive behaviour to take in an oligopolistic market and why? (12 marks)

6 If a government chooses to shift from direct to indirect taxation what would be:

   (a) the economic significance;
   (b) the implications for those marketing consumer goods. (20 marks)

7   (a)   What is the Exchange Rate Mechanism and how would the UK's membership of it affect its trade with Europe?   (12 marks)

        (b)   What differences would the exporter have to consider if he was trading with America as opposed to Spain at a time when both the UK and Spain are ERM members?   (8 marks)

[Question updated by BPP]

8   Economic growth is a desirable economic objective. Explain briefly what it means and the difficulties of maintaining steady economic growth rates.   (20 marks)

9   (a)   The size of the public sector within a country provides an indication of the balance of the command element of the mixed economy. How can a country reduce the size of its public sector and why might it want to do so?   (14 marks)

        (b)   What would you expect to be the major problems encountered in pursuing such a policy?   (6 marks)

10   (a)   Inflation is considered to be a serious economic problem. Why is this and what can be done to control inflation levels in the economy?   (14 marks)

        (b)   What is the impact of rising inflation on the marketing strategy of:

           (i)   a luxury branded product;
           (ii)   an inferior good.   (6 marks)

1 (a) Price elasticity of demand is a measure of the responsiveness of the demand for a good to change in its price. It is calculated using the following formula:

$$\frac{\text{\% change in quantity demanded}}{\text{\% change in price}}$$

Normally the quantity demanded goes up when the price falls and goes down when the price rises and so elasticity has a negative value, but it is usual to ignore the minus sign and consider only the absolute value of elasticity.

The value of elasticity may be anywhere between 0 and infinity but will fall into one of two broad categories.

(i) Above 1. This is classified as *elastic* demand and indicates that the quantity demanded changes by proportionately more than the change in price.

(ii) Below 1. This is *inelastic* demand, where the quantity changes by proportionately less than the change in price.

Where the value of elasticity is equal to one, demand is said to be of *unit elasticity* and quantity and price change by the same proportion. On a straight line demand curve, elasticity is different at different points of the curve but in general, provided the scales on each axis remain unchanged in proportion, the steeper the curve, the lower the elasticity, ie the less sensitive the demand is to a given change in price.

Figure 1

(a)   *(b)*

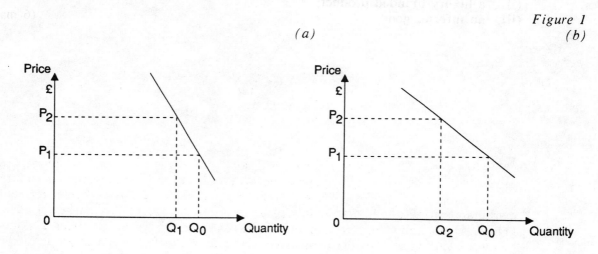

Hence in Figure 1 (a) the relative fall in quantity demanded is less than in (b) for the same proportionate increase in price of P_1 to P_2.

Marketers aim to make products less price-sensitive. Hence it is useful for them to be familiar with the characteristics which are likely to make the demand for a product more or less price elastic. In general, goods which are regarded as necessities, are addictive, have few available substitutes or which comprise only a small proportion of total spending will have inelastic demand whereas luxury items, those which have a range of substitutes or those which comprise a large proportion of total spending will have elastic demand. Hence the importance for marketers of trying to build up brand loyalty or to convert wants into needs.

Price elasticity of demand has a very important practical significance. Marketers can make use of information on elasticity which indicates how consumers will react to pricing decisions and hence what the effect on revenues and profits will be of different pricing strategies. For example, where the demand for a particular commodity is price elastic, a reduction in price produces an increase in total revenue and an increase in price would reduce total revenue. For a commodity whose demand is price inelastic, the opposite is true: a reduction in price would cause a fall in total revenue and an increase in price would increase total revenue from that commodity.

(b) There is a generally accepted lifecycle for most products comprising four stages: an introductory stage, growth, maturity and decline as illustrated below.

Figure 2
The product life cycle

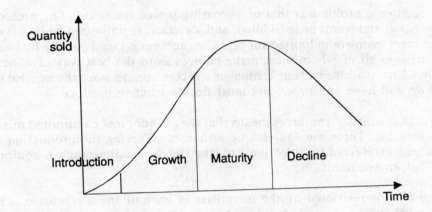

Not all products go through all of the stages and for different products the cycle may last a few weeks only, or extend for many years. The proportionate amount of time in each phase of the cycle also varies. But from the point of view of planning a marketing strategy it is important to recognise the steps through which the product will pass and, in particular, to adopt appropriate pricing at each stage.

In the introductory stage the product is unknown and the initial price may be the sole determinant of whether or not the product will be successful. At this stage, therefore, the price elasticity is likely to have a very high value and this is often reflected in marketers setting a deliberately low price in order to capture the market, a technique known as 'penetration pricing'. For an innovative new sound system, however, a 'skimming' policy of setting a high price initially might be preferred in an attempt to recover development costs as quickly as possible. With this type of pricing policy the price may gradually be lowered and this may assist the firm to expand its market share during the growth phase when the value of elasticity is still high. Elasticity remains high in the earlier stages of the cycle because many consumers who own a perfectly adequate sound system will regard the new one as an unnecessary luxury. It will probably be difficult at this stage to persuade them to switch to what is essentially a substitute for a product they already own, and they will certainly be sensitive to price.

As the market reaches maturity, growth tails off and at this stage the demand for the sound system is likely to become less elastic. The product reputation is becoming more established and greater numbers of consumers are likely to be switching to the new system with its innovative qualities which make it superior to their existing systems. As it becomes increasingly common to own this new type of system it becomes regarded as less and less of a luxury: as a result, the demand becomes more and more inelastic. This is borne out by the developments in the market for compact disc players, for example.

Finally, in the later stages of the product cycle the market for the product will probably decline as a result of other innovations in the industry and the introduction of improved products by competitors. Demand will once again revert to being more elastic – potential customers will be considering the new products coming on to the market and will be very sensitive to price.

2 (a) The basic economic problem is that of allocating scarce resources. The problem exists because the needs and wants of individuals and societies are unlimited while the resources available to meet them are in limited supply. The problem is faced equally by individuals, firms and nations all of whom must make choices as to the best way of allocating the resources they have available to them: consumers and communities must choose what goods and services they will have and producers must decide what to produce.

For a firm, the scarcity of resources means that they cannot make unlimited quantities of goods and services. There are four scarce resources affecting the production decision; natural resources (referred to collectively as land) labour, capital (such as equipment and tools) and entrepreneurship.

Because the firm is restricted by the quantities of each of these resources it has at its disposal, it must make a choice as to what goods and/or services to produce. Any decision about what to produce also implies a decision about how much of these items to produce but clearly, because resources are scarce, more of one thing implies less of something else. This introduces a central idea in economics: that of *opportunity cost*, which is a measure of the cost of an item, not in terms of financial outlay, but in terms of the best alternative foregone. Using opportunity cost as the basis for making production decisions emphasises the point that the firm must make a choice between alternative actions, this choice involving sacrifice of those options which it decides not to follow.

We can analyse the firm's problem of how to use its resources by using *production possibility curves*. A production possibility curve, also known as a transformation curve shows the maximum output the firm can produce of goods X and Y (or of good X and all other goods), given its existing resources at any moment in time. In other words, at all points on the curve the firm is operating at full productive capacity while a point inside the curve indicates that the firm is not utilising fully all the resources it has available. The production possibilities available to a firm which has the choice of producing good X and good Y may be illustrated as in the diagram below.

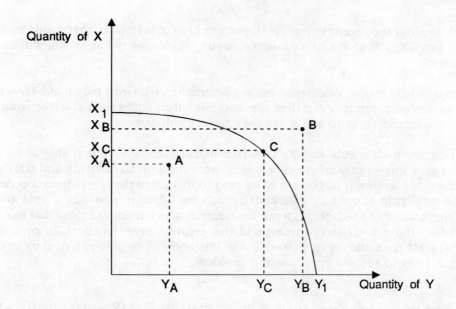

A point such as A in the diagram shown is within the production possibility curve. The firm has the resources available to make more of each product: it is operating below capacity. Point B, by contrast, is unattainable given the current resources and technology available to the firm.

The shape of the production possibility curve illustrates the principle of opportunity cost. If the firm is producing X_c units of X for example, the maximum amount of Y that can be produced is Y_c. However, if Y_1 units of Y are required then the firm can no longer produce any X. Thus the opportunity cost of producing an additional $Y_1 - Y_c$ units of Y is X_c units of X, as this is the amount of X whose production must be foregone in order to produce the additional Y.

The firm could choose to make X_1 units of X and no Y, or Y_1 units of Y and no X, or any combination of X and Y represented by points on the curve such as C. The decision which the firm makes about the combination of X and Y to be produced will depend on the benefits which the alternatives are perceived to offer, involving an assessment of the costs of production at each point and the demand characteristics. Therefore, the firm's decision will be based on the information it has acquired, for example through market research on market demand, so that it will allocate resources to producing those goods which will yield the greatest benefits.

(b) For a firm to resolve its economic problem of allocating the limited resources it has available to maximum benefit, it needs as much information as possible on the market demand for the various goods between which it is choosing to produce. The underlying assumption that producers always seek to maximise their profits means that a firm will seek to match its supply curve to the market demand for its product.

Marketing plays an important role in determining the allocation of resources. For the organisation to get the maximum benefit from its limited resources, it needs to ensure that the goods and services it produces are not wasted. The role of marketing in this process is to enable the firm to identify and anticipate customer wants and needs so that it can use its available resources to satisfy them. As a result, both the firm and the individual consumers can benefit from mutually profitable exchange. The concept of consumer sovereignty, which refers to the freedom of individuals in the free market to decide for themselves what they want to buy, is important here as it implies that goods and services will be provided that meets consumer needs, achieving what is known as 'market orientation'.

In practice, where market orientation has not been achieved, firms may themselves make the decision on what to produce and then use marketing techniques such as advertising to try to influence demand so as to sell what they have produced.

Marketing has a clear role to play in a free market economy but it should not only be regarded as helping the market process to operate through advertising and similar selling techniques. Marketing is important in helping to influence the level of market demand so that the available supply is matched by demand, but it also has a role to play in identifying consumer needs through market research which helps to ensure that resources are allocated to those activities which yield the greatest benefits, both to producers and consumers. Hence a marketing orientation to business can be seen as a dual mechanism for helping a firm to resolve its economic problem.

3 (a) In the long run when a firm expands its capacity, its fixed costs are increased but for most industries there will be some reduction of average costs. This is because if you double output, you do not necessarily double all the fixed costs.

If output increases more than proportionately to an increase in inputs (if doubling all inputs trebles output, for example) then the firm is enjoying *economies of scale* and in the long run average costs of production will fall as output volume arises. On the other hand, if output increases less than proportionately to inputs (for example, if trebling all inputs only doubles output) then the firm is experiencing *diseconomies of scale* and the long run average costs of production will rise as the volume of output rises. Alternatively, a firm may experience *constant returns to scale* where output increases in the same proportion as inputs. Returns to scale are improvements in productivity through increasing the scale of production – for example, by mass producing instead of producing in small batch quantities.

The economies of scale attainable from large scale production may be categorised as either *internal economies* arising within the firm from the organisation of production, or *external economies* attainable by the firm because of the growth of the industry as a whole.

Internal economies arise from the more effective use of available resources and from increased specialisation, when production capacity is enlarged. In a larger firm it is possible to achieve *specialisation of labour* with staff doing specific tasks to make full use of their skills, rather than doing a variety of tasks. It is also possible to achieve *division of labour* ie dividing work between several specialists rather than individuals switching between tasks. Extended capacity allows firms to make use of larger and more specialised machinery. Large capital items that are only justifiable economically at high volumes of output are known as *indivisibles*. There are also *dimensional* economies of scale, resulting from the relationship between the volume of output and the size of equipment needed to hold or process the output. The cost of a tank for storing 10,000 gallons of product will be much less than ten times the cost of a storage tank for 1,000 gallons.

Specialisation of labour and machines results in simplification and standardisation of operations which itself results in lower costs. In addition, specialisation of labour applies to management, and there are thus *managerial economies*; the cost per unit of management will fall as output rises.

There are also economies arising from the indivisibility of operations. There are operations which:

(i)   must be carried out at the same cost regardless of the size of the business, ie there are fixed costs, and average fixed costs always decline as production increases;

(ii) vary a little, but not proportionately with size, ie having semi-fixed costs;

(iii) are not worth considering below a certain level of output, for example advertising campaigns.

Larger companies are able to devote more resources to research and development, and in many industries this may be essential for survival. Larger companies will also find it easier, and generally cheaper, to raise finance. Quoted public companies, for example, have access to the Stock Exchange for new share issues and can borrow money more readily. A large firm can also undertake more investments in fixed assets and new operations than a small firm, allowing it to spread risks.

Buying economies may be available, reducing the cost of material purchases through bulk purchase discounts. *Stock holding* becomes more efficient as the most economic quantities of inventory to hold increase with the scale of operations, but at a lower proportionate rate of increase with the scale of operations, but at a lower proportionate rate of increase. Finally *marketing economies* are available because a firm can make more effective use of advertising, specialist salesmen and specialised channels of distribution.

External economies of scale occur as an industry grows in size. For example a large skilled labour force is created and educational services can be geared towards training new entrants, or specialised ancillary industries develop to provide components, transport finished goods, trade in by-products, provide special services etc. External economies of scale and potentially significant to smaller firms who specialise in the ancillary services to a larger industry than from its own internal economies of scale.

The diagram below shows the shape of the long-run average cost curve if there are economies of scale up to a certain output level and constant returns thereafter. It may be that the flat part of the curve is never reached, or it may be that diseconomies of scale are encountered, in which case the curve will begin to rise.

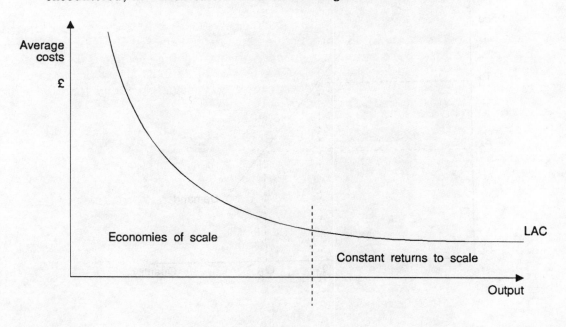

Diseconomies of scale might set in when a firm gets so large that it cannot operate efficiently or cannot be managed efficiently, so that average costs begin to rise.

(b) A successful advertising campaign may enable a firm, in the long run, to exploit economies of large scale production if it has sufficient impact on the market demand for the firm's product.

A concept which is useful to a marketer to measure the effectiveness of a campaign is the promotional elasticity of demand. This attempts to calculate the amount by which demand changes as a result of a change in the level of promotional spending using the following formula.

$$\frac{\text{\% change in demand for a product}}{\text{\% change in promotional expenditure}}$$

An inelastic product, indicating little demand change as a result of an advertising campaign, could reflect more on the quality of the campaign than on the nature of the demand for the product.

If promotional expenditure is successful it may generate sufficient additional demand for the product to enable the firm to expand its capacity and hence to benefit from lower long run average costs associated with the economies of scale discussed in part (a).

4 (a) In the discussion of demand, we are concerned only with 'effective demand', ie the number of units of a product which consumers not only *want* to buy but are also *able* to buy.

The total market demand for a commodity at any given price is the total of the amounts demanded by each consumer at that price at that particular time. Market demand curves are therefore simply the horizontal summation of each individual's demand curve. Since, for each individual, the quantity demanded varies inversely with price, this general relationship will be embodied in the market demand curve. A typical market demand curve therefore has the same general shape as the individual's demand curve (Figure 1).

Figure 1

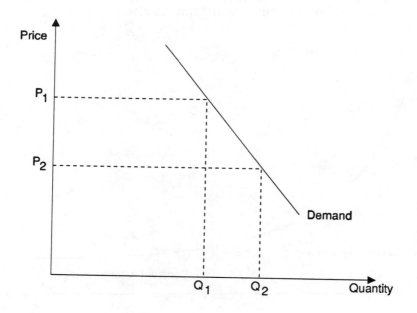

The market demand curve generally slopes down from left to right because the lower the price the greater the quantity demanded. For the individual consumer, a fall in the price of the good makes it relatively cheaper compared to other goods and, given the individual's limited budget, expenditure will be shifted to the good whose price has fallen. In addition, a fall in the price of the good means that people with lower incomes will also be able to afford it such that the overall size of the market for the good increases. In Figure 1, as price falls from P_1 to P_2, demand extends from Q_1 to Q_2.

(b) The demand for different types of products will be more or less price elastic or inelastic, ie more or less sensitive to price. Provided the proportionate scales of the axes remain unchanged, a demand curve with a steeper slope represents a product which is less price-sensitive, possibly because it has no close substitutes, is regarded as a necessity, is addictive or only represents a small proportion of the individual's total expenditure. A flatter demand curve indicates a greater change in demand for a given change in price and is characteristic of a luxury good, one with close substitutes or one representing a significant proportion of total spending.

Figure 2

(a)   *(b)*

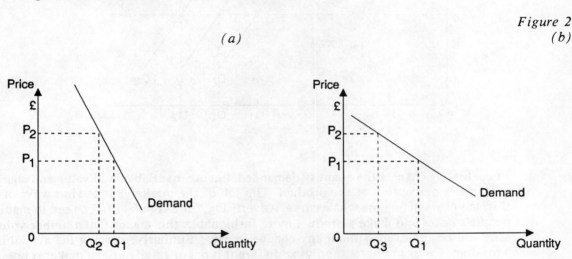

The demand for good (a) in Figure 2, for example, is less price-elastic than that for good (b) and so, for a given percentage increase in price from P_1 to P_2, the quantity demanded falls by proportionately less than is the case for good (b).

One of the main aims of marketing activity is to make the demand for products less price-elastic. Where the demand is price-inelastic, an increase in price by the firm, which may be necessary to cover increased costs, would increase the total revenue from that product. The same increase in price for a product with elastic demand would reduce total revenue. Marketing strategies to make the demand for a product less elastic include encouragement of brand loyalties, emphasising unique product characteristics and converting 'wants' into 'needs'.

Besides price, any other factor which influences the amount of a product demanded at a given point in time is referred to as a *condition of demand* and this may include: the price of other goods, income, fashions and tastes, and the number of people in the market. Changes in the conditions of demand result in shifts of the demand curve itself such that, for a given price, a different quantity is demanded (Figure 3).

Figure 3

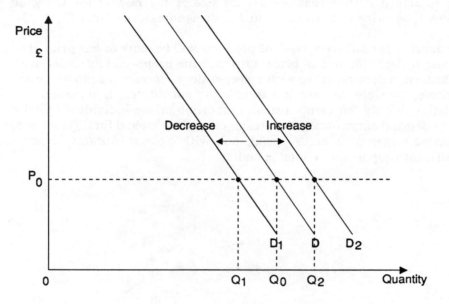

Price directly changes the quantity demanded, but other variables add value and change the customer's perception of the product. The job of the marketer is to find ways of doing this, thereby shifting the whole curve. Advertising, for example, can be used to manipulate people's tastes and make a product more fashionable: this means that a higher volume of sales can be achieved without any change in price. Similarly, altering the availability of a product, for example by supplying different types of retail outlets, makes it possible to alter the number of people in the market place.

Marketers have the job of making sure that the available supply of their organisation is matched by effective demand. The role of marketing is not limited to helping the market process operate through advertising or selling but also to influencing demand to match the available supply. Hence it is essential for the marketer to understand the factors which determine both the location and the shape of the market demand curve.

5   (a)   An effective monopoly can exist in a given industry when firms agree to cooperate with each other rather than compete. The closest type of agreement between producers is known as a *cartel* and this is when a group of firms in an oligopolistic market jointly coordinate their marketing policies and so act effectively as a single supplier. In practice, a cartel may operate through a single agency organising the marketing of a product supplied by several firms.

The rationale behind establishing a cartel is that, by acting as a single supplier of the product would, the member firms are able to exercise some degree of control over market price. The aim of the cartel is often to restrict market supply of the product, thereby forcing up price and increasing profits for the members.

A price cartel, also known as a price ring, is created when a group of firms combine to agree on a price at which they will sell their product to the market. The market might be willing to demand more of the product at a lower price, while the cartel agreement attempts to impose a higher price by restricting supply to the market to a level which is consistent with the volume of demand at the price they wish to charge.

Figure 1

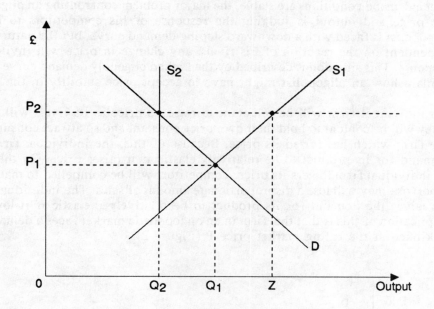

If the case illustrated in Figure 1 were a competitive market with supply S_1 and demand D, the price would be P_1 and output Q_1. However, a cartel of producers might agree to fix the price at P_2 but to do so they must also agree to cut market supply to Q_2, and so fix the supply curve at S_2.

Establishing a cartel depends on the firms in the cartel being able to control supply to the market, agreeing on a price (P_2) and agreeing on how much of the output each firm should produce. In the diagram above, if the market price is fixed at P_2, firms would want to supply an output of Z in a free market. This cannot be allowed to happen otherwise the price of P_2 could not be sustained.

Cartels are largely illegal in the UK, with just a few cartel-type organisations operating within the law. Among the most obvious examples are the agricultural marketing boards.

Where cartels do exist, both in the UK and abroad, they present a formidable barrier to entry into the market. Any potential entrant must either join the cartel or compete with it. Existing members may not allow the newcomer to join the cartel, and competing with the cartel may be uneconomic because of the need to produce on a large scale or because of the dampening effect on market price of a sizeable increase in industry output.

One of the best known cartels is OPEC, which has attempted to operate by assigning oil production quotas to each member country. Agreements have often broken down, however, because some member countries exceeded their quota or sold below the cartel's agreed price. The problem with all cartels is that once quotas have been agreed, the temptation for an individual producer is to increase covertly the amount it sells thereby raising its own profit. This is the main reason why cartels tend to be unstable.

311

(b) A market is oligopolistic when it is dominated by a few large-scale producers. Oligopolists may produce a homogeneous product such as oil, or there may be product differentiation (eg cars, cigarettes). The essence of oligopoly is that firms' production decisions are interdependent. One firm cannot set price and/or output without considering how the response of its competitors will affect its own profits.

When demand conditions are stable, the major problem confronting an oligopolist in fixing his price and output is judging the response of his competitors to his actions. An oligopolist is faced with a downward sloping demand curve, but the nature of the curve is dependent on the reaction of his rivals: any change in price will invite a competitive response. This situation is described by the kinked oligopoly demand curve which is used to explain how an oligopolist might have to accept price stability in the market.

An individual firm will be reluctant to raise its price as its rivals will not follow suit. They will be content to hold their own price constant and so attract consumers away from the firm which has raised its price. Because of this, the individual firm perceives the demand for its product to be relatively elastic if it raises price. On the other hand, if an individual firm lowers its price, competitors will be compelled to match the price cut otherwise they will lose a disproportionate amount of sales. The individual firm therefore perceives the demand for its product to be relatively inelastic if it lowers price. The implication of this is that the firm in an oligopolistic market faces a demand curve which is kinked at the ruling market price P (Figure 2).

Figure 2

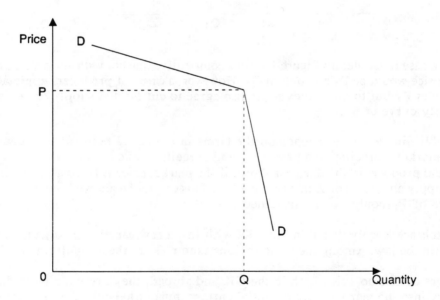

In general, oligopolists' prices will only rise if all the firms follow the lead of a rival in raising its price so that the demand curve shifts outwards with the kink at the new price level, which is again stable. This tendency for one firm to set the general industry price with the other firms following suit is called *price leadership*.

When demand conditions change, price stability might no longer exist. If total market demand falls, oligopolists might try to increase their share of the market by cutting prices, or if one firm begins to lose his market share he might try to restore it by cutting prices. The consequence would be a price war, as has been seen in the UK in recent years amongst supermarkets and oil companies, for example. The effect of price wars is often beneficial to consumers but they tend to be of limited duration because it is not in the firm's interests to sustain them for long.

Without the opportunity to compete on price, oligopolistic firms also have to compete through non-price variables. Non-price competition between rival producers in an oligopolistic market is often intense, and can take a number of forms. The main types of non-price competition are as follows.

(i) *Competitive advertising*

This is common in oligopolistic markets. Advertising is used to reinforce product differentiation and harden brand loyalties.

However, if firms get out of line with the industry norm for advertising spending or promotional activity, this can also cause adverse competitive responses. Advertising wars can be as damaging to profits as price wars.

(ii) *Promotional offers*

These are common in some markets such as household detergents and toothpaste. Such offers frequently take the form of veiled price reductions such as 'two for the price of one' or '25 per cent extra free'. In the case of petrol a common technique is to offer 'free gifts'.

(iii) *Extended guarantees*

This is an increasingly common technique in many of the markets for consumer durables. By offering free parts and labour guarantees for longer periods than their competitors, firms aim to increase the attractiveness of their product.

6 Taxation in the UK is usually classified as direct or indirect. Direct taxes are collected by the Inland Revenue and in the main are levied on incomes and transfers of capital. Indirect taxes, on the other hand, are collected by the Customs and Excise department and are sometimes referred to as expenditure taxes since they are levied mainly on spending. However, the traditional distinction between direct and indirect taxes is that the incidence, or burden, of a direct tax is borne by the person or entity on whom the tax is levied, and cannot be transferred on to another party. The burden of an indirect tax can, however, be passed on. In the case of VAT, for example, the tax burden can be passed on from the manufacturer to the retailer and subsequently to the customer.

Both direct and indirect taxes have some advantages and most economies will adopt a mixture of taxes in order to minimise their disadvantages. In the UK since 1979 there has been a significant shift from direct to indirect taxation, as well as a reduction in the overall level of taxation. Once of the political justifications for this shift was that indirect taxes are preferable because they only fall on those who choose to buy the goods and services on which they are levied. In other words, direct taxes are unavoidable which means that they must be paid by everyone, whereas indirect taxes are usually avoidable as people can, in theory, choose not to pay the tax by not buying the goods and services on which the tax is levied.

It is frequently alleged that high rates of direct taxation have strong disincentive effects on effort and initiative. Taxing profits through corporation tax might reduce the finance available to firms for investment in research and development as well as additional capacity, both of which can affect the future growth of output as well as the quality and competitiveness of the country and if the rate is too high corporation tax might discourage firms from seeking higher profits. Similarly, income taxes have a direct influence on an individual's disposal income and so, at very high marginal rates, might act as a disincentive to work. Hence one of the main arguments for shifting the burden of taxation away from direct taxes in favour of indirect taxes is that there would be fewer disincentive effects.

A shift from direct to indirect taxation has a number of other advantages. Indirect taxes can be used selectively, for example to discourage the consumption of certain domestic goods; they are cheaper and easier to administer in that the collection of VAT, the major indirect tax in the UK, is done on the government's behalf by tradesmen and businessmen; they are more flexible, and rates can be changed within certain limits by the Chancellor without parliamentary approval. It is also argued that indirect taxes, whether levied on a *specific* or *ad valorem* basis, are easier to understand.

There are also a number of disadvantages in a shift towards indirect taxation. Direct taxes have the advantage that they can be made progressive or proportional - in other words, the ability to pay can be recognised so that richer people pay a higher percentage of their income in tax. Indirect taxes, on the other hand, are generally regressive because they represent a larger proportion of the expenditure of lower income groups, although goods deemed as essentials like food and books can be zero-rated for tax purposes. Indirect taxes interfere directly with the market mechanism for goods and services: by increasing the price of certain goods they affect the basis on which consumers choose between alternative commodities. In addition, higher rates of indirect taxation have an immediate effect on the price index which may set in motion an inflationary spiral, while excessive indirect taxes on commodities will reduce the demand for them.

There are important implications for those marketing consumer goods of a shift from direct to indirect taxation. A government can exert a significant and unexpected impact on a product's marketing plan with a change in its taxation policy. Direct taxation has an impact on the purchasing power of broader market segments whereas indirect taxes can be targeted at specific goods and sectors, and a shift from one to the other can have far reaching effects on demand in many markets. Such a shift will affect individuals' disposable incomes and the prices of the goods and services on which the indirect taxes are levied. Hence it is important for the marketer to have an awareness of both the price and income elasticity of demand for their products.

Companies producing the types of goods which are likely to attract the attention of the Chancellor of the Exchequer need to pay particular attention to government opinion and the likelihood of fiscal policy changes which may affect them directly. Marketers can be faced on delivery of the Budget with the equivalent of immediate price rises with little or no warning and need to have sufficiently flexible marketing plans to respond to such events. Traditionally goods such as cigarettes, alcohol and gambling have been those which the government has taxed heavily and this tends to be reflected in the marketing strategies adopted in those particular industries. In the future any company offering products which, though perceived to be luxuries do in fact have relatively price-inelastic demand curves, could be subject to the same treatment.

7 (a) Within Europe, monetary and economic convergence is fostered within the European Monetary System (EMS) which comprises two main strands: the ecu (European Currency Unit) and the ERM. The ERM is the exchange rate mechanism whereby participating countries agree to maintain their exchange rates within a band of $2\frac{1}{4}$% either side of its central parity. The main margin of fluctuation has been $2\frac{1}{4}$%, until August 1993 when it was raised to 15%. When it was in the ERM, from October 1990 to September 1992, sterling was allowed a 6% margin as an exceptional case. Each currency must also keep within the same limit of each other currency within the system. Hence the ERM is composed of an 'adjustable peg' system, ie a scheme of margins around a central peg for exchange rates between the currencies of the member countries, and a policy of 'managed floating' between their currencies and the currencies of countries outside the system.

The value of the ecu is determined by a weighted average basket of the currencies of EC member countries. As well as there being an agreed rate between all participating countries in relation to each other, each currency has an agreed value against the ecu. The purpose of this is to generate a 'divergence indicator' equal to 75% of the agreed value of any currency against the ecu - it is presumed that the authorities of any country whose currency deviates by more than this will intervene to halt the divergence.

Exchange rate stability within a regime such as the ERM is seen as an encouragement to trade as it removes the uncertainty and risk for importers and exporters associated with a flexible system. Consequently, the volume of trade between the UK and the rest of Europe should have risen as a result of the reduction in uncertainty about exchange rate movements. Business confidence amongst UK exporters should have improved alongside the reduction in foreign exchange risks as well as allowing firms to plan and forecast with greater certainty. Imports from the other European countries are a significant part of the UK economy and so the ERM means there is less fluctuation in the level of expenditure on imports.

On sterling's entry into the ERM, a central parity rate equivalent to DM 2.95 per pound was set although this has been seen by many commentators as being too high. Although UK trade with Europe benefits from the reduction in uncertainty over the exchange rate, a rate that is too high is damaging to UK competitiveness - the price of a good from the UK in terms of another currency is higher, the higher the sterling exchange rate. This 'over-valuation' of sterling had the effect of 'squeezing' exporters who have to cut costs in order to remain operative.

Being locked into a semi-fixed exchange regime highlights the importance of being competitive. In particular, in order to be able to trade effectively in Europe, the UK has had to bring down its rate of inflation in line with the rates experienced by its European trading partners. Entry into the ERM at a high value for sterling and a relatively high inflation rate meant that the UK was not competitive and its balance of trade with the rest of Europe suffered as a result. At the same time it made it difficult for sterling, in the absence of official intervention, to remain within its permitted ERM bands. In September 1992, even official intervention proved to be inadequate and sterling's ERM membership was suspended.

(b) Within the ERM, sterling would be effectively fixed within specified limits against the Spanish peseta but would still float against the dollar. Hence, a UK exporter trading with America would potentially be faced by the problem of continuous adjustment of the exchange rate. The uncertainty over the exchange rate is regarded as a discouragement to trading although in practice a system of 'managed floating' exists between the pound and the dollar. The degree of uncertainty affecting trade with Spain will depend upon the percentage limits operating between the two countries within the exchange rate system.

315

Because the dollar value of the pound is not fixed, the dollar price of UK exports to America will fluctuate in line with the exchange rate and, in particular, if sterling appreciates relative to the dollar, Americans will find UK goods increasingly expensive. This may be quite damaging to the ability of British firms to maintain steady sales to their American customers, especially as the demand for British goods in the American market is likely to be fairly elastic given the extent of competition. A UK exporter would therefore have to consider whether maintaining the dollar price of his products and facing uncertainty over the sterling value of his sales would be less damaging. Exporting to Spain would not involve the same uncertainty given that the sterling-peseta rate is fixed, albeit within certain limits only, within the ERM. Consequently a UK business exporting to Spain is better able to plan and forecast, and this is a major factor determining the level of business confidence.

Because of the risk involved in trading within a floating system, a UK exporter to America would also have to consider the various options available for managing that risk. Most businesses are likely to undertake some form of 'hedging' against foreign exchange risks to protect themselves as far as possible against fluctuations in the sterling-dollar rate. Hence, they will be aware of the costs and benefits of the various types of forward exchange contracts, money market hedges and so on, or will need to seek specialist advice. By contrast the exporter to Spain would have less need for involvement in the foreign exchange market other than for standard currency transactions if he perceives the exchange rate risk to be low.

However, the events of September 1992, when pressure was put on many currencies in the ERM and sterling was one of the currencies which had to leave the system, illustrate that a risk of devaluation can still exist within a semi-fixed exchange rate system. Also, the ERM limits of 15% introduced in 1993 are so wide as to make the mechanism largely ineffectual.

8   There are many definitions of economic growth. It is sometimes taken to mean the growth of capacity of productive potential for the economy as a whole, represented by an outward movement of the economy's productive possibility curve, as this is the only way of increasing the size of real GDP in the long run. However, the usual definition is an increase in real GNP. Measuring in 'real' terms removes any increases in GNP caused solely by inflation, although it is not unusual to find economic growth measured simply as increases in total GNP.

In addition, it is often argued that economic growth should be measured by increase in GNP per head of population as this gives an indication of how the average standard of living is improving. If a country's GNP is rising by, say 2% per year but the population is also increasing at an annual rate of 2%, it may be that no increase in the individuals' standard of living is being achieved. Economic growth should mean that the population as a whole will be able to raise its standard of living in material terms, and that there should also be an improvement in economic welfare. A country experiencing economic growth is more easily able to provide a welfare state service without creating intolerable tax burdens on the community.

There are a number of key factors which contribute to economic growth. One of the main sources of growth is technological progress which means that the same amounts of the factors of production can now produce a higher output, and that new products will be developed, adding to output growth. The productivity of capital can be increased if machinery is updated so that firms use the latest technologies available and, although this might mean scrapping existing machinery, firms will be willing to do so because the higher productivity makes it more profitable for them. Since technological advances are encouraged when there is investment in research and development, greater expenditure on this will encourage a higher rate of economic growth. This points to the second key factor behind economic growth: business confidence. Sustained growth depends heavily on an adequate level of new investment which will only be undertaken if there are expectations of future growth in demand.

The quality of labour is another factor which is important in determining growth. It is dependent on education and training, which is often described as 'investment in human capital'. An educated labour force is easier to train and is likely to be more adaptable and enterprising. In addition, a highly trained labour force is likely to be more mobile and this can have an important bearing on the growth of productivity.

Productivity and technological progress together are two major factors contributing to economies of scale and encouraging the development of mass production industry which has been a feature of much economic growth in the past. The rate of technological advance is not constant, however, which means that the rate of economic growth it generates may be difficult to maintain.

For economic growth to occur, there must be sufficient availability of the factors of production. The rate of extraction of natural resources will impose a limit on the rate of growth. Natural resources are non-renewable and production which uses up a country's natural resources such as coal, oil and other minerals can be regarded as 'disinvestment' by depleting the stock of resources available. This suggests that the desirable rate of growth could be quite low, unless there is technological progress which reduces the use of non-renewable resources or replaces them - developments in nuclear and solar technology, for example, may be able to provide alternative energy sources to oil and coal, but any bottleneck in supply will prevent a steady growth rate from being achieved.

There are also external influences on the rate of economic growth in a country. For example, an improvement in the terms of trade means that more imports can be bought or a given volume of exports will earn higher profits. This in turn will boost investment and hence growth. The rate of growth of the rest of the world is important for an economy that has a large foreign trade sector. If a country's main trading partners are experiencing slow growth, the amount of exports which the country can sell to them will grow only slowly and this limits the opportunities for further investment and growth. International trade should be encouraged as a means to growth because it opens up markets for exporters and at the same time allows firms to benefit from economies of scale by supplying to larger markets than they could by selling to domestic customers only. For countries involved in international trade, however, maintaining a steady rate of growth is often hindered by developments in the world economy.

Economic growth is given a high priority as a policy objective because if the growth of output exceeds the growth of population, the standard of living as measured by per capita income, will rise. In the longer term, the compound effect on output of a constant rate of growth is impressive: for example if output grows by 2 per cent per year, GDP will double in approximately 36, years while if the growth of output can be increased to three per cent a year, output will double in approximately 24 years.

Alongside economic growth the other main policy objectives followed by most governments in the post war period in the UK have been stable prices, full employment and equilibrium in the balance of payments. A basic problem associated with the various objectives is that they are often in conflict so than an improvement in one of them can only be achieved at the expense of one or more of the others. A reduction in unemployment, for example, can normally be achieved by stimulating aggregate demand but this will tend to raise the level of imports and may lead to a trade deficit. Similarly, measures which are taken to remove a trade deficit, such as high interest rates, may have an adverse long-term impact on economic growth by discouraging investment.

Because it has proved impossible to achieve all of these aims simultaneously, governments have faced a conflict of policy objectives and have had to decide which they consider to be the most pressing. The level of unemployment a government could achieve has been determined in part by the rate of inflation it was prepared to accept and in part by its need to achieve balance of payments equilibrium. At times, full employment was the major aim, while at others it was sacrificed to the problems of containing inflation and restoring balance of payments. Successive governments have believed that economic growth should be encouraged by greater investment and that this was more likely to be forthcoming which aggregate demand was rising. The rising demand would create a growing market in which the additional output resulting from the increased investment could be sold. The management of demand to encourage growth has rarely, if ever, been a major policy objective in the UK; more often price stability and balance of payments equilibrium have taken precedence over other aims, including the commitment to a steady growth rate.

9 (a) A number of countries through the world, in addition to the UK, have been engaged in privatisation programs in a move to reduce the size of their public sector. The term privatisation is most commonly taken to imply the transfer of assets from the public to the private sector, involving a change in the ownership of assets. Privatisation can, however, cover other activities such as ceasing to provide such activities as refuse collection through the public sector and putting them out to private contract, or allowing private firms to compete against state-owned businesses where they were not allowed to compete before, as with the deregulation of bus and coach services, for example.

In general, it is the transfer of assets from the public to the private sector which has attracted most attention, and on which any discussion of privatisation or 'denationalisation' tends to concentrate. In recent years, the UK government has carried out a policy of denationalisation and British Gas, British Telecom and the main Water Authorities have been among the enterprises which have been privatised. In spite of some competition against British Telecom, these organisations are in general 'natural monopolies' and the government has not planned to break their monopoly hold on their markets, but has instead appointed 'consumer watchdogs' such as OFGAS and OFTEL to protect consumer interests.

Critics of a command economy or one with a large public sector point to the loss of consumer sovereignty as an important disadvantage of this type of system. In other words, it is the state which decides what is to be produced and consumers have limited influence in the marketplace, leading to shortages of certain commodities and surpluses of others with no automatic mechanism for their removal. In addition, there may be a tendency towards larger bureaucratic structures with large amounts of resources employed in government planning and administrative departments rather than being put to more productive use elsewhere. There are other arguments in favour of privatisation. One of the major aims is to increase efficiency in the allocation and utilisation of resources and another is to increase the extent of share ownership, partly for political reasons but also because it is thought to affect resource allocation and utilisation.

Privatisation is held to encourage efficiency for several reasons. One is that there will be less government interference in pricing and investment decisions. Another reason is that there will generally be increased competition. It is certainly true that governments have often deliberately prevented nationalised industries from increasing their prices as a means of tackling inflation, and have altered investment in different industries as a means of varying aggregate demand. As private organisations, firms are able to plan more effectively, and efficiency in the allocation of resources might also be improved. When prices are prevented from rising, too much may be consumed in relation to the optimum. In addition, it has been argued that increased investment in the nationalised industries has crowded out private sector investment, and the higher rate of return achieved in the private sector is evidence that investment there is more efficient.

The government has had some success in its aim of increasing share ownership: with the sale of British Gas, British Telecom and various other nationalised industries, there were nine million private individuals in the UK owning shares in 1988. It has been argued that this will encourage greater efficiency because management are now accountable to the shareholders, who have a vested interest in the profitability and efficiency of the companies in which they hold shares.

Denationalisation also provides an immediate source of funds for the government, enabling it to reduce its borrowing requirement. Much of the formulation of government policy in recent years has rested on the belief in a central link between the PSBR and the money supply such that reducing the PSBR allows the government greater control over the money supply and hence inflation. As a result of the major privatisations in the UK undertaken in the 1980s, the government raised some £25 billion.

(b) There are a number of problems associated with a policy of reducing the size of a country's public sector. In the privatisations undertaken in recent years in the UK for example, there has been much criticism of the pricing of some of the shares the government issued. As with any share issue, deciding on the price is a notoriously difficult problem: it should be low enough so as to ensure that a sufficient quantity is sold, yet sufficiently high to maximise the revenue generated. The first tranche of shares in British Telecom, for example, were issued at a price of £1.30 but by the end of the first day's trading they were quoted at £1.73, thus depriving the government of an extra £1.295 m in potential revenue. In addition, there were some who criticised the government for not issuing shares by tender. Although this was certainly a possibility, it was generally rejected probably because it was felt that it would not attract many small investors with little or no experience of buying shares.

Although one of the major aims of privatising state owned organisations is to increase efficiency, it may be difficult to achieve this in practice. In theory, management is made more accountable to the wider ownership, encouraging greater efficiency, but in practice few shareholders will attend the AGM and such organisations are, in effect, run along similar lines to a privately owned firm. In addition, there is little evidence of increased competition following some privatisations. Indeed, some organisations such as British Gas have been sold as monopolies to increase their attractiveness to shareholders. It might be claimed that the government had little alternative since some industries are quite clearly natural monopolies and that, in any case, as private sector organisations they must compete for funds on the capital market with other private sector organisations. Nevertheless, critics have argued that monopolies do not have to be efficient to be profitable, and that profitability is the main determinant of a firm's ability to raise funds.

10 (a) Inflation, which can be defined as a general and persistent rise in the price level (or fall in the value of money) has a number of undesirable features for the economy as a whole and for certain individuals or groups compared with others. At the outset it is important to distinguish between anticipated and unanticipated inflation. When inflation is fully anticipated, it is often possible for individuals and organisations to protect themselves against any adverse effects or to ensure that they reap maximum benefit whereas when inflation is unanticipated it is not possible to do either of these. Consequently, it is important to remember this distinction when considering the various costs and benefits.

Price stability is one of the main policy objectives of governments although price stability does not imply a commitment to zero inflation. Changing supply and demand conditions for various products will lead to price changes in the various product markets and consequently changes in the RPI, the most widely-used measure, are often held not to be an accurate measure of changes in the rate of inflation. Additionally, although academic opinion is divided, there is considerable support for maintaining a moderate rate of inflation rather than aiming to eliminate it altogether. A moderate rate of inflation is argued to provide a spur to investment by giving producers 'windfall' profits although there is no agreement about what constitutes such a rate. 1.5 to 2 per cent has been suggested.

In terms of the economy as a whole, one of the key disadvantages which inflation brings is the effect on competitiveness. Higher inflation in a country relative to its main trading partners, without a compensating adjustment in the foreign exchange rate, makes exports more expensive to foreign customers and hence dampens export trading. This in turn has an adverse effect on the country's trade balance and, as a result, may affect the exchange rate. Downward pressure on the country's currency together with the expectations of further inflation may also have the effect of undermining confidence in the economy and deterring the international trade.

As far as individuals are concerned, inflation has the effect of benefiting some groups relative to others. For example, a rising price level benefits borrowers at the expense of lenders as the real value of a debt falls. Hence the financial institutions are generally strong supporters of anti-inflation policy. Another group that is penalised by inflation is those on fixed incomes, as the real value of their income falls. In addition, where people have different expectations of inflation, distortions may arise in wage bargaining.

Inflation may have an adverse effect on the growth rate of the economy by discouraging investment. Firms' investment plans may be disrupted if they are unable to predict their future cash flows and interest rates. A high rate of inflation tends to dampen general business confidence. There are also structural and organisational costs associated with frequent price changes - the so-called 'menu costs' such as the costs of re-printing price lists and labels. It is also possible that inflation results in an increase in purchases of assets in particular property that provide a hedge against the effects of rising prices, as people attempt to preserve the real value of their wealth, while this diverts resources away from productive investments which could stimulate further growth.

Over time, different governments have resorted to a variety of anti-inflation policies influenced mainly by their analysis of the key causes of inflation. In the 1960s and 1970s prices and incomes policies were tried. Since 1979, monetarist weapons have been favoured. There are four main causes of inflation and policies to control it have varied according to the perceived cause.

Demand pull inflation occurs when there is excess demand for output at the existing price level: in other words, aggregate demand exceeds aggregate supply. Inflation of this type can be controlled by:

(i)   higher taxation;
(ii) lower government expenditure;
(iii) higher interest rates;

all of which serve to reduce the level of demand in the economy.

Cost push inflation occurs when increases in wages and other costs exert upward pressure on prices. This can be controlled by reducing production costs and price rises, either by encouraging greater productivity in industry or by applying controls over wage and price rises (prices and incomes policy).

Monetary inflation: the monetarist school of through argues that excessively fast growth in the money supply is inflationary and hence inflation can be controlled by reducing the rate of money supply growth.

Finally, persistent inflation may be caused by *inflationary expectations* and this points to the government pursuing clear policies which indicate its determination to reduce the inflation rate.

(b) The effect of rising inflation is to reduce the level of real incomes and this affects the demand for different types of products in different ways.

    (i) The demand for luxury goods tends to be fairly elastic and hence sales of luxury goods in general will be adversely affected by rising price levels, in addition to the income effect. The aim of a marketing strategy in this case must be to influence consumer perceptions such that the product is regarded as more of a necessity than a luxury. The marketer needs to persuade the consumer not only that this product is indispensable but also that their particular brand offers certain features if superior to the other brands in the market. The impact of the rising inflation is to make this particular market much more competitive pointing to the need for a more aggressive marketing strategy.

    (ii) An inferior good is defined as a good whose demand falls as income rises and rises and income falls. In a period of rising inflation, as the real value of incomes falls consumers are more likely to be switching to inferior goods, making the marketing process much easier. The impact of rising inflation is that firms need to devote less resources to marketing such goods. Marketing will still have an important role to play, however, to enable firms to exploit the potential increase in market demand to best advantage.

ILLUSTRATIVE QUESTIONS
AND
SUGGESTED SOLUTIONS

ILLUSTRATIVE QUESTIONS

All questions carry 20 marks

1 BASIC CONCEPTS

Explain the basic concepts of the science of economics.

2 OPPORTUNITY COST

Explain the concept of opportunity cost and give examples of its usefulness in the marketing context.

3 RESOURCES

How are resources allocated in a mixed economy?

4 UTILITY AND TIME

Explain how marginal utility theory accounts for:

(a) the behaviour of consumers;
(b) the allocation of time by consumers.

5 LEVEL OF DEMAND

What determines the level of demand for a product? How does the marketing person try to influence demand?

6 SUPPLY AND DEMAND

Assume a market where price is essentially determined by the forces of supply and demand. With the aid of diagrams, answer and explain the following.

(a) How would easier credit terms for compact disc players affect the price of vinyl disc players?

(b) How would an increase in the supply of oil affect the price of petrol?

(c) What would be the likely causes of a contraction in the demand for potatoes?

(d) How would an increase in demand for new houses affect the wages of bricklayers?

(e) How would a subsidy for beef producers affect the price of lamb?

7 INFERIOR GOODS

What is meant by the term 'inferior goods'? What can a marketing person do to sustain the demand of an 'inferior good'?

ILLUSTRATIVE QUESTIONS

8 TRANSPORT SERVICE

A provider of a major transport service (eg British Rail) is unlikely to announce a price rise without first considering the number of passengers likely to change their mode of travelling.

(a) Define:

    (i)   price elasticity of demand;

    (ii)   income elasticity of demand;

    (iii) cross elasticity of demand.

(b) Why would knowledge of these elasticities interest British Rail?

(c) Illustrate the effect of an income rise on the level of demand for transport facilities.

9 AVERAGE COST

How, and why, may the shape of the long-run average cost curve of a firm differ from that which is usual in the short-run?

10 ECONOMIC FACTORS

What economic factors might a manufacturing company take into account in deciding whether or not to move to a new location?

11 ADOPT A POLICY

Under what circumstances can a firm adopt a policy of price discrimination? What are the possible advantages and disadvantages of adopting such a policy?

12 OLIGOPOLY

Faced with increasing costs, the world's big five car manufacturing companies are considering raising the prices of their cars.

What factors would they, as individual firms, take into account in deciding whether or not to raise prices.

13 PRIVATE SECTOR FIRMS

Discuss the sources of finance available to private sector firms.

14 STANDARD OF LIVING

To what extent do national income figures accurately reflect changes in the standard of living of a country over a period of years?

15 RECESSION AND RECOVERY

Recession comes quickly; recovery is slow. Explain why this is so.

16 IMPLEMENTING POLICY

Discuss the general problems which the government of an industrial economy might face in attempting to implement a new economic policy.

17 HOW AND WHY

Discuss how and why governments seek to control the supply of money.

18 DIRECT AND INDIRECT

What are the advantages and disadvantages of direct taxation compared to indirect taxation?

19 VARIOUS TYPES

(a) Define inflation, distinguishing between the various types.
(b) How is inflation measured?

20 MAIN COST

Consider whether the main cost of controlling inflation is high unemployment.

21 ABSOLUTE ADVANTAGE

Demonstrate that specialisation and international trade can lead to an increase in the output of every commodity even if one country has absolute advantage in the production of all commodities. What are the important assumptions made in arriving at these conclusions?

22 DEFICIT

(a) Using a country of your choice briefly describe its balance of trade position over the last 10 years. Provide an explanation for this and any changes which occurred within the period.
(8 marks)

(b) What practical steps might a government take to improve the balance of trade and what factors might limit their success?
(12 marks)

23 DETERMINATION OF EXCHANGE RATES

By use of appropriate examples illustrate the ways in which exchange rates are determined.

24 INTERNATIONAL MARKETER

Why would an *international* marketer need to have an understanding of the concept of elasticity?

1 BASIC CONCEPTS

The word 'economics' comes from the Greek, meaning 'household management'. Today, the subject matter of economics is that part of human behaviour which relates to the production, exchange and use of goods and services.

This description of economics places the subject within the social sciences, the sciences that study and explain human behaviour. A science may be defined as an objective study to acquire knowledge through observation and experiment, with findings from these studies being critically tested, systematised (ie. reduced to or analysed into systems) and brought under general principles or theories. A social science is the study of the structure and functioning of elements of human society through the application of scientific methods of study. Economics is described as a science, because this reflects the way economists analyse problems. Economists aim to develop theories of human behaviour and to test them against the facts.

Economic theory provides a framework of analysis for interpreting facts about the real world, but, as with other social sciences, there are certain problems with the application of the science:

(a) Laboratory testing is not possible and so 'experiments' must be conducted in real world conditions where it is often impossible to isolate the specific factors that are being tested. The results from economic experiment are therefore unlikely to be conclusive because other factors will influence the situation and the results.

(b) Any scientific study of human behaviour involves making abstract conclusions from value judgements and the unpredictability of human behaviour. Because it is extremely difficult to formulate theories and predictions about what people will do, forecasts and predictions must be based on certain assumptions.

One of the basic assumptions in economics is the rationality of human behaviour; essentially this means that consumers and producers use the best information available to make consistent choices. Rational behaviour implies a motive behind decisions and actions and so it is conventional in economics to assume that consumers have the objective of maximising their level of satisfaction or utility, while it is assumed that producers wish to maximise profits. Although it is possible to challenge the assumption of rationality in particular instances, the assumption nevertheless contains a basic truth: that people try to act rationally in accordance with an objective. Its advantage lies in its simplicity and in the lack of agreement about a better alternative assumption.

In considering economics as a science it is useful to distinguish between positive and normative economics. Positive economics deals with objective or scientific explanation of the working of the economy. In contrast, normative economics offers prescriptions or recommendations based on value judgements. The purpose of positive economics is to enable economists to act as detached scientists.

A fundamental concept in economics is the scarcity of resources. For any society the central economic problem is how to reconcile the conflict between people's virtually limitless desires or wants for goods and services and the scarcity of resources with which these goods and services can be produced. For consumers, the scarcity of goods and services is quite apparent. Everyone would like to have more, for example, in our society, a larger house, bigger car, more and better consumer durables, more holidays or meals out. For producers the resources available to produce such goods and services are also scarce. These resources consist of labour, capital (eg machinery, tools), land (or natural resources) and entrepreneurship.

Since resources for production are scarce and there are not enough goods and services to satisfy the total potential demand, choices must be made. Consumers have limited incomes and so must choose which goods and services they will buy. Producers must choose how to use their available resources, and what to produce with them. Economics studies the nature of these choices. Because every society is faced with the problem of unlimited wants and scarce resources each society must solve three basic questions.

(a) What goods and services to produce?
(b) How to produce these goods and services? and
(c) For whom to produce these goods and services?

Economics is, fundamentally, the study of how society decides these basic questions of 'what', 'how' and 'for whom'.

Arising from the problem of choice is another basic concept in economics, that of opportunity cost. Making a choice involves a sacrifice. If a country has a choice of building either motor cars or tractors, and the country chooses to have tractors, it will be giving up motor cars in order to have tractors. The cost of having tractors can therefore be regarded as the sacrifice of not being able to have motor cars. Such choices also exist for individuals and producers. For example, the purchase of a compact disc may mean that a visit to the cinema is forgone. While if a producer decides to increase the production of tables with the resources available to him this may involve the sacrifice of chairs which would otherwise have been produced.

The cost of an item measured in terms of the alternatives forgone is the opportunity cost. Thus the opportunity cost to the country in deciding to build tractors is the motor cars forgone; the opportunity cost of buying the compact disc is the visit to the cinema, and so on. Opportunity cost is an important economic concept. It is the basis on which the economic cost of factors of production is measured, and so opportunity cost is fundamental to profit maximising production decisions.

In most industrialised countries the basic questions of 'what', 'how' and 'for whom' are determined through the operation of the market mechanism. Markets bring together buyers and sellers of goods and services, and market prices adjust to ensure that scarce resources are used to produce those goods and services that society demands. In essence markets are arrangements through which prices influence the allocation of scarce resources. It should be noted though that the basic economic questions may be settled without the use of markets, for instance through the command economy, in which government planners would take decisions about production and consumption.

Finally, it is possible in economics to classify branches of the subject according to the subject matter of the approach that is used. In this there is a broad division of approach into microeconomics and macroeconomics. Microeconomics is the study of individual economic units or particular parts of the economy, for example how are the wage levels of bricklayers determined, or how does an individual firm decide what volume of output to produce or what products to make? Macroeconomics is the study of 'global' or collective decisions by individual households or producers. It examines the economy as a whole, for example the aggregate price level, total output, the level of unemployment, etc and what economic policies a government can pursue to influence the condition of the national economy.

2   OPPORTUNITY COST

Economics is about choice. Choice is necessary because resources are scarce and limited, yet needs and wants are unlimited. It is not therefore possible to satisfy all needs and firms, countries and individuals all have to choose between competing uses for their limited resources. In choosing one use for a quantity of resources, there is a cost, called an opportunity cost.

Opportunity cost may be defined as the cost of an item measured in terms of the alternatives foregone.

The concept of opportunity cost arises because resources are scarce. In choosing which goods to produce from scarce resources, society is forced to do without other goods which might otherwise be produced. The next best alternative foregone or sacrificed is the opportunity cost of what is produced.

The income of individuals restricts the range of goods and services they are able to consume and they are thus forced to choose between alternatives. In choosing to purchase a textbook, for example, a student may forgo a meal in a restaurant. The meal forgone is therefore the opportunity cost of the textbook. For another individual the decision to choose to purchase a new compact disc player may involve the sacrifice of a foreign holiday. The individual's income is such that he/she can have one or the other but not both. The foreign holiday, being the next best alternative to purchasing a compact disc player, therefore represents the opportunity cost of the compact disc player.

A limited income is the main kind of resource constraint which the individual faces thus giving rise to the need to choose between alternatives. Time, however, is also a scarce resource for the individual. If a student decides to spend an evening at home revising for an economics examination, for example, the opportunity cost of such revision may be the time not spent revising for a marketing examination.

Opportunity cost does not compare just the financial price of these alternatives. It is necessary to take a much wider view of cost encompassing the benefit which would be derived if the product was purchased or the decision taken. The new compact disc player may provide hours of relaxing and cheap entertainment at home, but the holiday may represent a much needed break without which your health might suffer and future income could be lost.

The concept of opportunity cost provides marketers with a model which explains how customers might make decisions about which goods to buy. It emphasises the underlying truth that all goods are in competition for the individual's scarce income resource, and not just brands of the same generic product competing for a share of the sales of that product category. In this way strategies which help car producers compete with holiday firms may be more effective in increasing sales than campaigns promoting the merits of one car model over another.

The concept of opportunity cost also helps the marketer concentrate his or her thoughts on the importance of the whole package of benefits, and encourages a 'value added' competitive approach rather than a price-cutting one.

Businesses and marketing is about decision making. Firms also have limited resources and an opportunity cost approach to decision making encourages all the implications and alternatives to be assessed and evaluated. Turning down a large one-off order which would prevent the delivery of a smaller but regular client's products may be of more value to the company in the long term. A sponsorship deal which generates good public relations in the town and has publicity spin-offs may prove a better use of budget than an advertising campaign.

SUGGESTED SOLUTIONS

 The marketer needs to recognise that the broad concept of opportunity cost aids his or her decision making as well as providing an insight into customer/buyer behaviour and decision making.

3 RESOURCES

Economics is fundamentally about how best to use the scarce resources of the world. The central economic problem of resource allocation exists for individuals, firms and nations. At whatever level you look you can find the dilemma caused by unlimited needs and wants but limited resources to satisfy them:

(a) a company can use its machines and workforce to produce one product or another;

(b) an individual can spend his/her limited income and time on the garden or on home improvement, and so on;

(c) a government can use its resource to build either roads or new schools.

Economics is the study of the consequences of these decisions. At national level a number of economic systems have evolved which have been used to try and solve a country's economic problem.

There are two extreme types of economic system.

(a) *The market economy*
Here the forces of the market place operate and the 'invisible hand' of price allocates and reallocates resources as producers seek to maximise their profits.

(b) *The planned economy*
Here the rational approach of centralised planning means that resources are owned collectively, controlled centrally and all allocated according to the objectives of the planning authorities (the government).

Although some countries have tried to apply these systems in their extreme forms, the disadvantages of both have resulted most in some form of mixed economy, in an attempt to gain the advantages inherent in both systems.

In a mixed economy there will be two identifiable sectors, a private sector and a public one. Resources are allocated differently in each.

The private sector relies on the profit motive and the price mechanism to ensure that resources are used to produce the goods and services which are most in demand. Productivity increases profitability, so there is an incentive to find ways of getting the most output from the least input. Finished goods and services go to those who can afford them. Shortages or increases in demand lead to higher prices and profits, therefore signalling the desirability of more resources in a sector.

The public sector is financed largely through taxation and allocates resources centrally to ensure that community and social needs are satisfied. Decisions are made centrally on the level of defence, health, education and justice systems which should be provided. Allocation of these is usually on the basis of need: you are entitled to education when you are young, to health care when you are sick, and to police help when you need it, and so on.

In a mixed economy the government can intervene to prevent the excesses of a market driven system, legislating to control industrial pollution, protecting consumers and employees and providing a welfare 'net' to protect the unemployed and the disadvantaged. At the same time the disciplines of the private sector can help to reduce inefficiencies in the public sector and competition between the two sectors, if balanced, comes close to offering the best of both systems.

Managing a mixed economy is not without its own difficulties. Some can be seen as the Eastern European bloc countries begin to establish private sectors in their previously centrally planned systems.

In a mixed economy, private sector monopolies may act against consumers' interests. On the other hand, public sector organisations may be less efficient because they are driven by different objectives from profit maximisation.

However on balance the mixed economy does appear to offer the best option available and seems likely to remain the route chosen by most economies in the foreseeable future.

4   UTILITY AND TIME

Tutorial note. Including one or two practical examples in your answer may help you to demonstrate that you understand the concepts and can apply them.

Suggested solution

(a)   Marginal utility theory is one of the theories that enables economists to explain consumer behaviour. More specifically, it helps to explain why, when the price of a normal good declines, the quantity consumed of that good rises.

The term 'utility' refers to the satisfaction that the consumer derives from consuming a commodity. Total utility is the total satisfaction that is gained by consuming a particular quantity of a commodity. Marginal utility refers to the change in satisfaction resulting from consuming marginally more or marginally less of that commodity. As an individual consumes more and more of a particular commodity, the total utility which he gains will increase, but successive units of the item will yield less and less utility as consumption increases. In other words, marginal utility declines as the total consumption of a particular commodity increases, the consumption of all other commodities being held constant. This is called the hypothesis or law of diminishing marginal utility. Marginal utility may actually become negative for some goods, since the total utility derived from consumption of a good may begin to fall if consumption extends beyond the level at which the consumer is satiated.

Utility theory makes the assumption that a consumer seeks to maximise his total satisfaction within the constraints imposed by his budget (ie his income), and the prices of all the commodities he can choose to consume. The consumer's budget is allocated among the various commodities so as to maximise his total utility. In other words, the consumer seeks to reach a point at which no reallocation of his expenditure will increase his total utility. This position can be established by comparing the marginal utilities of the various commodities consumed with their respective prices, and deriving the marginal utility for each penny spent on the various goods. Equilibrium is attained when the marginal utility of the last penny spent on each good is equal. If this is not the case then the consumer can increase his total utility by shifting his expenditure away from the commodity whose marginal utility per penny spent is lower to one whose marginal utility per penny spent is higher. The process of re-allocation is continued until the marginal utility of the last penny spent on one commodity equals the marginal utility of the last penny spent on another. To maximise total utility, marginal utilities must be equalised with respect to price, thus:

$$\frac{MU_x}{p_x} = \frac{MU_y}{p_y}$$

ie: Marginal utility   =   Marginal utility
    per penny for good X   per penny for good Y

Now if the price of good X rises, the consumer's marginal utility per penny spent on good X is less than that for good Y. So the consumer shifts his expenditure away from X, buying buys less of good X and more of good Y. Because of the principle of diminishing marginal utility, this decreases the marginal utility of Y and increases the marginal utility of X. Eventually a situation is reached in which, again,

$$\frac{MU_x}{p_x} = \frac{MU_y}{p_y}$$

This is the new equilibrium position.

Thus an increase in the price of good X is seen to have reduced the quantity demanded of good X. This is how the marginal utility theory helps us to explain the downward slope of the demand curve for normal goods.

(b)   Since no one has infinite time at their disposal, the use of time implies the utilisation of a scarce resource. If a consumer spends a certain amount of time on consuming one commodity, then that time is not available for use in the consumption of any other commodity. That time has an opportunity cost, which amounts to the value of the alternative use of that time. Consequently when comparing the costs of consuming different commodities, we need to take into account not only the prices of these commodities as quoted in the market but also the value of time required for the consumption of each of these commodities.

Marginal utility theory can accommodate this additional factor. We have seen that in order to maximise their total satisfaction, consumers need to allocate their budget among the different commodities available to them in such a way as to equalise their marginal utilities with respect to their prices,

$$\text{ie} \quad \frac{MU_A}{p_A + t_A} = \frac{MU_B}{p_B + t_B} = \frac{MU_C}{p_C + t_C}$$

where p_A = the market price of good A in monetary terms
and t_A = the value of time required in the consumption of good A
and so on.

The value of time will be the opportunity cost of the alternative use of that time.

For example, an individual may need to choose how many journeys to make by public transport and how many by using his own car. The marginal utility of each additional journey may be judged to be similar whichever method is chosen: the individual does, after all, reach his destination. But the individual will not simply compare prices of the two methods and always choose the cheaper. He is likely also to consider the relative amounts of time taken. For example, a journey by high speed train may cost £20 more than the marginal cost of travelling the same journey by car. But if three hours are saved in travelling by rail rather than car and the individual values his time at £8 per hour, then the choice of the rail journey in preference to car travel will be advantageous to him. The individual might value his time in terms of the money he would earn in that time.

5   LEVEL OF DEMAND

Economists are concerned with 'effective demand', that is the number of units of a product which the market not only *wants* to buy, but is also *able to* buy. Marketers may take a rather long term view of demand, accepting that decision making, particularly for luxury goods, and acceptance of a product by consumers can take time. Marketers may promote a product today in anticipation of future sales. However it is revenue in the short run which determines the organisation's financial health and I will consider effective demand from the short run standpoint.

Market demand is the sum of all individual demands and represents the volume of goods being purchased at a particular price and at a particular time. A number of factors influence how much this quantity will be.

Firstly the price charged for the product will affect the demand. For normal goods higher prices usually mean less demand, but as price falls, more people can afford the product and individuals may buy more units of the product, finding a second or third purchase worthwhile at lower prices.

Figure 1
As price falls from P to P_1,
demand extends from Q to Q_1

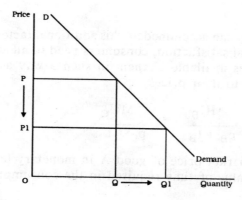

Demand for different categories of product will be more or less sensitive to price, ie more or less price elastic or inelastic. A steeper slope on a demand curve illustrates a product which is less price sensitive, possibly because it has no close substitutes, is a product which is a necessity, is addictive or only represents a trivial proportion of an individual's expenditure. Flatter curves indicate that demand changes greatly with changes in price and are characteristic of a luxury product, one with close substitutes or one representing a significant proportion of income spent.

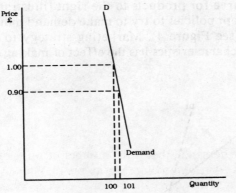

(a)
A steep slope indicates
price-inelastic demand

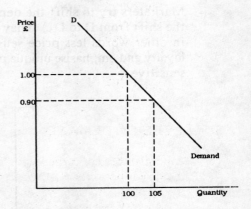

Figure 2
(b)
A flatter curve indicates
a price-sensitive product

Besides price, any other factor which influences the amount of a product demanded at a point in time is referred to as a condition of demand. The conditions of demand include:

(a) the price of other goods;
(b) income;
(c) expectations;
(d) fashion and taste;
(e) the number of people in the market.

Changes in the conditions of demand result in a shift in the demand curve (an increase or decrease in demand), as shown in Figure 3.

Figure 3
Changes in the conditions
of demand cause the
demand curve to shift

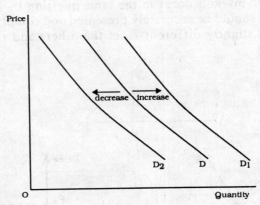

Marketers have the job of making sure that the available supply of the organisation is matched by demand. Understanding the factors which influence demand is therefore essential to the marketer. The marketing mix, the 4Ps of product, price, place and promotion, are the controllable variables the marketer can use to influence demand.

As we have explained, price directly changes the quantity demanded, but other variables add value and change the customer's perception of the product. Advertising can make the product more 'fashionable', shifting the whole curve. By altering its availability of the product it is possible to alter the number of people in the market place.

Marketers try to shift the demand curve for products to the right (illustrated in Figure 3 as the shift from D to D_1). They also adopt policies to try to make demand more price-inelastic, in other words less price sensitive, (see Figure 4). Marketing strategy to encourage brand loyalty and emphasise unique product characteristics has the effect of making demand less price sensitive.

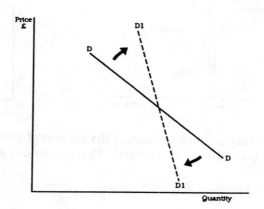

Figure 4

Understanding the mechanics of demand is essential for developing marketing strategy.

6 SUPPLY AND DEMAND

Tutorial note. Questions on simple supply and demand analysis can provide candidates with high marks so long as the subject is fully understood and a thorough treatment is given. In each market changes in price and quantity, and shifts and movements along the curves, should be explained. Where two markets occur in the same question their inter-relationship should be identified. Diagrams should be accurately presented and comply with the written description. Note that part (c) is slightly different from the others and requires an explanation of the conditions of supply.

Suggested solution

(a)

Figure 1

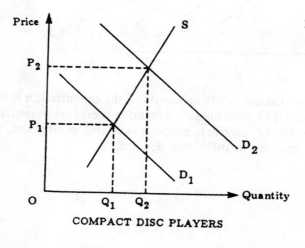

COMPACT DISC PLAYERS

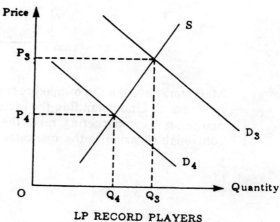

LP RECORD PLAYERS

Easier credit terms will increase demand for compact disc players causing the demand curve to shift to the right from D_1 to D_2. This will have the effect of raising the price from P_1 to P_2 and quantity supplied will extend, bringing about an increase in quantity traded from Q_1 to Q_2.

As compact disc players and vinyl disc (LP) players are in competitive demand – they are substitutes for each other – there will now be a fall in the demand for record players, shown as a leftward shift of the demand curve from D_3 to D_4. This will result in the price falling from P_3 to P_4, and quantity supplied will contract, bringing about a decrease in quantity traded from Q_3 to Q_4.

(b)

Figure 2

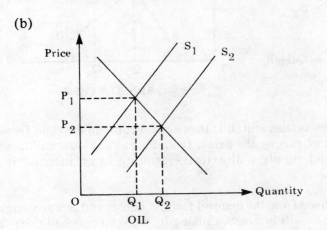

An increase in the supply of oil will shift the supply curve to the right from S_1 to S_2. This will have the effect of pushing the price down from P_1 to P_2 and quantity demanded will extend, bringing about an increase in quantity traded from Q_1 to Q_2.

As oil and petrol are in joint supply, increased supplies of oil will lead to increased supplies of petrol, causing the supply curve for petrol to also shift from S_3 to S_4. Consequently the price of petrol will fall from P_3 to P_4 and the quantity supplied will extend from Q_3 to Q_4.

(c) The demand for potatoes will contract as a result of a price increase, caused by a contraction in supply.

Figure 3

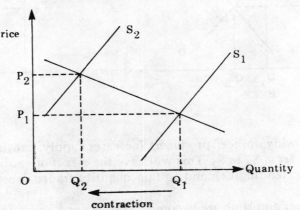

A contraction in supply might be caused by increases in the cost of production (higher wages, increased cost of pesticides, poor growing conditions etc), changes in taxation, withdrawal of firms from the market, or more profitable uses of resources for alternative purposes.

(d)   *Figure 4*

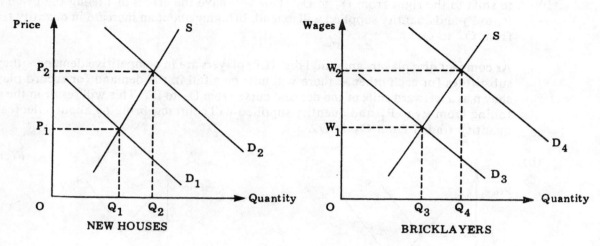

NEW HOUSES   BRICKLAYERS

An increase in the demand for new houses will shift the demand curve to the right from D_1 to D_2. This will have the effect of raising the price, from P_1 to P_2. Housebuilders will respond to the higher prices and supply will extend, resulting in an increase in the quantity traded from Q_1 to Q_4

The demand for bricklayers is derived from the demand for new houses and as a consequence the demand for this type of labour will increase, causing its demand curve to shift from D_3 to D_4. The wages of bricklayers will rise, shown as W_1 to W_2, and the quantity employed will extend from Q_3 to Q_4.

(e)   *Figure 5*

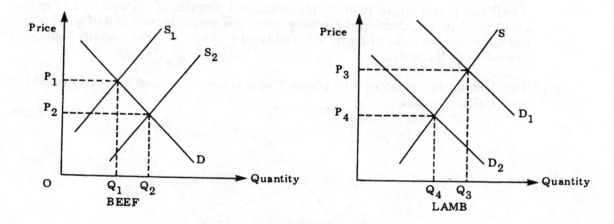

BEEF   LAMB

A subsidy on beef producers increases supply, causing the supply curve to shift to the right from S_1 to S_2. This will have the effect of causing the price to fall from P_1 to P_2, and extending demand so that quantity traded increases from Q_1 to Q_2.

As beef and lamb are in competitive demand – they are substitutes for each other – there will now be a decrease in the conditions of demand for lamb, shown by a leftward shift of the supply curve from D_1 to D_2. This will have the effect of causing lamb prices to fall from P_3 to P_4 and the quantity supplied by farmers will contract, causing a decrease in the quantity traded from Q_3 to Q_4.

7   INFERIOR GOODS

An inferior good is a product for which there is a preferred, but more expensive, substitute or alternative. Limitations of income force the consumer to choose the cheaper option. Examples might include bus travel instead of taxis, domestic holidays instead of overseas holidays or mince meat instead of steak.

It should be noted that the term 'inferior' does not refer to the quality of the product. Inferior goods are *not* necessarily shoddy or substandard. The bus service could be the best in the world and the mince of the highest quality, but they are perceived by the consumer to be less desirable than the more expensive alternative. The significant factor for the marketer lies in the *perception* of the inferior product. Any marketing strategy for an inferior good has to tackle this directly.

Demand for an inferior good falls as income rises, giving an inferior good a negative value of income elasticity.

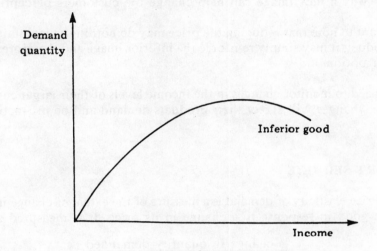

The income elasticity of demand calculates how sensitive demand is to changes in income level. Inferior goods are sensitive to income changes. In other words, the quantity demanded changes significantly as a result of a change in income.

For example, if income increases by 10% and the quantity demanded falls by 15% the value of income elasticity would be -1.5.

$$\text{YED} = \frac{\% \, \Delta \text{ in } Q_D}{\% \, \Delta \text{ in } Y} = \frac{-15}{+10} = -1\tfrac{1}{2}$$

Y = income
Δ = change
Q_D = quantity demanded

For every 1% change in income the quantity demanded will move in the opposite direction $1\tfrac{1}{2}$%. Income elasticity has a negative value of more than 1.

However inferior goods can also be income inelastic. In this case the value of income elasticity would still be negative but the value would be less than 1. Here although there is a tendency to buy less as income rises and of course more as income falls, the change in demand is not so significant as income changes.

The marketer may be faced with the problem of decreasing demand for an inferior good in a situation where the standard of living of the target customers is increasing. Sustaining demand in this situation can be done in two ways.

(a) By finding new customers for the product, who are in a lower income group and/or who have a different perception of the product, thus extending the life cycle of the product.

(b) By repositioning the product through added value and a new image. Examples could include selling bus travel on the grounds of it being more environmentally friendly than alternatives, and margarine on the grounds of being a healthier product than butter.

In this way a new image can help change the customers perception of the product.

It is important to note that reducing the price may do nothing to maintain the demand for an inferior product; it may simply reinforce the inferior image and therefore the income effect of the cheaper option.

Marketers need to monitor changes in the income levels of their target customers, be aware of how income changes will effect their products demand and be pro-active in their strategic response.

8 TRANSPORT SERVICE

(a) (i) Price elasticity of demand is a measure of the extent of change in market demand for a good in response to a change in its price. It is measured as:

$$\frac{\% \text{ change in quantity demanded}}{\% \text{ change in price}}$$

Since the demand goes up when the price falls, and goes down when the price rises, elasticity is strictly a negative value, but it is usual to ignore the minus sign. Goods with a price elasticity of demand less than 1 are said to have an inelastic demand, and goods with an elasticity greater than 1 are said to have an elastic demand.

(ii) Income elasticity of demand for a good indicates the responsiveness of demand to changes in household incomes. It is measured as:

$$\frac{\% \text{ change in quantity demanded}}{\% \text{ change in household incomes}}$$

The change in demand for normal goods rises if household incomes rise, and falls if household incomes fall. A good is income elastic if this value is greater than 1 and income inelastic if its value is less than 1 but more than 0. Inferior goods have an income elasticity of less than 0, which means that as household incomes rise, demand for the goods falls.

(iii) Cross-elasticity of demand refers to the responsiveness of demand for one good to changes in the price of another good. It is measured as:

$$\frac{\text{\% change in quantity of good A demanded}}{\text{\% change in price of good B}}$$

Cross-elasticity therefore involves a comparison between two products. Cross elasticity is potentially significant where the two goods are close substitutes for each other, so that a rise in the price of B, say, is likely to result in an increase in the demand for A. Cross-elasticity of demand between two complementary products can also be significant, because a rise in the price of B would result in some fall in demand for A (because of a fall in demand for B).

(b) British Rail, like any other firm, should be interested in all three elasticities. However, firms such as British Rail operate with a high proportion of their costs being fixed, and not many variable costs.

(i) Price elasticity of demand is therefore significant because if demand is elastic, an increase in price would result in a fall in total revenues. Given the high level of fixed costs, the reduction in the volume of passengers resulting from a price increase would not cause a significant fall in costs, and so the price increase would be loss-making. On the other hand, if demand were inelastic in response to a price increase, an increase in price would result in an increase in profits. Reductions in price could be considered in much the same way, because if prices were lowered, the increase in traffic demand would not increase operating costs by much, and so the profitability or otherwise of a price reduction would depend on price elasticity and the effect of the price change on total revenue.

If the policy of British Rail were to attract more customers to its services, price elasticity of demand would also be of importance in estimating the likely response to a price reduction to attract more business.

(ii) Income elasticity of demand would help British Rail to assess the effect of changes in household income on demand for its services. It is particularly useful for longer-term forecasting - eg will a rise in household incomes over time result in a significant shift of traffic from rail to private cars on the road?

(iii) Cross-elasticity of demand between the demand for rail services and the prices of close substitutes, such as bus services and car prices, would also help BR's management to plan its own pricing policy. For example, if the bus transport organisations announced an increase in their prices, BR could decide whether to take the opportunity to raise its prices too, or hope for an increase in traffic by keeping its prices unchanged.

(c) The effect of an income rise is likely to result in a shift in the demand curve for transport services. If transport services are 'normal' goods, the shift in the demand curve will be to the right - ie demand will be higher than before at the same price levels.

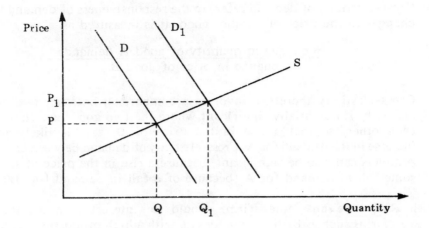

The effect of a shift in the demand curve from D to D₁ is that British Rail would be able to put up its prices from P to a new equilibrium price of P_1 and achieve an increase in demand from Q to Q_1. Total revenue would rise, and given the fixed cost nature of BR's business, profits would rise too.

9   AVERAGE COST

Short run AC curve
The shape of a short run average cost curve is dependent on two factors.

(a)   The fall in unit costs as the output of a firm during a period rises, because of the wider spread of fixed costs. For example, a firm with fixed costs of £10,000 per annum would incur fixed costs per unit of £10 if it produced 1,000 units in the year, but only £1 if it produced 10,000 units.

(b)   The law of diminishing returns explains why short run average costs begin to rise after a certain level of output. In the short run, either capital or labour as a factor of production is limited in supply, and so extra amounts of that factor cannot be obtained. More quantities of the other factor can be obtained, but given the restricted availability of the fixed factor, additional quantities of the variable factor that are used become increasingly less productive.

The law of diminishing returns states that beyond some point of increase in the amount of the variable factor that is used, the marginal addition to total output falls (ie the 'marginal physical product' of the factor of production falls). As a consequence unit costs of extra output rise, and the average cost of total output will also rise when the *marginal* cost of extra output begins to exceed the average cost of all output up to that point.

These two factors explain why the short run average cost curve is U-shaped.

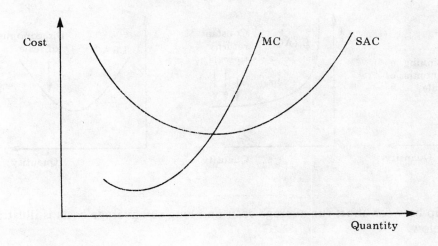

The marginal cost curve (MC) cuts the short run average cost curve (SAC) at its lowest point, because if MC is below SAC, SAC must be falling, but when MC exceeds SAC, SAC must rise.

Long run AC curve
The shape of the long run cost curve is different, because in the long run, all factors of production ('inputs') are assumed to be variable in supply. This means that the law of diminishing returns does not apply. However, *economies of scale* affect long run costs.

(a) Internal economies of scale are reductions in unit costs that can be achieved by producing output on a larger scale. The sources of internal economies include greater division and specialisation of labour and the use of larger or more specialised machines, which a smaller producer would find uneconomic but a large producer can exploit to improve productivity.

(b) External economies of scale occur as an industry as a whole gets larger, so that an experienced specialist labour force and specialised ancillary industries develop around it.

Economies of scale can only be properly exploited in the long run, because it takes time for a firm to get bigger - ie to overcome the fixed nature of one or more 'inputs' (factors of production) in the short term.

Once a firm gets above a certain size, further economies of scale cease to be achievable, and constant returns to scale might occur - ie it would then cost the same per unit to produce extra output, because twice as many resources would then be needed to produce twice as many units. Classical economic theory also predicts that there will be *diseconomies of scale* when a firm grows beyond a certain size. The cause of diseconomies is generally assumed to be the inability of management to manage a large firm efficiently, due to the problems of its sheer size.

A long run average cost curve might therefore be continually downward-sloping (if there are never-ending economies of scale to be obtained) or it might level off (if there are constant returns to scale above a certain size) or it might be U-shaped (if there are diseconomies of scale above a certain size).

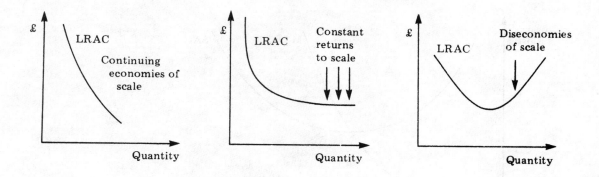

The relationship between short run average costs and long run average costs is illustrated in the diagram below.

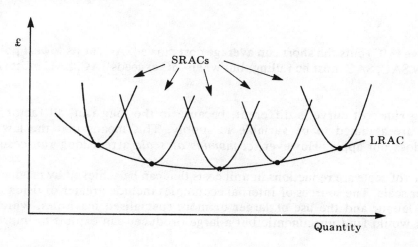

10 ECONOMIC FACTORS

Tutorial note. Although you might be able to draw on your general knowledge to answer this question, make sure that the points you make concern the *economic* factors involved. The impact of government regional policy is clearly a factor which should be discussed.

Suggested solution

The geographical location of the enterprise is usually a fundamental decision for an entrepreneur. There will be a number of influences on this decision including social factors. For example, the top management might prefer to live in a particular part of the country and hence locate the firm in what they consider to be a pleasant area to live. There are a number of other economic factors which influence the choice of location.

It is usually assumed that firms will wish to minimise their costs of operation, so firms will be mainly concerned with the effects of different location on the cost of production. Usually, several locations are possible sites from which the firm might operate and the management will thus choose that site which minimises the costs of production. Such a decision may not be as easy as it sounds. However as in deciding what to produce, a firm may face a number of trade-offs; for example its needs as a manufacturer might conflict with its requirements as a seller. Although one location might be optimal in relation to the source of major raw material inputs, another site might be more favourable in relation to access to markets. The ultimate decision of where to locate will depend on the assessment of the maximum net advantages of alternative sites.

The advantages of different localities may be considered in terms of natural advantages, acquired advantages and government policy. The natural advantages may be considered in terms of transport costs and proximity to markets. The two main ways in which transport costs affect the location of a firm are in the movement of its raw materials and in the movement of its finished product. Where a firm is faced with the choice of a site near to its sources of supply or a site near to its markets, the strength of the attractions of the alternative sites will basically depend on the nature of the manufacturing process carried out by the firm.

If the firm's raw materials are bulky, heavy and costly to transport while the finished product is light, compact and relatively cheap to transport, the firm will be attracted to the sources of its raw materials. When the manufacturing process greatly reduces the weight and bulk of the raw materials used, the quantity to be transported will be much less when the firm is located near the source of its raw materials.

On the other hand, when the transport costs of finished goods are much higher than those for the basic materials there will be a strong attraction to locations near to the market. This will clearly be the case where the manufacturing process increases bulk, as it does for instance in the furniture industry. Transport costs will also be relatively high where the product is perishable or fragile.

Access to markets may also be important for reasons other than those associated with transport costs. The development of the European Community, with the abolition of internal tariff barriers and the coming of the Single European Market at the end of 1992, has encouraged some firms, particularly Japanese owned, to locate manufacturing plants within the EC in order not to be excluded from those developments. The establishment of the Nissan car plant on Teesside is an example in this respect.

As far as manufacturing activities are concerned, supplies of capital and land are not usually important determinants of location, as these inputs are usually available in a number of alternative locations. The availability of labour may however be an important influence on location. Labour is relatively immobile which means that labour may be in surplus in some regions but in short supply in other areas. A firm may find, therefore, that labour costs are higher in some areas – those of labour shortage – than in other areas. Where there are regional differences in the costs of labour these will clearly influence a firm's decision on where to locate. The availability of labour with particular types of skills will also be important to many firms and the speed with which unskilled labour may be trained and retrained will influence location decisions.

Other natural advantages include physical features and accessibility. For some firms, the physical features of the site are of prime importance. Firms which require very large quantities of water in their production processes will be attracted to river locations. Those firms which have serious problems of waste disposal, especially chemical industries, are also usually located on river-bank sites, while the problem of dust control has made it necessary to site cement works in fairly remote locations.

Firms may historically have been attracted to a particular location by the natural advantages of a site, such as the availability of raw materials or access to sources of energy. When these natural advantages have disappeared, for example following the exhaustion of a mineral deposit, or have become unimportant, the location may remain attractive because it yields important acquired advantages. These acquired advantages develop as the concentration of firms, and hence the industry, grows larger. Such advantages may include a skilled labour force, communications, marketing and commercial organisation, nearby ancillary industries, training colleges in the locality and a widespread reputation for products of the region. All of these factors can help to lower the costs of production and hence make some locations more attractive than others when a firm is considering the relocation of its plant.

In the UK and in many other developed countries, the geographical distribution of industry is not decided entirely by market forces: there are often government restrictions on the freedom of managers to decide the location of their firm's operations. Since the Second World War, successive UK governments have introduced various types of measures in order to control industrial location, basically in order to try and achieve a better regional balance of economic activity. The government, therefore, has had to interfere in the decisions of firms when siting their plants. Often this has involved providing incentives by way of grants and soft loans to firms which are prepared to move to areas of high unemployment, while also curtailing expansion in the more prosperous areas by limiting the granting of Industrial Development Certificates.

Over the past 14 years, however, many of the traditional features of regional policy have been removed by the Conservative government which has reduced the amount of state interference in the location decision of managers, including the abolition of IDCs and reducing the availability of grants and loans. Despite this, some government incentives do remain. In 1980 the government introduced the first of a number of Enterprise Zones which provide various inducements for firms to move back to city areas. Firms which locate in Enterprise Zones have a long period of exemption from rates, very favourable tax treatment of capital expenditure, and speedy planning approvals. Such inducements, as well as other continuing aspects of regional policy, will have an influence on managers contemplating the relocation of their manufacturing capacity.

11 ADOPT A POLICY

Price discrimination occurs when the same commodity or service is sold at different prices to different customers. If the products are differentiated, as in the case of first and second class travel, or stalls and balcony theatre tickets, this is not a case of price discrimination.

If a producer is able to charge two different prices for the same product this is equivalent to there being different market segments. For this position to be maintained the two market segments must be kept separate and neither the goods nor the consumers should be able to move from one segment to another. An example of price discrimination would be the different prices of the same good sold in the home market and sold in a foreign market. A consumer living in the foreign market, if that was the more expensive market, would be discouraged from buying in the cheaper market because of transport costs, tariffs or indeed ignorance of the price variation. A doctor may charge different prices for the same private medical treatment because the service cannot be transferred (ie re-sold). Equally electricity companies can charge domestic and industrial users a different rate and telephone calls after 6pm and at weekends are cheaper than at peak times.

Keeping the market segments separate is an essential prerequisite for price discrimination to work. The lowering of trade restrictions in Europe is going to make it increasingly difficult for car manufacturers to charge different prices in different European markets. This will have implications for international pricing strategy and may restrict the opportunities of varying price to reflect different market conditions across Europe.

If we assume that the producer is a profit maximiser, it will be in his interest to take advantage of price discrimination if he can increase his profits by doing so. He can increase his profits in this way if the price elasticity of demand for the product is different in each market. Differences in such elasticity mean different proportionate changes in quantities purchased in the light of the same proportionate changes in price. Such differences may occur because there are more substitutes available in one market, because consumers have larger incomes in one market or because rival firms react more quickly to competition in one market.

In the case of commuter travel there are often no really viable alternatives, so demand is price inelastic. Off peak travellers have other options including staying at home, so this market segment faces price elastic demand.

By pricing high in the inelastic market and low in the elastic market, revenue will be higher than charging a single price to both segments.

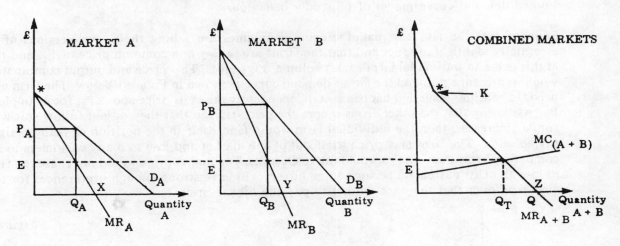

In the above diagram, the two separate markets are shown as market A and market B. The demand curves are shown as straight lines, both downward-sloping. Demand is more inelastic in market B, as illustrated by the steeper downward-sloping demand curve. The MR curves are also straight lines (they must be because the demand curves are straight lines). The monopolist will sell each extra unit of output in either market A or market B, depending on where the most extra revenue could be obtained - ie where the MR is higher. The MR curves of the two markets are combined to produce the 'aggregate' MR curve facing the firm.

Profits are maximised where MC = MR. In this case this is where $MC = MR_{A+B} = MR_A = MR_B$ (shown by price E = equilibrium price in the diagram). This establishes the profit-maximising output Q_T and the profit-maximising sales quantities in market A (Q_A) and market B (Q_B). $Q_A + Q_B = Q_T$. The price charged in each market will be different because the demand curves are different. This means that there must be price discrimination in order to maximise profits. The prices to be charged to maximise profits in this case are P_A and P_B in markets A and B respectively.

The advantages of a policy of price discrimination are mainly financial, increased total revenue and the opportunity to maximise sales in a variety of market segments by varying price according to the nature and conditions of demand. The main drawbacks to price discrimination are related to customer attitudes. If they are aware of it, customers may be disgruntled and are less likely to remain loyal if in the future alternative products become available. It can therefore cost the firm loss of goodwill as well as the costs of 'policing' the different markets.

12   OLIGOPOLY

The world's big five car manufacturing companies operate in a market structure which is termed oligopoly. Markets are said to be oligopolistic whenever a small number of firms supply the dominant share of an industry's total output. In oligopoly, firms are large relative to the size of the total market they serve, and in the case of giant corporations they are large not just relatively but absolutely as well.

In an oligopoly each firm has a prominent market position, such that its decisions and actions have significant repercussions on rival firms: what one firm does affects the others. If one firm should announce a price change, for instance, its competitors would quickly take notice and consider whether and how to respond. There is thus a great deal of interdependence and competitive interaction among firms in an oligopoly. One answer to the question of how rival firms would respond to a decision of one firm to raise its selling price is contained in the kinked demand curve model of oligopoly behaviour.

Suppose that the five car manufacturing companies are selling their own versions of an essentially identical product and that the firms are selling at a common price of P_1, and that at this price an individual firm's sales volume is Q_1 units. This price and output combination would represent a point on the firm's demand curve as shown in Figure 1 below. The firm now needs to consider what will happen if it independently raises its price above P_1, for example to P_2. Assuming that the other firms ignore the price rise, in that they do not follow suit with similar increases, then the individual firm would find itself in the position of being a high-priced seller. The firm may price itself out of the market and lose so many customers to the competing firms that its sales would fall to Q_2 units. The higher price would not cause the firm to lose all of its customers because some buyers will have strong enough preferences for this firm's product that they are willing to pay the higher price.

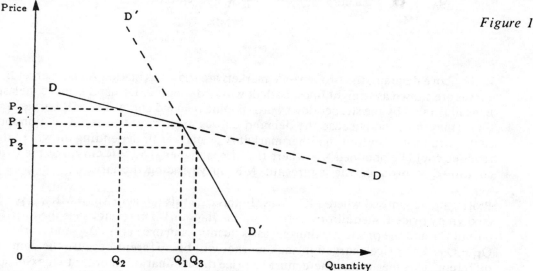

Figure 1

In the converse situation of the firm lowering its selling price, say to P_3, it is likely that the competitor firms will follow suit, reducing their prices by a similar amount in order to prevent the first firm from attracting their customers and so reducing their sales. Such a retaliatory move will tend to have the effect of limiting the individual firm's gain in sales to its proportionate share of the increased market which all firms in the industry will tend to realise because they are now selling at a lower price. Figure 1 shows that when rival firms match price cuts then the individual firm's sales will only expand to Q_3 units.

An individual firm can, therefore, expect that price increases will be ignored, because rivals of the price-raising firm will gain the business lost by the firm which raises price, while price cuts will be matched as rivals react to prevent the price-cutter from gaining customers at their expense. This means that each firm will have a kinked demand curve for its product like the solid line DD[1] in Figure 1, with the kink occurring at the prevailing price. The demand curve for each oligopolist thus tends to be highly elastic above the ruling price and inelastic below the ruling price. The competitive situation among the firms is, therefore, such that an independent price increase will cause a drastic decline in a firm's sales volume.

When a firm's demand (and hence its average revenue) curve is kinked, its corresponding marginal revenue curve consists of two disjointed segments, as shown in Figure 2. The upper segment corresponds to the more elastic portion of the demand curve, while the lower segment corresponds to the less elastic portion of the demand curve. The vertical discontinuity in the MR curve is at the prevailing price and output rate.

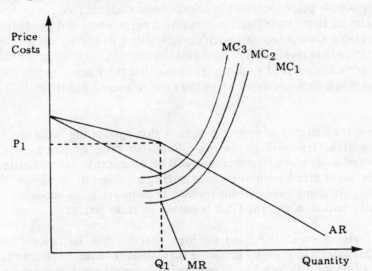

Figure 2

Assuming that the firm's marginal cost curve is MC_1, as shown in Figure 2, then the profit maximising output level for the firm, ie where MC = MR, is output level Q_1. In the situation of rising costs, for example wage increases or increases in raw material prices, the firm's marginal cost curve will shift upwards, say to MC_2 in Figure 2. Given the discontinuity in the MR curve, the most profitable output level of the firm remains Q_1 units because MC_2 = MR at this volume of output. An increase in costs resulting in a shift in the marginal cost curve to MC_2 will thus leave the price-output combination of firms in the oligopoly unchanged at P_1 - Q_1. In fact, the firm's marginal cost function must rise above MC_3 before it would be advantageous to change either price or output. As long as the marginal cost curve intersects the discontinuous portion of the MR curve, the firm's profit maximising point is fixed at the kink in the demand curve. The price and output level of an oligopolistic firm will, therefore, not necessarily change even though costs change.

Although the kinked demand curve is a widely used model of oligopoly behaviour it is subject to several criticisms. An important limitation of the model is its inability to explain how oligopolists initially arrive at the prevailing prices. The model is much better at explaining why price persists at the kink than how it reached that level in the first place or why and how it might change.

Alternative explanations for price rigidity can be found. Firms may, for instance, be reluctant to change prices frequently or independently so as not to disrupt customer relations by introducing an element of uncertainty as to future prices. Some firms argue that it is better to raise prices in large amounts and to do so infrequently than to raise prices frequently but by small amounts. Thus oligopoly prices may be 'sticky' because firms are cautious about making price changes until cost (or demand) conditions have clearly changed in a well-defined way.

The assumption in the model that price cuts will be matched and price increases ignored does not always hold. When a firm reduces its price, rivals may not interpret this as a sign that the firm is seeking a larger share of the market. Rivals may interpret the price cut to mean that the item is about to be replaced by a new model or that the company is hoping the whole industry will reduce its prices in the interests of stimulating total demand. Competitors may react differently depending on whether they view the price change as temporary or permanent and each rival firm's reaction will be based on what it thinks is motivating the company's price cut.

With respect to price increases, when rivals experience similar shifts in cost conditions, the incentive to change price may be generally recognised and mutually advantageous to all concerned. Industry-wide price increases in oligopolistic markets frequently follow wage and tax increases imposed on all firms by collective bargaining agreements and governments respectively. Knowing that its rivals are confronted with comparable cost increases, a firm can raise prices with more confidence that rivals will follow suit. Moreover, linking price rises to wage or tax increases has the added benefit of making it appear that the blame rests with the trade unions or the government. Such an association helps the firm to escape public criticism and charges of profiteering.

When the incentives for a price rise appear generally throughout the industry, the main problem becomes that of which firm will be daring enough to raise its price first, after making a careful assessment of what size price increase will be acceptable to competitors. The tendency to ignore price increases also becomes remote during a period of inflation. When prices have been rising generally for some time consumers may become resigned to higher prices, and firms, both independently and as a group, find it easier to raise prices.

If in the face of rising costs the firm decides not to raise its price it may adopt other measures to increase sales and thereby generate sufficient revenue to cover the cost increase. A common feature of oligopolistic markets is non-price competition. Consumers buy a product not merely upon the basis of price, but also after consideration of many other factors which the firm can influence. A car manufacturer may therefore attempt to change the design and quality of its products, engage in a large scale advertising campaign or improve after sales service.

It is also possible for the group of oligopolists to form a cartel, that is to engage in collusion, by making an agreement relating to the prices to be charged and the level of output to be produced. The objective would be for the oligopolists to act collectively like a monopolist, by restricting output and raising price, thereby earning the maximum profit that can be attained in the industry.

13 PRIVATE SECTOR FIRMS

Tutorial note. It's easy to forget the most important and cheapest source of finance - retained profits - in answering this CIM past question.

Suggested solution

A private sector firm may finance its activities by various combinations of equity and debt. Equity applies to companies and refers to ordinary share capital and reserves while debt usually refers to long-term and medium-term liabilities. Preference share capital falls between the two. The proportion of equity and debt in the capital structure of a firm varies from one company to another, and for a particular company over time. Major differences between equity and debt relate to risk and profit. From the holders' point of view, ordinary shares are riskier than loans, but their potential profit - either in dividends or in residual market value - may be much higher. Equity holders receive any residual profit after tax and after the fixed commitments to pay interest on loans and dividends on preference capital. From a company's point of view the reverse is true - debt capital is cheaper than equity, partly because interest is tax-deductible; but it is also riskier because of the fixed nature of the legal commitments.

Ordinary shares are shares in the ownership of the company and give ultimate rights of control over its effects. The number of shares which a company is authorised to issue is indicated in its constitution (memorandum of association) which also specifies the nominal amount of each share, eg ordinary shares of £1 each. Once issued, ordinary shares represent permanent capital, not normally redeemed during a company's existence. If an individual shareholder wants to recover his capital investment while the company continues in business, he must sell his shares to someone else. Such a sale does not affect the company directly, unless it changes the controlling interest.

A public limited company ('plc') may increase its ordinary share capital in order to raise further finance in two ways.

(a) *Issues for cash or other assets*
The directors of the company may decide to issue a further tranche of ordinary shares in order to acquire more assets. Members of the public and investing institutions such as pension funds would be invited to offer to buy the shares.

(b) *Right issues*
The company may make a rights issue to existing shareholders. This involves the company offering additional shares to existing shareholders at a price which is generally a little below the current market price. Rights are issued to existing shareholders in proportion to their existing shareholdings, eg on the basis of a '1 for 5' rights issue. If a shareholder did not wish to invest more cash, he could sell his rights in the market. If he did neither, the company could normally sell the rights in the market on his behalf. The buyer of the rights would then be able to subscribe for the new shares.

The extent to which new equity issues to new or existing shareholders can be carried out will partly depend on the valuation the stock market places on the company, which in turn will be heavily influenced by the dividends paid out and/or expected and prospects for future growth of the company. A private company is not allowed in law to offer shares for sale to the public.

A company may obtain finance from retained earnings, ie retained profits or undistributed profits. These are any after-tax profits that are reinvested - or ploughed back - into the firm rather than being paid out to the shareholders in dividends. Such retained earnings form a valuable source of capital which may be invested in additional fixed capital and current assets. They serve to swell the value of the company to the shareholders and increase shareholders' capital employed by adding to revenue reserves any profit not paid out in dividends or added to the accumulated retained earnings figure on the balance sheet.

Preference shares fall between ordinary shares and debt. Legally they form part of a company's share capital, but with limited rights to participate in profits. Preference dividends are normally 'cumulative', so that no ordinary dividends can be paid until all preference dividends due (including any arrears) have been paid. Preference shares have lost favour with investors and with companies seeking to raise capital. Although preference shares are still common they are usually a relatively unimportant source of finance.

Apart from equity a company may borrow in order to finance its activities. Such borrowing may be considered in terms of long-term liabilities and medium-term liabilities. Companies may raise long term debt from merchant banks, insurance companies or other institutions and for large companies from the stock exchange. In certain cases government loans may be available for companies unable to borrow commercially.

The company must repay the amount borrowed at the promised time and pay interest outstanding on the debt in the meantime. Failure to do either entitles the lender to take legal action to recover the amount due; and in the event of a company going into liquidation, all debts must be paid in full before any amounts can be paid to preference or ordinary shareholders. Sometimes a loan will be 'secured' by a charge or mortgage on some or all of the assets of the company. In the event of a liquidation this will entitle the lender to recover his debt in full before trade and other 'unsecured' creditors can receive any proceeds from the charged assets.

The terms of a long term loan can vary considerably, but will often be for a period between 10 and 20 years. The rate of interest will depend on prevailing conditions and expectations in the market at the time of issue, and on the financial status of the borrower. The greater the risk perceived by the lender, the higher the interest rate that will be required for a loan, or the more stringent the other conditions that may be insisted on.

A special category of debt can be 'converted' on pre-arranged terms with ordinary share capital at the holder's option, after which it is indistinguishable from other ordinary share capital. If not converted during the option period, convertible debt simply becomes straight debt capital when the conversion rights lapse.

Loans payable between 1 and 5 years from the balance sheet date are sometimes referred to as 'medium-term'. Apart from loans with a specified repayment date, certain overdrafts may also be classified as medium-term. Although in theory bank overdrafts are repayable on demand, it is not unusual for companies to go through refinancing cycles in which overdrafts fulfil a bridging role between the dates at which the company raises more permanent capital - either equity or long term debt.

For the purposes of short-term credit, almost all businesses make use of trade credit, which is the credit provided by suppliers of raw materials, components and other goods and services in the normal course of trade. Trade credit is typically granted for 30, 60 or 90 days before invoices must be paid. Trade credit permits a producer to defer payment until after materials or services purchased have been used in production, and thus reduces the level of working capital which would otherwise be necessary for the business to operate. If the business supplies on trade credit to other businesses, it will effectively be providing short-term finance through trade credit to its customers on the one hand, and receiving short-term finance from suppliers on the other hand. Many retail businesses can gain a significant cash flow advantage from the fact that they receive payment from customers in cash at the time of sale, but do not need to pay their suppliers promptly.

The proportion of debt and equity within a company's capital structure is decided by its directors. A company with a large proportion of debt in its capital structure is said to be highly 'geared'. The higher the financial gearing the greater the risk for owners of equity capital, but the greater their prospect of profit if all goes well.

14 STANDARD OF LIVING

National income is a measure of the value of the output of goods and services produced by an economy over a period of time. The national income can be measured in any one of three ways.

(a) *The output (or production) method*

This measures the value of output of each industry and then aggregates these output measures to arrive at an estimate of aggregate output. This does not mean, however, that the value of each firm's output is added together as to do so would give an aggregate many times greater than the national income because of double counting which arises because the outputs of some firms are the inputs of other firms. Double counting is avoided by summing the value added at each stage of production, or by adding together the final value of output produced.

(b) *The income method*

This measures factor incomes directly. It is important to ensure that only factor rewards are included, ie only those incomes paid in return for some productive activity, and for which there is a corresponding output.

(c) *The expenditure method*

This measures the flow of expenditure on domestic final output.

In theory these three measures should all give exactly the same total. In practice, however, this is unlikely to be the case. First, because the aggregates are extremely large, arising out of tens of millions of transactions of varying amounts paid over varying time periods, it would be surprising if all three measures gave exactly the same result. Second, the existence of the 'black economy' means that some transactions are recorded in one measure of national income but, because of largely illegal dealings, there is no counterpart in other measures. It is unlikely, therefore, that all three aggregates will balance.

The standard of living is usually taken to mean the quantity of goods and services available to the citizens of a country measured in money terms. As a measure of the standard of living, the national income figures are not entirely accurate because of several problems associated with the compiling of the national income accounts.

(a) As noted above there is a great deal of economic activity which is unrecorded - usually referred to as the 'black economy' or the 'hidden economy'. If the black economy is of a significant size then this will cast doubt on the credibility of the official statistics. A number of estimates have been made of the black economy in the UK which range from about $3\frac{1}{2}$% of measured national income up to about 15% of national income.

(b) Over time there will be qualitative changes in the goods society consumes. For example, the washing machines, televisions and cars available today are much better than the models available ten years ago. Accurate comparisons of national income over time must make some allowance for the additional satisfaction this confers on consumers. However making such allowances is inevitably as much of an art as a science.

(c) Services produced by the government are valued at resource cost, ie the cost of provision. However, since the consumer often has no choice about whether or not to purchase those commodities, for example police services, defence and education, the estimate of their 'worth' is arbitrary. Indeed, if it over-estimates their worth for a particular country it is possible that a shift from public sector provision of services to private sector provision would raise the level of social welfare without markedly affecting the size of the national income.

(d) Many goods and services are produced neither by the government nor sold through the market and therefore do not appear in the national income figures. For example, the services of parents in terms of running a home and raising children; the produce obtained from domestic gardens such as vegetables, fruit and flowers; home repairs and do-it-yourself activities performed by members of the family. In some countries the level of this output is considerable and hence the national income figures do not fully reflect the quantities of goods and services available to the citizens.

(e) The national income figures do not account for the value of leisure. Between two periods changes in national income may be influenced by changes in the number of hours worked. It is possible for instance to have the same or a greater level of total output but with people working fewer hours per year, for example because of a shorter working week or longer holidays. Comparison of living standards should therefore include a measure of the increased value of leisure. However, this may be difficult to determine.

As a measure of changes in the standard of living it would be misleading simply to compare the money value of output produced in two separate years because inflation will lead to a higher money value in later years, irrespective of whether the volume of output has increased. In order to see what has happened to real national income when two years are compared it is necessary to remove the effect of inflation. This is accomplished by deflating the money measure of national income by the GDP deflator, which is a measure of price increases throughout the economy.

It is also necessary to adjust the national income figures for changes in the size of the population. A measure of the real national income would give a picture of the standard of living in a country, however a rise in the real national income may be associated with a fall in the standard of living of most individuals if the population rose more rapidly. As far as the citizens of a country are concerned, the standard of living depends much more on the average level of purchasing power per person than on the total measure of national income. It is necessary therefore to consider the changes in real national income per capita over time when discussing changes in the standard of living.

As far as the citizens of a country are concerned, the average standard of living will not only depend on the total income available but also on its distribution. It is possible for the national income figure to rise but the standard of living of many citizens to fall, for example if total income were rising in a period when the rich were getting richer and the poor were getting poorer.

Apart from any distributional considerations, there are other reasons why living standards in a country may not move in step with changes in its total income.

(a) Increased lending abroad or increased investment abroad will mean that domestic residents have fewer goods and services available for themselves and so will have lower living standards.

(b) An increased output of capital goods and the production of fewer consumer goods, ie investment is raised at the expense of consumers' expenditure and living standards.

(c) Increased spending on items that do not affect what is ordinarily understood as the standard of living at the expense of items which do. Increased spending on armaments for defence purposes is an example, at the expense of consumer durables.

Although calculation of real national income per capital over time gives a useful indication of changes in living standards, there are other factors which impact on the standard of living which are not reflected in the national income calculations. The welfare of the citizens might change, for example welfare might fall if there was a threat of war, or if some citizens became less law abiding. However, this change in welfare cannot be quantified in a clear way. It is the welfare of the population which is fundamentally important but welfare itself cannot be measured. So, although increases in real national income per head give some indication that there has been an increase in living standards such figures ignore any offsetting costs such as pollutions and environmental degradation, the nature of work and urban living.

15 RECESSION AND RECOVERY

Tutorial note. The statement which this question asks to be explained concerns the fluctuations in levels of economic activity which are referred to as the 'trade cycle'. Your answer should cover the characteristics of recession and should describe the processes which lead to recovery.

Suggested solution

While over a long period of time, levels of output tend to rise, over a shorter timescale a series of 'booms' and 'slumps' in economic growth often occurs. Cyclical activity affects all economies to some extent, and no economy is entirely insulated from cyclical trends occurring internationally. This cyclical tendency is known as the 'trade cycle' or business cycle, and is illustrated in the diagram below.

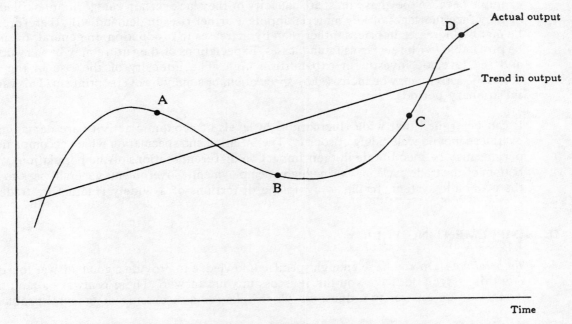

At point A, the economy is entering into a recession. In the recession phase, consumer demand falls and many investment projects already undertaken begin to look unprofitable. Orders will be cut, stock levels will be reduced and business failures will occur as firms find themselves unable to sell their goods. Production and employment will fall. This will lead to a fall in income and expenditure and, as the aggregate level of demand falls, an increasing number of firms will face financial difficulties. The general price level will begin to fall. Business and consumer confidence are diminished and investment remains low, while the economic outlook appears to be poor. Eventually, in the absence of any stimulus to aggregate demand, a period of full depression sets in and the economy will reach point B.

Recession can begin relatively quickly because of the speed with which the effects of declining demand will be felt by businesses suffering a loss in sales revenue. The 'knock-on' effects of destocking and cutting back on investment exacerbate the situation and add momentum to the recession. Recovery can be slow to begin because of the effect of recession on levels of confidence. It can take some time for confidence to return, and initial moves towards expansion of activity are likely to be tentative.

At point C the economy has reached the recovery phase of the cycle. Once begun, the phase of recovery is likely to quicken as confidence returns. Output, employment and income will all begin to rise. Rising production, sales and profit levels will lead to optimistic business expectations, and new investment will be more readily undertaken. The rising level of demand can be met through increased production by bringing existing capacity into use and by hiring unemployed labour. The average price level will remain constant or begin to rise slowly.

In the recovery phase, decisions to purchase new materials and machinery may lead to benefits in efficiency from the fact that it will be possible to take advantage of new technology. This can enhance the relative rate of economic growth in the recovery phase once it is under way.

As recovery proceeds, the output level climbs above its trend path, reaching point D, which is the boom phase of the cycle. During the boom, capacity and labour will be fully utilised. This may cause bottlenecks in some industries which are unable to meet increases in demand, for example because they have no spare capacity or they lack certain categories of skilled labour, or they face shortages of key material inputs. Further rises in demand will, therefore, tend to be met by increases in prices rather than by increases in production. In general, business will be profitable, with few firms facing losses. Expectations of the future may be very optimistic and the level of investment expenditure high. The intensity of the rise in the level of economic activity may be increased by speculation, or simply by over-optimism. This can lead to inflationary periods.

It can be argued that wide fluctuations in levels of economic activity are damaging to the overall economic well-being of society. The inflation and speculation which accompanies boom periods may be inequitable in their impact on different sections of the population, while the bottom of the trade cycle may bring high unemployment. Governments generally seek to stabilise the economic system, trying to avoid the distortions of a widely fluctuating trade cycle.

16   IMPLEMENTING POLICY

Tutorial note. Do you have enough specific knowledge to provide a good answer to a question like this? If you do, have you put it across in your answer? There is always a temptation to 'waffle' in an answer to a question which asks for a discussion of 'general problems'.

Suggested solution

The primary objective of the policy maker is likely to be to ensure a standard of living for all citizens that is as high as possible, both now and in the future. This overriding objective is somewhat vague but can be made more precise by considering the following main objectives of economic policy which have been followed by most governments of the UK since the Second World War.

(a) Stable prices. The rate of inflation should be as low as possible.
(b) Full employment. The level of unemployment should be as low as possible.
(c) Economic growth. The rate of growth of real output should be as high as possible.
(d) Equilibrium in the balance of payments.

To these four major economic objectives could be added many others, for example, to achieve an acceptable distribution of real income amongst the population or to achieve a reduction in regional disparities in income and employment.

A basic problem associated with the four major objectives set out above is that they are often in conflict so that an improvement in one of them can only be achieved at the expense of one or more of the others. A reduction in unemployment, for example, can normally be achieved by stimulating aggregate demand, but this increase in activity will tend to raise the demand for imports and thus may lead to a trade deficit. Similarly, measures which are taken to remove a trade deficit, such as high interest rates, may have an adverse long-term impact on economic growth by discouraging investment.

The policy maker has a variety of instruments available with which to achieve the often conflicting objectives. These can be classified as either fiscal or monetary or direct controls. Fiscal policy consists of changes in taxation and public spending. Monetary policy consists of change in interest rates and the growth of the money supply. Direct control covers any remaining policy instruments, eg prices and income policy; import controls.

Each of the instruments will have an impact on several of the objectives. An increase in public spending, for example, may reduce unemployment but at the same time it may increase imports leading to a balance of payments deficit. The balance of payments deficit may be eased by raising interest rates which encourages an inflow of short term capital. Higher interest rates may though discourage firms from investing, so a third instrument such as a tax-cut may be required to boost demand for domestic output, and so encourage investment. The further stimulation to domestic demand and income may lead to an even greater demand for imports.

This example illustrates that the macroeconomy is a very complex set of inter-relationships between variables, which poses fundamental questions for the government when it formulates economic policy. There are in fact several stages in the formulation of economic policy. The first stage, and the essential starting point, is to have some idea about the way in which the economy works. These ideas are formalised in terms of an economic model which will take the form of a set of equations which describe the inter-relationships between the variables in the system. The problem for the policy maker, however, is that economists cannot provide a model of the economy that is universally agreed upon. The real economy is so complex and the development of economic thought is, as yet, so limited that there is fundamental disagreement between different sets of economists as to exactly how the economy works. The Neo Classical School adopts the view, for example, that the economy is automatically self correcting and will self adjust to attain a full employment equilibrium. In contrast, Keynesians would argue that it is possible for the economy to reach equilibrium at less than full employment and to remain at this level for long periods unless corrective action is taken by the government.

Assuming that the government has adopted an economic model of the economy, the second stage in the process of policy formulation is to use the model to forecast the future levels of target variables, ie the objectives of policy, if the instruments are changed in a particular way. For example, the effect of reducing the level of income tax can be predicted by setting the tax rate at a new lower level, while leaving all other variables unchanged. In this way a series of 'laboratory experiments' or simulations can be conducted, whose purpose is to investigate the effects on the targets of changes in the instruments. A problem for the policy maker is that in the real world experimentation is not possible. However, simulations - made possible by advances in statistical techniques and sophisticated computer programmes - do enable the policy maker to predict the likely outcome of any change to a policy instrument. This still leaves some basic problems for the policy maker. Firstly, there may not be agreement on the impact of an instrument on a target variable. Keynesians, for example, would argue that controlling the rate of growth of the money supply would only have a limited impact on the rate of inflation (especially if the inflation is believed to be caused by cost-push factors), while Monetarists would contend that control of the money supply would always eventually have an effect on the rate of inflation. The value judgements of the government will therefore be crucial in determining which policy action is taken.

The policy once implemented may produce an outcome which is not the same as the predicted outcome. There may be two basic reasons for this. First, the economy is subject to random shocks which cannot be predicted. Events such as a war, a strike, or exceptionally severe weather conditions will affect the target variables and throw the economy off course. Second, there may be a problem of structural change which makes the structural relationships assumed in the underlying economic model obsolete. For example, the model may assume a constant propensity to save but over the period of time when the policy was implemented the propensity to save may have fallen considerably.

A further important aspect of economic policy is that it will be subject to long and variable time lags. The existence of these lags, which are difficult to judge precisely, could mean that a policy designed to stabilise the level of demand could end up by producing a destabilising effect on the economy. A demand management policy for example may attempt to reduce the level of demand during the peaks of the economic cycle (through a budget surplus) and attempts to increase demand during the troughs (through a budget deficit). It is however extremely difficult to correctly implement both the magnitude and the timing of such a policy. Timing problems are of various sorts: collecting statistics; diagnosing problems; planning appropriate measures; predicting accurately when the measures will have an effect. The technical problems of timing and magnitude may result in the policy having a destabilising rather than a stabilising effect on the economy, exacerbating demand at the peak of a cycle and cutting back demand in a trough.

All of these features mean that economic policy is not a neat mechanistic choice about the correct levels of policy instruments. Rather the government must pick its way forward from a present which is highly constrained to a future which is highly uncertain. Policy must be seen as a strategy and, given uncertainty, the government must ask how sensitive any given strategy is to particular assumptions - and what happens if these assumptions go wrong. Policy formulation is incomplete without an analysis of the risks.

17   HOW AND WHY

The idea that government should seek to control the supply of money strongly influenced the Conservative government of the early 1980s in the UK. The idea derives largely from the monetarist view that an increase in the supply of money above the rate of increase in output will lead to rising prices.

The monetarists' view may be expressed in terms of Irving Fisher's 'fundamental equation of exchange' (the 'quantity theory of money'):

$$MV = PT$$

where   M is the total money stock

V is the velocity of circulation of money, ie the average number of times that a unit of currency is used to make a transaction in a given period of time.

P is the average price level of transactions

T is the total number of transactions.

In itself the equation is a truism, as MV equals the total value of all expenditure and PT equals the total value of all sales, so, by definition, MV must be equal to PT. The equation becomes the basis of an explanation of inflation if certain assumptions are made, as follows.

(a) *Full employment:* the price mechanism will work efficiently and that the economy will adjust automatically to the full employment output level. Hence the volume of transactions (T) will be fixed at a constant level which reflects the full employment level of output.

(b) *The velocity of circulation is constant:* the velocity is determined by institutional factors, eg the average time between income payments. These institutional factors change only slowly over time, so that V may be treated as a constant.

(c) *The money supply is determined by the government.* Also the money supply is independent of V, P and T and at any point in time can be taken as fixed.

Applying these assumptions to the equation, the average price level of all transactions (P) will be determined solely by the quantity of money in circulation. An increase in the money supply will result in a proportionate rise in the general price level.

The rationale for this result is that people are assumed to hold money only as a medium of exchange, ie there is a transactions motive for holding money but no speculative motive for holding money. Starting from a position of equilibrium money holdings, if the money supply rises people will find they are holding more money than they desire to cover transaction needs. They will therefore spend the excess balance on all forms of goods, services and assets. Assuming full employment, the result is that with an increased level of money demand, as output cannot increase, prices will rise. The rising price level leads to an increase in the transactions demand for money until the demand for money matches the new higher level of money supply.

There are three basic ways to control the money supply. These are:

(a) direct quantitative controls;
(b) control through interest rates; and
(c) monetary base control.

Quantitative controls
The simplest form of monetary control is where the central bank simply orders the commercial banks to limit the growth of their lending and deposits. This has the virtue of simplicity and a major advantage is that it is effective, at least in the short term. Unfortunately, it has a series of undesirable side-effects which render it less attractive as an option in the long run. The first of these disadvantages is known as 'financial disintermediation'. The normal process of financial intermediation is for borrowers and lenders to be linked together through the banking system. However if the amount of business which the banks can carry out is limited by regulation, other, less efficient, means will be found of carrying out the same functions. New institutions will grow up, exempt from the controls, and only able to do business because the more efficient banks are restricted. Such a situation involves a less efficient financial system and discrimination against the banks. Quantitative controls also have the undesirable effect of stifling competition as the banks cannot compete with each other for business; they must simply ration out limited lending. A further major disadvantage is that, in today's deregulated financial markets, lending will simply be driven overseas, and the controls will thereby be circumvented.

SUGGESTED SOLUTIONS

Control through interest rates

Instead of controlling the amount of bank lending directly, government may control it indirectly, through price. By raising interest rates, credit is made more expensive, so that the demand for lending is reduced. In that case the banks will lend less, and monetary growth will have been restricted by 'riding up the demand for credit curve'. This approach has been used in Britain, but has a number of disadvantages. In the first place, the demand for credit may not be very sensitive to interest rates. Various commentators have noted recently that despite very high interest rates on some forms of credit, consumers seem to be undeterred from borrowing. Many borrowers seem unconcerned about interest rates, considering only whether they can meet the monthly payments. If this is the case, interest rate controls may be ineffective. For companies having a high level of debt finance, higher interest rates may produce such substantial cash flow problems that they are actually forced to borrow more in order to avoid defaulting. Even if interest rate controls are effective it may be necessary to raise rates to unpopular levels to secure the degree of control required.

Interest rate controls can be particularly difficult to use effectively if a government commits itself to a clearly defined quantitative target for the size of the money supply, as Figure 1 indicates.

Figure 1

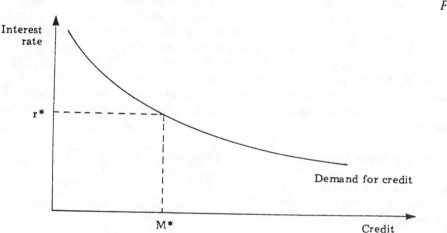

If the government sets itself a target for the money supply of M^*, it has to set interest rate r^*. However, that assumes that the government has perfect knowledge of the demand for credit curve, which it does not. It will therefore have to guess at the appropriate interest rate. Furthermore, there is no reason to suppose that the demand for credit curve remains in the same position. If it moves, the interest rate which is required to meet the monetary target will also move. Government will find it difficult to set the correct rate and may find itself involved in frequent changes, which are de-stabilising and impede sensible decision-making. Interest rates become a less flexible policy tool for controlling money supply growth for a country in a semi-fixed exchange rate system, such as the European exchange rate mechanism, since then interest rate changes are constrained by the need to keep the exchange rate within its permitted limits.

Monetary base control

There are two forms of 'monetary base control'. The first involves a mandatory requirement that the banks hold a certain proportion of their assets or liabilities in the form of reserves or 'monetary base'. Under that system, if the government can control the level of reserves held by the banks it can control the amount of their lending and monetary growth. In many respects such a system resembles a form of quantitative controls, with its advantages and disadvantages.

The second form of monetary base control is sometimes referred to as the 'pure' form in which no mandatory controls are placed on the banks at all. However, banks need to have 'mandatory base', (defined as notes and coin and deposits in the central bank), because these are liabilities of the government, not the bank, and can be used to settle transactions between banks and to satisfy customers who require cash rather than cheques in payment. The banks need monetary base for 'prudential' reasons. Under the 'pure' system of monetary base control the government would control the amount of monetary base available and would provide an indirect way of controlling bank lending and the money supply. The easiest way to conceptualise the workings of the method is to think of the banks as an industry which uses inputs of labour, capital and monetary base to produce credit. If the availability of monetary base is controlled then there are limits on the amount of an input available and the level of output is limited. Milton Friedman has drawn the analogy with controlling the output of cars by controlling the availability of steel to the car industry.

Monetary base control will be effective if the banks really need monetary base, and if the amount they require bears a stable relationship to the amount of lending they carry out. Clearly if they do not need monetary base, or the amount they require is variable for the same level of business, control of the monetary base will not be an effective means of controlling the money supply.

Clearly, the control of the money supply is an extremely difficult area of policy for governments, none of which have found wholly satisfactory solutions.

18   DIRECT AND INDIRECT

Taxation is the major source of revenue to government and so is essential to allow the financing of public sector goods and services. The larger the public sector the more financing it requires and so the greater the proportion of national income the government will need to fund its expenditure. There are two basic approaches to taxation, either to tax individuals or companies directly as in the case with income tax, or to tax indirectly.

Indirect taxation is where the person legally responsible for the tax is in fact only an intermediary and can hand on the burden of it to someone else, as in the case of VAT, which is a tax on the supply of goods and services. Here the manufacturer and retailer act as collectors of VAT although the tax is effectively borne by the end user of the product – the consumer.

The relative advantages and disadvantages of the two approaches to taxation depend from whose perspective you are examining them. Adam Smith identified four characteristics of a good tax as follows.

(a)   People pay according to their ability.
(b)   It should be certain and understood by all.
(c)   It should be related to how and when people receive or spend their income.
(d)   The cost of collection should be small relative to the tax yield.

Even in these four basic features it is possible to identify benefits from both the individual and the government point of view.

Direct taxes have the qualities that they can be made progressive or proportional. In other words the ability to pay can be recognised so that richer people pay a higher percentage of their income in tax.

Indirect taxes are generally regressive. The greater burden is on the poorest in society because they spend a higher proportion of their income on consumption than the better off. However, goods deemed as essentials like food and books can be zero-rated for tax.

The incidence of progressive, proportional and regressive taxation is illustrated in the diagram below.

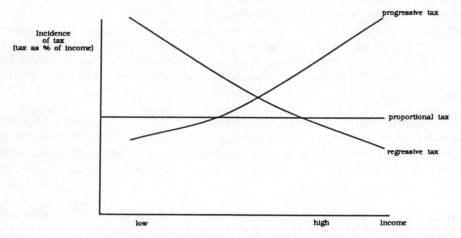

Direct taxes influence the individual's disposable income and so at very high marginal rates of tax they might act as a disincentive to work. However, they are easily understood and collected relatively cheaply through 'PAYE' systems at the point where income is earned.

Both direct and indirect taxes have some advantages and most economies will adopt a mixture of taxes in order to minimise their disadvantages. One issue in countries like the UK is how the balance between the two approaches shifts. The years of the Conservative administration since 1979 have seen a significant shift from direct taxation to indirect taxation as well as a reduction in the overall taxation level. One of the political justifications for this shift was that indirect taxes are preferable because they only fall on those who *choose* to buy the goods on which they are levied.

19   VARIOUS TYPES

(a)   Inflation is an increase in the general level of prices, which thus reduces the purchasing power or real value of money.

'Inflation' is a term that is associated with a situation in which there is a *continuous* tendency for prices to rise, and the increase in output of goods and services is continually less than the increase in spending in money terms.

Extremely high rates of inflation are sometimes referred to as runaway inflation or hyperinflation.

Types of inflation

The two basic types of inflation are *demand-pull* inflation and *cost-push* inflation.

(i)   *Demand-pull inflation* describes a situation in which there is excessive demand for goods and services, which 'pulls' prices up to a higher level.

One way in which demand-pull inflation occurs is an increase in credit lending by building societies and banks (including credit card companies). Borrowers use their loans to spend more, and there is an increase in the money supply because the money lent by the banks (which is an asset of the banks) finds its way back into the banks as customers' deposits (and these liabilities of the banks are included in various definitions of the money supply). Another way in which demand-pull inflation occurs is excessive borrowing by the government (also from banks), caused by government expenditure exceeding government income from taxation and other sources.

(ii)   *Cost-push inflation* occurs when the cost of factors of production increases at a rate in excess of the current rate of inflation.

Wages costs are often regarded as a major cause of cost-push inflation. There is an *expectations theory* of inflation that the work force will try to achieve wage increases in anticipation of what inflation will be; this anticipation becomes a self-fulfilling prophecy, since actual wage increases themselves become a cause of inflation. Firms that award higher wages without improvements in productivity taking place must either accept a reduction in profits or pass on the higher costs to customers in the form of higher prices. Unless the workforce becomes more productive, and is able to create more output in exchange for higher wages, it is argued, inflation will be caused by this process of passing on higher costs into higher prices.

Import costs are another possible cause of cost-push inflation. The UK is heavily dependent on imports, and if there is a fall in the foreign exchange value of sterling, the cost of imports will rise. Higher import costs either add to the cost of raw materials of UK manufacturers, who must pass on the higher costs into higher prices, or else directly affect the price of goods in the shops.

(b)   Inflation can only be measured broadly because:

(i)   individuals buy different goods and services and in differing quantities and so the rate of inflation for one individual will not be the same as the rate of inflation for another;

(ii)   it would be impossible to monitor the prices of all goods and services.

An inflation index (or price index) can be constructed by taking a selected 'basket' of items and monitoring their prices at regular intervals (typically monthly). A base year (eg January 1981) is selected for a price index level of 100 and subsequent changes in prices are measured as a monthly change in the index level.

In the UK, the main index for measuring inflation is the Retail Prices Index, which measures prices of a 'basket' of hundreds of items including the cost of housing, such as mortgage repayments for an average-sized mortgage.

Although the RPI is a very broad measure of inflation, it is nevertheless an indicator of inflation which receives wide publicity and attention from the government, trade unions and employers. It is also used for such purposes as the updating of social security benefits and the calculation of capital gains for taxation purposes.

The annual increase in RPI excluding mortgage costs from the calculation is referred to as the 'underlying' rate of inflation. The purpose of this measure is to provide an indicator of inflationary pressures in the economy which removes the direct effect of interest rate changes on the mortgage rate.

20   MAIN COST

Inflation and unemployment are two of the major economic problems which plague economies. The links between the two and trade off between them cause division and disagreement among politicians and economists alike. Keynes, working against the background of the great depression of the 1930s, first put together a model to explain the workings of the economy. His work in analysing that the cyclical peaks and troughs of the trade cycle were inevitable without government intervention led to the adoption of demand management economic policies.

Unemployment was characteristic of recession and depression, caused according to Keynes by insufficient demand in the economy to sustain full employment. The solution was simply to reflate the economy with policies which increased injections or reduced leakages from the circular flow. Reducing taxation or increasing government spending were favourite strategies because the government had direct control of this pair of leakage and injection.

Inflation, a persistent and significant rise in the general level of prices was associated with the top of the trade cycle - the boom. In this instance too much demand overheating the economy led to the raising of prices and the sucking into the system of imported goods, with consequent balance of payments problems.

Again the principle behind the Keynesian solution was simple: deflate the economy by policies designed to decrease demand.

Unfortunately the short term effect of such demand-reducing policies is to cause unemployment. This situation is made worse as the multiplier and accelerator further magnify the impact of the reduced demand levels.

The statistician Phillips illustrated the trade off between inflation and unemployment with the Phillips curve.

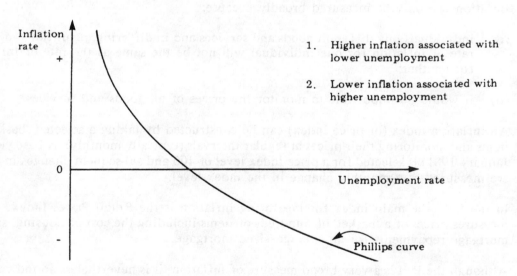

1. Higher inflation associated with lower unemployment

2. Lower inflation associated with higher unemployment

This curve demonstrated how inflation fell as unemployment grew and vice versa. The best government could do was target for a low level of both. After the mid-1970s when the Phillips curve relationship had been deemed to have broken down, as both inflation and unemployment were increasing simultaneously, the economic baton was passed to the monetarists. Their view was that controlling inflation was a priority in establishing a healthy economic climate. Caused by a too rapid growth in the money supply, ie purchasing power, inflation could be controlled by tight monetary controls.

As we have experienced twice since 1979 in the UK, the cost of such policies is rising unemployment. However, some would argue that the reward is lower inflation, which in the long term protects our competitiveness and therefore employment.

An alternative to these two approaches, both of which accept unemployment as the cost of lowering inflation, might be a prices and incomes policy. This strategy depends on governments intervening in the market mechanism to prevent both prices and incomes rising. Although tried by both Labour and Conservative governments, such policies have failed to work in the past and have often resulted in distortions in the market place. At the most they provide a short term relief from the symptoms of inflation, but more direct action is needed to eradicate its causes. Experience was that once released, pressure on wages and prices exploded: the inflation had still been there but was 'pent up'.

Inflation is a potentially serious economic problem, which if not controlled can lead to both economic and political instability. The most obvious solutions appear to lead inevitably to unemployment with its high social costs and wasted resources. Perhaps the best one can hope is that government policy on inflation will include mechanisms for sharing the burden of this cost more equitably across the community.

21   ABSOLUTE ADVANTAGE

Absolute advantage is a concept relevant to the situation in which some countries are more efficient than others in producing certain goods and services. This may occur because of a more skilled workforce, or a superior commercial environment. When one country can produce a good more efficiently than another country, it is said to have an advantage over the other country.

Suppose that a country is more efficient in production of all goods or services than another country. Can it still be of benefit for the country to trade in those goods and to specialise? The easiest way to demonstrate this is to consider two commodities; the argument can then be extrapolated to cover all commodities.

Suppose that the two commodities produced in the economy of the UK are fish and chips. One unit of resource - one person-week - produces:

Either   400 kg of fish
Or   800 kg of chips

If the cost of one person-week is £200, the selling price of 1 kg of fish must be at least 200 ÷ 400 = £0.50, and the selling price of 1 kg of chips must be at least 200 ÷ 800 = £0.25.

Assuming the economy of the UK operates at full capacity, the opportunity cost of producing 1 kg of fish is 2 kg of chips, and the opportunity cost of 1 kg of chips is $\frac{1}{2}$ kg of fish.

Suppose that in the USA the same products are made and one person-week costing $200 (exchange rate £1 = $1) can produce:

Either   300 kg of fish
Or   400 kg of chips

The opportunity cost of producing 1 kg of fish in the USA is 400 ÷ 300 = $1\frac{1}{3}$ kg of chips, while the opportunity cost of 1 kg of chips is 300 ÷ 400 = $\frac{3}{4}$ kg of fish.

The UK has an absolute advantage over the USA in both commodities - fish and chips. It can produce both more efficiently than the USA.

Suppose that each country has 2,000 units of production resource. If there is no international trade and each country devotes half of its resources to producing each commodity, production will be as follows.

		UK	US	Total
Production resources:	Fish	1,000	1,000	2,000
	Chips	1,000	1,000	2,000
	Total	2,000	2,000	4,000
		Kg	Kg	Kg
Output:	Fish	400,000	300,000	700,000
	Chips	800,000	400,000	1,200,000

Can output be increased by a reallocation of production resources? Suppose that production resources are reallocated as follows:

		UK	US	Total
Production resources:	Fish	850	1,250	2,100
	Chips	1,150	750	1,900
	Total	2,000	2,000	4,000

With these production resources, the levels of output achieved are as follows:

		Kg	Kg	Kg
Output:	Fish	340,000	375,000	715,000
	Chips	920,000	300,000	1,240,000

The reallocation of production resources has led to an increase in the output of both fish (increased by 15,000 kg to 715,000 kg) and of chips (increased by 40,000 kg to 1,240,000 kg). Thus, the output of each commodity has been increased by a measure of 'specialisation'. It will be in the interests of each country to trade in the commodities so that supply can be matched with demand in each country.

The argument may be extrapolated to cover a situation involving many different commodities, and therefore corresponding more closely to a real situation.

A number of assumptions have been made in arriving at the above conclusions. Firstly, it is assumed for the sake of simplicity that there are constant returns to scale, so that the number of units of output produced by each unit of resource (each 'person-week' in our example) is the same whatever the level of output. Secondly, it is assumed that factors of production (labour, capital goods etc) are readily transferable between the commodities: fish-processing workers can easily be switched to processing chips instead. This assumption is consistent with the first assumption of constant returns to scale. A third assumption is that the costs (in terms of production foregone) of transporting the goods between the countries in the course of the international trade activities are negligible or at least are less than the value of the increase in output obtained from specialisation.

SUGGESTED SOLUTIONS

22 BALANCE OF TRADE

Tutorial note. This question, set in the June 1993 CIM Economics paper, is answered here with reference to the UK.

Suggested solution

(a) The balance of payments is the record of all transactions between a country and other countries. Technically the balance of payments has to balance, but the term deficit or surplus are used to indicate an imbalance of *trade* between countries. A deficit which is persistent, significant or unplanned is a potential problem and needs to be tackled by government action.

The major influences on the UK balance of payments over the last ten year period have been as follows.

(i) The visible trade section of the current account shows imports and exports of goods. During the early 1980's the UK was a net exporter of oil. Oil exports grew until they peaked in the mid 1980s. The 1980s also saw a decline in the size and competitiveness of UK manufacturing industry; production costs, particularly wages, were seen to rise at comparatively higher rates in the UK than in many other countries. The decline in net oil exports and the decline of manufacturing industry helped to create substantial deficits on the visible balance by the second half of the 1980s. Rapid economic growth in the late 1980s boosted consumer demand, which came to be met by increasing imports, thus pushing the visible balance further into deficit.

(ii) Since the early 1980s, the UK has enjoyed a substantial surplus in the invisibles section of the balance of payments. The data shows the three main components of the invisibles balance.

(1) Services have earned a substantial surplus in each year covered by the data. Financial services, with London being a major world financial centre, and tourism are important elements of this surplus.

(2) The balance on interest, profits and dividends (IPD) was in deficit at the beginning of the 1980s. The removal of exchange controls in 1979 led to substantial subsequent growth in sums invested abroad by UK residents. This led to inflows of income in the form of IPD, outweighing the outflows to overseas residents investing in the UK, although these too have risen significantly.

(3) The negative transfers balance reflects substantial net payments by the UK to the European Community (EC), for example, to pay for the subsidies under the Common Agricultural Policy. The net transfer payments have reduced the surplus on invisibles throughout the period.

(iii) The UK's membership of the EC has exerted an important influence on external trade as well as in respect of transfers. Over 50% of the UK's external trade is now with other EC member countries, and the UK is heavily in deficit on current account trade with the rest of the EC.

(iv) By the late 1980s, the UK was experiencing substantial deficits on the overall current balance, with a deficit of over £20 billion being recorded for 1989. More recently, dampened consumer demand and economic recession following a period of sustained high interest rates in 1989 and 1990 have helped to suppress the level of deficit. However, the propensity of UK consumers to buy imported goods remains and the prospect is that economic recovery bringing an accompanying boost to consumer demand will exert upward pressure on the level of current account deficit. One mitigating factor could be the effect of the devaluation of sterling following its suspension from the European exchange rate mechanism (ERM).

(b) Policies to eliminate a balance of trade deficit can be grouped into three kinds. Those which deflate the domestic economy; those which alter the exchange rate through devaluation or depreciation; and direct controls on trade between countries.

Domestic demand can be reduced by the government cutting purchasing power through increased taxation, by reductions in government expenditure and by restricting the growth of the money supply and raising interest rates. The impact of the policy would be two-fold. Reduced demand at home should help reduce inflationary pressures and thus help exports as the home country's price level comes more in line with its competitors. The lower level of economic activity at home would also reduce the demand for imports. These deflationary measures are likely to increase unemployment and hinder the long term growth rate. Whether or not such a policy is successful would depend on the income elasticity of demand for imports (the greater this is the bigger the fall in imports from a given deflation of domestic income) and the causes of the home economy's lack of price competitiveness (if the inflation rate was due to cost-push rather than demand pressures the deflation would not have such a direct effect on the price level).

If it is recognised that the existing exchange rate is in disequilibrium, then the balance of payments deficit might be corrected by lowering the exchange rate. If a system of fixed or semi-fixed rates is in operation, a once-and-for-all devaluation might be announced; if a floating rate operates, then market forces can be allowed to operate, with the central bank withdrawing support for the currency on the foreign exchange market until a new equilibrium rate has been established. The success of policies which operate through changes in the price of exports and imports (caused by the exchange rate changes) depends on the degree of responsiveness of exports and imports on both the supply side and the demand side to price changes. The most successful results occur where there is a high degree of price elasticity for both imports and exports. Where the price elasticity of demand for exports and imports is so low that when the two elasticity values are added together the resultant sum is less than one, devaluation worsens the balance of payments. The effectiveness of depreciation will be reduced if a number of countries simultaneously depreciate their currencies. Although these kinds of policy do not involve a government in abandoning any policies it may have for full employment, the depreciation will be inflationary and may provoke as a result demands for wage increases in compensation. The further twist to the inflationary spiral from this may offset the competitive advantage gained by the depreciation.

If a government is unwilling to adopt policies which will harm their progress in terms of the objectives of full employment and of price stability, the alternative is for some form of direct controls on trade between the country in question and the rest of the world. Controls can be imposed on the movement of capital out of the country and on imports of goods by quotas which limit the amount of particular imports allowed, and tariffs which artificially raise the price of imports compared to that of a domestic substitute. These may be justifiable in the short run to meet emergency conditions if a country's trading partners agree. The danger is that other countries would retaliate and a general restriction on world trade would result. The 'Single European Market' rules prevent the UK adopting such measures in handling trade imbalances with the rest of Europe.

23   DETERMINATION OF EXCHANGE RATES

Tutorial note. The application of demand and supply analysis to the determination of exchange rates is required, together with a demonstration of knowledge of the main influences on demand and supply.

Suggested solution

A major influence on the exchange rates of currencies is the policy of governments towards exchange rate management. Different exchange rate systems are possible as frameworks within which exchange rates are determined. At one extreme, a system of floating exchange rates between currencies may be in operation. In this case, the exchange rates are determined by demand and supply conditions in the currency markets. At the other extreme, a system of fully fixed exchange rates must involve means of counteracting the pressures on exchange rates which are exerted by supply and demand conditions, generally through government intervention in the foreign exchange markets. The European exchange rate mechanism (ERM) allows member currencies to fluctuate within predetermined margins around central parity rates.

A system of 'dirty' floating exchange rates, such as that which was in operation in the UK before sterling joined the ERM in October 1990, is one in which the government intervenes in the market at times when it appears appropriate to do so. Under the chancellorship of Nigel Lawson, sterling 'shadowed' the German deutschmark while not being a member of the ERM. This involved government intervention without there being official membership of any exchange rate agreement.

The determination of freely floating exchange rates can be illustrated by considering the supply and demand conditions for currencies. Consider, for example, the exchange rate between pounds sterling and the US dollar. Even while sterling was a member of the ERM, sterling effectively floated against other non-ERM currencies, including the US dollar. The demand curve for sterling, which will be downward sloping, is illustrated by D in the diagram below. The supply curve of sterling will be upward sloping (S in Figure 1).

Figure 1

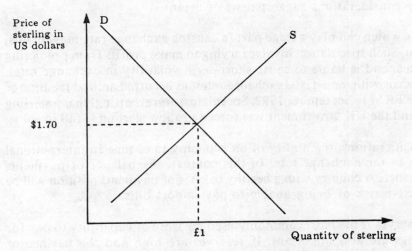

The fact that the demand curve is downward sloping illustrates that, as the price of the pound in terms of dollars falls, British goods will become cheaper in dollars. As a result, more British goods will be purchased by US residents, and larger amounts of pounds sterling will be purchased in order to buy these goods. As the price of the pound expressed in dollars rises, British people will tend to buy more US goods because they will be able to get more US goods per pound. Consequently, the supply curve S will be upward sloping.

Various factors influence the demand for and the supply of a currency. The exchange rate of a currency is a measure of its value relative to that of other currencies, and as such that relative value tends to reflect the internal strengths and weaknesses of the respective economies. Consequently, one of the chief determinants of the exchange rate between sterling and the US dollar is the relative strength of the UK and American economies. A problem arises, however, of defining the means by which economic strength is to be measured; it may be in terms of national income levels, growth rates, foreign reserve holdings, inflation rate and consequently to a certain extent the judgement becomes subjective in nature and dependent on the criteria used. Also of importance in this context is the extent to which external observers consider the economy to be under control. The economy suffering from hyper-inflation is likely to witness very rapid degeneration of the exchange rate for its currency whilst the economy which is experiencing high but stable, if not declining rates of inflation, and is characterised by government attempts at 'economic management', may have a much less volatile exchange rate. As a result the political colour and economic strategy of the government may influence the exchange rate; it may be remembered that the pound sterling reached a short-term high in the days immediately following the election of the Conservative Government in 1979. Future confidence in the economy's prospects can be as important as the current state of the economy in determining the exchange rate.

As indicated above, relative inflation rates affect the exchange rates between countries. The economy experiencing relatively high domestic inflation will find a steady devaluation in its exchange rate for the stronger currency. One theory of exchange rates argues that they move in such a way as to ensure purchasing power parity between currencies; in other words, differences in domestic inflation rates will be eliminated via movements in the exchange rate.

Another feature of the domestic economy of importance in establishing the exchange rate is the level of the interest rates, and in particular, their level relative to rates prevalent in other countries. This is of importance because if interest rates in an economy are high relative to the rates available elsewhere in the world, capital investment funds will be attracted into the economy, and demand for its currency will rise. The rise in demand for the currency then raises the exchange rate. It was argued that the need to maintain sterling's value within the ERM soon after the entry of the UK into the ERM in 1990 necessitated maintenance of higher interest rates than other economic policy considerations suggested was warranted.

Speculation is another factor which can play a large part in causing exchange rate movements, particularly in the short term. Such speculation involves trying to make profits from predicting movements in exchange rates, and is liable to cause short-term volatility in exchange rates. Large speculative flows can occur with semi-fixed exchange rates, as occurred around the time of sterling's departure from the ERM in September 1992. Speculators were 'betting' that a sterling devaluation was imminent, and the UK government was forced to allow sterling to fall in value.

In addition to domestic considerations, the ability of an economy to engage in international trade is of direct relevance to the exchange rate. In this context, the balance of payments position is of primary importance. A country with a healthy balance of payments position will be able to trade without excessive risk of being unable to pay import bills.

Since the level of foreign reserves is the most commonly used measure of capability to pay for imports, the reserve holdings are also important. If reserves are high and the balance of payments in equilibrium or surplus, the exchange rate is likely to be favourable.

24   INTERNATIONAL MARKETER

Elasticity is a measure of the responsiveness of demand or supply to a particular variable such as price or consumers' income. As in the case of a marketer who is engaged in marketing within the domestic economy, it is important for the international marketer to assess and understand elasticities of demand in the various markets with which he is concerned.

However, a special consideration for the international marketer is the possible effect of movements in the exchange rate on the marketer's pricing strategy.

Devaluation of a country's currency might mean, for instance, that the UK's exchange rate in terms of the USA dollar moves from £ = $1.80 to £ = $1.40. The trading effects of this would be that exports become cheaper to buy in overseas markets while imports into the devaluing country become more expensive. By no means all of the possible effects would follow immediately. There could be noticeable 'leads and lags' in the system. Thus, some importers might have anticipated the exchange rate adjustment by forward deals in foreign exchange so might not have to pass on price increases for some time; while many exporters might be slow to adjust to the new situation.

Exporters might respond to the changed situation in different ways.

(a)   Some might not adjust their UK list prices, fully passing on the price benefit to their customers. This is more likely if demand in the selling market is noticeably elastic and supply can easily respond.

(b)   Other might adjust list prices by an amount equivalent to the exchange rate adjustment (assuming that the foreign exchange rate is sufficiently stable to permit this). This is the more likely where margins have contracted in recent times even though the market is rather much of a 'sellers' market'.

(c)   Still others might make only minor adjustments in their list prices, passing on some, but not all, of the price benefit to their customers.

Economic conditions in the devaluing country at and following the exchange rate adjustment would determine the subsequent events. Any strong inflationary pressures, whether domestic or 'imported', could within say 18 months substantially erode much of the initial price advantage so that gradually any export competitiveness would be lost. Apart from this, those manufacturers whose goods contain a high level of import content might quickly find that they have lost much of any apparent price advantage. Clearly, critical to any pricing and/or output decisions is the calculation of how long any price advantage is likely to last.

The producer operating in conditions of imperfect competition might be part of an oligopoly market structure, with product differentiation a likely significant element. Are the overseas customers highly 'price sensitive', with price elasticity of demand playing a key role? Or are they buying largely on grounds other than price? For instance, in the supply of capital equipment, major determining factors could be existence of well-established trading relationships, product design, quality and reliability, meeting delivery dates, meeting specific customer requirements. If the firm is selling (say) a 'consumer good', customers could be fairly price sensitive and there might be a high underlying cross-elasticity of demand between the different supplying firms, eg in the TV receiver market. Beyond this, any firm would need to have regard to its longer-term market strategy: for instance, is it aiming to build volume now, and to become stronger on selling prices at a later stage?

Other matters must also be considered. What is the practice of foreign competitors who also are selling in the home market? Have their exchange rates strengthened relatively? Or have their currencies also been devalued, and, if so, to what extent? Are they cutting their margins in order to hold their share of the market? All of these factors could be important in affecting relative competitiveness.

If the firm has a quasi-monopoly position it might be possible to practice price discrimination as between the home and the export markets. The ability to do this depends on the means of keeping the market separate, such that it is impossible for arbitrage to be practised between the different 'sub-markets' (the re-selling of goods from a low-price into a high-price market, thus tending to eliminate price differentials).

INDEX

FURTHER READING

You may wish to test your grasp of economics by tackling short questions in multiple choice format. BPP publish the Password series of books, each of which incorporates a large collection of multiple choice questions with solutions, comments and marking guides. The Password title relevant to CIM Economics is called Password *Economics*. This is priced at £6.95 and contains about 300 questions.

To order Password books, ring our credit card hotline on 081-740 6808. Alternatively, fill out this page and send it to our Freepost address or fax it to us on 081-740 1184.

To: BPP Publishing Ltd, FREEPOST, London W12 8BR   **Tel: 081-740 6808**
                                                              Fax: 081-740 1184

Forenames (Mr / Ms) : _____

Surname : _____

Address : _____

_____

Post code : _____

Please send me the following books:	*Quantity*	*Price*	*Total*
Password *Economics*	....	£6.95	....

Please include postage:

UK: £1.50 for first plus £0.50 for each extra book   ....

Europe (inc ROI): £2.50 for first plus £1.00 for each extra book   ....

Outside Europe: £4.00 for first plus £2.00 for each extra book   ....

I enclose a cheque for £_____ or charge to Access/Visa

Card number ☐☐☐☐☐☐☐☐☐☐☐☐☐☐☐☐

Expiry date _____ Signature _____

On the reverse of this page there is a Review Form, which you can send in to us (at the Freepost address above) with comments and suggestions on the Study Text you have just finished. Your feedback really does make a difference: it helps us to make the next edition that bit better.

Name: _____

How have you used this Text?

Home study (book only) ☐

On a course: college_____ ☐ Other _____

How did you obtain this Text?

From us by mail order ☐ From us by phone ☐

From a bookshop ☐ From your college ☐

Where did you hear about BPP Texts?

At bookshop ☐ Recommended by lecturer ☐

Recommended by friend ☐ Mailshot from BPP ☐

Advertisement in _____ ☐ Other _____

Your comments and suggestions would be appreciated on the following areas.

Syllabus coverage

Illustrative questions

Errors (please specify, and refer to a page number)

Presentation

Other